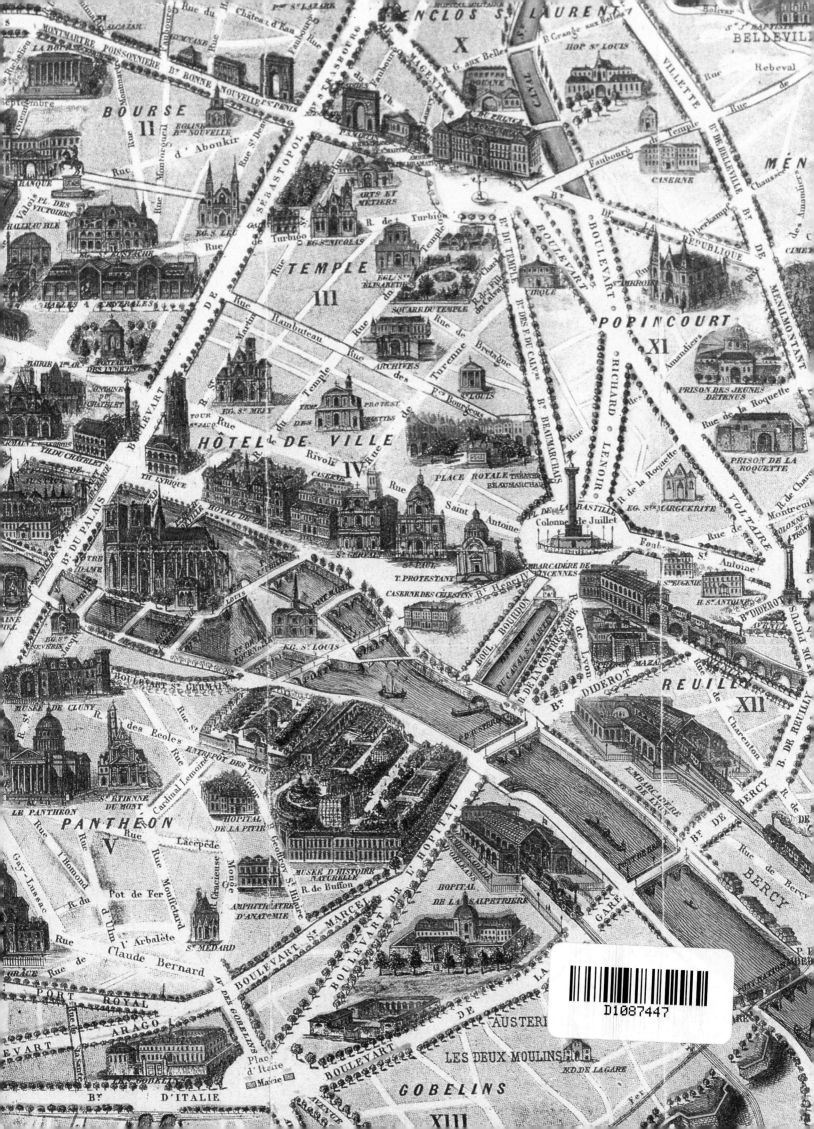

PARIS
NINETEENTH CENTURY

ARCHITECTURE
AND
URBANISM

PARIS
NINETEENTH CENTURY

✤

ARCHITECTURE AND URBANISM

FRANÇOIS LOYER

TRANSLATED BY
Charles Lynn Clark

✤

ABBEVILLE PRESS
PUBLISHERS
NEW YORK

✤

Endpapers: Maison Logerot, *Souvenir du Nouveau Paris* (detail).
J. Gaultier, Paris, 1889. Courtesy of the Map Division,
The New York Public Library, Astor, Lenox and Tilden Foundations.

This work has been published with the cooperation of the
French Ministry of Culture and Communication.

Design: Roman Cieslewicz.
Picture Research: Nathalie Beaud, Hélène Guéné

Printed and bound in France.

Copyright © 1988, Editions Hazan.

First American Edition.

Library of Congress Cataloging-in-Publication Data

Loyer, François.
[Paris XIXe siècle (L'Immeuble et la rue). English]
Paris nineteenth century : architecture and urbanism /
François Loyer.
p.   cm.
Translation of: Paris XIXe siècle : l'immeuble et la rue.
Bibliography: p.
Includes index.
ISBN 0-89659-885-3
1. Architecture, Modern—19th century—France—Paris. 2. City
planning—France—Paris—History—19th century. 3. Paris (France)
—Buildings, structures, etc.   I. Title.
NA1050.L6713 1988
720′.944′361—dc19   88-071658
                                                            CIP

CONTENTS

The map supplement between pages 288 and 289 is paginated I–VIII.

Preface

Writing to his friend Carla Seligson on June 5, 1913, the essayist who was later to call Paris "the capital of the nineteenth century" summed up his first impressions of the city as follows: "The rows of houses seem to stretch out endlessly, not to be lived in, but to pass between—the way one passes through the wings in a theater." What astonishes one immediately is how appropriate Walter Benjamin's description still is today. Indeed, as over half of present-day Paris was built during the nineteenth century, the city remains, on a purely statistical level, the "capital" of that century—so near and yet so far! Having tried everything we could to get away from it, we now passionately and anxiously contemplate the nineteenth century, as we would perhaps a brother. Thus the first thing that will interest readers in François Loyer's book on the reality of Parisian buildings is that it brings to life the city of Balzac, Baudelaire, and the Impressionists, retracing the city's sometimes stormy architectural evolution from neoclassicism to art nouveau—or, if you will, from the age that discovered photography to the age that discovered cinema. Like a pendulum swinging back and forth between moving pictures and stills, Loyer's book—sometimes using close-ups to focus in on details, sometimes using impressive panoramic shots—tells the story of what makes Paris the city we see today. Since much of the texture imposed by the nineteenth century (which the book examines in its most minute ramifications) can still be seen by residents and visitors, the book's historical interest is coupled with what might be called a practical interest: as one advances in the book and scrutinizes a row of balconies or cornices with it, one is thrust into the street and the city as they really exist. And the experience of reading a book that can be constantly verified—the experience of a history so alive and so continually linked to every step we take and the very air we breathe—is somehow uncanny.

François Loyer shows us the height of the city's cornices and their varied yet monotonous horizontal composition, the roofing materials and forms of the roofs, the strongly structured rows of balconies and harmoniously striped shutters, lined up as if on parade, and the ornaments hanging in clusters on the fine stone façades. He shows us the window openings that seem to form a stairway to the sky, the network of tensions that bestows on the city as a whole the symbolic power of a monument, and the precise urban structure that makes of each block a fixed movement, and of each building a distinct note, in a full and repetitive symphony. He shows us the courtyards and staircases with their secrets and shadows, as well as the trees, streetlights, and fountains that punctuate the cityscape. Neither a hymn nor a guide, the book is a serious historical study, but the author is not afraid to sing the city's praises and gladly helps the reader find his way through its streets.

What the book is really about, what it really reveals about the forms that make up the great, gray fugue of the city (inside and out, in its smallest details and its structure as a whole) is what might be called the mystery of local tonality. A city can be nothing but itself, and this limitation is what makes it what it is. In the following pages we see Paris as it is, with all its attributes, as one sees it on a stroll or as it appears in a blur when observed from above: always identical to itself and, though heterogeneous, extremely uncolorful and quite uneclectic.

What strikes one first about Paris is no doubt its dull coloring. The city is an infinite modulation of grays: slate lends a blue cast, brick a red one, and stone a yellow one. Gray does not have a good name; but in the very special light of Paris, it becomes a sort of receptacle for every nuance, creating a pearly refinement that excludes all shrillness.

What strikes one next is probably the strong alignment of the buildings, the way the façades combine, and the strange solidarity that holds the buildings together, as Loyer suggests, a bit like books in a library—books with the same binding, closed on their contents. The rows in the library of the city stretch out in a maze of secretiveness; each building is a book sheltering the private lives inside. It is as if the city had been written by Jorge Luis Borges in dense, infinite prose.

Looking up, one notices another row, formed by the nearly constant heights that the capital of the nineteenth century chose for itself, favoring the public space and rigor to arbitrary individual feats. Finally, turning to the details, one gets lost in the ornamental and architectural profusion that an apparently monotonous and monochromatic style conceals; but here, too, beyond distraction and diversity, a sense of constancy and, at heart, a unity of style again emerge. And that unity, we can be sure, was anything but an accident.

Perhaps nothing better illustrates Erwin Panofsky's notion of the formative strength of habits than the harmonious Parisian fabric, and the permanent link of its tiniest stitches to the pattern that structures (and indeed almost saturates) the whole. In the city's unity, above all, a community expressed itself. That is probably the case with all stylistic unity, but Paris is different in that the community intuitively expressed itself in the form of the city as a whole, rather than in isolated, individual monuments. In fact, everything leads one to believe that nineteenth-century Paris—the city we have inherited—lived between symbol and function, between the prestigious royal universe of representation and show and the worker's very different world—that is, and there is little doubt about this, between the spirit of classical architecture and the beginnings of architectural modernity. Yet this situation was not amorphous, but dual: it bound the two together, and in so doing invented a world.

That world was first and foremost the apogee of the bourgeoisie. It was at once symbolic and functionalistic but never purely figurative nor purely functionalist: a continual, all-encompassing oscillation, it did not have time to be one *or* the other. Caught in the stranglehold of an unprecedented level of real-estate speculation, the city had inherited representational values that had to be transcribed onto a vast new

9

expanse, but it was also faced with the responsibility of providing basic structures and services in an urban system characterized by its perpetual growth. This growth involved a kind of improvisation with no real theoretical underpinnings to speak of. There were great symbolic packages—for example, the Opera House—as well as second thoughts, regrets, and failures, and collisions with the social problems the century preferred to ignore, even when that meant attempting to settle things later in an absurdly bloody way.

If we can reconstruct the mentalities and rites of the nineteenth-century bourgeois universe (which in so many ways still provides the framework of our lives), and if we can read its "façades" as a kind of veil drawn over reality (a reality that could on occasion be terribly mean and obscene), it is because that veil still structures the entire city and indeed makes it breathe magically. For we have inherited what Benjamin called the city's "wings"—its streets, boulevards, and passageways—and more generally speaking, the spatial structuring that makes Paris a mosaic city in which the alternation between residential and nonresidential neighborhoods seems perfectly balanced. The nature of a legacy is to present the past as having value for the present. A legacy can turn out to be a burden, but in the case of Paris, whatever its faults, it does offer a valuable lesson. What François Loyer's book reveals is not just the city's material reality but also the quasi-organic link, the necessary accord between the city's fabric and its life. Even with its quirks, the Parisian fabric that the nineteenth century wove to fit its needs and tastes—a smooth and endless echo of itself—is not so much just one fabric among others as it is the conscious expression of the need for that fabric, woven into a dreamworld of stones.

The Paris that Baron Georges-Eugène Haussmann built had in fact long been in the making. François Loyer clearly shows that, when Chabrol and Rambuteau were prefects, Paris was already changing, as if irresistibly drawn to its destiny to become a metropolis—a destiny that Haussmann took it upon himself to fulfill. Haussmann's Paris was doubtless more pragmatic and less systematic than Ildefonso Cerda's Barcelona, its exact contemporary, but its texture, which always gave the street and public space the force of an ever acting principle, both demonstrates the need for that principle and offers a valuable lesson for urban planners today.

Loyer's point is not to pillory modernity. On the contrary, he shows us that the nineteenth century invented modernity, and that it must now be reinvented to make up for the damage done by the systematic negligence of twentieth-century urban planners, who have emphasized isolated architectural works at the expense of the city's overall structure. The discussion that is now beginning—and Loyer's book makes a major contribution to it—is most certainly not a discussion of architectural forms but rather a reevaluation of the contexts in which those forms arise. The contexts in which architecture exists are of infinite complexity, and the city is living proof of that complexity. The joy of being able to meet Baudelaire on a street corner also contains the possibility of all new encounters. It is in its prose, and because it is prose, that the city is also poetry—our song of self in space. François Loyer has written a poetics of the city: he describes the syntax and paradigms of the city's flowing prose, such as they interact in the language, the living language, that is Paris. Pointing out a balcony's ornate railings or a perspective forming an estuary for a crowd, the historian accompanies us through the city. But he also leaves us alone with the city, which becomes each reader's own fabulous story.

Jean-Christophe Bailly

INTRODUCTORY NOTE BY THE ATELIER PARISIEN D'URBANISME*

François Loyer began his research on nineteenth-century Paris in 1974, at the request of the Atelier Parisien d'Urbanisme (APUR). The APUR published the first results of Loyer's research in 1980 under the title *Paris au XIXe siècle; l'immeuble et l'espace urbain*; the map supplement included here first appeared in that earlier publication.

Long underestimated and even scorned, nineteenth-century architecture began to be taken more seriously in the second half of the 1970s. The study we asked Loyer to do was meant to facilitate decision-making concerning the protection of nineteenth-century buildings, which are particularly numerous in Paris. Our goal was to improve evaluation of the architectural expression of a period that was incredibly rich yet often repetitive.

Loyer's very innovative research has become a reference point. However, it would be a mistake to interpret his work as advocating the systematic preservation of buildings that is sometimes called for today. In the long run, such an attitude would rule out the modernization and improvement of a large part of Paris.

Loyer's book is the first comprehensive treatment of the architectural and urban features of a key era in the urban history of Paris that accounts in large part for the way the city looks today. It recalls the foundations of Haussmann's approach to urbanism: the hierarchy of spaces, streets, and constructions, the primacy of public spaces and architectural wholes over individual constructions, and so forth.

In conceptions such as these, contemporary urban planners are sure to find lessons worth pondering.

Indeed, the new building regulations adopted in Paris in 1977 (while Loyer's study was under way) incorporated urbanistic principles that had first been formulated during the nineteenth century (without, of course, copying that century's architectural forms). Since then, a greater concern for the city and the urban environment has emerged: public spaces have been accorded greater importance; buildings have been designed to be more in proportion to the constructions around them; and there has been a return to the strict alignment of construction on the building line.

To a certain extent, the city policies that determine a new neighborhood's heart and soul can henceforth draw inspiration—in an extremely undogmatic way—from this same nineteenth-century approach. This is especially true for the design of public spaces in areas in which the urban system remains unfinished.

In other words, the study of an epoch that strongly affirmed its confidence in the city must under no circumstances lead to a withdrawal into the past. Indeed, the nineteenth-century example should be taken as an invitation to complete and expand the city.

* The Atelier Parisien d'Urbanisme (APUR) is a nonprofit agency for urban studies sponsored by the city of Paris and the French government.

Foreword

The architecture of the urban environment is a subject as fascinating as it is difficult, particularly for an art historian. Indeed, the concepts art historians are used to handling are better suited to "great" architecture—monuments and exceptional works—than to everyday construction. To speak about ordinary buildings in terms of style is an exaggeration that furthermore underscores the extreme formalism of a discipline that tends to overlook the socioeconomic implications of artistic production and isolate the individual work within a trivial aesthetic debate. And yet, in the pages that follow, we have not hesitated to analyze the plastic aspects of Parisian buildings at considerable length. At times, the reader may even be surprised by how closely we have studied such apparently minor details as the graphic patterns of façades from the Haussmann era or the formal repertory of cast-iron ornament.

We have not adopted this approach out of blind conformity to an obsolete formalism, but rather as the best way to understand the meaning of nineteenth-century architectural production in Paris, a subject but slightly explored and usually misunderstood in the past. In some ways the apparent banality of our subject, which has not given rise to much discussion in intellectual circles, justified the method we decided on: when correctly analyzed, form will reveal the ideologies that underlie it. Indeed, in a formal system as codified as architecture is, it is not hard to distinguish families of edifices, to situate them geographically and historically, and then to formulate a socioeconomic hypothesis—which subsequent analysis of various source material will either confirm or invalidate. Nothing could be more rigorous than this kind of scientific approach based on hypothesis and verification—poles apart from the subjectivity that is generally thought to reign supreme in art and art criticism. Our method is a purely archaeological one, based on locating, describing, comparing, and contrasting buildings. Description is the first step on the road to interpretation, since only by patiently describing and comparing buildings can one hope to decipher the ideogrammatic language that architecture so often is. Every structure has something to tell us about how and why it was built. It expresses the cultural context that existed when it was designed and the socioeconomic level of those for whom it was built. A culture is a complex network of interactions. The

13

historian's job is to discover the diverging trends and great issues of an epoch—that is, to show how a culture came to be.

The fact that history is made up of contrasting and even contradictory aesthetic ideals broadens a historian's perception of contemporary artistic debates and, similarly, forces him to reflect more deeply on the real meaning of current tastes. This is particularly true today, when, after undergoing half a century of punishment, history has come back into fashion. At times our generation seems to be wallowing in simultaneous and somewhat superficial admiration for the successive phases of contemporary history—art nouveau, art deco, the 1940s and—why not?—even the 1960s. In the face of such cultural inflation, the historian's task is a thankless one: he must address the past and the present, relive a bygone era and filter the judgments (and misjudgments) of his own day. Past and present are so tightly intertwined that it is impossible to think seriously about the past without taking it, at least to some extent, as a model. Rather than try to hide it, we feel it necessary to warn the reader of our bias: in our opinion, the Haussmann era provides part of the answer for which our own urban planners have been looking.

Indeed, Paris offers an extraordinary lesson. Although the city of the nineteenth century had inherited a classical cultural system, it adapted perfectly to the demands of an industrial economy. Moreover, it succeeded in gradually transposing that system into the language of modernity. The history presented in the following pages is that of an eighteenth-century city whose fundamental values survived the enormous upheavals of the nineteenth century. Worked out during the Renaissance, the classical city came to maturity during the reign of Louis XVI. Throughout the nineteenth century—and for that matter well into our own—artists and architects succeeded in keeping the city alive despite the brutally obsolete socioeconomic system underlying it. But when they changed course and adopted new values stemming from the industrial system, the city collapsed, leaving our generation the difficult task of reinventing a lost urban culture—a task for which we are all too often novices, as lacking in knowledge as in subtlety. (The generally crude imitations of the old city offered us today are blatant proof of our ignorance and would certainly have made our more civilized ancestors smile.)

My interest in the buildings of the Haussmann era began when I noticed how they were being altered by sloppy repairs and rash renovations during my youth. Having seen so many cast-iron pipes, zinc roofs, molded doors and cornices, and marble fireplaces disappear, I had the impression that by the time narrow-minded admirers of modernity got through modernizing, nothing would be left of the typical Parisian building. As my interest grew, I quite naturally discovered the architectural quality of nineteenth-century buildings (which at the time were seriously underrated and completely misunderstood) and even thought about writing a thesis on the subject.

For various reasons, that project—which dates back some twenty years—never came to fruition, but then, an exceptional opportunity was given to me by the Atelier Parisien d'Urbanisme. In 1974—the year the nineteenth century was "rediscovered"—Pierre-Yves Ligen asked me to do an inventory of nineteenth-century Parisian buildings. After five years of work the inventory and maps were finished, and I published an analysis of the Parisian building and Haussmann's approach to urban planning. For the present book, I thought it necessary to recast the various elements of that previous study in a substantial chronological synthesis retracing the architectural and urban history of Paris from the French Revolution down to World War II.

It might seem surprising that such an extensive investigation draws but slightly on the enormous number of available primary sources and turns only occasionally to contemporary scholarship. But when one's aim is to formulate a broad synthesis in a field dominated by very specialized monographs, one cannot let oneself be overwhelmed by the masses of available documents and the relatively partial opinions and theories that other scholars and critics have set out. I have quite deliberately carried out my study using purely visual criteria: I have studied the buildings themselves, and not what has been or is being said about them. Even so, a huge number of documents had to be consulted; just getting through them was a big job in itself. (In the notes, I have mentioned only those individuals to whom I am directly indebted.)

This study is only a beginning: it is hypothetical and will have to be fully verified by future investigations. Over the last ten years some essential inventories have been done—for example, the building permits in the Archives de la Seine (by the Commission du Vieux Paris) and nineteenth-century periodicals (by researchers at the Musée d'Orsay). But much remains to be done. We must now investigate the individual careers of a multitude of artists and builders, define schools and trends, and delve into the mysteries of professional contacts and influences. Moreover, in order to flesh out the present study, we need to consider the many debates and disagreements that accompanied the urban and architectural history of nineteenth-century Paris and, perhaps most important, study the socioeconomic archives that will prove or disprove the analyses found in the following pages. My greatest hope is that such research will facilitate the reevaluation of the urban culture I have tried so hard to bring back to life.

Rue Coquillière, looking from the Rue Jean-Jacques Rousseau toward the Rue du Jour. Photo: Marville, 1874.

17

Rue du Temple, looking from the Rue Dupetit-Thouars toward the future Rue de Turbigo. Photo: Marville, 1866.

Chapter I
The Traditional City

Well before the effects of industrial capitalism began to be felt, Paris was already a major city. Long the largest metropolis in Europe, it served as a guide for other cities.[1] Around the time of the Revolution, the city counted more than half a million inhabitants in the vast area inside the Farmers-General Wall, but that expanse was far from completely developed. Indeed, the city filled scarcely a third of the area inside the official city limits, for it had never really broken out of the old ramparts built by Charles V in the fourteenth century (and somewhat enlarged to the west during the Wars of Religion). Radiating out from the city's compact core there were, however, extensive faubourgs, some of which spread beyond the Farmers-General Wall, outside the city limits.

The large reserves of undeveloped land made it possible for the city to grow steadily until the midnineteenth century. The conveyance of old monasteries, convents, and feudal estates provided centrally located land to be developed, and a number of new districts were built on the eve of the French Revolution: for example, the Odéon district (on the site of the old Condé mansion); the Palais-Royal district (on the Duc d'Orléans's appanage); and the Val-Sainte-Cathérine (Rue de Turenne), Choiseul (Opéra-Comique), Luxembourg (Rue des Fleurs), and Faubourg du Temple. Furthermore, the confiscation of the clergy's property came at just the right moment and satisfied the quickly growing urban center's appetite: starting in 1793, some 1,000 acres—of the 8,330 the city contained at that time—were turned over to real-estate developers.[2]

The city's growth was governed by customs and traditions that had withstood the test of time. Consequently, the vast agglomeration had a profoundly unified appearance in the late eighteenth century, nuanced only by the traditional opposition between city and faubourg (and the nascent distinction between residential and working-class neighborhoods). Even today one still finds many traces of the traditional urban configuration on which the New Paris was built in the nineteenth century.

Before analyzing how the city changed in the nineteenth century, one must determine the traditional characteristics of the old Parisian cityscape. Deeply rooted in a tradition of medieval origin, the architectural and urban accomplishments of the nineteenth century

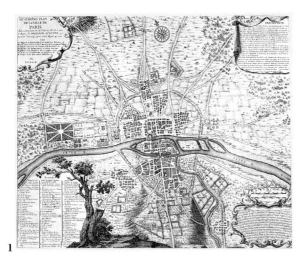

1

2

3

Above: three maps showing the growth of Paris. Reprinted from *Traité de la police*, Delamare, 1713.
1. The city under Philip Augustus.
2. The fourth wall, begun in 1367 under Charles V, and completed in 1383 under Charles VI.
3. The city's growth beyond the walls from 1422, under Charles VII, to the end of Henri III's reign in 1589.

Right: the successive walls and city limits of Paris, from the late Roman Empire down to 1845 (map prepared by Michel Fleury, 1964).

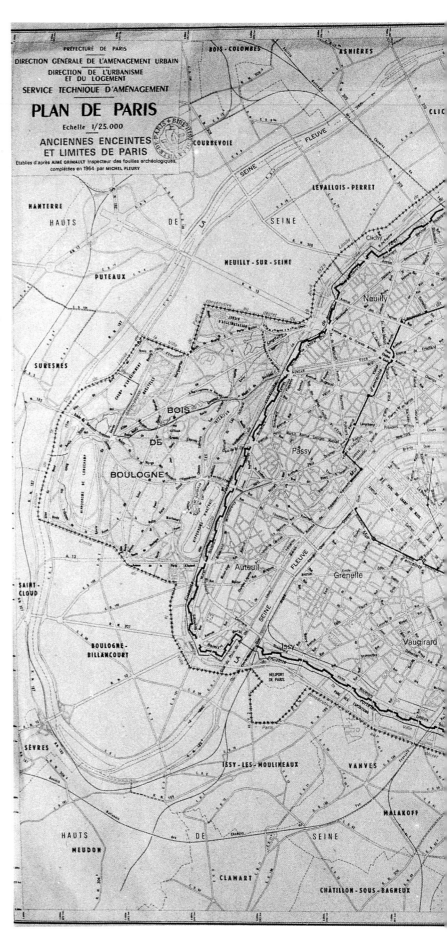

PRÉFECTURE DE PARIS
DIRECTION GÉNÉRALE DE L'AMÉNAGEMENT URBAIN
DIRECTION DE L'URBANISME
ET DU LOGEMENT
SERVICE TECHNIQUE D'AMÉNAGEMENT

PLAN DE PARIS
Echelle 1/25.000

ANCIENNES ENCEINTES
ET LIMITES DE PARIS
Etablies d'après AIMÉ GRIMAULT Inspecteur des fouilles archéologiques,
complétées en 1964 par MICHEL FLEURY

would be incomprehensible without some knowledge of the earlier models that inspired them, since nineteenth-century architects and administrators by no means rejected the city's past. On the contrary, they did their best to adapt and enhance principles that had proved their worth over the years. If they rejected anything, it was the deterioration of the urban environment caused by the city's skyrocketing population density: in the same area, the city's population rose from half a million to over a million between 1801 and 1846. The city was loyal to its past; we shall therefore begin our study with a retrospective glance at Paris as it was in the eighteenth century.

A Structure of Medieval Origin

A Dense and Heterogeneous Center

Prior to the nineteenth century, Paris was characterized by a limited surface area, high density, and the multifunctionality of its neighborhoods, which went hand in hand with a close intermingling of the social classes. Since the Middle Ages, city life had revolved around the street, which had multiple functions, ranging from communications to commerce and craft. Many trades were pursued more or less on the roadway itself, where produce vendors, blacksmiths, carpenters, and masons could all be found. Conversely, activity decreased proportionately with distance from the street, driveways and courtyards being tributaries of the street's seething river of life. The most sought-after dwellings were those closest to the street, with a door opening onto it or a second-floor balcony directly overlooking it; more modest dwellings were located on the upper floors and the courtyards, where one did not enjoy direct contact with the hustle and bustle of the outside world.

The priority given to the street was so strong that it conditioned the parceling of land into narrow strips that, though barely six meters across, were sometimes as much as forty meters deep.[3] A neighborhood's size and importance were directly reflected by the activity of its major streets: a neighborhood started as a linear flow (the main street in the faubourg); then, once the saturation point had been reached on the main street, parallel street networks were created. However, before that stage was reached, the main roadway had been completely developed from one end to the other, as had the intersecting secondary streets (benefiting, along varying lengths, from its proximity).

Limitation of the city's surface area was the golden rule of occupancy, which was based on the principle of exchange—to the detriment of traffic, when necessary. Since the city's structure was not adapted to any other means of transport, the only way to get around was on foot. In other words, the city had a pedestrian scale. Its

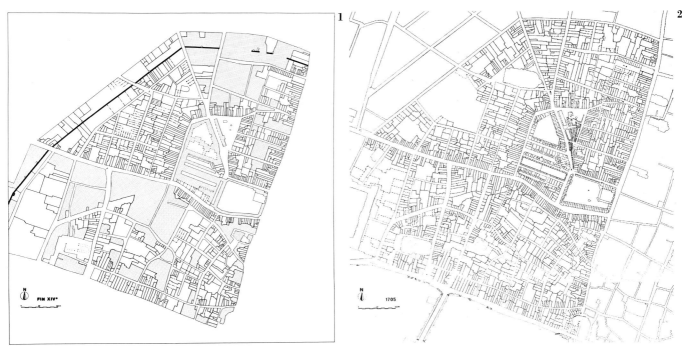

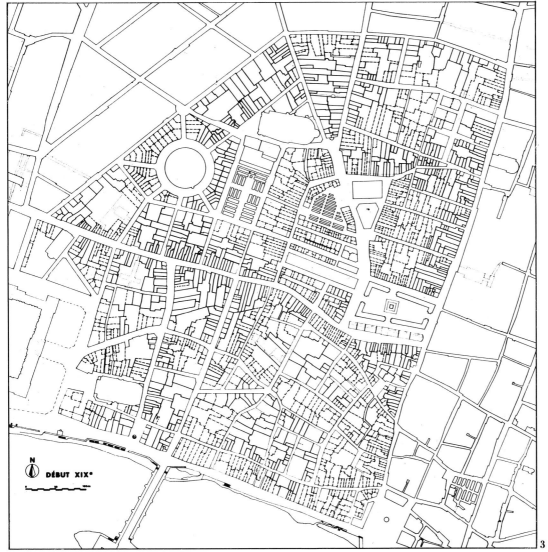

Three maps showing the lot pattern of the Halles district. Reprinted from Françoise Boudon, André Chastel, Hélène Couzy, and Françoise Hamon, *Système de l'architecture urbaine* (Paris: C.N.R.S., 1977).

1. Late fourteenth century.
2. Early eighteenth century.
3. Early nineteenth century.

The maps show the great stability of lot patterns in Old Paris. The traditional pattern was not significantly modified until Louis-Philippe's reign, when laws were enacted authorizing land expropriation for public use. Until then, new construction meant building up the old lots more densely.

maximum diameter was three kilometers—half an hour's walk, or a quarter hour's from the center to the edge of town. As soon as the land along a neighborhood's main and secondary streets had been developed, the old lots were built up with additional constructions, then new stories were added to existing buildings, filling the lots even more and gradually eating up all remaining space. New expansion was conceived of only in terms of developing land that had not been used earlier because it was liable to flooding, and sites that, being abandoned, were recoverable (e.g., old mansions and church and military property). Or, alternatively, expansion resulted from opening up access to areas in the center of town that had previously been hard to reach. Thus the Pont-Neuf and the Pont-Marie made it possible to develop, respectively, the Pré-aux-Clercs and the Ile Saint-Louis.

The key principle of centrality (and its direct consequence, high density) ruled out any secondary development of a suburban type—the suburb being, by definition, a noncentral place dependent on the city and complementing the constructed area agriculturally.[4] Trades were seldom forced out of the city's center for being too specialized or harmful. Although butchers, tanners, weavers, and boatmen were found in specific neighborhoods that were sometimes outside the city limits proper, they were always within easy reach of the center and, of course, the waterway. Not even the market gardeners were far from the center of town.

Consequently, there was a close blend of activities throughout the entire city: dwellings were located over shops, and the latter were next door to craftsmen whose workshops were usually located in the courtyards behind the shops facing the street. Similarly, there was no clear separation between rich and poor: the rule was juxtaposition (the Sully mansion on the bustling Rue Saint-Antoine) and superposition (the ground floor for commerce, the second floor for prestigious dwellings, and the attic for the working class). Finally, the functions that took up the most space—such as storing foodstuffs and parking vehicles—were attended to in the middle of large blocks whose outer crust was made up of tight strips of narrow, shallow houses. These large blocks ensured the existence of reserves of land to be built up in the future, when passageways were built through them, thus forming intricate mazes of little courtyards linked by narrow paths.

These general principles determined the configuration of an extremely dense urban center that was small in scale and incredibly complex, since the tight mesh formed by the narrow roads and chopped-up lots simultaneously served all functions, the essential value being proximity, which favored exchange. The architectural typology of the city's buildings closely reflected the tight interweaving of shops, residences, and workshops on which the urban system was based.

Soon cramped by the old ramparts around it, the city spontaneously
overflowed into faubourgs, which were the beginning of what would
later become urban neighborhoods. It would hardly be an
exaggeration to say that every street in the city started off as a faubourg
and then, as its density rose, became a part of the urban center. Each
new faubourg began and was built up in the same way.

The physiognomies of city and faubourg were very different: an
area's population density was expressed in the amount of empty space
and the heights of buildings found there. The loose mesh of the
outlying areas corresponded to large reserves of space that allowed
huge blocks and wide lots, courtyards, and gardens. The airiness of the
outlying areas would, however, not have been visible when seen from
the street, if the low buildings had not immediately informed one of a
section's noncentral status.

Indeed, prior to the city's spatial explosion in the nineteenth
century, Paris was based on a clear articulation of buildings and houses
in an obvious hierarchy of sizes (from two to six stories). Traces of that
hierarchy are still visible in the structure of concentric rings indicating
successive additions. The practices of cramming a lot with new
constructions and adding extra stories to existing buildings allowed the
city's density to be increased, first in the center and then farther out.

The architectural typology prevailing at the end of the Ancien
Régime was unambiguous. At the top of the hierarchy was the building
with a freestone façade, modeled after the impressive buildings on the
old royal squares: above an arcaded ground floor and mezzanine used
for shops, there were two floors of living space, the lower being more
prestigious; the top of the building was formed by an attic with a
mansard roof with one or two levels of living space, generally used as
servants' quarters. It goes without saying that this type of building was
not very widespread.

This preeminent type—close to the Italian palazzo—had several
less prestigious variants that were actually modifications of the
medieval house. The mezzanine floor was eliminated, and the arcade
was lowered to a single high level used for shops; three main stories of
living space were placed above the arcade, each level being of
approximately the same prestige; finally, the attic was turned into an
apartment. Typologically uncertain, this hybrid model was moving
away from the traditional house toward a new form, the apartment
building.

The ordinary building was an economical version of the preceding
models. The arcades were replaced by simple, straight lintels on a
ground floor reduced in height (it was no higher than the other floors);
the upper floors were of equal ceiling height and prestige, and their
number increased to four; the façade was built not of stone but of wood
and plaster. This model seems to have already existed in the
seventeenth century (e.g., the Rue de Cléry and Rue d'Aboukir); the
eighteenth century simply strengthened its graphic systems and

1. Lambert mansion, Quai d'Anjou. The section on the right is the rental building where the architect Le Vau once lived. 2. House of Jules Hardouin Mansart, on the corner of the Rue des Petits-Champs and the Rue Sainte-Anne: the top of the urban hierarchy. 3. Rue de la Harpe. Flanked by ordinary houses, a handsome eighteenth-century façade with arcades.

Three examples of how the working-class faubourgs once looked.

1. Rue Mouffetard (site of the present Avenue des Gobelins), looking north. In the background, the Pantheon. Photo: Marville, ca. 1867. **2.** Intersection of the Rue du Faubourg-Saint-Jacques and the Rue Leclerc, photographed from the Rue Humboldt (now the Rue Jean-Dolent). Photo: Marville, ca. 1865.

3. Rue de Port-Royal. On the left, the Faubourg Saint-Jacques. On the right, the Rue Saint-Jacques. Photo: Marville, ca. 1865.

The center of Paris: tall, narrow houses from the seventeenth century, next to the wider buildings that began to appear when adjacent lots were joined in the eighteenth century. **1.** Rue Saint-Honoré. **2.** Rue de la Montagne-Sainte-Geneviève.

considerably increased the size of the window openings at the expense of the piers. The very severe appearance of these constructions, built in blocks that became increasingly uniform as time went by, was relieved by wrought-iron ornaments that account for most of the charm of mideighteenth-century buildings.

Outside the medieval center of Paris, a completely different architectural typology was found: before the Revolution, the Marais, for example, was still a suburban neighborhood whose only densely populated sections were the larger arteries. Behind the urban surface found along the main streets in the faubourgs, a provincial typology based on three-story houses dominated. The most luxurious of these were the mansions in the aristocratic faubourgs, which were built back from the street, where the building line was maintained by a one-story wall. This model, which can still be seen on the Rue de Grenelle in the Faubourg Saint-Germain, was first modified when porched houses were constructed on the street in front of the mansion (as was often the case in the Marais, starting in the late seventeenth century).

At lower levels of social standing, simpler materials and decorative features were used, but the number of stories and the overall size of buildings did not change. Thus even the village houses in Auteuil and Belleville remained loyal to the three-story height. Most exceptions can be explained by the fact that the buildings in a given district were not all built at the same time. At the Pré-aux-Clercs and on the Rue de Charenton, for instance, the earliest constructions (sometimes dating back to the late sixteenth century) still included ground floors on stone posts, flat façades with window openings of varying sizes (expressing the internal functions and layout of the rooms), and big dormer windows at the base of the roof. Later, four-story houses became more common; then the mansard roof—so typical of the eighteenth century—appeared. During the first half of the nineteenth century, five-story houses were added, the top story in neoclassical style with a low ceiling of about 2.30 meters. Fairly commonplace in the east of Paris, this was the last embodiment of the traditional house on the outskirts of town.

What is striking is that the upper, middle, and lower classes lived together in the same neighborhoods and indeed on the same streets. Differences in social position could still be seen in the often quite dissimilar buildings on a street, ranging from small stone mansions decorated with wrought-iron elements, sculptures, or moldings to extremely modest little wood-and-plaster houses. Similarly, slate roofs, synonymous with upper-class constructions, neighbored the tile roofs of working-class constructions steeped in the rural tradition of the countryside around Paris. In the late eighteenth century the geographic segregation of the social classes was just beginning.

One more aspect of the traditional typology should be mentioned. Established by strict regulations, the city limits were still quite perceptible; the phenomenon of the suburb as a group of detached buildings existed neither topographically nor typologically. Buildings and houses formed a continuous, uninterrupted façade on both sides of every street; indeed, building regulations constantly insisted on this. As density lessened, the reserves of land at the back of lots increased while, farther out, buildings decreased in size. But even in areas where there were no buildings, the city's landowners were systematically required to wall off their lots in order to maintain a solid façade along the street. This walling off of city lots (including those that had not been built on) strengthened the mineral character of the urban world while opposing it to the open spaces of the surrounding countryside. When a tree could be found in the faubourgs, it was always behind a wall—a little piece of the country hemmed in by the expanding city. The city could be stretched, but the chain was never broken.

The old faubourgs. Rue Saint-Jacques, photographed from the Rue Royer-Collard.

A direct outgrowth of the Middle Ages, the faubourg tradition began to change when segregation of the social classes appeared in the eighteenth century. Until then the luxurious mansions in the Marais, for example, had neighbored the Rue des Francs-Bourgeois and the Rue Saint-Antoine, and residential areas could not be sharply distinguished from working-class districts—unless we were to distinguish between a neighborhood and the façade formed by its outer crust, which would ignore their close complementarity. The situation was completely different in the Faubourg Saint-Germain: at the branching intersection formed by the Rue de Grenelle, Rue de Varenne, and Rue de Babylone, the Rue du Bac clearly separated the traditional faubourg on one side of the intersection from the modern residential neighborhood on the other. Although the alignment of the buildings along the streets was maintained (as was the medieval custom of building mansions between a courtyard and a garden), the urban façade was weak, and the mixing of functions nonexistent.

The loose alignment found in the eighteenth-century neighborhoods of the Faubourg Saint-Germain. Rue de Grenelle, beyond the Rue du Bac.

The Matignon mansion on the Rue de Babylone was an important symbol in itself: the gate in the long wall around the mansion, allowing a backdrop of foliage to be glimpsed, created a total break with the mineral unity of the urban world. The mansion was on the last frontier between city and country; just a little beyond, one found little villages (Gros-Caillou) surrounded by vegetable gardens and fields. Matignon was the symbol of a world that was tending to assert itself as antiurban: the mansion was subtly turned into a château, and the garden into a formal park. The traditional hierarchy of urban space was turned upside down: it was no longer the street that counted, but the plot of ground—the inside, which is private, and not the outside, which is collective. In short, the faubourg had become a suburb: it was no longer a prolongation of the city, but its opposite.

As the Faubourg Saint-Germain was becoming a residential area, the eastern faubourgs were specializing in working-class functions. On the old lumber yards around the Bastille and the Arsenal, sheds and warehouses proliferated, built to fill the pressing needs of craftsmen. By the end of the eighteenth century, the extremely attractive picture

31

1 and **2.** Alleys lined with workshops, Faubourg Saint-Antoine (173 and 155 respectively). **3.** Detail of Turgot's map (1734). The Faubourg Saint-Antoine runs northeast from the Bastille, lined with market gardens.

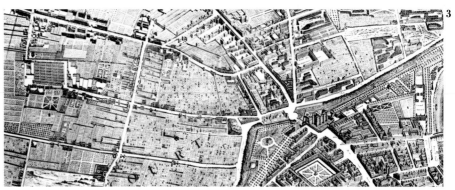

of the district found on Turgot's 1739 map no longer in any way corresponded to reality. The deep lots with vegetable gardens behind the rows of faubourg houses had given way to a maze of narrow passageways lined with workshops. While the Faubourg Saint-Germain was of low density, each lot in the eastern faubourgs was used intensively. Soon there was no reserve space left; worse still, because of overcrowding and the total disappearance of green spaces, health was endangered. In fact, the eastern faubourgs were no better off than the most saturated sections in the center of town. Reflecting the new economic structure that emerged in the eighteenth century, the geographic separation of the social classes had decisive consequences for the city. Once a part of the social body had isolated itself from the whole to invent new forms of residential space, defined in *opposition* to the city (the place of exchange and proximity), the medieval continuum—the complementarity and mixture of functions—was no more than a memory.

While the working-class faubourgs long respected the urban and architectural traditions handed down from the Middle Ages, the new residential neighborhoods were quick to adopt specific models that broke with tradition. This is why the old faubourgs of Paris are today just about the last remaining evidence of an urban culture that has otherwise disappeared. Although they have been allowed to deteriorate for purely economic reasons, the faubourgs are still very instructive to anyone interested in the city's history and structure. Much of Old Paris was demolished in the nineteenth century, but the faubourgs have miraculously retained enough of their identity to allow one to piece together a fairly accurate picture of what Paris was like before the Industrial Revolution—a Paris that contemporary society is tending to destroy. It is quite important to have some idea of what Paris was like in the late eighteenth century, since the deterioration of the old urban structure led directly to the nineteenth century's determination to reshape the face of the city.

1

401. – PARIS. – La Rue des Saules et la Rue de l'Abreuvoir à Montmartre

2

Facing page: **1.** Corner of the Rue des Saules and the Rue de l'Abreuvoir in Montmartre. Postcard. **2.** Rue de la Brèche-aux-Loups. Anon., 1898. An old country house to which a workshop was later attached.

3. Passage des Deux-Sœurs, looking from the Rue Lafayette toward the Rue du Faubourg-Montmartre. Photo: Marville, ca. 1868.

Vestiges of a Bygone Landscape

The Heart of Old Paris

1. Quai aux Fleurs and Rue des Ursins, front view. Photo: Atget, 190**2. 2.** The same place, side view, 1986.

In truth, only fragments remain. The last variant of a structure that had endured since the Middle Ages, eighteenth-century Paris has really survived only in certain districts on the Right Bank—essentially, the Marais, the Halles, and the Sentier. Despite the many new streets built in conjunction with the redevelopment of the Halles that began during the reign of Louis-Philippe (Rue Rambuteau, Halles Centrales, Rue de Turbigo, Boulevard de Sébastopol, Avenue de l'Opéra, Rue Etienne-Marcel, and the extension of the Rue de Rivoli), the area was able to hold its own.[5] However, as a result of the successive enlargements of the Louvre and the reorganization of the Châtelet and the Hôtel de Ville, the buildings that once graced the banks of the Seine have disappeared almost entirely. If the projects proposed between World War I and World War II for the Saint-Gervais neighborhood had been carried through to completion, the whole riverfront on the Right Bank would have been destroyed (a destruction actually begun on the Rue des Nonnains-d'Hyères).

Generally speaking, the high density and old lot pattern of the central neighborhoods on the Right Bank saved them from being entirely renovated. Even in those areas where construction of new streets was most energetic, large residual pockets went untouched, though some were left in a sorry state indeed (e.g., the Sainte-Anne neighborhood, cut in two by the Avenue de l'Opéra).[6]

At the very center of Paris, the Ile de la Cité and its neighbor, the Ile Saint-Louis, experienced completely different fates. If the Ile Saint-Louis was left intact, the Ile de la Cité was totally destroyed by the "administrative reorganization" carried out there during the nineteenth century. The three big complexes built for the Palais de Justice, the Préfecture de Police, and the Hôtel-Dieu eliminated practically every trace of the medieval fabric preserved there hitherto. Not even the area around the Rue du Cloître was spared: constructed on the site of the gardens of the canons of Notre-Dame, the current buildings were all rebuilt in the late nineteenth century to fit in with the constructions on the Rue d'Arcole and the Rue Jean-du-Bellay. The mansion on the Rue des Ursins is a unique remnant of the island's medieval past; since it has been restored, however, it must be considered with great caution.

On the Left Bank, urban renovation was carried out with particular zeal in the nineteenth century. Paradoxically, it had less effect on the riverfront, where no monumental projects were envisaged (which was certainly not the case on the Right Bank), but it disrupted the inner unity of the neighborhoods much more profoundly.

When the Saint-Michel/Saint-Germain intersection was built at the foot of the hills south of the Seine, a number of self-sufficient pockets were left along the river—Maître-Albert, Saint-Julien-le-Pauvre,

Several vestiges of medieval Paris.
1. Corner of the Rue de Buci and the Rue de Seine.
2. The old Rue de l'Ecole-de-Médecine at the corner of the Rue Larrey, 1866. **3.** Half-timbered houses, Rue François-Miron.

Saint-Séverin, and Saint-André-des-Arts, all inside the medieval wall.

Major projects were realized throughout the eastern part of the Left Bank, where two new sets of parallel streets—the Rue des Ecoles and the Boulevard Saint-Germain (the product of two rather contradictory projects for developing the Left Bank), and the Rue Saint-Jacques and the Boulevard Saint-Michel—completely reorganized the neighborhood.

Although the following observation is not directly related to the subject, it is interesting to note how few traces of the medieval environment could be found in eighteenth-century Paris, which —despite a timid spurt of growth to the west—had scarcely budged from its medieval perimeters. Aside from foundations and a very few scattered examples (Rue de Buci, Rue François-Miron), the medieval house had already practically disappeared from Paris.[7] Built of exposed wood, the corbeled medieval houses were the object of exceedingly severe regulations from the seventeenth century on. If some medieval elements can still be found in Paris, it is because, traditionally, lots were seldom completely reconstructed and, whenever feasible, building materials were salvaged and used for new constructions. (The practice of reusing materials survived well into the nineteenth century, and even later for working-class constructions.) Thus, particularly around the Halles, a certain number of medieval vestiges can still be found.

Though medieval constructions are practically nonexistent in present-day Paris, sixteenth- and seventeenth-century buildings are still plentiful (e.g., Saint-Paul/Saint-Antoine, Ségurier/Dauphine, and naturally the Ile Saint-Louis and the Pré-aux-Clercs). They are modest constructions of mediocre quality, built of wood or masonry and rubblestone, tightly packed together on narrow lots. Freestone façades are rare, having become popular in the eighteenth century; indeed, they reflect that century's interest in a building's outside appearance, as do the decorative frames around window openings and wrought ironwork.

Constructed in the seventeenth century, the Saint-Sulpice and Pré-aux-Clercs districts were able to hold their own when the Boulevard Saint-Germain was built through them, although the Saint-Germain market did suffer greatly. These seventeenth-century neighborhoods were laid out on an almost regular orthogonal grid. The absence of inner gardens (replaced by narrow inner courtyards in the middle of the lot) characterized all the constructions, from the humblest to the fanciest. The arrangement of the courtyard was closed in by the lot: parallel main buildings at the front and back were connected by closed passageways built along the sides of the lot, leaving a courtyard in the middle. The architectural treatment of the courtyards was generally mediocre, if not nonexistent.

Despite the many transformations it has undergone, the Saint-Germain district can still be seen to have been completely different in nature. A neighborhood of mansions, it was morphologically close to the initial state of the Marais and the Faubourg Saint-Honoré, characterized by low constructions on large semisuburban lots with gardens and even parks behind the edifices, and by a particular architectural typology.

The Parisian mansion[8] was always placed between a courtyard and a garden and so was isolated from the street and other residences. The street façade was maintained by a wall with a big entry gate. On the other side of the wall, a courtyard preceded the main building and was flanked by low wings used as sheds and stables. (Later the wings took on more prestigious functions, and service activities were relegated to an annex area of less elegant architecture.) The mansion itself was based on the traditional dialectic of reception rooms (the salons) and private apartments. The rear façade opened onto a pleasure garden; only a few prestigious edifices included a rear wing with a monumental gallery. When the government transformed these mansions into offices, the wall along the street was often replaced by a building, but the mansion itself was left intact. Consequently, the Faubourg Saint-Germain is today a "two-faced" neighborhood: on the street, the arrangement is nineteenth century; within, the prestigious big mansions reveal their earlier suburban origins.

The working-class faubourgs to the east, Saint-Médard and Saint-

The Faubourgs: Mansions and Workers

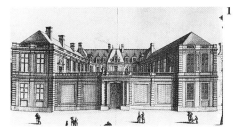

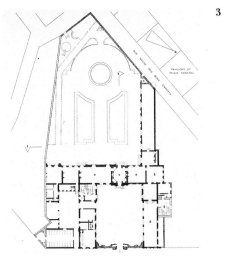

François Mansart's Vrillière mansion. **1.** Street façade. **2.** Garden façade. **3.** Plan of the ground floor. Engravings after Marot.

Aspects of the old outlying villages. **1.** Rue de Tourtille in Belleville. **2.** Corner of the Rue Singer and the Rue Alfred-Bruneau in Passy. **3.** Beginning of the Rue de la Roquette (even numbers), near the Place de la Bastille. **4.** Rue de Charenton.

Antoine, were comparable in lot pattern, but the lots were built up in a radically different way, each being packed full, drastically reducing the courtyards in size. The degree to which a given lot could be built up varied greatly, but building always meant adding on. As a result, constructions in the eastern faubourgs are seldom as old as they look. If a building on the street was built in the seventeenth or eighteenth century, it was often profoundly transformed later by the addition of extra stories and secondary constructions—especially during the Restoration, when, for want of a coherent approach to urbanization, dense new constructions prevailed. Notably in the Faubourg Saint-Antoine,[9] most of the existing workshops on the courtyards were built between 1800 and 1850, after which construction activity gradually slowed down, until the last years of the Second Empire. The practice of totally reconstructing a lot did not begin until the Third Republic. The rise of capitalism was certainly not unrelated to the end of piecemeal reconstruction of lots—one building at a time, rather than all the buildings at once.

The best-preserved parts of Old Paris are certainly the faubourgs, which modern urbanization has often bypassed, since city planners have preferred to build new developments adjacent to them (e.g., Saint-Honoré/Rivoli and Mouffetard/Monge). Thus the faubourgs Saint-Germain, Saint-Honoré, Montmartre, Saint-Denis/Saint-Martin, du Temple, Saint-Antoine, and Mouffetard have all retained significant traces of the seventeenth- and eighteenth-century environment. Indeed, in some cases the old buildings have been almost fully preserved and deserve to be more carefully protected than they have been up to now. The fate of the Erasme/Mouffetard intersection offers striking proof of the urgency of protecting the old faubourgs.

The Villages around Paris

The last aspect of Old Paris, the villages outside the Farmers-General Wall, has long been ignored by historians of the capital. It has too often been forgotten that the outlying villages, which were important commercial centers, played a significant role in the city's history.[10] Passy and Auteuil had been preserved until recently, but have suffered greatly over the last few years. On the Left Bank the incoherent urbanization of the fifteenth arrondissement has not left many traces of Grenelle and Vaugirard. In the thirteenth and fourteenth arrondissements, the villages of Montrouge and Gentilly were too far out to be annexed to the capital when the Thiers fortifications were built; only Butte-aux-Cailles, a modest hamlet, was annexed to Paris at that time. On the other hand, in the east of Paris Charonne, Belleville, Ménilmontant, La Villette, and La Chapelle —like Montmartre to the north—all acted as stops on the outward growth of Paris. However, recent renovations have partially or completely wiped them off the map, just as Haussmann's urban policies had earlier destroyed the village of Ternes.

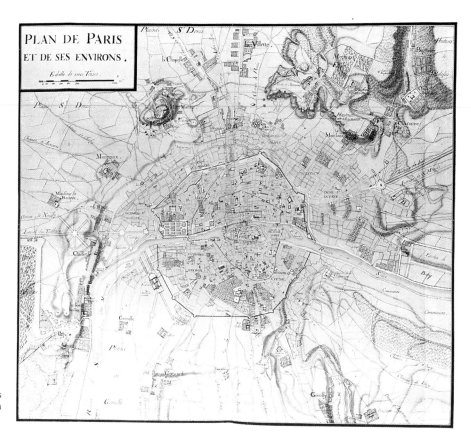

Early eighteenth-century map showing the villages outside the Farmers-General Wall. Reprinted from *Oisivetés de M. de Vauban*.

The evolution of the villages from a rural to a craft or industrial function was closely related to that of the faubourgs. In many cases the transformation was recent. Thus the transfer of the city's fiscal limits from the Louis XIV wall to the Farmers-General Wall rendered obsolete the Faubourg Saint-Antoine's initial function as a relay for horses and a storage place for fodder, wood, and other raw materials; then, as industry developed, the old stables and grain lofts between the Bastille and La Nation became workshops.

When this happened, Charonne and Belleville, eastern villages located outside the new Farmers-General Wall, took on the functions of the old faubourgs, then were themselves transformed into faubourgs, adopting all the latter's morphological characteristics. Bypassed by Haussmann (who was more interested in filling in the big gaps between the villages around Paris after their annexation in 1860), the old villages resisted nineteenth-century urbanization fairly well, but recent urban renewal projects have razed them in favor of totally heterogeneous structures. If nothing else, their destruction has at least demonstrated, *a contrario*, the urban qualities of areas that, however deteriorated, were far richer in potential than the simplistic renovations that have replaced them.

The Paris described here has little to do with what has been called the "sacred perimeter" of the Farmers-General Wall. In fact, the official city limits during the reign of Louis XVI defined a much larger area than the actual city. The latter had only recently expanded beyond the medieval ramparts and adjacent faubourgs. At best, the city of Louis XVI covered the area within the Louis XIV wall. Beyond, it developed along several diverging or even splintered axes in the suburban villages.

For appropriate protective measures to be taken, it should not be forgotten that the medieval and postmedieval fabric of Old Paris is found in two types of clearly demarcated neighborhoods: in the extremely dense inner city, and in the much more loosely structured faubourgs and villages. Especially for the faubourgs and villages, strong protective measures are sorely needed: the low densities and deteriorating constructions of those areas combine to threaten their very survival, whereas the old neighborhoods in the center of the city are much more strongly structured.

The Impending Saturation Point

The city that had begun as a small Roman town on Mont Sainte-Geneviève continued to grow smoothly, expanding little by little, down to the nineteenth century. Yet by the age of classicism growth had already approached a critical limit, and a rather anarchic series of new streets, as for instance the connection of the Rue du Roule with the Monnaie/Pont-Neuf axis in the seventeenth century, merely delayed the inevitable crisis.[11]

When the population of Paris reached the million mark, communications in the tight, dense network of medieval origin became so difficult that the specialization of functions began to appear. Thus the new residential faubourgs were soon followed by sections outside the walls (with the Louis XIV wall constituting the real city limits down to the Restoration). The conveyance of national property had already allowed the creation of huge developments such as those around the Bourse and on the Rue d'Assas. Farther out, the Right-Bank districts between the Madeleine and the Bastille were built up until the old faubourgs were completely joined together. By the eve of the Revolution, the city had reached the slopes of Montmartre.

To deal with this situation, which was particularly critical on the Right Bank, a network of pedestrian passageways began to form. Descending via the Passage des Panoramas from the Faubourg Montmartre, and via the Passerelle des Arts from the slopes of Sainte-Geneviève, the pedestrian network allowed inhabitants of both banks to get to the Bourse, the business center, more easily. The beginning of a general dissociation of functions, the pedestrian passageways are proof of how clogged the urban structure had become. The city was no longer able to meet its growing population's needs in the limits of its traditional scale. The old medieval structure had been built up as much as it could be; with all reserves of space used up, the saturation point was at hand.

The Crisis
of the Medieval
Space

43

Rue des Orties, photographed from the Rue de
l'Evêque and the Rue des Moineaux, in the Sainte-
Anne district. Photo: Marville, ca. 1864.

Rue Beaubourg, looking south from the Rue au
Maire. Photo: Marville, ca. 1868.

The Birth of Superimposed Residences

The shortage of space in the dense inner city had important ramifications for housing. Indeed, it would not be an exaggeration to say that the nineteenth century utterly revolutionized the formal typology of the Parisian building. The increase in population density caused by the revival of industry and commerce during the First Empire (owing to the double impetus of military activity and territorial expansion) necessitated a complete transformation of the way the population was housed. In a general transition from the private house to the apartment building, the "rental property" was born.

At first only large edifices of the mansion type were divided up into apartments. (The very term *apartment* is proof enough of the aristocratic origin of the expression.) What was new in these buildings was the distribution of dwellings by floor (and the further possibility of subdividing the floors) so as to allow several households to be lodged on a single lot. Previously, the owner of a piece of ground had occupied the whole house built on it; it would not have occurred to anyone to stack up houses, so to speak, inside a single shell.

During the reign of Louis XV, when Paris was still a four-story city, the densest districts in the center did contain six- and seven-story constructions with certain similarities to apartment buildings. But examination of how those constructions were actually used reveals that they were *shared houses* rather than true apartment buildings. Seventeenth-century examples show that the floors above the ground floor had a rather ill-defined layout of large and small rooms that notarial inventories designated as *chambre* and *cabinet*.[12] As this vague terminology suggests, the rooms in a building were not strictly defined in functional terms. Staircase landings opened directly into a large number of interconnected rooms. Floor plans carefully indicated the arrangement of beds in the rooms—double beds in the *chambres*, single beds in the adjoining *cabinets* (where a servant or child might be lodged).

But the rooms did not have clearly defined functions, and the basic *chambre*/*cabinet* unit could be used in a variety of ways. Thus the main room could pass as a salon and the smaller one be used as a kitchen. Finances permitting, a tenant was free to adapt his dwelling to his own particular life-style. As for the owner, he lived in all or part of the other rooms in much the same fashion. This way of dividing up a constructed volume linked tenants and owners closely, for they basically lived together—from one floor to the next, and indeed even from one room to the next—without having, strictly speaking, an apartment of their own. Things changed completely when the rental property was created, for it was made up of identical superimposed units defining on each floor the main volumes of a traditional residence: a kitchen, a salon, bedrooms, and dressing rooms. Moreover, in rental buildings the rooms in each residence were laid out around an entry hall separated from the staircase and landing.

The multiplication of residences in a house seems to have already

An example of how the 1784 building code affected the city's appearance on the Rue de l'Odéon. The void formed by the street is governed by a traditional harmonious proportion: the street width is two-thirds the height of the façades.

Detail of Turgot's map, showing the low constructions that characterized Old Paris (here, the Saint-Merry section).

existed in the early eighteenth century (e.g., the Marquis de Pompal's Lisbonne). In any case, it was definitely in widespread use during the reign of Louis XVI: numerous Parisian buildings from that epoch have been preserved—as for instance the Choppin d'Arnouville building (61 Rue Dauphine, 1769), the Montholon building (Buci intersection, 1771), the Martin building (Boulevard Beaumarchais and Rue du Pont-aux-Choux, 1775), and the Doublet de Persan building (7-9 Rue Bonaparte, 1772).[13] Despite the newness of the conception, the generic model for all the aforementioned buildings remained the structures on the royal squares built during the reign of Louis XIV: the Place des Victoires and the Place Vendôme. These constructions included three main parts: a ground floor and a mezzanine for shops; two floors of living space, the lower being the more prestigious (in some rental properties, the number of floors of living space rose to three or even four); and an attic under a big 45-degree tile roof with several small dormer windows. However, neither the full balcony on the third floor (except in the Montholon building, which in this respect was ahead of its time) nor the recessed top story was yet widespread. The latter was introduced a bit later, as a way of getting around a 1784 regulation. It allowed an additional floor to be added without going over the stipulated size: by creating a recess equal to the height of the new story, an extra story could be constructed "under" the 45-degree slope of the roof (i.e., without changing the cornice height). The complex volumetrics of neoclassical buildings (whatever their shortcomings) is partly related to the use of recessed stories with terraces, traditionally clad in lead.

The development of the apartment building transformed the capital's silhouette by raising the number of floors on an average from four to seven. As Turgot's map shows, in the second third of the eighteenth century Paris was still a low city, made up of three- and four-story private houses topped by big tile roofs—the latter usually covering an attic rather than a permanent residence. In the central districts, where construction was thickest, certain houses were already being used as apartment buildings, usually as the result of random construction of simple residences over a family house.

In the second half of the eighteenth century the situation began to change, because of the population influx. Existing houses were built as high as regulations allowed. For new construction, moreover, lots were grouped together to form the big lots needed to build real apartment buildings and redistribute residences by floor.

The first way of increasing density that came to mind was to cram the traditional lots—deep, narrow strips—with additional constructions. Lots were always built up in the same unchanging way. After a construction had been built on the street, another was placed behind it; then the empty space between the front and back buildings was progressively built up.

Until the appearance of common courtyards shared by buildings on adjacent parcels in the mideighteenth century, the parallel buildings constructed across the front and back of a lot were, following the medieval model, linked together with connecting spaces used for staircases, kitchens, and bathrooms.

A hierarchy of human activities, based on each building's distance from the street, was implicit in the way lots were built up: at the top of the hierarchy, dwellings and shops on the street; on the courtyard, less luxurious residences, storerooms, and workshops. Until the industrial explosion in the nineteenth century, the bottom of the front-to-back hierarchy was the vegetable garden, located at the core of blocks having very deep lots.

Later, to meet the needs of the capital's growing population, new buildings were placed farther back in the lots. Often the buildings separating the front and back courtyards were used as service areas. Thus the kitchen was relegated to the second building, detached from the building on the street.

Next came the modification of the connecting volumes on the sides of lots, which were divided up (and sometimes widened) in order to be used for housing. The staircase at the back of the main building was first used for the building on the street, but then allowed the development of a wing at a right angle behind it, built along the edge of the lot. The layout of the wing was slowly transformed and eventually became a separate residence. When that happened, access to the constructions at the back of the lot was cut off, and new ways of reaching the rear volumes had to be devised.

Once the sides of a lot had been completely built up, the only remaining way to fill a lot was to put constructions in the courtyard itself. As a general rule, light buildings were built—simple one-story sheds and warehouses. They almost completely ate up the remaining space and reduced the courtyard to a mere passageway; however, they did not prevent sunlight from reaching the dwellings located in the other buildings, and also allowed the survival of craft and manufacturing activities at a time when the shortage of space was tending to drive craftsmen out of the center of the city.

This buildup occurred slowly and differed from one neighborhood to another. Indeed, it continued in some areas until a relatively recent date and, surprisingly enough, was still going on in the 1930s, when a city regulation finally limited the degree to which a lot could be built up. Consequently, a seventeenth-century façade sometimes conceals extremely heterogeneous constructions, including brick buildings from the 1930s.

The Cramming
of the Lots

Examples of how the city's narrow lots were built up.
1. 169 Rue Saint-Jacques. **2.** 23 Rue de l'Annonciation. **3.** How a lot was built up. Diagrams reprinted
courtesy of the Atelier Parisien d'Urbanisme. (a) A
building on the street. The arrows indicate a tendency to expand into the courtyard. (b) A second
building is gradually extended across the back of the
lot and then along the sides. (c) The back and sides
have been built up. Expansion into the courtyard follows. (d) Various sheds spring up in the courtyard.

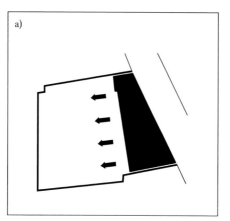

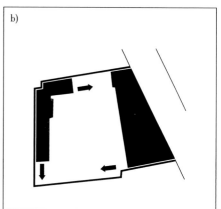

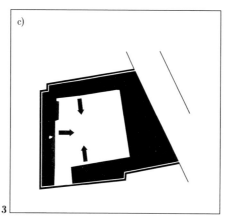

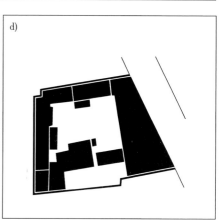

Heightening Buildings

In a city whose limits remained fixed by how long it took to walk somewhere, the main way to increase density, once the ground had been filled to capacity, was to add new stories onto buildings. In a preindustrial society, salvaged materials played an important role. Materials salvaged from the demolition of dilapidated constructions were used to construct new buildings or, if it was at all possible to save the shell, a building was simply heightened. In postmedieval construction, renovating an existing building by adding on extra stories had become an art allowing the wildest heightenings of the most structurally unsound bases, since the systematic use of wooden construction allowed buildings to be raised considerably without overloading the foundation masonry.

The simplest way to heighten a building was to put a bigger roof on it. When this was done, an attic could easily be transformed into two or even three floors of living space. The old house below remained unchanged, oddly topped by a new roof as high as itself.

A second technique consisted in modifying the form of the roof. The transition from the traditional roof (two slopes) to the mansard roof, with its row of dormer windows, made it easier to use an attic as living space. In a good number of cases, close analysis would show that the old frame had not even been touched and that the upper slopes of the new roof had simply been added on over it (or else that the frame had been mounted on posts and raised one story).

Starting in the early nineteenth century, masonry was used more and more to heighten buildings; doubtless the advent of brick —extremely light when used in a single row—was not unrelated to this. It was thus possible, starting from the old cornice level, to build a front wall on which the new rafters could rest. (Here too, the old frame remained intact beneath this dressing.)

During the Restoration the recessed top story came into fashion. Set back from the façade, a new recessed story hardly weighed on it; indeed, it contributed to the façade's stability by shifting the weight to the back. An extremely light story was constructed in wood or a combination of wood and brick. The roof, now almost horizontal (since the height of the old rooftop had not changed), was clad with a new material that was particularly effective on low slopes: zinc. When money allowed, the little terrace in front of the recessed story was given a lead floor, which made it accessible and thus contributed to the new floor's charm.

In the final analysis, these simple techniques were just ways of making full use of the space beneath the roof. Yet they did often make it possible to double the number of people housed in a building.

By the midnineteenth century, urban density had become so great that renovating attic space was no longer enough. The only way to remedy the situation was to add on new main stories. Buildings were raised from three stories to five and then to seven. The new stories were seldom all added at once, and many buildings still show traces of

1. An eighteenth-century house heightened with a recessed story during the Restoration, corner of the Rue du Faubourg-Saint-Antoine and the Rue de la Roquette. **2.** Successive stories added to eighteenth-century houses on the Rue de la Roquette.

the gradual addition of floors: recesses in the masonry, changes in material, and alterations of the chimney, especially when, starting in the Second Empire, an old flue was raised in clay.

These various technical indications are confirmed by stylistic ones. In a good many cases the earliest buildings to be heightened respected the principle of a decrease in ceiling heights between the prestigious lower floors and the less prestigious upper ones. (The difference in ceiling height from one floor to another was sometimes as much as a meter.) When previously heightened buildings were raised again—often toward the end of the century, during the new surge of industrialization that marked the beginning of the Third Republic, and even well into the twentieth century—there was a tendency to go back to the normal regulation height of about 2.85 meters per floor. Thus the upper floors were given visibly higher ceiling heights than the middle floors.

Rue de l'Abbaye, 1898.

Because of the plaster used in Paris from the late sixteenth century on, transformations are extremely difficult to date: first, because the plastered surface—redone at least twice a century—covers over any structural alterations (which are easy to see in the wood underneath, when the buildings are replastered), and second, because the ornamentation usually dates from the last time the surface was redone (using cement in the 1850s).

Only construction materials, which can be dated in terms of when a product was industrialized, can be considered reliable indicators. This is particularly so for elements of an ornamental nature, such as balcony railings and indoor fittings (e.g., door and window frames, chimney mantels). Yet even here one must be quite cautious. A lot of old woodwork has been renovated with stuck-on moldings, so that solid wooden doors dating from as early as the sixteenth century are sometimes found beneath a nineteenth-century dressing. On the other hand, it must be remembered that building materials were often salvaged from demolition sites in the nineteenth century—especially during the Second Empire, when half of Paris was torn down and used to build the other half! Finally, changing fashion sometimes led to a complete overhaul of a building's ornamentation—notably, its windows and balcony railings, for cast iron was a very economical way to modernize a building's appearance. (This was still the case twenty years ago, when tubular metal railings were popular.)

The astonishing growth of Paris from the Revolution to the midtwentieth century was marked by several key periods: the reign of Louis XVI, the beginning of the reign of Louis-Philippe, the fin de siècle, the 1930s.

Yet, the casual Paris visitor does not even suspect the complexity and incoherence of the city's architectural evolution, since the use of plastered façades, the strong tradition of light construction, and the absolute respect of a single building height (set at 22.41 meters in the 1784 regulations) have totally concealed it. Paradoxically the old

55

The vertical style.
1. Rue Vauvilliers, in the Halle au Blé section. Postcard. 2. Rue Saint-Honoré, corner of the Rue Saint-Roche. 3. Rue de Valois. 4. Rue Saint-Honoré, corner of the Rue des Bons-Enfants, 1913.

neighborhoods, whose chronology is the least coherent, look the most unified today, whereas the more recent residential districts in western Paris have had much trouble concealing structural modifications.

A Vertical Style

Provided for in rental leases, which required tenants to put up with the inconvenience, the heightening of buildings was an old tradition in Paris, and was not unrelated to the construction methods used there down to the nineteenth century. It might be thought that the addition of extra stories to a building would be disastrous to its architectural appearance, but that was not the case. As the same construction methods had been handed down from century to century, there was no real difference between a seventeenth-century construction and the nineteenth-century stories added to it. Ever since exposed wooden siding had begun to be plastered over to protect it from fire (an imperative mentioned in many sixteenth-century regulations), façade decoration had been limited to a nearly constant spacing of solids and voids with discreet wrought-iron accents. Being neutral surfaces characterized by the regular alternation of window openings and piers of identical width, the façades of traditional Parisian buildings were devoid of individuality—so much so, in fact, that they could support constant breaks in cornice height (a function of a building's number of floors) and turn what might have been a defect into a distinctive architectural feature: a strong vertical style. Thanks to the latter, the unity of the cityscape triumphed over the profusion of individual constructions, which were reconciled in a harmonious whole.

The strong vertical style that characterized constructions built before the nineteenth century can be attributed to several concomitant

factors. It results in particular from the narrow lots of medieval origin that had been laid out to allow a minimum of façade for a maximum of depth (and thereby a relatively loose, hence economical, road network). The use of narrow lots was combined with a mode of construction based on short spans (a façade's width not exceeding six to eight meters). The result was the rows of tightly packed individual houses, taller than they are wide and deeper than they are high that can be seen today in Flemish towns still faithful to the medieval typology. In Paris the tendency to heighten buildings—transforming the three- and four-story city of Louis XV into the six-story city of Louis-Philippe—almost turned to caricature.

The style of façades was deeply affected. Starting in the mideighteenth century, the traditional composition based on horizontal bands to reduce the vertiginous aspect of the tight systems of tall windows was replaced by a new mode of composition that multiplied the tall window openings and accentuated the vertical rows formed by the windows and narrow piers. The technical principle adopted—light wooden façades and heavy masonry sidewalls—destroyed the façade as a solid. The result was to strengthen the role of the sidewalls, where the chimneys were located, their tall stacks sticking up over the roofs. A technical device for the evacuation of smoke and a firebreak system, the heavy sidewalls were also a stylistic device emphasizing the vertical perpendicular to the street.

These various technical and visual systems helped to integrate the constructions, of varying scale, into the urban continuum that had been handed down from the Middle Ages. The heightening of buildings, a simple way of dealing with density (linked to an archaic stage of capitalization), was perfectly adapted to such a system. Since

horizontals always existed only in short sequences—ranging from the width of a pier or lintel to that of a lot (i.e., in a very limited range of one to ten meters, at most)—a building's long verticals (fifteen to twenty meters), which were extremely close together, easily won out on the graphic level. Mass was defined only by the powerful perpendicular screens formed by the heavy sidewalls and chimneys. The transparent screen formed by the façade mattered little (indeed, it was hardly perceptible); thus, it could be raised without damaging a building's appearance.

The city's overall architectural unity being assured by the principle of verticality, a building's various levels could be played on contradictorily. The aesthetics of the ground floor was determined by the shops found there, and this aesthetics was based much less on the transparency of the windows than on the lively colors and surfaces of the storefronts. This architecture of colors and solids broke off abruptly a little above eye level where commercial activity ended and no one would ever have thought to look.

A building's upper stories, used as living space, were done in a totally different style, based on the creamy white and ocher yellow of the stone, an abundance of glass, and the graphic patterns formed by the frames around the window openings. The vertical wall on the street was a curtain drawn between bedroom and pavement.

In silhouette, everything changed. The highly individualized tops of the houses were like faces in a crowd that, when seen from afar, blend together in a continuous vibration. Two-story houses neighbored seven-story buildings in harmony. When seen from a certain distance, the rigid rows of façades formed a powerful pattern in which each portion of space on a street, marked off with a character of its own, played a role.

The combination of similar and dissimilar forms in the traditional rows of buildings in Paris was an astonishing success: breaks in size and stylistic contradictions were easily digested, even when a building had been built several centuries later than its neighbors. Differences were easily assimilated and space defined on a certain, unchanging scale, based on seeing a unit at a middle distance, between the blend of the panoramic view and the compact, polymorphous close-up with detail. More than anything else, the architecture of Old Paris reveals how important it is to take relations of scale into account, when one considers and designs urban spaces and forms.

The Twilight of Classicism

The extreme unity given Paris by its architectural typology—a unity based on a scale and materials shared by most of the edifices and the possibility of constantly enlarging constructions with new stories—allowed the city to cope with its growing population for half a century, down to the beginning of the Restoration. To understand the situation fully, a few figures need to be mentioned.[14]

If we compare the surface area inside the Charles V wall (1,085 acres) with that of the city of Louis XIV (2,720 acres), the increase is completely normal, since the city had grown to 400,000 inhabitants by the late seventeenth century. Measured in terms of the distance from the center out to the city limits, this increase was of little consequence: the most outlying points in the city were two kilometers from the center, and the last house in the faubourgs less than four, or a little over half-an-hour's walk.

On the other hand, when the Farmers-General Wall was built, the tripling of the city's surface area (8,280 acres) did not correspond to a real increase in the area the city occupied: in the eighteenth century, the city, as we have seen, remained inside the old boundaries, though it did spread out in a number of faubourgs. As the city's natural scale was surpassed, an opposition between center and outskirts was created. The center then became a predominantly residential area, while work activities were driven out to the edge of town. Population growth was manifested by an increase in density of constructed surfaces, not by a geographic expansion into new areas.

The situation worsened considerably in the nineteenth century. The 100,000 people who had moved to Paris in the course of the eighteenth century were joined by 170,000 more between 1801 and 1817, then by 150,000 in the following twenty years and another 185,000 ten years later. In 1846, Paris went over the million population mark. But even then the city had still not managed to completely fill up the area inside the Farmers-General Wall. If it had overflowed to the north, where it finally joined up with the village of Montmartre at Abbesses, enormous sections were left unoccupied or underoccupied around the Arch of Triumph, Monceau, La Villette, and La Nation on the Right Bank, and around the Champ-de-Mars, Montparnasse, and Salpêtrière on the Left Bank. In certain areas, density had soared to over a hundred thousand inhabitants per square kilometer; in others, it was under a thousand. In fact, the city refused to budge from its old limits and rashly continued to build up the old center, to the detriment of its health.

Traditional construction techniques and approaches to urban development simply could not deal with the population influx. Clearly, what was needed was a more dynamic approach to construction and urban expansion, following the models first elaborated in the eighteenth century for the Odéon and Italiens districts. The rental building was really born only with the big, new nineteenth-century districts and, like them, reflected the economic vitality of a flourishing society in the golden age of industrial capitalism. More so than the Empire—too short an interlude—the Restoration was the period that consecrated the birth of the Parisian apartment building.

Behind the formal appearance of the city's classical façades, a different state of mind then emerged. As it did so, everything changed: the scale and financing of operations, the typology and style of buildings, and even the construction techniques used. Long before Haussmann, the Haussmann era was in the making. A whole conception of the city—one that classicism had inherited from the Middle Ages and in which it had evolved with ease—disappeared. In order to survive, the old style had to be adapted to the techniques of the industrial age. The history of the Parisian building in the nineteenth century reveals a constant concern with preserving the values of the classical tradition, as transposed to the world of mass production and the large scale of contemporary capitalism. More than the transition from one system to another, however, what must be emphasized is how a culture and its values resisted the new imperatives of the marketplace. If nineteenth-century architecture was so perfectly adapted to the emerging modern world, it is because it conceded nothing.

NOTES

1. Paris was the biggest city in Europe for many years, before losing that distinction and then winning it back. In the late eighteenth century, London—with a population of over a million—was the largest metropolis in Europe. In France industrialization did not really begin until the law abolishing guilds—a decisive law, if ever there was one, in the economic history of France—which was enacted in 1791.

2. This information is taken from Bernard Rouleau, *Le Tracé des rues de Paris. Formation, typologie, fonctions* (Paris: C.N.R.S., 1967). The structure of the Parisian system is remarkably well analyzed by Rouleau, as is the history of its formation. We have made constant use of this fundamental study.

3. Since Paris was a tight mesh of small properties, most lots were not this deep. Indeed, they were seldom over twelve to fifteen meters deep. Thus most of the lots inside the city's earliest wall (built by Philip Augustus) were quite small (sixty to seventy square meters). Farther out, the lot structure and street network were looser and the lots deeper. This is the case for the section of the Rue Saint-Antoine from the church of Saint-Paul on, which was a faubourg until the fifteenth century. The best treatment of lot structure is unquestionably found in Françoise Boudon, André Chastel, Hélène Couzy, and Françoise Hamon, *Système de l'architecture urbaine. Le quartier des Halles à Paris*, 2 vols. (Paris: C.N.R.S., 1977). The C.R.H.A.M. team's study deals mostly with the formation of the medieval fabric and its subsequent historical evolution.

4. The *banlieue* was the place where the *ban* was pronounced—i.e., an area placed under the legal jurisdiction of a neighboring town and not, as lovers of false etymologies might claim, a place that had been banished (*banni*). An agricultural area with few constructions, it was complementary to the town and provided it with food and raw materials.

5. One of the most accessible documentary sources on the center of Paris—far more precise than Jacques Hilairet's *Dictionnaire des rues de Paris*—is Adolphe Berty's twenty-volume *Topographique historique du Vieux Paris* (Paris: Imprimerie Impériale, starting in 1866). Marius Barroux's *Le département de la Seine et la Ville de Paris* (Paris,

1910) and Marcel Poëte's *Formation et évolution de Paris* (Paris, 1910) can also be helpful. Bernard Rouleau's study includes an intelligent critical bibliography.

6. Much could certainly be done to bind the two networks closer together. In particular, the intersections could be developed into focal points similar to the lively intersections along the Boulevard Saint-Germain on the Left Bank.

7. The most striking proof of the disappearance of medieval constructions in Paris is found in studies of the Marais neighborhood: only cellars (notably in the Rue François Miron) have been located, in buildings that were partially or totally rebuilt in the eighteenth and nineteenth centuries.

8. Unlike the private house and the apartment building, the mansion, a prestige construction, has given rise to numerous and often luxurious books published by Guérinet and others. Given the wealth of monographs on the subject, we will not go into great detail here. It should, however, be mentioned that many of these studies, while rich in historical information, neglect the architecture itself, make little or no effort to establish a typology of the mansion, and say practically nothing about a mansion's relationship to the neighborhood around it.

9. A fairly modest analysis of the Saint-Antoine district was attempted by Catherine Aubert in an unpublished paper (U.P.6., Paris: E.N.S.B.A., 1977). More recently the city has undertaken a complete inventory of the area.

10. Forgotten, at least until the publication of Bernard Rouleau's book *Villages et faubourgs de l'ancien Paris* (Paris: Le Seuil, 1985).

11. Françoise Boudon, André Chastel, Hélène Couzy, Françoise Hamon, "L'Ilot de la rue du Roule et ses abords," in *Paris-Ile-de-France. Mémoires de la Fédération*, vols. 16-17, 1966, pp. 1-129.

12. To date, the best study of living space during the age of classicism is Jean-Pierre Babelon's *Demeures parisiennes sous Henri IV et Louis XIII* (Paris: Le Temps, 1965). Our observations are close to his own.

13. For further information, see Michel Gallet's remarkable book *Demeures parisiennes à l'époque de Louis XVI* (Paris: Le Temps, 1964), which we have relied on heav-

ily. A revised edition of this work has been published under the title *Paris Domestic Architecture of the 18th Century* (London: Barry and Jenkins, 1972).

14. For further information, see the general article "Paris," by Jean-Pierre Babelon, Jean Tulard, and Jean Bastié, in the *Encyclopedia universalis*, vol. 12 (Paris, 1972), pp. 533-42.

Facing page
: **1.** Marché des Innocents. Photo: Marville, 1853. **2.** The Seine around the old Pont des Saints-Pères. Photo: Ferrier, 1865.

3. Rue Saint-Georges, looking from the Rue Saint-Lazare toward the Rue de Provence. Photo: Marville, ca. 1865.

Chapter II

The New Paris during the Restoration and the July Monarchy

The accession of Charles X in 1824, ten years after the restoration of monarchy, was a turning point in the history of Parisian urbanism. In a complete break with the old faubourg tradition, the capital's first big apartment-building developments were now initiated. Though their subsequent history had its ups and downs, these new sections profoundly modified the cityscape. Indeed, the juxtaposition of distinct urban structures inside the city created the mosaic composition that so strongly characterizes Paris today.

Born during the reign of Louis XVI, the apartment building had disappeared during the economically unstable Revolutionary period and resurfaced only timidly during the Empire. Following the great upheaval in social structure brought about by the abolition of feudal law and fortune (the Civil Code and national property), the return to order that characterized the Restoration was accompanied by a new phase of expansion. Construction activity picked up considerably as promoters started building apartment houses. As before, the buildings were grouped together in new districts, but this time on a vast scale (the Odéon and Italiens developments were small operations that covered little more than a block). The sections in the New Paris that Balzac so enthusiastically extolled were big—indeed, out of all proportion to the reality of the city's population and the means of its financiers. Inevitably, many of the new projects ended in failure. The first phase in the revival of building activity after the Revolution turned out to be short-lived. By 1826 there were already signs of an economic slowdown. Then, in 1828, all activity came to a standstill and remained there for a decade. Things picked up again in the 1840s—especially after 1842, when the typology that was to be Haussmann's suddenly emerged. (Thus the typology in actual fact preceded its "inventor" by over ten years.)

One could speak, then, of a sort of dress rehearsal in two acts. During the reigns of Charles X and Louis-Philippe, Paris was getting ready for the great transformation that came at midcentury; indeed, it had already set that transformation as its goal. The Restoration brought a first, if fleeting, taste of things to come. Then, during the July Monarchy, an essay in true grandeur began. Apartment buildings

66

sprang up throughout the city, and new, wider streets, essential to the city's transformation, were designed, built, and landscaped. In the late 1840s the Boulevard de Strasbourg foreshadowed the city's future. Between the fall of the First Empire and the rise of the Second, Paris was nothing short of an urban laboratory where the typology of the bourgeois apartment building was being invented, plus a city to go with it. The history of the city's transformation is an exciting one, especially given its rapidity. In less than a quarter of a century, Paris became a new city.

1 and 2. Boulevard de Strasbourg, 1868 and 1908.

The Neoclassical City

The *Tableau de Paris*, published in 1782, contains a fascinating description of the city's growth: "Huge buildings are rising out of the ground as if by magic, and new sections are being filled with the most stately edifices. A passion for building has taken hold of the city, whence its new air of grandeur and majesty.... With a blueprint in one hand and an estimate in the other, the city's contractors are firing the imagination of our capitalists."[1] It would be hard to find a better description of the relation between the rental building and the birth of capitalism.

One of capitalism's most important effects on construction was to transform the scale of projects. In the eighteenth century, the old lot pattern, adapted to the private house, began to evolve as lots were joined together and, moreover, whole new districts were created *ex nihilo*.

The new developments were built on big, empty pieces of ground in the capital and yielded substantial profits to the important men behind them: the Duc de Chartres, who developed the land around the Palais-Royal; the Comte de Provence (the future Louis XVIII), who was responsible for the Odéon[2] and had big plans for the Luxembourg area

Apartment-Building Developments

Two neoclassical buildings framing the beginning of the Rue de l'Odéon.

67

Rue de Viarmes. Anon., n.d. *Insert*: map showing
how the area around the Halle au Blé was subdivided
by Le Camus de Mézières.

Facing page: panoramic views of the Halle au Blé
section. **1.** Anon., 1885. **2.** Photo: Godefroy, 1909.

(abandoned after the Revolution); and the Duc de Choiseul, who speculated in the Italiens neighborhood. The oldest venture of this sort would seem to have been the development of the Halle au Blé on the site of the old Soissons mansion in 1763, the year the Seven Years' War ended.[3]

Public Interest, Private Interests

Having large sums of money at their disposal, the developers of the new sections built solid edifices with stone façades and regularized elevations. Working on an unprecedented scale, they helped define a

The 1796 Artists' Map, drawn up in accordance with the law of April 4, 1793, on subdividing state property. The map shows many of the new streets to be built in the nineteenth century.

new architectural typology, as all the buildings were based on a standard model and reflected a desire for monumentality in the city's appearance—a desire that was quite pronounced in the late eighteenth century, when the bourgeoisie began to think about what form "their" city should take. (The first plans for new streets and urban improvements date from 1769, at which date Moreau-Desproux, the superintendent of buildings for the city of Paris, submitted them to the king for approval.)

In the late eighteenth century it became obvious that something would have to be done to unclog the city's congested streets. On the eve of the French Revolution, Moreau-Desproux began the first clearing operations and, in particular, had the houses on the bridges and the medieval fortifications around the Châtelet torn down. The Artists' Map from the time of the Convention visualized these projects in a style that in some respects was still baroque, but also shows an unmistakable concern for efficiency.

The major urban projects during the Empire and the early

Restoration were designed above all to beautify the city. The development of the landscaped paths around the Observatory, at the far end of the Luxembourg Gardens, and the construction of the Rue de Rivoli on the Terrasse des Feuillants (Tuileries Gardens) were, strictly speaking, beautification projects. The property transfers brought about by the Revolution allowed vast green spaces in the center of the city to be transformed into public parks and esplanades. When this occurred, the urban façade of the park was formed: rows of grillwork echoed by regular English-style terraces parallel to them. The city's parks were also given a monumental role: the alignment of regular façades on the Rue de Rivoli was but one element in a larger urban design, opening, via the Rue de Castiglione, on the old royal square and the mock-antique triumphal column erected in the emperor's honor. In comparison, the apartment houses built on the site of the old Capuchin convent and the opening of the Rue de la Paix were quite modest undertakings: a large piece of land was developed merely by building several streets to service it, along which rows of

Rue de Rivoli. **1.** Looking toward the Place de la Concorde. Anon., n.d. **2.** Looking toward the Hôtel de Ville. Anon., 1907.

Place de la Bourse and Théâtre du Vaudeville.
Photo: Marville, 1867.

Drawing of Gilbert Robert Gaspard, Comte de Chabrol de Volvic.

ordinary houses were constructed. The case was the same around the Bourse (on the site of the Filles-Saint-Thomas convent) and at Saint-Martin-des-Champs and La Roquette.

Despite the opportunities created by the transfer of church property, neither the Empire nor the early Restoration were particularly innovative in urbanism. Economic conditions were not yet right for big projects to be launched with some chance of success. Moreover, city officials were preoccupied by other matters—city management and public health. Over a period of twenty years a city administration was set up that undertook a considerable effort at rational organization. One of the highest priorities was the Cadastral Survey of Paris, to which an examination of the sewers and the underground quarries was added. A generation of surveyors worked on these projects: without their contribution, no public projects of any size would have been possible in later years. But public health and provisioning were just as important: as soon as he was named prefect of the capital in 1812, Chabrol undertook to reorganize the city's markets[4] and simultaneously to restructure the navigation system and the ports of Paris, thereby also solving the capital's water-supply problems.

Gilbert de Chabrol de Volvic (1773-1843), who was prefect of Paris until 1830, had been the driving force behind the reconstruction of Pontivy during the Empire, applying a certain number of ideas on city structures and services.[5] But, like all his contemporaries, he left residential construction to private investors, considering it to be outside the realm of state responsibility. Thus when the city intervened, it did so only in order to enforce the building code (e.g., concerning the building line and the height of buildings). The notion of public interest was interpreted as applying only to big public edifices, major boulevards, and by extension parks and gardens designed in conjunction with certain monuments and public buildings. Everything else was in the hands of private investors. Yet Chabrol was aware of the economic risks in real-estate speculation and of the shaky financial structures of early capitalism. Consequently, he showed a marked preference for small projects, the success of big ventures being far from guaranteed in advance.[6]

The First Big Projects

It was, however, big new projects (and their failure) that were to mark Chabrol's tenure as the capital's chief administrator. 1824 was a watershed year in the city's development: the election of the *Chambre retrouvée* and the accession of Charles X added to the confidence resulting from the strengthening of the economy over the previous ten years. Enthusiasm about the nation's economic prospects was reflected in a wide array of urban projects.

The first important project, dating from 1823, was the François Ier development near the Champs-Elysées. The totally original design brought together three distinct traditions. The first was the airy composition of the London square, a mixed landscape combining city and country (though nature was completely rearranged). The second was also English: the cottage tradition of architectural quaintness, which triumphed in the juxtaposition of villas and mansions whose cultural references were totally heterogeneous.[7] But the third tradition could not have been more French: the star network, an outgrowth of the layout of parks and forests in the classical era, which had been used in the design of large suburban spaces since the eighteenth century. The supple diagonals of which the eighteenth century had been so fond (e.g., the Quinconces in Bordeaux and the Odéon in Paris) were combined with the ideal image of a construction-filled park to form a neighborhood of houses deep in verdure. What the Tour-des-Dames section had expressed in a modest way a generation earlier was powerfully expressed by the François Ier district, which became a model for developments to come.

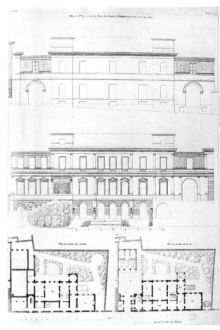

Talma mansion, 9 Rue de la Tour-des-Dames. Front and back façades, plans of the first and second floors (bottom left and bottom right, respectively).

Saint-Vincent-de-Paul and Europe

In 1824 the biggest new developments Paris had even seen were created: inside the Farmers-General Wall, Saint-Vincent-de-Paul and Europe (on either side of the Nouvelle Athènes); and outside the Wall, Beaugrenelle and Passy. Bernard Rouleau is quite right to emphasize the utterly new conception of urban space realized in these primarily residential neighborhoods (in this respect, similar to London).[8]

The typology was more varied than it might seem at first glance: Saint-Vincent-de-Paul and Europe form a dense urban network characteristic of the center of a city. Thus in Saint-Vincent-de-Paul the only verdure was on the future Boulevard Magenta and around the stairs leading up to the church of Saint-Vincent-de-Paul, framing the

73

The François Ier development.
1. Plan of the Solkykoff mansion. **2.** Garden façade.
3. Courtyard façade. **4.** Details of the chimneys. **5.**
Details of the balustrades. **6.** House, Rue Lord-
Byron.

Facing page: **1.** Place François Ier. Anon., 1910. **2.**
Prince Napoleon's Pompeiian house on the Avenue
Montaigne, and the Solkykoff mansion.

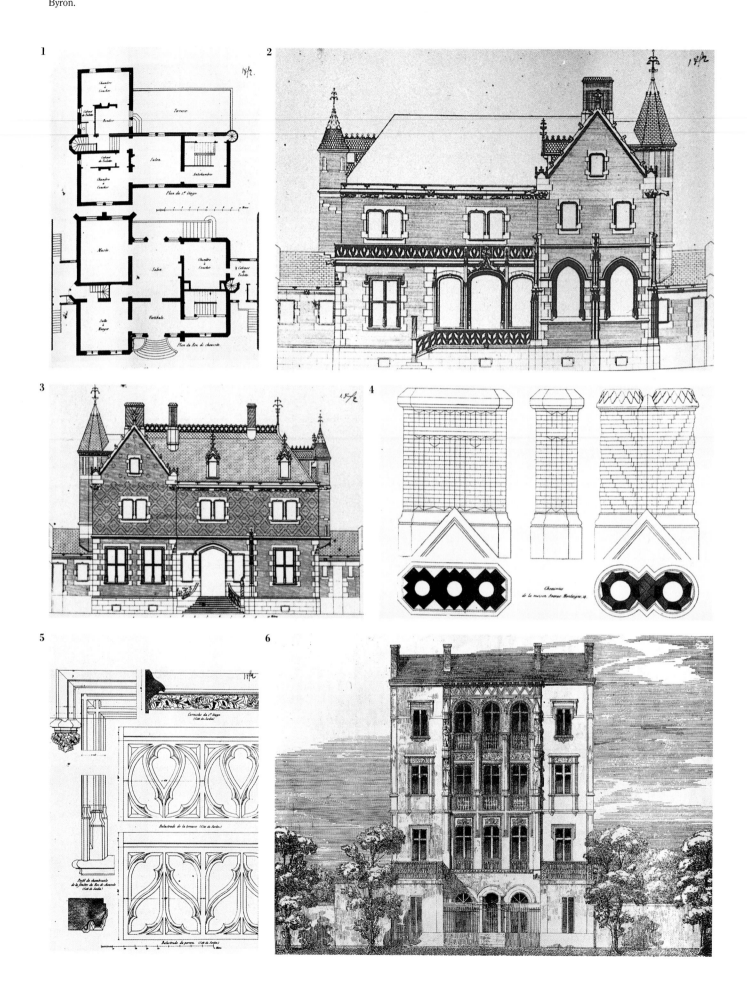

Elévation des Maisons Place Lafayette
No 9

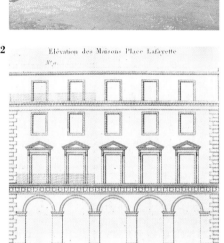

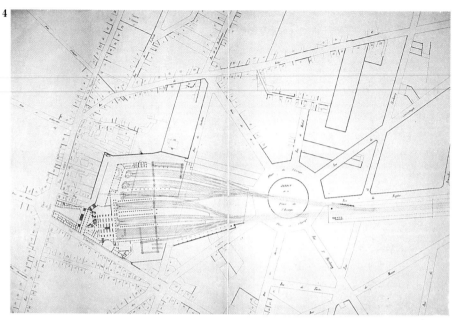

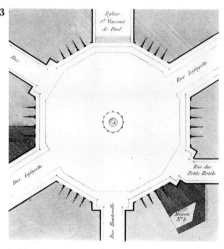

1. Place Franz-Liszt, photographed from the garden of the church of Saint-Vincent-de-Paul. **2.** Façades of houses. **3.** Plan of the square. Illustrations 2 and 3 are reprinted from Charles Normand, *Paris moderne* (Paris, 1843). **4.** Map of the Europe district before 1859. In the center, the Gare Saint-Lazare.

church façade on the Roman model of the Trinità dei Monti. The district was, however, quite different from the old city in that a clear hierarchy of streets was established. The network included two major streets, the Rue La Fayette and Boulevard Magenta, annexed to squares (the Place Franz-Liszt and Place de Valenciennes). The remainder of the street network was designed on a much more modest scale, to meet the district's internal needs. The overall layout reveals the beginnings of a practice that became widespread during the Haussmann era: the Rue d'Hauteville and the church of Saint-Vincent-de-Paul are part of the neighborhood's internal structure and reveal its basically residential vocation. On the other hand, though this was but a beginning, the Boulevard Magenta and the Rue La Fayette were designed to be arteries of greater importance. The Place Franz-Liszt does in fact connect the two networks at the foot of the church, but the Place de Valenciennes became a square/intersection dissociated from the district's monuments and internal structure. Thus the district could be said to foreshadow Haussmann's use of a hierarchy of street networks and, in particular, the principle of dissociating intersections of major citywide arteries from squares providing the internal structure of specific neighborhoods.

Though it is harder to visualize today (since a railway line has cut it in half), the Europe district was originally comparable in structure: a simple orthogonal network of parallels set out in tiered rows on a hill, the top of which, on the Boulevard des Batignolles, was to have been embellished with a church. Two diagonals intersecting at the Place de l'Europe were superimposed on the orthogonal grid, while two other diagonals—the Rue du Rocher and the Rue d'Amsterdam—cut through the remaining tiercerons, creating additional diagonal vistas. However, though the diagonal streets were well adapted to the slope of the hill, they were not as interesting as the hierarchy of streets in the Saint-Vincent-de-Paul neighborhood.

Beaugrenelle and Passy

Although the Beaugrenelle and Passy sections were laid out to resemble Europe and Saint-Vincent-de-Paul, a totally different typology was used. As these areas were outside the Farmers-General Wall, the problem of density did not exist in the same way.

Based on a fairly unoriginal orthogonal grid, the Beaugrenelle section had two parallel axes: the house of the developer Léonard Violet and the church of Saint-Jean-Baptiste de Grenelle, the heart of the development. Perpendicular to these axes, a town hall and a theater formed secondary centers of interest. Within the basic structure, activities were distinctly divided up on a block-to-block basis. Thus industry and warehouses were located along the Seine near the port, whereas shops were in the center along the Rue du Commerce, which, via the Rue Frémincourt (the beginning of what later became the Avenue Emile-Zola), led to the Ecole Militaire, from which point one could continue on to the Rue du Four and the Rue de Buci. The residential section was located between the industrial and shopping districts, around the Rue Violet and on the Place Violet. The sharp dissociation of industry, shopping, and housing constituted one of the most original things about the Beaugrenelle development, which, stretching out over some 250 acres, was the biggest district in Paris.

Nearly as large, the Passy section covered the northern half of the sixteenth arrondissement, between the sites where the Trocadéro and the Arch of Triumph were later built. The star network used in the layout of the François Ier section (which Passy hoped to match in prestige) was applied on a very large scale. The hierarchy of streets characterizing the Saint-Vincent-de-Paul district was also used, but was adapted to the verdant landscape of a suburban neighborhood. All functional and social differences aside, the outlying Beaugrenelle and Passy sections shared a suburban vocation implying a return to small lots and individual houses. Such a return had, in fact, been in the offing since the beginning of the Empire. Thus the earlier Goutte d'Or and Batignolles neighborhoods were characterized by small-scale buildings and streets; outlying sections of modest residences, they were like autonomous villages inside the city, and can be said to have initiated the mosaic composition of the Parisian cityscape mentioned above.

Fountain, Square de Boufflers, in Auteuil.

The Outskirts

These new districts and their heirs—Charonne, Plaisance (Avenue du Maine), and the Villa Montmorency (in Auteuil)—were added to the traditional structuring of the city into a center and faubourgs. The urban continuum was thus replaced by a center and outskirts: as one moved away from the center, attached buildings were replaced by detached houses, verdure appeared between constructions, and

77

The church of Saint-Vin-
cent-de-Paul and its
garden, Place Franz-Liszt.

Map of the new village of Grenelle during the Restoration. The heavy line across the top represents "the
route to be taken by crosstown traffic." The lots
shaded in gray, above the Champs-de-Mars, "belong
to the company."

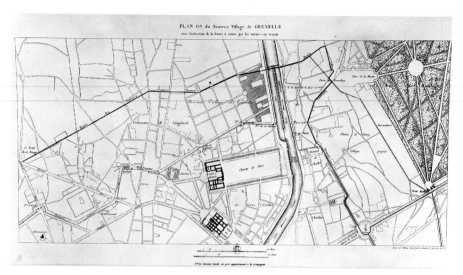

Map of Auteuil, Passy, and Chaillot in 1859.

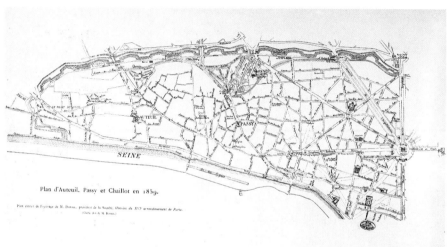

Map showing the subdivision of Passy (1824).

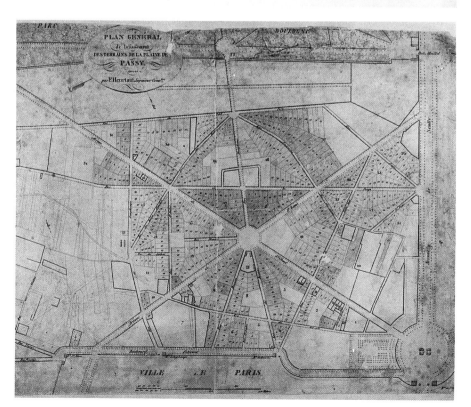

building size gradually decreased (from six-story edifices in the center to low houses on the outskirts, with every stage in between). As the city expanded beyond its natural scale (materialized by the limits of the Louis XIV ramparts), secondary organisms sprang up spontaneously; possessing structures of their own, they coexisted with the urban center proper but did not depend on it. Some of the new sections were quite successful: Saint-Vincent-de-Paul, Beaugrenelle, and Batignolles, for example, had a strong urban flavor. Others, however, were much less fortunate: Europe, severed by a railway line built through the heart of it and by the continuation of the Rue de Rome (though the Place de l'Europe is quite beautiful); and Passy, which, designed as a residential area, is notorious for its lack of a center (the Place Victor-Hugo and the church of Saint-Honoré-d'Eylau act as one, at a poorly adapted intersection).

The partial failure of the new developments was primarily due to their excessive size. The rampant speculation that began when Charles X came to the throne in 1824 soon led to disaster. By 1826 a serious economic crisis was under way, and the new districts had to be left unfinished. They were not completed until the annexation of 1860, and not without changes in the initial layout and typology. One can understand Chabrol's suspicion of big real-estate ventures!

The Hameau Montmorency in Passy, 12 Avenue des Tilleuls.

The Emergence of an Architectural Style

The construction of outlying districts went hand in hand with the development of covered passageways in the center of the city. As the urban scale grew, passageways were built through the big older blocks to create shortcuts to the center. Covered passageways first appeared around the time of the Revolution, when the Parisian tradition of building little paths through a block (many still to be seen in the Faubourg Saint-Antoine, the Faubourg Saint-Denis, and Charonne) was combined with the new technology of glass-and-steel roofing. The earliest example was the Passage du Caire, built in 1799, followed a year later by the Passage des Panoramas. The first covered passageway, like the many open passageways in its vicinity, was simply an extension of the Rue Saint-Denis, a busy shopping street; the second, as already mentioned, was a real shortcut between Montmartre and the Bourse. A new distinction between street and passageway was thus established. A lighted shopping area, the covered passageway can be considered the forerunner of both the department store (which appeared in Paris during the Second Empire) and today's shopping malls.

Covered Passageways: A Symbol of Centrality

The Passage du Caire and the Passage des Panoramas remained isolated cases for a number of years. Then, in 1823, the covered passageway suddenly came back into fashion, and a specific architectural typology emerged.[9] The Galerie Vivienne and the

Passage de l'Opéra, Galerie du Baromètre. Photo: Marville, ca. 1870.

Passage du Grand-Cerf. Photo: Atget, n.d.

1. Place du Caire. **2.** Passage du Caire.

Passage Choiseul were built through blocks in the extremely dense area around the Bourse and the Palais-Royal. They were soon followed by ten or so additional passageways that put the principle into general use. A new group of passageways was built in the 1840s (when economic recovery led to a revival in the building trade); but that was to be the last spurt of passageway-building in Paris. The covered passageway's official death sentence came with the 1860 annexation: the expansion of the city's scale and, relatedly, the construction of major new arteries made these small projects on the edges of the old center obsolete.

Decentralization

Restoration Paris, the city of Balzac, underwent profound changes. The conquest of new outlying spaces was one, but certainly not the only, significant change. Just as important was the center's creeping expansion beyond the medieval wall. No longer confined to the small shopping and entertainment district around the Halles and the Palais-Royal, the heart of Paris now extended out to the Right Bank boulevards between the Madeleine and Le Temple. There, along the tree-lined esplanades created on the site of the old Louis XIV ramparts in the eighteenth century, were the chic cafés (the Café Anglais, the Maison Dorée, and Tortoni, on the Boulevard des Italiens), as well as most of the theaters.

Deserting the Left Bank, Paris pushed north, and the old ramparts became the city's center. The most beautiful Restoration buildings were built between Trinité and the Gare de l'Est, around the most prestigious churches of the day, Notre-Dame-de-Lorette and Saint-Vincent-de-Paul. These major monuments were complemented by the mansions in the Saint-Georges section and by coherently planned groups of buildings located, for example, on the Rue des Petites-

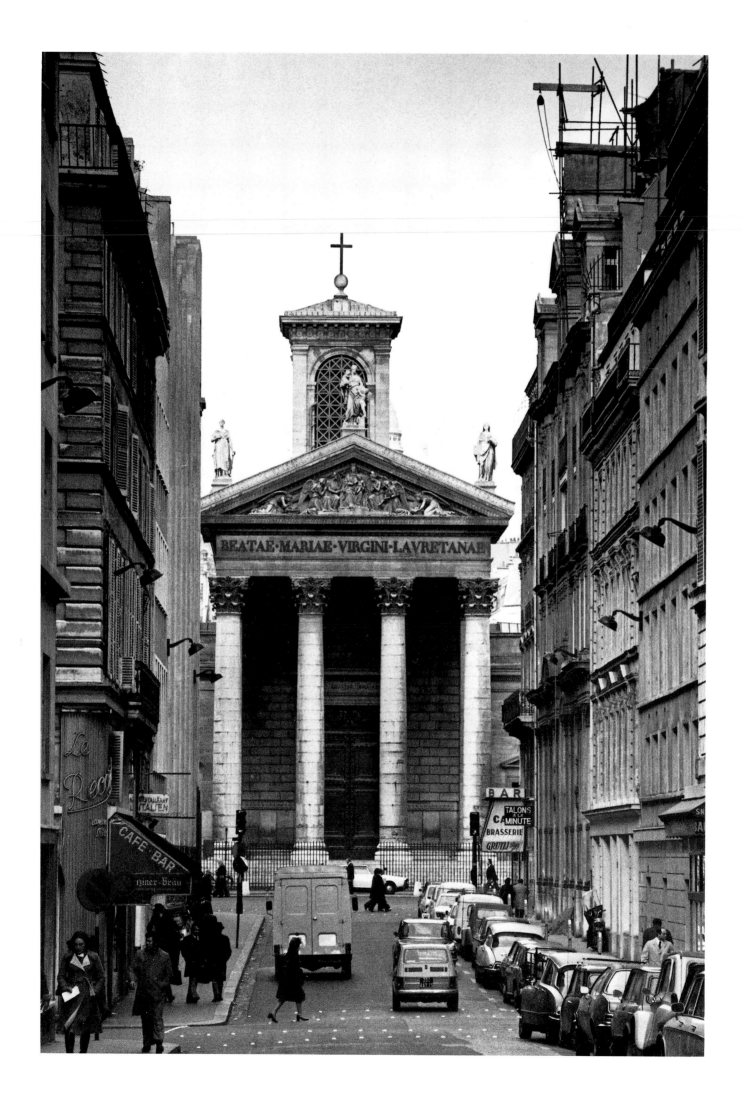

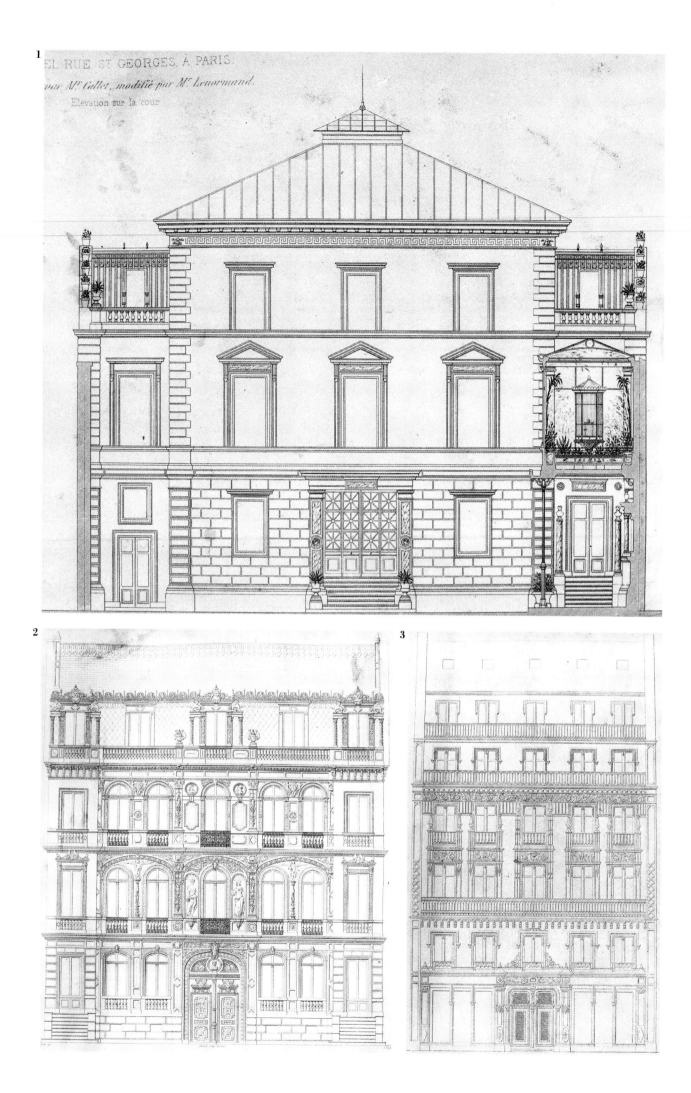

EL RUE ST GEORGES, À PARIS.

par Mr Gallet, modifié par Mr Lenormand.

Elévation sur la cour

2

par Mr Gallet, modifié par Mr Lenormand.

3

Facing page: **1.** Mansion, Rue Saint-Georges, court-yard façade. **2.** 26 Place Saint-Georges, 1843. (See p. 85, no. **1**). **3.** 45 Rue de la Chaussée-d'Antin, 1848.

Ecuries and the Rue d'Hauteville. The city's northward thrust also stretched, though the quality of constructions was somewhat lower, to the slopes of Montmartre (around Abbesses and Goutte d'Or, which at that time were neighborhoods of low houses). Blocked to the north by the village of Montmartre, the city threaded its way east along the Rue de Clignancourt and continued into the Château-Rouge area. By comparison, westward expansion was quite weak: the Madeleine district expanded somewhat on the Rue Saint-Honoré, but not much farther than the Rue des Mathurins. But the district, in existence since the eighteenth century, did slowly get denser, as the old mansions were torn down to make room for new buildings. Thus the Thélusson mansion, one of Ledoux's masterpieces, was destroyed in 1826 "by an awful tailor named Berchut who demolished it and built plaster houses on the site."[10] On the other hand the Left Bank, with its big stately mansions and gardens, would seem to have dropped off into peaceful slumber. Indeed, it was years before the section south of the Luxembourg Gardens was finished.

The construction of tall buildings would seem to have come to a standstill during the Restoration, when the private house—ranging from the most modest (Rue Damesne, for instance) to the most luxurious (Place François Ier)—enjoyed great popularity. Though many had been built during the reign of Louis XVI, big buildings were used less systematically in the early nineteenth century, when a number of intermediate categories crept in between the six-floor edifice and the mansion or villa. During the Empire the numerous little real-estate ventures brought about by the sale of state-owned land had already been characterized by an obvious typological uncertainty in a number of cases. One of the most revealing of these is the Rue de l'Abbaye, built on the site of the old Saint-Germain-des-Prés convent, using what could be salvaged from the convent, as was customary at the time. (The big window from the refectory of Pierre de Montreuil was recently found intact, buried in the wall between two buildings.) On the Rue de l'Abbaye one finds a four-story wood-and-plaster house on stone posts next to a five-story rubblestone building, as well as a large four-story stone house, including a basement with mezzanine.

There was no shortage of building sites during the Restoration, thanks to the city's considerable expansion beyond the medieval ramparts. Outside the center, buildings were not very tall. Three upper stories (one of them recessed) over a basement with mezzanine characterized the very prestigious Place Franz-Liszt (on which the regular façades were, however, meant to be monumental), while only three floors were used in the Cité Bergère, though extra stories were later added to some structures.

Typological Uncertainty

Rue de l'Abbaye, photographed from the Place Saint-Germain-des-Prés.

89

The emergence of a new architectural category: the
apartment house. Rue Saint-Lazare, even numbers,
seen from the church of Notre-Dame-de-Lorette.

The emergence of the apartment building as an architectural category depended above all on the size of the lots. The difference in size between lots used for traditional townhouses and modern rental buildings is easy to see on cadastral maps. In fact, only one dimension counted: a lot's width. The increase in width that resulted from attempts to group lots together during reconstruction in the eighteenth century has been pointed out by Françoise Boudon in a study of the Halles area.[11] The transition from lots that were six to eight meters across to lots of around twenty meters in width was decisive.

The joining of two lots did not create the wide lots needed for a total change in architectural typology. When lots were less than a dozen meters wide, it was difficult to build more than a single apartment per floor since, according to tradition, three rooms had to overlook the street (the living room, the master bedroom, and a *cabinet*, giving a total width of over ten meters). Starting in the late eighteenth century, builders began tackling the problem of lot width and gradually worked out a solution. The structure that prevailed until the midnineteenth century was based on a width of twelve meters (e.g., the Odéon and Rue d'Hauteville). The same structure was also used on the Boulevard de Strasbourg, and on the Rue de Rivoli when it was extended early in the Haussmann era, but was no longer found on the Boulevard Saint-Michel just a few years later. We are thus dealing with a transition that can be divided into two periods: lots were first widened from six to twelve meters and then, at midcentury, from twelve to eighteen meters.[12]

The result was two distinct types of apartment buildings. In the first case, a lot's depth was exploited in the traditional way: the nicest apartments overlooked the street, while more modest ones, accessible by the service staircase, were placed at the back of the courtyard. For this, a width of twelve meters was quite sufficient, as long as the lot was deep enough—at least twenty meters, meaning lots of around 250 square meters. In the second case, two symmetrical apartments were placed on each floor, on either side of a common staircase, overlooking the street; the depth of the lot was built up according to the space available. Toward the end of the century there was a tendency to use very deep lots (a much more profitable approach) filled with parallel buildings of almost the same status, though the front building remained somewhat more prestigious. The surface area of lots then soared beyond the 450-500 square meters common up to that time.

Restoration buildings were in general fairly modest constructions; each floor contained a single apartment with five to seven windows opening onto the street. (Tradition thus remained loyal to the uneven numbers that Blondel had advocated as being more harmonious.) The elevation, including basement and upper stories, adhered to the monumental tradition of classicism, but some subtle nuances were introduced. Thus the basement could contain one or two levels: a ground floor alone with a shop, or, in more elaborate constructions, a ground floor and a mezzanine. (Though common in Italy, the use of the mezzanine for shops is not really a Parisian tradition, the prevailing usage in France being to place a small residence behind the shop itself.) Above the basement, the colossal orders of the baroque style were seldom used. There were commonly three upper floors with approximately the same ceiling height, ranging from 3.1 meters in the lowest apartment to 2.6 in the topmost, as opposed to the 4.5-2.5 range found in earlier buildings. Inspired by Quattrocento palaces and notably by the Chancellery in Rome, a building's composition was framed only by flat, fluted pilasters or cornerstones linked together by thin cordons. The traditional double cordon disappeared, as did the vertical treatment of the bay, replaced by a simple frame around the window opening.

There was an obvious taste for geometry; the basement and the stories above it were unadorned, the attic and the cut-off corner were avoided, and the roof was slanted at a 45-degree slope interrupted only by a few dormer windows. Detail was simplified and remained purely graphic—fluting (never any bosses!), pediments, and frames around the window openings. The economy of formal means became so great that only a single element was used to structure a building's mass: either a cornice with modillions outlining the arris at the base of the roof, or a balcony running across the top story, but not both. The same simplicity was found in a building's details. The only thing that could be seen from the base of a façade was the pattern formed by the arcades or, in other cases, the consoles beneath a light iron balcony. The combination of both motifs would have been too rich.

The Restoration building was the product of a systematic codification of compositional elements; in that respect, it remained perfectly neoclassical. The overall volumetrics of buildings, the structuring of their façades, and their decorative details formed coherent wholes whose function it was to express the social level of the city's various streets. A comparison of façades in the Saint-Vincent-de-Paul section is most revealing. On the Place Franz-Liszt the summit of the architectural and social hierarchy is represented by arcaded basements with mezzanines; by two-story elevations with pedimented windows, varied proportions, and balcony; and by the recessed last story, emphasized by a second balcony across the front. On the Rue La Fayette one notices the elimination of monumental proportions in favor of three-story elevations above the basement in buildings possessing either an arcaded basement or a recessed top story. Finally, on the Rue d'Hauteville one finds completely flat, unadorned façades with no visual breaks between stories.

Restoration architecture eliminated ornament or at least restricted it to some focal point like the entryway or the partial balcony on the floor above the basement. Thus, when seen from a distance, Restoration façades have no real specificity. The sole decorative elements allowed

1. Rue La Fayette. 2. Rue Richer, seen from the Rue Saulnier. 3. 95 Rue La Fayette. 4. Rue Bleue.

were those that would catch the eye at close range only, and even these were to be used with restraint. It is precisely this acute sense of *propriety* that eclecticism was later to fight with such violence.

Outdoor Shutters, a Unifying Element

A general formal unity was, however, created with a stylistic device common to all new constructions, from the simplest to the most luxurious. Indeed, whether built out of freestone in the best of cases, or more often out of plastered rubblework, all Restoration façades were based on a particular decorative system: the grid or checkerboard pattern. Whereas seventeenth-century plaster houses had traditional flat façades with odd little dormer windows and no ornament, and the eighteenth century developed a vertical style, the Restoration building used a very elaborate graphic network of cornices, cordons, and sometimes frames around the window openings in vertical bays linking the stories together. Geometrical and abstract, this graphic system replaced the tradition of ornament.

In traditional architecture a building had contained more solids than voids, the latter being perceived as holes in a wall. The Restoration and the July Monarchy preferred transparent façades in which the thin perpend or wooden walls gave an equal, if not greater, place to openings.

In Restoration façades, with their elementary decoration and simple profiles, the windows took on considerable importance when a building did not have shutters; the empty walls looked flimsy, and the many window openings created a strange greenhouse impression. There was an obvious advantage inside, for each room contained two, if not three, windows. This transparency was made possible by the use of advanced construction techniques (the façade was no longer load-bearing) as well as by the development of lower-priced industrial materials: glass was the first material whose price plummeted because of industrialization. Be that as it may, nothing is more typical of the 1830s than the transparent façade, and the tight grid formed by its cordons and by the frames around its window openings.

The checkerboard pattern was strengthened by the systematic regularization of the spacing and dimensions of window openings, as opposed to the medieval custom of determining an opening's size and location according to the volume to be lighted inside.[13]

The typical Restoration façade was in itself quite monotonous; the only thing to break that monotony was the outdoor shutter. Covering the façade with thin parallel stripes, Venetian shutters helped to destroy the materiality of the solid-void relation in favor of a purely graphic system of light, rigorously horizontal hachures. If nobody knows exactly when outdoor shutters were first adopted in Paris (they had long been used in the Mediterranean countries), it can at least be said that they became widespread and tended to replace indoor shutters at the very end of the eighteenth century.

1. Rue Racine. 2. Cité de Trévise.

Several examples of "transparent" façades.
1. Corner of the Rue Madame and the Rue de Fleurus. **2.** Rue de Castellane. **3.** Intersection of the Rue de Moscou, the Rue de Bucarest, and the Rue de Turin. **4.** Rue Madame. **5.** Rue de La Rochefoucauld.

Above and facing page:
two views of the Cité de Trévise.

The advantage of indoor shutters was that they did not interfere with a façade's architectural lines. In addition, as solid panels they were particularly efficient at blocking out light. On the other hand, they had the double drawback of not protecting windows from attempted break-ins (for that, iron bars had to be added), and of being difficult to manipulate, since the shutting mechanism was shared by shutters and window. The outdoor shutter was introduced shortly before the espagnolette bolt, a more precise and efficient system not really designed to be used with indoor shutters.

Outdoor shutters were, however, adopted much more for stylistic than for purely technical reasons: the graphic interplay of the outdoor shutters discreetly broke the monotony of the otherwise unadorned neoclassical surfaces, making them vibrate as delicately as the grain and meticulous bonding of the stone itself. In a period of strict decorative austerity, they were a very subtle way of livening up façades. The charm of certain Restoration neighborhoods in Paris (notably, around Saint-Georges) is almost exclusively due to the insistent presence of outdoor shutters that unify the various façades into a coherent decorative system based on graphism and horizontality. Intentionally banal, the use of outdoor shutters as a decorative device thrust the building into anonymity and thereby linked it even more strongly to the whole formed by a street or a neighborhood.

If, strictly speaking, there is no generic model for the Restoration

building (which partook of a long classical tradition), one can assert with some confidence that there was a dominant stylistic system that reflected an underlying desire for regularity and order. In fact, that desire characterized the entire nineteenth century, and was so strong that it succeeded in totally controlling the wildest decorative extravagances of three generations. It is indeed paradoxical that, though plastic means changed and were enriched, the principle of unity was maintained throughout the nineteenth century with as much firmness as in Restoration architecture. Thus, all ornamental differences between periods aside, Restoration buildings must be considered the prototype of the nineteenth-century bourgeois building.

In point of fact, Restoration architecture drew on two rather contradictory sources. The first, architectural in the accepted sense of the word, was the Rue de Rivoli. The second, more decorative than purely architectural, was the little buildings in the center, particularly those on the Rue du Bac. The Rue de Rivoli includes not only the arcades that Percier and Fontaine built along the Terrasse des Feuillants (whose buildings originally opened directly onto the garden). It is also a rigorous, almost cubic, volumetrics, a repetitive and absolutely regular trabeation stripped of all ornamentation, a rhythm created by the decreasing ceiling heights of the three main stories

Monumentality or Decoration?

The contrast between imposing architecture and the vernacular tradition. **1.** Rue de Rivoli. **2.** Rue du Bac, even numbers, between the Boulevard Raspail and the Rue de Grenelle.

above the basements, the last set back slightly from the façades, and finally the big curved roofs—so Palladian—that inspired the regulation circular arcs of the late nineteenth century. Characterized by strong lines and a lack of ornamentation, the Rue de Rivoli is especially noteworthy for the excellent proportions of its buildings (levels and window openings) and its overall impression of unity.

Ordinary architecture could retain neither the impressive site nor the monumental rigor of the Rue de Rivoli. But it could draw on the harmonious relationships between proportions, the spirit of bare, unadorned simplicity, and the beautiful stonework found there. Thus the Rue de Rivoli inspired a number of handsome groups of flat stone houses whose only ornament consists of their cordons and the frames around their window openings.

Given the small lots in the old center, the Rue de Rivoli model could hardly have been used there. In the center the composition of private dwellings was purely decorative, and was sometimes just a transposition of a building's indoor ornament onto its façade. The use of the orders on façades betrays a naive attempt at academic art. Yet the small proportions of the stories, the systematic neoclassical simplicity, and the subtle scales of detail found in Restoration buildings in central Paris do give the ornamental façades great charm. Though the decorative treatment of architectural surfaces was not really appreciated in the imposing architecture of the Restoration, which had to be sober and severe, it later came into great favor and led to the rich ornamental repertoire of the July Monarchy. The decorative approach was often preferred in shopping districts; it seems fair to suppose that some rich Restoration façades were quite simply architectural advertisements for shops. In any case, what is certain is that ornament was already an unresolved issue during the Restoration; a bit later, that issue was to become an open conflict.

In outlying sections, where the larger lots were much better adapted to apartment buildings, façades were radically different in style. The typology was usually based on six-floor constructions. Beneath the four main floors was an arcaded basement with a mezzanine. Two balconies were built across the front, on the prestigious third floor and the top floor, powerfully structuring the levels of the composition. This model—clearly seen on the Rue Saint-Lazare—is an obvious transposition of the Rue de Rivoli model, which inspired the use of decreasing ceiling heights (and decreasing ornamentation, the frames around the upper windows being considerably simpler than those around the lower ones). But the Rue de Rivoli model was adapted to the more mundane context of simple plaster façades, and the stately curving roofs were replaced by regulation roofs pitched at a 45-degree slope and by big dormer windows above the façades.

Though formally inconsistent at first, Restoration architecture later became much more homogeneous (one might even say banal), as the visual links between the successive buildings on a street were strengthened. By the time of the July Monarchy, new rows of buildings were almost *too* coherent, as cordons, frames, and cornices were placed at the same height from one building to the next, and windows always spaced at the same regular intervals. Graphically, façades were reduced to the shallow surface vibration of the little horizontal system formed by the shutter slats.

Broken by similarly sized, regularly spaced window openings, Restoration façades so closely resemble one another that they seem to have been traced on a single pattern and have no individuality whatever. The ornamental repertoire was extremely limited. The aesthetics of the Rue de Rivoli triumphed on the lower slopes of Montmartre—on the Rue de la Rochefoucauld, Rue d'Aumale, and Rue de Trévise.

A purely horizontal composition thus emerged: the superposition of window openings emphasized trabeation; all vertical links were eliminated; and relatedly, the horizontal lines of the cordons and cornices were strengthened. As façades risked a lack of relief, two powerful balconies were projected out from the façade, running across its entire length in the best of cases. The taste for uninterrupted horizontals was so pronounced that the city had to strengthen regulations concerning the separation of adjacent buildings. Thus a balcony slab could not continue from one building to the next, and wrought-iron barriers had to be installed to section off a balcony when more than one apartment opened onto it.

Nurtured on a neoclassical vision of mass and line, the Restoration created a "horizontal composition" strongly opposed to the traditional vertical style. These austere rows of buildings and repetitive façades can be denigrated, as indeed they were during the Second Empire. But the eminently bourgeois architecture that emerged in the 1830s can also be seen as the triumph of a neoclassical aesthetic in gestation since the reign of Louis XVI.

A Rigid Urban Model

Implicitly based on a distinction between the center and outskirts of the city (and between rich districts and poor ones), the expanding neoclassical system gave the city a definitive global configuration that was meant to express the hierarchy of social classes. Public spaces and private constructions alike contributed to establishing a strict correlation between the city's form and the social hierarchy. The system's advantage was its clear and logical structure: architectural form reflected the social level of each street and section in the city. The drawback of the system, on the other hand, was that it could not be modified even slightly; if a section's situation or urban function changed, all its architecture became obsolete. Thus when the social structures underlying city life began to change in the nineteenth century, the city fell apart. The rigid spatial model, based on the stable social system of the Ancien Régime, that was set up during the

21 Rue Bréa.

Restoration obviously could not satisfy the demands of social groups seeking to better their status and gain access to privileges previously reserved for an aristocratic elite.

A Monotonous Landscape

The clear organization of Restoration Paris—which seems so admirable today, now that it has been replaced by anarchy—had various drawbacks. The negative side effects of the fundamentally rational neoclassical style, such as it evolved in the first quarter of the nineteenth century (definitively eliminating the old way of doing things handed down from medieval times), were particularly obvious in the capital's poorer sections—the mushrooming working-class districts outside the city limits.

Leaving the prestigious neighborhoods located near the fashionable boulevards on the Right Bank, one found vast stretches of identical constructions in districts without big, tree-lined streets, public squares, or edifices with character. A unique architectural typology was repeated ad nauseam along uniform streets that consequently all looked alike. The things for which Haussmann would incur such blame could already be found in several Restoration neighborhoods, notably in the eleventh and thirteenth arrondissements, already well on their way to becoming exclusively working-class districts.

Four- or five-story elevations continued uninterrupted up and down the streets with no recesses or projections whatsoever and, needless to say, no balconies. Identically sized windows were spaced at regular intervals on plain, undecorated walls, so that the wood and plaster constructions were at least well lighted. On the flat façades ornamentation was reduced to cordons uniting the bases of the windows, and to roof cornices. Molded cast-iron railings were placed outside the windows in the extremely shallow wells—the only system allowing installation of outdoor shutters, which cannot be used when a balustrade is placed outside the well. Because of their thin walls, the monotonous spacing of the window openings, and the complete absence of projections, the façades found in working-class neighborhoods were extraordinarily uniform and, for that matter, were used with a surprising sameness from one neighborhood to the next.

When money allowed, the "poor man's version" of the Restoration building (poor also inside, for the buildings usually contained very small apartments) was improved with features from the more sophisticated neoclassical model, the Florentine-style palace with its high, bossed basement and heavy cornice. But that was seldom the case; the Restoration's "barracks"—every bit as bad as certain apartment complexes built recently—must be judged by the tradition of the private house, still thriving at the end of the eighteenth century.

1. Rue de Charenton. **2.** Rue du Chemin-Vert.

Traditionally, the poorest man had been able to build himself a modest house (albeit little more than a shack) and organize his living space as he saw fit. Industrial society put an end to that, and housing became one of the most visible forms of the proletarianization of the working classes.

The Number of Stories

The monotony of the outer districts was somewhat compensated for by a gradual decrease in building heights. The city's outward expansion led to the construction of developments that, though urban in flavor, were noticeably lower than those in the center. Moving away from the center, one came across more and more individual houses with successive decreases in size; buildings with three, then two, main floors above a one-story basement were common near the Farmers-General Wall, as also in the centers of the old villages around Paris. When one crossed from one side of the wall to the other, buildings quite often lost a story.[14]

Two- or three-story houses were the bottom rung on the ladder. They signified that one was relatively far from the architecturally harmonious center of the city. Obvious architectural coding certainly contributed to defining the city's very clear form for as long as the latter was and wanted to be visible. An examination of the map of building heights in Restoration Paris is very instructive. If such an examination is possible, it is because city officials classified districts not in terms of density but according to the number of floors in their buildings. Thus whenever civil engineers were working in the field, they systematically noted down the number of stories (and the materials used) in the constructions on the building line.

The hierarchy of building heights—traces of which can still be seen in the city's neoclassical constructions—was a very obvious and very sure way of maintaining clearly structured spaces in the city. A building's height told passersby how far they were from the center.

The Birth of the Suburb

At the very bottom of the urban hierarchy, one found vast outlying areas opened to construction during the reign of Charles X, but soon abandoned as a result of the economic downturn. On the cheap ground outside the city, little houses and shacks were built with thin, plastered wooden walls and no foundations. Anarchy reigned as sheds and little houses sprang up next to four- and five-story buildings. Since the surface area available for construction was too big, it could not be built up as coherently as the old faubourgs were. There were numerous streets of about the same size and importance; chance alone governed their development. A unified urban façade of blocks could not be formed for the good reason that utterly different functions had been thrown together with no underlying logic. The resulting incoherence was plain to see, and later hurt the evolution of the outlying districts by

Views of the old suburbs in the outer arrondissements. **1.** Boulevard de la Villette. **2.** Rue de la Pompe. **3.** Rue Duban. **4.** Rue de Charenton. **5.** Impasse du Mont-Tonnerre.

giving them a negative image of uncertainty and disorder. In other words, the suburb was born.

The rigid neoclassical order of the center did not stop the proliferation of suburban anarchy. The city was simply unable to coordinate its own expansion: in a totally uncontrolled free-market economy, the authorities, even if they disapproved, could not prevent real-estate speculation and moreover were even less able to deal with its consequences. To avoid this break in urban structure—the first in the city's contemporary history—it would have been necessary to revive restrictions on development.

Suburban growth extended far beyond the area just outside the Farmers-General Wall (Gros-Caillou, Plaisance, Batignolles). In fact, it affected all the suburban villages—Passy, Auteuil, La Chapelle, Belleville, Charonne, Gentilly, Montrouge. As a result the Thiers fortifications, built between 1841 and 1845, had to contain a huge space, that of present-day Paris. After the annexation of most of the villages around Paris in 1860, the city had to take on the difficult task of coordinating the metropolitan area's chaotic expansion. In particular, it had to alleviate the critical situation in the old, saturated centers of the villages.

Between 1825 and 1830 the centers of the villages around Paris began to be built up with four- and five-story buildings that gave certain streets like the Rue de Passy a highly urban look. Elsewhere, as real-estate speculation increased, there was a good deal of variation from one building to the next, as for example on the Rue de Flandre, where adjacent constructions vary from two to four stories. In still other areas, such as the Butte-aux-Cailles and Montmartre, a rural fabric was maintained and built up in an utterly anarchic way.

Eventually, all the available space between neighboring villages was filled up with low (generally two-story) constructions of which many traces can still be found today. The simple little wooden houses with tile roofs and plaster façades were unfailingly decorated with a molding around each window opening (as well as the traditional window ledges). The suburban spaces were sometimes built up in so perfunctory a way that they turned into shantytowns (as for example the Rue Vitruve, near the Place de la Réunion in Charonne). These constructions were in complete keeping with the rural tradition of the Ile-de-France, which explains the village charm still found in certain neighborhoods of Paris. It must, however, be recognized that the architectural quality of these sections is far poorer than the "atmosphere." As they were built on highly limited budgets, the architecture was often highly limited, too, though some of the old suburban neighborhoods do reflect an astonishingly fine comprehension of the sites and vistas of the urban landscape.

Not all the new suburban districts were working-class: the residential vocation of western Paris could already be seen in the many country houses built on the airy hillocks between Ternes and Passy. Grouped together in clusters, they soon gave birth to the little neighborhoods of private houses that still dot the landscape of the fourteenth and sixteenth arrondissements. These groups of low houses were the bourgeois version of the proletarian suburbs to the east and southeast of the city. By 1830 the sociological division of Paris was clearly under way, quickly pivoting from a north-south axis (Saint-Georges/Plaisance) to an east-west axis (Ternes-Auteuil/La Chapelle-Butte-aux-Cailles).

The last thing that must be emphasized about Restoration Paris is the separation of the working class and the bourgeoisie inside the urban organism: the poor migrated to the east, while the rich headed west. If the Left Bank had been abandoned for some time, the heights of eastern Paris became more and more a working-class area in the years that followed. The phenomenon had been foreshadowed during the classical period in the divergent development of the Faubourg Saint-Germain and the Faubourg Saint-Honoré to the west, and the Faubourg Saint-Antoine to the east. During the Restoration, what would happen remained unclear for a while, but the destiny of the unfinished developments eventually settled the matter once and for all. The die was cast: as Beaugrenelle, Plaisance, Charonne, and La Chapelle turned into proletarian neighborhoods, Europe, Monceau, Passy, and Auteuil were covered with the residential constructions of the bourgeoisie.

The Industrial Era

New Vistas

The advent of the July Monarchy and subsequent replacement of Chabrol by a new prefect were not in themselves as important as some observers have hastily claimed. The cholera epidemic that ravaged France two years later—its victims included the prime minister, Casimir Périer—was much more decisive. At a time when the study of hygiene was making great progress,[15] political leaders could not remain indifferent to the issue of public health. In 1833 a new prefect was appointed: Claude Berthelot de Rambuteau (1781-1869). His pioneering efforts were as important as Chabrol's, for they cleared the way for the urban transformations usually associated with Haussmann. Indeed, for fifteen years Rambuteau's administrative decisions totally modified urban practices in Paris. He considerably broadened the notion of urban space—its specific features and general organization—and contributed to a new definition of the public interest in a rapidly changing world.

In a city that was still growing fast (the population went over the million mark in 1846), the new prefect's role was all the more difficult, as the very conditions of urbanization were changing. Since the old city was clearly obsolete, architects, engineers, landscape gardeners, doctors, and lawyers devoted their energies to setting up a new urban model.

The change in urbanistic conceptions during the July Monarchy was directly related to the transportation revolution that, in just a few short years, drastically changed the relationship of time and distance. Two primordial inventions marked the end of Charles X's reign: the omnibus and the railroad.

The omnibus replaced earlier elementary forms of public transit like the traditional horse-drawn barges on the Seine, and offered the lower classes what had previously been the prerogative of the rich: a relatively rapid mode of transport. But the "poor man's coach" was not so much a victory for the working classes as an important means of urban growth. Humble horse-drawn carriages, crammed with fifteen passengers or more, provided a shuttle service between places of work in the center and modest homes in neighborhoods outside the city's walls, where a population of clerks, shopkeepers, and laborers settled. Paris outgrew its pedestrian scale. There is an obvious link between the opening of the first new districts outside the Farmers-General Wall in 1824 and the advent of the omnibus four years later.

The importance of the transportation revolution as a factor in the city's growth has usually been underestimated. Prior to the introduction of the omnibus, the city had not been able to expand beyond certain limits; in the necessarily confined geographical area that resulted, overcrowding and public health became critical issues. When public transport modified the traditional relationship between space and time, it brought all kinds of immediate advantages. Outside the city there was ground and fresh air to spare. Suburban land was healthier and also cheaper, which meant lower rents. Last but not least, living outside the city limits considerably lowered the cost of merchandise, since one did not have to pay the taxes collected on goods entering the city. For a population with modest incomes, the argument was an important one—and blinded workers to the disadvantages (like commuter fatigue) of living in the suburbs. As a result, the center of Paris was drained of a whole segment of its population, which clustered together in outlying villages and developments.

Space-Time

Claude Berthelot de Rambuteau (1781-1869).

A Legal Instrument

The other new mode of transportation, rail, affected the city differently. The railroad was introduced in France during the reign of Charles X. The first steam railway line had been opened in England in 1825; two years later, in 1827, Marc Séguin opened the line from Andrézieux to Saint-Etienne, and it was extended to Lyons in 1832. The railroad arrived in the capital relatively late, and rather timidly, when the line from the Gare Saint-Lazare to Saint-Germain-en-Laye was opened in 1837. Between the 1833 law that established a national rail network and the 1842 charter that turned the operation of the network over to a certain number of big companies, there were ten years of debate on the issue of public interest and the priority it must sometimes take over the free use of private property as defined in the Civil Code. The law of May 3, 1841, on expropriating private property in the public interest finally settled the matter, allowing the fairly rapid establishment of a national rail system without endless negotiations with divergent and highly speculative private parties. Though originally drafted to facilitate rail construction, the new law was soon interpreted as allowing land to be expropriated for urban development also. As a result, the new arteries that public opinion was calling for—an absolute necessity in the unhealthy, overcrowded capital—could be built.

Armed with the 1841 law, Rambuteau undertook to restructure the city of Paris; thus the city's transformation got well under way during the reign of Louis-Philippe. The problem was twofold: first, density had to be lessened in the saturated center by tearing down existing structures; second, wide arteries adapted to the development of large-scale public transportation had to be built to facilitate travel from one part of town to another. The Haussmann boulevard was born, to become simultaneously a thoroughfare allowing faster travel and the lungs of a choking city. The 1841 law on the expropriation of private property in the public interest can thus be said to have played a primordial role in the city's development. It could even be called the birth certificate of the Haussmann era.

A Cleaner and Healthier City

Analyzed in an official report, the 1832 cholera epidemic was found to have been all the more devastating because of overcrowding. Thus, well before the definition of "unhealthy blocks" according to the mortality rate caused by tuberculosis, Parisian hygienists noted the relationship between population density and insalubrity. Pointing out that half the city's population was concentrated on a fifth of the city's surface area, the cholera report went on to reveal that the death rate had been highest precisely in the densest part of town, on the Ile de la Cité and around the Hôtel de Ville (6.4% of the population on the Rue de la Mortellerie, 13.6% on the Place de l'Hôtel de Ville, and 24.4% on the Quai de Grève).[16] Understandably, the highest priorities of city officials were to lessen density in the center by developing new outlying areas (inside the the Farmers-General Wall, which was still far from

Cast-iron urinal (installed in 1848, with funds collected from neighborhood residents), Rue du Faubourg-Saint-Martin, behind the church of Saint-Laurent. Photo: Marville, ca. 1870.

Urinal, Chaussée de la Muette. Photo: Marville, ca. 1865-70.

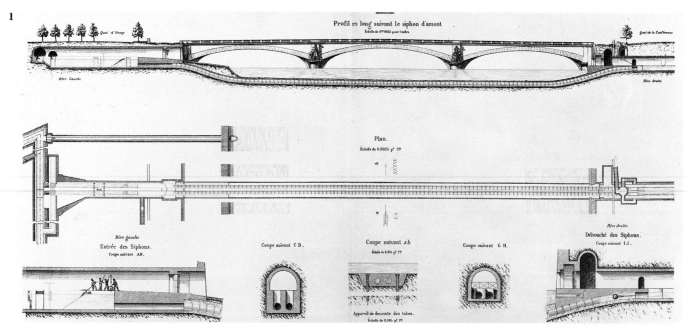

1. Siphon of the Left Bank sewer at the Pont de l'Alma. **2.** Drawing of the tunnel under the Boulevard de Sébastopol, where it intersects with the tunnel under the Rue de Rivoli. Illustrations reprinted from *Travaux souterrains de Paris* (Belgrand, 1887).

being filled up), and to make the city a cleaner place by installing fountains and sewers. Somewhat later, the idea of building new streets through the city caught on, largely because of the press, which was in favor of radically restructuring the city. As the idea gained popularity, architects, intellectuals, and speculators came up with the most diverse, contradictory, and far-fetched solutions imaginable. However, the new thoroughfares being built were slow to increase in size. The Boulevard de Strasbourg was the first new street over eighteen meters wide, but the principle of the wide artery was not really put into general use until the Haussmann era.

To make the city a cleaner and healthier place, Rambuteau began by improving the sewer system, which the hygienist Parent-Duchâlet had studied in great detail in his *Essai sur les cloaques ou égouts de Paris* (1824). A system of pipes under the roadway was not enough: liquid wastes also had to be carried off by a permanent stream of water (the chance flow of rainwater along the roadway had previously been relied on all too often). Thus the city decided to install a system of mains to carry water from the river to a network of hydrants that would provide a permanent stream of water in the gutters to help clean the cobblestone streets. This went hand in hand with the adoption of English-style sidewalks raised higher than the roadway,[17] and the subsequent installation of roof gutters and drainpipes to collect rainwater and channel it directly to the curb, so as to increase the flushing. In 1832 there were 39 kilometers of water mains and 217 hydrants in Paris; by 1850, the network contained 358 kilometers of mains and 1,837 hydrants. The prefect's interest in sanitation also led him to introduce public urinals (which the Parisians mischievously nicknamed after him!). Finally, he had gas street lighting installed throughout the city. By the end of Louis-Philippe's reign, Paris was a properly lighted and cobbled city with sidewalks and public fountains. Yet Rambuteau and his collaborators had a basically traditional outlook. Thus the water supplied by the Canal de l'Ourcq fed only the public fountains: the lack of pressure still made it impossible to install running water on every floor in private constructions.

Part of a long tradition from medieval times, the development of public spaces took precedence over private interests. Private real-estate ventures were counterbalanced by what the municipality saw as its responsibility to maintain and improve public property. The major idea was *beautification*, a good example of which can be found in the fountains that appeared around the city: a simple faucet could have supplied a street or neighborhood with water; instead, veritable monuments were erected. The city commissioned Louis Visconti (who had designed the Gaillon fountain ten years earlier) to do the colossal constructions on the Square Louvois and the Place Saint-Sulpice, as well as the Molière fountain, while J. I. Hittorff designed the basins on the Place de la Concorde. In the dream of a city with a thousand fountains, enormous gardens, and tree-shaded esplanades, one can see the long neoclassical tradition of the pilgrimage to Italy, the very essence of fine-arts education in nineteenth-century France. Indeed, Italian models have deeply influenced the way the city looks today. Though Visconti's references were basically French (the Fontaine des Innocents and the Fontaine de Grenelle), his treatment of jets of water and use of monumental environments breaking with the scale of the city's buildings were utterly Roman—almost more so, in fact, than Hittorff's reference to Bernini and the Piazza Navona.

Shaping the Urban Organism

The idea of beautifying the city played an equally important role in Rambuteau's decision to create tree-lined esplanades along the banks of the Seine; along with the inner boulevards, these promenades prefigured the thoroughfares Haussmann was later to build. Unlike the mall and the bowling green—where a central lane was treated as a landscaped dividing strip or lawn, and traffic was prohibited[18]—the Parisian boulevard was designed with three parallel lanes for pedestrians and vehicles. Traffic flowed down the middle while the side lanes, protected from passing vehicles by a row of trees, were devoted to walking and leisure. The formula was invented by accident, when the old Louis XIV ramparts were transformed into public esplanades (the trees had originally been planted for purely military purposes).[19] The boulevard soon came to exemplify the the city's center, if for no other reason than the considerable success enjoyed by the Right Bank boulevards, the vortex of nineteenth-century Parisian life. Busy shopping areas that might be seen as a strange combination of the fashionable covered passageways and the busiest arteries, the tree-shaded boulevards became the principal model used to restructure centrally located spaces. Their function was in fact threefold: the sidewalks were for shoppers and shopping; the roadway itself allowed rapid transportation from one part of town to another; and finally, the double row of trees separating roadway and sidewalks created a break between two distinctly different functions. Moreover, the boulevards created the large-scale network needed to give the city as a

Facing page: **1.** Saint-Sulpice fountain. Anon., 1853.
2. Gaillon fountain. Photo: Atget, 1902.

3. Molière fountain. Photo: Edmonds, 1869.

Boulevard de Sébastopol, looking north from the Rue de Rivoli. Photo: Marville (?), ca. 1875.

whole a clearly defined structure. A line of communication and a boundary line, the boulevard played a complex role in shaping the urban organism.

The boulevards enjoyed such great success that the model spread to the quays,[20] where the city's booksellers, deserting the arcades of the Odéon and the Palais-Royal, set up shop. The boulevard was soon recognized as the best way of aerating and structuring the huge conglomeration that the capital had become. First tested on the natural breaks, topographical or historical, between the city's neighborhoods, the boulevard later became the model for all major new streets, and was finally realized in true grandeur when, after five years of construction work, the Boulevard de Strasbourg was opened in 1852.

The First Boulevards: Trial and Error

The Boulevard de Strasbourg was the outcome of more than twenty years of trial and error, and in some ways was still deficient: Haussmann criticized it for not opening onto a major monument on the south end, which, had it existed, would have determined the boulevard's scale of depth. The first attempts to create wider streets date back to the beginning of Louis-Philippe's reign. Shortly after the Citizen King's accession to the throne, a number of measures were taken to aerate the urban space and in particular to widen existing streets. The usual method consisted in moving the building line back, and closely resembled the technique civil engineers had been using for about a century to straighten certain streets.[21] The principle was simple. The official building line on a given street was moved back; then, whenever a building on that street was demolished, the construction replacing it had to be set on the new line. City officials hoped that, in the long run, existing streets would thus be widened at the lowest possible cost. Indeed, the operation cost nothing; as years passed, a street would gradually be widened.

For the long run, the principle itself cannot be contested. It should be noted, however, that corbeled façades, prohibited in France since the sixteenth century, can still be found today. Urban constructions have a very long life span, to be counted not in years but in centuries. In the final analysis, buildings are totally rebuilt much less frequently than they are transformed. Not surprisingly, the widened roadways that this measure, adopted for a considerable number of streets, was expected to create are still being awaited today. Indeed, the streets that were actually widened in this way were rare exceptions to the rule. Moreover, the method had disastrous consequences for the many streets that were never widened. As constructions were placed on the new building line, jagged rows of buildings were created; the gables of the old constructions were left exposed and the old alignment was totally destroyed, creating an anarchic landscape of short, choppy sequences. It did not take long for the ineffectiveness of this policy to be felt—even if the relevant city ordinances were not revoked until 1974! For Paris to be restructured, a much bolder approach had to be found.

In reaction to public opinion, Rambuteau soon undertook to build the first big new street through an existing part of town—the street in the Halles district that today bears his name. Just as that district's total failure to meet the growing capital's needs was being noticed, medical studies on city hygiene[22] were stressing the old district's saturation. But at first the only issue was traffic: the objective of the ordinance of March 5, 1838, establishing the route to be followed by the Rue Rambuteau, was to alleviate the traffic situation between Saint-Antoine and Saint-Honoré by connecting the Rue des Francs-Bourgeois with the Rue des Petits-Champs. When the street was built, two distinct approaches were tested: the first was to tear down the north side of the Rue Coquillière (an approach also used a bit later to widen the Rue Montmartre); the second was to build a new roadway through certain blocks, cutting through the gardens of old mansions and monasteries whenever possible and sometimes incorporating short streets that coincided with the new route. Though these methods tended to spare the old urban fabric, the buildings they left behind to camouflage the scar were often little more than closets. Rambuteau's approach was in fact the exact opposite of Haussmann's, inasmuch as the latter destroyed much more of the urban fabric and then grafted new buildings onto the new streets. An advantage can also be a drawback: though it disrupted the city's existing structure less, Rambuteau's approach was often too timid.

The opening of the Rue Rambuteau proved to be a turning point: it showed the city fathers that they absolutely had to think big and build more and wider streets through the saturated center. In 1842 the restructuring of the Halles and the construction of a wholesale market in proportion to the city's size became a hot issue. (The first proposals

Learning to Think Big

Examples of the jagged rows caused by moving the building line back on certain narrow streets. **1.** Rue Quincampoix. **2.** Rue de l'Annonciation, corner of the Rue Levain.

1. Rue Coquillière. 2. Rue Rambuteau. 3. Widened streets and new streets in the Halles district, 1833-53. Map reprinted from *Système de l'architecture urbaine* (Paris: C.N.R.S., 1977).

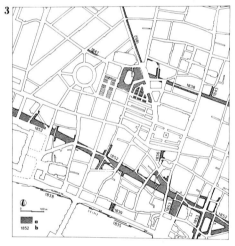

conceived the new market in a very traditional way, with supplies still coming into the city on the Seine.) Construction work finally began in 1851, involving not only the reconstruction of the market itself, but also a new road to extend the Rue de Rivoli east to the Hôtel de Ville, where it would join up with the Rue Saint-Antoine. A continuation of the route (designed during the First Empire) between the Concorde and the Pavillon de Marsan, the new road was twenty-two meters wide. The prestigious new route was meant to play a fundamental role in the city's street network, as was the Boulevard de Strasbourg, the big artery that the city soon decided to extend down to Châtelet. Thirty meters wide, the Boulevard de Strasbourg was even broader than the Rue de Rivoli. A comparison of the Rue Rambuteau and the Boulevard de Strasbourg, thirteen and thirty meters wide respectively, speaks for itself: there had been a major change in urban scale. Significantly, the building of the new boulevard corresponded to the opening of the Gare de l'Est, the first of the big Paris train stations (at a time when Saint-Lazare was still little more than a platform).

There was a good deal of improvising in these first, highly experimental street projects. Thus the need to connect the new section of the Rue de Rivoli with the Boulevard de Strasbourg was not seen until work was already under way. Next it became apparent that the Place du Châtelet, the area around the Hôtel de Ville, and the Halles also needed restructuring. Finally, the problems of planimetry brought about by the building of new streets were discovered when workers came up against the hillock known as the Butte Saint-Jacques, which had to be leveled. Along with improvisation, there was also a lot of utopian thinking. Railroad tracks were installed under the Halles

The first pavilion constructed by Baltard, in 1851: the meat market. Photo: Marville, n.d.

market and connected to a hugh turntable under the Boulevard de Sébastopol, so that produce could be shipped directly into the city's market. Before long, the system proved completely unworkable.

In spite of these many uncertainties, the efforts of Rambuteau and his collaborators eventually bore fruit: the wide street was born. In the traditional city the largest conceivable street width had been eighteen meters. An ordinance of August 25, 1784, distinguished three categories of street: those under 4 *toises* (7.80 meters), those under 5 *toises* (9.75 meters), and those over 5 *toises*, though in actual practice, this "over" was limited to 9 *toises* (17.54 meters). The main reason for these narrow streets was the harmonious two-thirds proportion that had traditionally existed between a street's width and the height of the buildings on it: thus, a street width of twelve meters was typically paired with a cornice height of eighteen meters (maximum regulation height).

Just after the Revolution the hierarchy of street sizes became somewhat more explicit when functional categories were introduced: six meters for "short routes," ten meters for "intermediate routes," twelve meters for "inner arteries," and fourteen meters for "big thoroughfares leading from one end of Paris to the other."[23] Remembering that sidewalks did not yet exist, we can calculate that streets allowed between three and seven lanes of traffic, parking included. When English-style sidewalks were built, the width of the roadway was reduced, and it became necessary to build streets that did not respect the old two-thirds proportion between street width and building height.

Even so, a street width of thirty meters was inconceivable before the specific typology of the boulevard was adopted. The boulevard was seen not as a single unit but as three distinct routes—the two sidewalks and the roadway itself—separated from each other by rows of trees. This conception allowed the traditional two-thirds proportion to be

The Invention of the Wide Street

Facing page: wide streets. **1.** Boulevard Beaumarchais, seen from the Colonne de Juillet. Anon., 1907.
2. Rue Etienne-Marcel and Rue de Turbigo. Anon.,
1906.

Narrow streets in the Halles district. **1.** Rue de la Fer-
ronnerie. Photo: Atget, 1907. **2.** Rue de la Grande-
Truanderie, seen from the Rue Pierre-Lescot. Photo:
Atget, 1907.

maintained. The roadway itself was about a dozen meters wide and was flanked by narrower pedestrian lanes six to eight meters wide. Thus, the sidewalks not being taken into account, the traditional proportion was preserved, which may well explain why the formula was so successful. Rambuteau's approach—in this respect very different from Haussmann's—remained loyal to a strong urban tradition and modified it in a perfectly acceptable way. He used the existing boulevards, with an average width of thirty-four meters, as a model, but in no way disrupted the traditional typology of streets and public spaces, which remained closely linked to the old pedestrian scale.

Indeed, Rambuteau proceeded with obvious caution. The Rue de Rambuteau was his laboratory, the testing ground for the various possible ways of widening the city's streets. The most economical solution (found in all earlier ordinances concerning the building line) was to move back only one side of a street, as on the Rue Coquillière and then on the Rue Montmartre. The results were disappointing: a disequilibrium between the two sides of the street was created, since the new side did not preserve the old typology (lot size, building height, stylistic detail). Even worse, when a street was widened, the area that had to be reconstructed was slight: often a veneer was simply placed over the remnants of the old constructions. The new façades closed off severely amputated buildings.

The problems created by this approach led city officials to prefer the construction of new roads through the centers of old blocks. In other words, old roads were not widened but were paralleled by wider new ones that relieved them of some of their congestion. Paradoxically enough, the new roads caused the saturated center to become even denser. When they were built, new land became available for construction. Indeed, had it not, there would have been no chance for profits, hence no investors, and the streets would not have been built. Although the Rue Rambuteau was not as wide as it should have been (the thirteen meters across did not even fit the definition of a "big thoroughfare leading from one end of Paris to the other"), it did show investors that the building of new streets could simultaneously open up land for construction. Unfortunately, the new lots were seldom deep enough. Consequently, the lots were hard to build on; there was not enough room for inner courtyards of any size, nor for staircases behind the buildings, nor sometimes even for a layout into front and back rooms. Architecture, lot size, and profitability are closely interrelated. During the July Monarchy profitability dictated certain architectural features such as a layout with two rows of rooms per floor (and, when feasible, the creation of a core between them for halls and closets), and the location of the staircase in a wing behind the building itself. In an old system of lots adapted to individual residences, the lots cut off when a building line was moved back were neither wide nor deep enough. On the other hand, when a new street was built through the middle of a block, the new lots could be made as wide as desired,

478. PARIS. — Le Boulevard Beaumarchais. - G.I.

TOUT PARIS

235 — Les Halles le matin - Rue Etienne Marcel et Turbigo (I° arr)

1906

though they too proved to be too shallow when insufficient land had been acquired around the new route.

Organization and Financing

Rambuteau's first experiment was no less revealing from a legal standpoint. An ordinance of March 5, 1838, "in the public interest" made it possible to build the Rue Rambuteau. But for other streets to be built, the city lacked an appropriate legal tool until the 1841 law on expropriation gave it one. Significantly, Hippolyte Meynadier's work on *La Grande Circulation de Paris*, defining the principal new streets built during the Haussmann era, was published two years later.[24] Studies for the reconstruction of the Halles district started in 1842. The project was ready three years later, but it took a long time to organize and finance the controversial operation. On August 2, 1849, city and state reached an agreement; two years later, government bonds were issued to pay for the construction work. Finally, the reconstruction was carried out from 1852 to 1854, with city and state sharing the construction work. For the completion of the Rue de Rivoli (the city's responsibility between the Louvre and the Hôtel de Ville), there was so much concern about landowners not having enough money to rebuild that a law was enacted to exempt "full-size" constructions (i.e., of regulation six-story volume) from taxes for twenty years.

Napoleon III's attitude was utterly different. Designed to encourage huge ventures and stimulate the real-estate market, the decisive decree came on March 26, 1852. It authorized the expropriation, for reasons of public utility, not only of buildings along new streets but also of any surrounding land needed to complete an operation. The imperial decree went hand in hand with the formation of associations of landowners that had the power to decide to reconstruct a section or block and moreover to impose the majority's decision on any recalcitrant parties. Generally speaking, the Second Empire approach was the outcome of the successive alterations of models and regulations during the reign of Louis-Philippe. Between Rambuteau's first timid experiment and the major restructuring brought about by the Boulevard de Strasbourg, there had been a radical change in thinking about urban development.

Block Planning

The transition from houses to apartment buildings, that is, from family property to investment property, seriously affected the city's traditional configuration. During the reign of Louis-Philippe, the pace of that transition quickened as the nation and private investors began working together. Speculators took advantage of the government's power and support to realize major projects, though sometimes after long and difficult negotiations. The transition from state monopoly,

Courtyard, 47 Rue du Montparnasse.

whereby the city itself was in charge of overseeing the construction of big projects, to the use of concessions, whereby it delegated power to the private sector, was highly significant, and allowed the Rue des Ecoles and the Boulevard de Strasbourg to be built shortly before the coup d'état that ended the Second Republic. Urbanistically speaking, the use of government-granted concessions led to the transition from lot-by-lot construction to what has been called "block planning."[25] Based on shared courtyards and coordinated façades, a totally new type of rental property emerged.

The Shared Courtyard

Traditionally, a separate courtyard had been placed in the middle of every lot between two parallel buildings joined by wings on either side of the lot. Although courtyards shared by adjacent lots appeared sporadically in the eighteenth century, the traditional closed courtyard prevailed until the end of the Restoration. The shared courtyard, a formula developed by architects and city officials, was used only when towns were reconstructed after disasters[26] and in big developments on large pieces of ground, as in the area around the Halle au Blé (1762). In ordinary neighborhoods, where construction took place on a lot-by-lot basis and there was no overall plan, the structuring of courtyards was

125

rather haphazard. Though courtyards did more or less coincide from one building to the next, fairly big recesses in their alignment, and thus exposed gables (which blocked the neighboring building's sunlight) were tolerated. The police ordinance forbidding access between buildings on adjacent lots for security reasons[27] was no doubt related to the slowness with which the use of shared courtyards caught on.

For shared courtyards to exist, several buildings had to be designed to form a single unit. When this was done, the advantages were considerable. Whereas, on lots about a dozen meters wide, courtyards had to remain quite small (four to five meters wide and six to seven meters deep, hence no more than about thirty square meters in the best of cases), shared courtyards were sometimes over a hundred square meters in size. As a result, a second façade was created on the courtyard side. The street façade's "little brother," it was a simplified replica built of cheaper materials (wood) and with simpler decoration (balustrades in the window wells and cordons).

The building regulations themselves had nothing to do with the evolution of Paris courtyards. Indeed, the first regulation concerning them dates from 1884. It set the minimum surface area of a courtyard at thirty square meters for buildings eighteen meters high or less, while for taller constructions there was an additional requirement that buildings be set at least six meters apart. The real reason for the creation of larger courtyards was quite down-to-earth: the more modest apartments in the rear building could not be rented out if they were too dark. Thus the size requirements stipulated in the 1884 regulation had in fact been in use for some time. The distance between a building on the street and the parallel building behind it was unofficially set at about a third of the height of the buildings. A courtyard's width was determined mainly by the width of the lot itself and of course by the way the sides of the lot had been built up.

An Ambiguous Space

Nevertheless, even when buildings on adjacent lots were designed around a common courtyard, the courtyard itself was often fairly small and unattractive, since toilets, wells, fountains, garbage cans, sheds, and various outbuildings were still located there. But even if the courtyard was often extremely cramped and unattractive, its status began to change as the buildings around it were set farther apart and given regular, decorated façades. Thus the courtyard was a highly ambiguous space, a service area with aristocratic pretensions.

Two contrasting approaches to window openings reveal this ambiguity. In some cases, following the Gothic lesson, the size of a window opening was based on the volume to be lighted inside. Each window revealed the function of the room behind it: a bedroom window could be distinguished from a lavatory window, owing to the difference in size and the different levels at which they were placed. In keeping with this logic, one later found shuttered food-storage containers hanging outside the kitchen window, and larger window openings for the reception rooms. A façade's style was determined by the irregularity of the window openings, whose size signified their function. There was a transposition of each floor's layout onto the style of the building's façade.

Diametrically opposed to the functional approach was the principle of a neutral and uniform street façade, which had prevailed since the late eighteenth century. As the buildings on the courtyard came to be seen as forming a second façade, they were given regular, decorated façades that resembled the ones on the street. The main difference was that the window openings were smaller on the courtyard and the piers narrower; windows were generally a meter wide (as opposed to an average of 1.20 meters on the street), while the piers varied between thirty to forty centimeters and a meter. The impression of uniformity was strengthened by the use of openings with ledges and balustrades identical to those on the street, as well as by the repetition of cordons on each story. The other difference from the street façade was in the quality of the construction: throughout the nineteenth century the ancestral tradition of plastered wooden walls prevailed in the courtyards of Paris.

One last problem, the short distance between the windows in buildings built directly opposite each other, does not seem to have bothered builders much. The old tradition of staggering windows made it possible to avoid having one window open directly onto another: when one looked out a window, the staggered windows in the building across the courtyard were simply glimpsed as a zigzag of background transparencies. But as the buildings around the courtyard were given a façade, regularization eventually won out. Thus the windows on facing façades were systematically aligned with each other—a problem alleviated by the well-established custom of using sheer curtains to veil rooms from the outside. Obviously, the common courtyard went hand in hand with the regularization of window openings; both elements signified a strong new emphasis on enhancing the inside of the block. Here already is an example of the kind of block planning that was perfected in the early twentieth century.

Courtyard, 37 Rue de Seine.

Another problem was solved with the introduction of wells that allowed light and air to enter rooms in the core of a construction (staircases, halls, lavatories, etc.). The wells were designed to fit the needs of individual buildings, but with little or no regard for how they might affect neighboring constructions. The only regulation concerning them was found in the Civil Code, which required a distance of 1.90 meters between parallel walls. Thus it was common to find wells no more than two meters wide. Wells varied in depth, but

Air Wells

Air wells, 37 Rue de Seine and 8 Rue du Mont-Thabor (in the background, the courtyard of 229 Rue Saint-Honoré).

their total surface area seldom exceeded ten square meters and was sometimes as little as three or four. Whatever their size, they were useful, for a little light is better than no light at all (as is usually the case today). Finally, the presence of windows opening onto the wells created an appreciable flow of air to ventilate apartments, especially in the summer months. It is indeed unfortunate that these light and ventilation shafts were later abandoned by architects.

Originating, it would seem, during the reign of Louis XVI (Lenoir-le-Romain used them frequently in the many buildings he designed), wells allowed a building to be used to greatest advantage by lighting and ventilating the core. They were directly related to the emergence of big buildings. Traditionally, buildings had been relatively shallow: each room had windows on the front and back façades—an inviolable principle of medieval architecture. The end of the sixteenth century saw the creation of the double row of rooms, one on the street and the other on the courtyard[28]—a model that prevailed down to the mideighteenth century. Then, during the reign of Louis XVI, an extra, fairly narrow series of rooms was inserted between the two rows, which were thus isolated from each other. Often used to create alcoves and lavatories, this arrangement was not always accompanied by reflection on the problems of lighting and ventilation; the core was simply lighted and ventilated by the windows in the other rooms. And all too often, the traditional coupling of a building's staircase with the lavatories resulted in the latter's being ventilated through the former. When the well appeared in the eighteenth century, problems of this kind were resolved. After a period of disfavor during the Restoration, wells reappeared, albeit less systematically, during the reign of Louis-Philippe.

The shared courtyard and the air well are signs of the new conception of the apartment building evolving since the late eighteenth century. The determining element was the transition in scale from lot to block. That transition was just as important for the façade, which was profoundly transformed. The traditional "bouquet" composition of groups of buildings of unequal height linked together by a common vertical style was replaced by a new, more homogeneous composition that differentiated between the treatment of mass and the treatment of detail, in perfect keeping with the logic of neoclassicism. The block was given a very strong unity based on the use of a single volumetrics (maximum regulation height) and by the powerful emphasis on the two horizontals formed by the balconies on the prestigious first floor above the basement and on the top story. However, on the heavy mass formed by the block as a whole, stylistic detail remained faithful to tradition: at close range, vertical bays still dominated, structuring buildings by means of the traditional technique used when the scale was the single lot. Foreshadowed by the monumental architecture of eighteenth-century squares, this particular combination of mass and verticality came to define the architecture of the block during the reign of Louis-Philippe.

The Rambuteau Building

The Birth of Regulation Architecture

The most important aspect of the typological transformation that began in the 1840s was the systematic use of the maximum height allowed by the building code. Encouraged by a municipal administration that favored regular, homogeneous blocks, the use of a standard size for all buildings went hand in hand with a change in methods of financing: investors now had the capital needed to begin the huge rental buildings that were to characterize construction during the second half of the nineteenth century and the beginning of the twentieth. Architecturally, the consequences of this approach were considerable: during the reign of Louis-Philippe regulation architecture was born and its forms determined by city statutes that were numerous and increasingly precise.

The first formulation of the classical building code had been the Desgodets code, named for its author, the architect Antoine Desgodets (1653-1728), who as the king's superintendent of buildings had drafted a compendium of the habits and customs governing the construction of buildings in Paris. That individual initiative was followed, during the reign of Louis XVI, by the first real regulation: the "Declaration of the King on Building Lines and Window Openings in Paris," dated April 10, 1783, which was soon followed by an ordinance of August 25, 1784, defining the major principles of regulation architecture: determination of a façade's height in function of a street's width, fixing of the cornice height, the number of floors, the slope of the roof, and so forth.

When edifices of maximum regulation size finally began to be built, the systematic reproduction of a single size of building generated an astounding unity, which was further strengthened when the city began forcing builders to respect the unity of the block even in compositional detail: floor levels of equal height, a standard projection for balconies and cornices, a standard spacing of solids and voids, and even standard decorative details like pilasters, frames around window and door openings, and pediments. Unchanged until 1859, the Parisian regulations set the cornice height at 9 *toises* (17.54 meters) above street level for streets over 9.75 meters wide. Six stories of 2.92 meters each were to be used. In narrower streets, buildings were to be lower: five floors for streets less than 9.75 meters wide, and only four for streets less than 7.80 meters wide (i.e., verticals of 14.62 and 11.70 respectively). The roof, whose slope was set at 45 degrees, could not be more than 4.87 meters high. Thus the theoretical height of the city was set at 22.29 meters above street level (any slope in the land being corrected for at regular intervals). Following the classical tradition, façades were structured in three parts: a two-floor basement, three main floors, and a top floor, the roof not being visible from the street.

The drawback of this system was that it did not completely respect the harmonious classical proportions between stories. The model used in drafting the regulations was the elevations found on the big royal squares (Place des Victoires and Place Vendôme) designed by Hardouin-Mansart, and the Palladian palaces of Vicenza, which were never more than five stories tall (a mezzanine floor, two main floors, and a low top floor). In the narrowest streets, the low fifth floor was eliminated; in the widest, an extra main floor was added. The generalized use of streets more than ten meters wide (for reasons already discussed) eventually led the nineteenth century to use six stories on a systematic basis, that is, to use a cornice of 17.54 instead of 14.62 meters. The tradition of recessing the last story made that story's presence completely acceptable.[29] On the other hand, the fifth floor did not fit into the totally modular classical model. Parisian architects attempted to conceal the disproportion created by the fifth floor in numerous ways, the commonest being to use a double cornice to structure the middle section of the elevation in two parts. There can be little doubt that the question of proportions long hindered the transition from five-story buildings to the six-story edifices so characteristic of the Haussmann era.

The Rambuteau years were a period of transition. At the beginning of Louis-Philippe's reign, buildings were classically proportioned; but after 1840, the six-story elevation began to catch on. The transition from the scale of the lot to the scale of the block made this transformation possible; once the block had become the basic architectural unit, an individual building's proportions were less important than the overall mass. As this change in scale took place, graphism gave way to a sculptural sense of form. Important new architectural details then appeared. The most important of these was the cut-off corner, used to break sharp edges and merge perpendicular façades together, thus transforming their static style into a kind of subtle surface vibration. The cut-off corner accompanied the almost systematic use of the star network in the layout of streets, which created extremely rich diagonal vistas—much more interesting, at any rate, than the purely frontal perspectives of the classical style. Finally, the roof reappeared above the recessed top floor. Completely contrary to the logic of the regulations, mansard roofs began to become widespread in the late 1840s. With their six stories, continuous balconies, cut-off corners, and big roofs, the new Paris buildings soon had nothing in common with their predecessors. The architectural typology changed so quickly that the Rambuteau building of the early 1840s can be clearly distinguished from the pre-Haussmann buildings constructed toward the end of that same decade.

Rambuteau or Haussmann?

131

Limited to the width of a bay, the first cut-off corners were quite narrow. They created a smooth transition between a corner building's two façades, and were much less elaborate than the cut-off corners of the Second Empire and the Third Republic.
1 and **2**. Corners of the Rue d'Hauteville and the Rue de l'Echiquier. **3**. Rue de Trévise. **4**. Intersection of the Rue de Moscou and the Rue de Bucarest. **5**. Corner of the Rue de Provence and the Rue Laffitte (with three window openings grouped together on the corner of the building). **6**. Rue Montmartre. Anon., ca. 1896. In no. 6, the windows on the cut-off corner were closed off to draw attention to the building, which housed the offices of a newspaper.

Apartment building, 72 Boulevard de Sébastopol, 1860.

This question deserves all the more attention because a chronological distinction between a Haussmann and a Rambuteau typology turns out, on analysis, to account for only part of the actual facts. Many buildings with plaster façades and Louis-Philippe ornament (frames, cast iron) cannot have been built before the Second Empire, if only because of their location and their similarity to neighboring constructions. Closer study reveals certain technical and stylistic details (e.g., moldings used around window openings) proving that the traditional typology was still alive and well in the middle of the Second Empire and even during the early Third Republic. In light of this, the distinction between the Rambuteau building and the Haussmann building is not to be viewed chronologically but sociologically. In fact, the geographical distribution of the two types of buildings and that of certain social classes match up in a most significant way. The Rambuteau typology was maintained by and for a conservative petite bourgeoisie that settled in such characteristic outlying areas as Batignolles, Gros-Caillou, and Beaugrenelle. That class was quite different from the new bourgeoisie of the Second Empire, which preferred to live on the Right Bank boulevards, and differed even more from the Third Republic tenants who moved to the big residential districts on the western edge of the city. Architectural and social stratification mirror each other here with a fair degree of precision.

Although the birth of the Haussmann building is difficult to date precisely, the transformation that occurred around 1850 was as profound as it was obvious. That transformation was the real watershed between neoclassical tradition and the new socioeconomic system. Perhaps the most important thing to remember is that the typological, technological, and sociological evolution of the city's architecture corresponded closely to the transportation revolution brought about by the railroad after 1842.

The Art of the Façade

An utterly new formal system emerged. Its originality was such that one must again pause to consider its specific features more closely. The new architectural and urban type that characterized the Rambuteau years was the last embodiment of the classical conception that had been shaping Paris for centuries. At first glance, one might think the new type a loyal descendant of that conception. In point of fact, though the new type was deeply rooted in European history, it was also an unmistakable sign of the cultural transformation brought about by industrial capitalism.

The Unity of the Block

The new type retained the rigorous horizontal composition that had characterized neoclassical architecture during the Empire. But the compositional principle was systematically applied to entire blocks,

and in some cases even to entire neighborhoods. The urban whole was given more importance than the subtle hierarchy of scale and architectural quality on which the entire classical system had been based. The result was a kind of monotony, stately in its regularity, but so anonymous as to be disconcerting.

Standardization, latent since the Restoration, first affected the size of buildings. The hierarchy that had determined a building's number of floors according to its distance from the center of the city was replaced by a standard six-story structure: a two-level basement (under the main balcony), three main floors of equal height, and a recessed top floor under a 45-degree roof (with the attic transformed into servants' quarters). As early as 1840 a number of examples could be found, like the building at 1 Rue de Trévise.

The powerful masses that had given neoclassical buildings a palatial fullness were destroyed by the use of large window openings (the "transparent building") and the systematic elimination of a volume's edges; the little recessed top story would rob even the most monumental cornice of its power. The clear division into a basement and upper floors was dissolved by the practically identical treatment of the two surfaces (the horizontal joints in the masonry below, the slats of the outdoor shutters above) and by the use of similar window openings on all floors (elimination of the arcade). Finally, Louis-Philippe architecture waged a vigorous war on the corner: whereas the entire neoclassical tradition had emphasized the meeting of orthogonal planes to create clear geometrical forms, the new architecture generalized use of the cut-off corner on the pretext that it increased visibility at intersections.

Before Haussmann, the cut-off corner was a slanted bay that allowed one façade to continue into another without interruption. At the start, it was in no way used to emphasize the corner as a visual focal point (as seen in the steeple and fountain of Borromini's San Carlo Church). The cut-off corner's fundamental role was to destroy the perception of a building's characteristic volumetrics by turning its façades into a continuous curtain drawn around the block. Numerous eighteenth-century examples could be invoked as precursors, but the nineteenth century went much further, using the cut-off corner not merely to soften the "collision" of two surfaces, but also to destroy systematically the autonomy of architectural volumes.

Finally, verticality was brought back and combined with horizontal composition. The tops of the frames around the windows on the first floor above the basement came to resemble the window ledges on the floors above; they were often nothing but portions of the cordon, whose horizontal continuity was broken by projections above the window openings. Thus the division between the three main floors above the basement was weakened, and the vertical pattern formed by the projections around the window openings and portions of the cornice took on new importance. This renascence of a common vertical style linked façades together, while also tending to conceal any imperfections in the organization of individual façades.

Only two horizontals resisted the reappearance of a vertical style after the "horizontal" Restoration years: the balcony and the cornice. The cornice as such was seriously altered, being seen now as just another continuous balcony whose plastic interest, in any event, was created more and more often by projecting modillions. The least elaborate model limited the balcony to the recessed story; but normally at least a partial balcony (and preferably a full one) was used to indicate the break between the basement and the stories above. Emphasized by the use of decorative cast-iron balustrades (especially on the lower balcony), the balconies created two strong horizontals in front of the façade, where the black cast iron stood out against the ocherous white of the walls.

A counterpoint to the strong vertical bays, the horizontals established two powerful unifying strips—a bit like the string around a package. The animation and diversity of eighteenth-century building rows and the arbitrary unity of Empire neoclassicism came together to create the Rambuteau building, a middle way that reconciled individual initiative and architectural fancy with the overall unity of the block. The notion of block unity was extremely important in the subsequent evolution of the Parisian building, and played a role in all later revisions of the building code. Even the most individualistic revision, that of 1902, continued to invoke the criterion of a block's global unity as overriding considerations of diversity in architectural and decorative detail.

The Recessed Story

Toward the end of Louis-Philippe's reign the building's typological evolution, closely linked to the emphasis on coherent blocks, was profound. In fact, the change in the scale of conception necessitated a change in the size of buildings. If a three- or four-story elevation was understandable when the basic architectural unit was the façade (seldom over ten or so meters across), the expansion of the scale of perception to the block as a whole—a distance that might be several hundred meters long—imposed an increase in proportions and a systematic strengthening of architectural lines.

The change in scale also led to the recessed story's becoming a part of the elevation. Though the building code determined how far it was to be set back, the recessed story was increasingly used as a constituent of the façade. It began to be built out of freestone (owing to advances in construction techniques and in particular to a better mastery of the cantilever), and the ornament on the rest of the façade was continued up onto it.

In point of fact, the regulations would seem to have been violated very early on, and the top stories set back less and less (thirty to forty centimeters from the perpendicular of the façade). At about the same time the upper slopes of the mansard roof began to be raised, and more and more often big dormer windows (usually made of wood) were built flush with the façade. This double transformation was closely related to the use of the recessed floor as a bourgeois apartment and the attic as servants' quarters. If the widespread use of mansard roofs does not, in itself, tell the whole story, it does indicate that buildings were being conceived in a new way. Another indication of the new social homogeneity of buildings, and a reflection of the nascent segregation of the city into bourgeois and working-class neighborhoods, appeared about this time: the equalization of ceiling heights on all floors.

These changes resulted in a modification of the façade: the continuous balcony on the sixth floor became a major compositional element, as did the roof, because of the raising of its upper slopes. At the same time, the line separating the basement from the story above was strengthened. Indeed, once frontal composition—the façade in the traditional sense of the term, perceived as a decorated surface with window openings—became less important than the silhouette of the whole block seen in perspective, buildings tended to take on a harder profile; the recessed crown and steep roof topping the mass were balanced by a heavy base pressing up against the third-floor balcony.

At first partial, the third-floor balcony soon ran across the entire length of the façade—like the balcony on the recessed story—and thus marked the structure with a second horizontal strip providing a strong graphic emphasis (mostly owing to the molded cast-iron balustrades that were increasingly used to adorn it). Its projection, though weak, was emphasized by the heavy, accentuated silhouette of the console beneath it, which in purely technical terms was obviously oversized.

The Balcony

Like the transformation of the roof, the introduction of the balcony on the floor above the basement is a significant indication of the typological change that affected the Parisian building at the very end of the July Monarchy. That addition was, however, quite paradoxical: just as the ceiling heights of the floors were being equalized, an exterior sign of prestige was added to set the third floor apart. Plastic reasons (and the link with the initial model) partially explain the introduction of the third-floor balcony, as do technical advances that led to an improvement in the dressing of stone.

Yet plastic and technical explanations do not fully account for such a paradoxical development. To understand what happened, one must admit an implicit hierarchy of quality and price—a hierarchy even within a social category as tightly unified as the bourgeoisie.

Thus a subtle hierarchy distinguished the "gentleman on the third floor" (above the shopkeeper's mezzanine), with a balcony overlooking the avenue, from the increasingly modest tenants on the floors above. The tenant on the top floor paid a bit less rent to compensate for living right under the servants' quarters and having to climb five flights of

Third-floor balconies. **1.** 43 Rue de Provence. **2.** 23 Rue d'Hauteville. **3.** Rue de Cluny, corner of the Boulevard Saint-Germain.

stairs. (Additional compensation was provided by the fact that he had more air, more light, and a big balcony.) In this way the class hierarchy inherited from the Ancien Régime was transmitted smoothly to the new bourgeois society.

The formal evolution of bourgeois architecture was in fact slower than that of the class itself, for in many cases a hierarchy of floors persisted into the Second Empire. Nevertheless, the trend toward equality eventually proved stronger than considerations of prestige, and led to the curious development that characterized the period from the last years of the Second Empire into the 1890s: all bourgeois tenants being supposed equal, balconies were built on every floor. This practice was so typical of the period that it constitutes a very reliable criterion for dating buildings.

Thus the window with a balustrade in the window well itself was often replaced by French windows with shallow little balconies, which created the illusion of continuity between indoors and out that characterizes the principle of the balcony. In other cases, several windows opened onto a partial balcony that had the double merit of showing the world outside the location and size of an apartment's salon (the balcony being almost imperatively linked to the idea of receiving guests), and of allowing an axial composition that made the façade autonomous vis-à-vis its neighbors without affecting the regularity of the general organization of the block. After 1890 this system was modified by the introduction of the closed balcony, or bay window.

Retractable Shutters

Collapsible shutters.
1. 28 Rue de Richelieu. **2.** 44 Rue de Provence.

Outdoor shutters had been adopted as a function of the flat, stripped-down architecture of neoclassicism and its cold, geometrical surfaces. When the rental building began to undergo a stylistic development of its own during the reign of Louis-Philippe, these outdoor shutters tended to be eliminated in order to put clearer emphasis on the lines of the sculpted ornament that was reintroduced at that time. A new sense of monumentality was emerging, reemphasizing the decorative liveliness of wall surfaces.

A new kind of outdoor shutters appeared as early as 1840-45: folding shutters (in that respect, similar to indoor shutters) that retracted into a housing concealed by the frame around the window opening. These retractable shutters were used for some years during the Second Empire, but were later abandoned in favor of metal shutters.

A balustrade's form and the type of shutters that can be used are closely related, which explains why both elements changed at the same time during this key period in the history of the Parisian building. The old style of outdoor shutters had made it necessary to move the balustrade back into the window well or to renounce using full-length shutters at all, since a projecting balustrade made it impossible to close them. Conversely, the use of a projecting balustrade—or better still, of a shallow little balcony with French windows replacing the traditional window—made it necessary to abandon the old style of outdoor shutters and replace them with folding, retractable ones.

Insignificant as they may seem, these details are very important and indeed reveal the profound typological change that took place during the reign of Louis-Philippe. Nothing could better express the era's desire for monumentality than the decision to conceal a practical element, the shutters, and thereby emphasize the general lines of the framing around the window opening—the ledge and in some cases its consoles, the balustrade, and the frame itself.

The desire to turn the apartment building's façade into a monumental palace façade was also manifested in the total regularization of the spacing of window openings, regardless of a building's layout inside. The use of stone and ornamental scuptures obviously went hand in hand with the palatial ambitions of the bourgeois apartment building. Promoters of course had their reasons: buildings that looked like palaces were no doubt much more appealing to prospective tenants, especially given the distinctly mediocre quality of traditional housing in Paris.

Monumental edifices did, however, suffer from not fitting in with the rest of the urban environment. The mansion, an exceptional event inside the ordinary fabric, was indeed set off by its contrast with the mediocre environment. But the big apartment buildings' placement in rows destroyed their architectural autonomy. Compensation for this was sought in an absolute respect for the coherence of the block as a whole. As a result, an individual edifice was perceived as a constituent part of a larger whole—the block or the neighborhood—and was judged less for itself than for its ability to fit in with the other constructions. This phenomenon was of course already perceptible in the regular elevations of the façades on the royal squares.

Organized in coherent groups on a large scale, Rambuteau buildings totally transformed the way in which the city was perceived, the scale of perception changing from the lot to the block. A building had to blend with those around it. The same verticality, expressed in the rows of bays rising up to the dormer windows on the roofs, characterized the block as a whole. Moreover, the levels of each building matched up with its neighbors' levels, and cordons and cornices continued uninterrupted along the city's streets.[30]

Another consequence of the standardization of the block was that axial compositions tended to disappear. When such compositions did exist, the rigorously identical appearance of the window openings robbed them of much of their visual impact.

As ornament now intervened only around the evenly spaced window openings, the role of the horizontal link provided by cornices was considerably strengthened.

Moreover, the observer's point of view changed. Although architects still designed façades to be seen as a plane (a point of view that cannot exist in reality), an awareness that façades were not autonomous led to the abandoning of the centralized, axial model of classical tradition in favor of an ornamental system based on the profile of elements projecting from the façade. Thus perspective played a much greater role in the nineteenth century than it had during the previous one. Decorative projections were used to pattern façades, whence the widespread adoption of the balcony console and the use of relief around window openings (including, in particular, the transformation of the recessed balustrade into a little balcony).

Frontality
or Perspective

Plates showing façades, originally published in nineteenth-century architectural reviews.
1. 31 Boulevard du Temple, 1847. **2.** 26 Rue Notre-Dame-des-Victoires, 1848. **3.** 20 Rue Drouot, 1854.
4. 82 Boulevard Beaumarchais, 1849.

A.D.

The Embellished Building

The Stone Façade

Boulevard Montmartre, corner of the Rue de Richelieu.

The typological transformation of the Rambuteau building also affected the choice of construction materials: freestone definitively triumphed over wood on the street façade. The building code played an important role in the change. For safety reasons, lawmakers differentiated the maximum height of freestone façades from the maximum height of those in wood (which was lighter, hence not as solid). That distinction later disappeared, but before it did, it had helped establish the use of stone for façades, which became systematic in bourgeois constructions during the reign of Louis-Philippe. In point of fact, however, the stone façade was nothing but a mask. Behind their magnificent façades, bourgeois constructions (the floors, the walls, and the courtyard façades) were still made entirely of wood. The traditional hierarchy of heavy and light elements was maintained. A construction's solidity and fire resistance were ensured by its heavy rubblestone sidewalls (which also contained the chimney flues). Consequently, the façade could contain a lot of window openings, which cut down on the amount of stone needed and at the same time enhanced contact with the street. On the other hand, all of a building's secondary divisions—courtyard façades and partition walls—were still built out of wood, which allowed changes of layout at the lowest cost.

Quarried in what is today the fourteenth arrondissement of Paris, the stone came through the city toll in impressive quantities: 40,000 cubic meters in 1810, 90,000 in 1839, and 120,000 in 1847. The toll figures provide a good indication of building activity on a year-to-year basis, confirming a slowdown in 1828, gradual recovery after 1830, and a short but violent downturn in 1840-42.[31] Never in the previous history of architecture had housing attained such a high level of quality. In the nineteenth century the art of the stonecutter triumphed. Aided by the mechanization of his equipment as much as by the astounding growth of the real-estate market, the stonecutter rose to a kind of artistic nobility; it is no accident that the signatures of sculptors can be seen on so many buildings. In the nineteenth century the façade became an enormous monumental sculpture facing the street.

The Triumph of Ornament

The popularity of the embellished building during the last years of Louis-Philippe's reign marked the definitive break with half a century of neoclassicism. The shock was a deep one. Closely linked to the rise of industrial capitalism, a new city emerged.

At first, the break with neoclassicism was decorative: the reappearance of façade ornament brought a break with the repetitive patterns of academic architecture. Rich decoration had been limited to a few isolated edifices during the first third of the century, and used in a very architectural spirit to enhance the superimposed orders and emphasize the façade's division into stories; now it spread to all new construction. As it did so, ornament was interpreted in a new way. The

29 Rue de l'Université. **1.** Façade. **2.** Detail of the fourth story. **3.** Detail of the second story. **4.** Detail of the main balcony.

1

2

4

3

Détails du 1ᵉʳ Étage.

Facing page: Cité des Italiens, Rue Laffitte, 1841.

Above: Maison Dorée (before renovation), Rue Laffitte and Boulevard des Italiens, 1839.
Left: Boulevard des Italiens.

emphasis was now on the architecture of the bay, exoticism as a stylistic theme, and wrought iron as a decorative material.

A Monumental Anonymity

The ornamental repertoire of the Rambuteau building evolved rapidly. Soon the only acceptable decoration was one that, projecting from the façade, could be seen in profile without disturbing the general effort toward block unity. That effort tended to dissolve the originality of façades altogether, reducing them to modest participant modules in the more general structure of the urban whole. The result was monumental—and profoundly anonymous. When the Second Empire and the Third Republic built whole developments of sumptuous yet monotonous buildings, they were merely expressing in a more bombastic way how the bourgeoisie of Rambuteau's day had seen the city.

Much has been said about bourgeois individualism in the nineteenth century. In architectural matters the concept is utterly ridiculous, for conformity was the general rule. Indeed, when buildings ceased being a family's private property and became financial investments,[32] they tended to lose their originality and become products, sinking into an increasingly stereotyped interpretation of their role, form, and purpose. This phenomenon was fundamental in the nineteenth century, when the bourgeois apartment building was born in Paris. Conversely the private house, and the suburban house in particular, quickly became a place for the most astonishing extravagances and whims, individuality being the defining characteristic of a family's private property and permanent residence. This was in marked contrast to the anonymity of the rental building, in which occupancy by the owner remained a pure coincidence.

The key edifice in this transformation was the 1839 Maison Dorée, designed by the architect Lemaire and the sculptor Rouillard. If successive transformations had not completely eliminated the ornament and reduced the building to a mere façade, we would still be able to see the principal model of a new kind of architecture whose ambition was to break with the neoclassical tradition. The designers emphasized verticality by using superimposed pilasters (which reduce the horizontal impact of the cornice) and by visually linking the window openings on the various floors with rich frames and balustrades. Stylistically speaking, the neoclassical repertoire was enriched with motifs quite reminiscent of the Renaissance (as was also the case with the astonishing façades on the Place Jussieu) or even of the eighteenth century. Finally, ornamental cast iron was allowed to reign supreme in the sumptuous Moorish arabesque of the third-floor balcony. The façade decor of the Maison Dorée continued as a very rich decor inside, as was also the case in several big cafés of the day (Frascati, Véron). Appealing examples of this repetition of ornament can still be found in the provinces, as in the Café de la Renaissance in Alençon.

149

The success of this stylistic approach was by no means limited to café ornament. Between 1840 and 1850, numerous buildings in Paris were given incredible façade decors that, in no way influenced by the stylistics of neoclassicism, could be Louis XV, Manueline, Gothic, Oriental, or Borrominian. All these richly decorated buildings were affected by the new cast-iron craze. Indeed, after 1840 the architecture of Paris buildings became an architecture of cast-iron ornament.

Ornament and Class

The profound contradiction between the proliferation of ornament and its systematization on the façades of buildings during the second half of Louis-Philippe's reign is curious, to say the least, and demands some explanation. The upheaval in technical, economic, and social structures brought about by industrialization largely accounts for the disturbance of traditional values, which turned the question of ornament into a critical issue in nineteenth-century art. As the segregation of the social classes became increasingly pronounced, a hierarchy of materials and decoration emerged, richness of ornament being seen as the equivalent of wealth. The Louis-Philippe building was distinctly more speculative in nature than the late-eighteenth-century building. At a time when the lower classes, after a good deal of urban strife (e.g., the Rue Transnonain riot in 1834), were being isolated in specific parts of town rather than stacked on top of the upper classes, the stories of buildings were equalized in height in order to correspond better to tenants of uniform social origin. New apartment-building developments were thus a reflection of a class system and ranged from the residential (the area around the Madeleine and the Champs-Elysées) to the mediocre (Batignolles, Clichy, La Goutte d'Or), with the middle class in between (Montmartre, Abbesses). However, a distinction between qualities of construction—freestone or wood—did exist within each particular category, ornamental richness being the outer sign of high social position.

But at the same time, radical changes were taking place in industry. The invention of industrial techniques of reproduction (molded cast iron, terra-cotta, staff) lowered the price of ornament and consequently broke the link between ornament and wealth. When that happened, the lower middle class could afford to copy the rich ornamentation on the façades of bourgeois buildings. Needless to say, this provoked a reverse reaction in constructions meant for the upper class. Since ornamental simplicity was tolerable when sumptuous materials abounded, the upper class soon distinguished itself by preferring monumentality and austerity, as opposed to the exuberant tastes of the lower middle class.

This change became extremely obvious after 1850, when the decorative overload of the Maison Dorée (1839) gave way to an austere style emphasizing the fine stonework of broad, bare walls with discreetly decorated cordons and bays. When moldings were used, what counted was the originality of their design. Once mass-production techniques had been developed, there was a tendency to value a design for its uniqueness; consequently, new designs were in constant demand.

Recourse to past historical styles made it possible to broaden the decorative repertoire and create a great number of new and original combinations. Stylistic eclecticism was born. It reflected a subtle class hierarchy and moreover helped keep the lower middle class—who, as all readers of Balzac know, were eager to improve their social position—from transgressing that hierarchy.

The Hierarchy's Last Blaze

At a time when the typology of the six-story building was being increasingly used in Paris, one might expect all other models to have disappeared. Oddly enough, that did not happen. Though the center/outskirts hierarchy was weakened, certain areas continued to affirm their residential vocation by rejecting the six-story model of the center. This was notably the case around the Luxembourg Gardens, Saint-Sulpice, and Vaugirard, and throughout the Europe district from Saint-Augustin to Clichy.

Five Stories or Six?

In those areas, as in the center, elevations included a basement and a recessed top story, but in between there were two main stories instead of three. As mentioned earlier, the five-story model corresponded better to classical tradition, since it facilitated use of the colossal order (frequently used, for example, in the Europe district). But that would not seem to be the sole reason for which the model was chosen, especially since the use of one-story pilasters (or of none at all) was common. Rather, it would appear that the principle of a hierarchy of districts exerted a strong influence for quite some time. In predominantly residential areas like the Saint-Georges section, smaller buildings with noncommercial ground floors were used, and the basement as such—directly linked to the notion of shops—disappeared.

These five-story districts had an atmosphere of their own. One found discreet, rather squat-looking buildings whose façades were in direct contact with the street, whereas, in the center, shop fronts separated the façade proper from the street. The problem was that the five-story model, not having been provided for in the regulations, was beleaguered with shortcomings and uncertainties. Was there to be a basement or not? If not, where was the lower balcony to be placed? Was the ground floor to be used residentially, and if so, in what form—an apartment off the lobby, or a townhouse embedded in the building with direct access from the street? How were the streets inside a district to be related to the avenues on its borders? Thus, on the Boulevard Malesherbes, was the five-story model found in the rest of the neighborhood to be maintained, or the larger six-story model introduced?

151

Though problematic, the five-story model did nonetheless determine the character of certain sections—notably the Europe district, built up during the Second Empire with a five-story model predominating. It is unfortunate that size variations of this kind—also found around Monceau (e.g., the interesting elevations with recessed roofs on the squares in the Pereire section)—were not better respected in the years that followed. When these developments were completed in the last quarter of the nineteenth century, the initial model was often profoundly altered: because a land shortage had developed, the maximum regulation height was increasingly used for new buildings.

Villas and Townhouses

The most striking thing about neoclassical districts was their regular organization. They have often been compared to English terraces and in particular to the town of Bath, as developed in the eighteenth century. In Bath, however, regularity as such was secondary. The town was designed to form a landscaped composition of constructed volumes and open spaces. From big, monumental circular intersections to small, tightly spaced individual houses, all types of urban development intermingled there.

Restoration Paris had retained the principle of typological variation between areas defined by the morphological unity of their component parts. The striking variation of densities and building sizes used by the developers has been heavily altered today; it did, however, continue to play a certain role during the Second Empire. The model furthest removed from the apartment building—the most suburban in design—was the "villa," interpreted according to the Italian model as a cube set down in the midst of a verdant space. Areas where villas were built were the opposite of the totally mineral center of town, which was structured wholly on the urban void and not on architectural form. In the villa sections, streets were merely little paths, and the volumetrics of architecture reasserted itself.

In between the villa and the apartment building, the mansion and the townhouse were maintained as the middle degrees in the scale. Still persistent during the reign of Louis-Philippe, the neoclassical tradition leaned more toward the townhouse, clearly more urban in nature (e.g., Duban's Pourtalès house on the Rue Tronchet), though during the Second Empire townhouses did tend to be countrified with little gardens in front of them. These constructions, all three stories high, were arranged in sumptuous new developments or inserted in empty spaces in the urban fabric, but were rarely mixed with groups of apartment buildings; the desire for homogeneousness in the size of constructions necessarily led to a certain specialization in the urban fabric. That specialization was strengthened as the pre-Haussmann type of building began to emerge: the identical appearance of apartment buildings in some districts was echoed in others by the

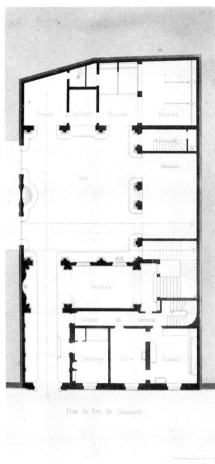

The neoclassical tradition during the reign of Louis-Philippe. Pourtalès mansion, Rue Tronchet. Street façade; plan of the ground floor.

strengthening of the private house's typological characteristics. There too, mixtures were no longer acceptable. Soon the variety of types itself was eliminated in favor of the unifying model of the six-story apartment building customarily associated with the Haussmann era.

The Exodus of the Working Class

The worker's residence would seem, at least for a while, to have gone untouched by the technological, economic, and architectural transformations of the day. The revolution that affected the working class was geographic, not typological. The decision to renovate the center—the restructuring of the Halles and the first projects for the "transformation of Paris"—along with the advent of public transportation, pushed the working class out of town. Earlier, it was seen how the creation of the Farmers-General Wall had caused the Faubourg Saint-Antoine and the Rue de Charonne to specialize in craft activities to the detriment of their original functions—stables and storehouses—which were moved outside the city's fiscal limits to the Montreuil area. Similarly, the workers took over La Chapelle, Belleville, Ménilmontant, and Charonne on the Right Bank, and Gentilly, Montrouge, and Plaisance on the Left.

153

Home of the actress Rachel, 4 Rue Trudon. **1.** Street façade. **2.** Cross section. **3.** Longitudinal section. **4.** Plan of the ground floor.

COUPE LONGITUDINALE

Sellerie

Cour

Remise

Avenerie

Grande

Parloir

Remise

Porte

Cochère

Suisse

Cuisine

Goutte-d'Or district. **1.** Corner of the Rue Cavé and the Rue Saint-Luc. **2.** Rue de Chartres.

Regardless of how a working-class area was built up—whether new lots were created or existing structures renovated—builders remained unshakably faithful to the Ile-de-France tradition of wood-and-plaster houses with tile roofs (replaced more and more by zinc, which was extremely economical). Moreover, the old techniques used to build up the inside of a lot and to heighten buildings were applied here also. Thus the cityscape of the old center of medieval origin was reconstituted in the villages around the capital.

Victims of the Industrial Revolution, which lowered them to the most unenviable status of proletarians, workers were perhaps the last segment of the population to feel the effects of that revolution on the city's architectural typology. If they perceived them, they did so as mere spectators passing through the sumptuous new districts on the Right Bank.

More than anything else, Paris, the capital of a country undergoing rapid industrial expansion, feared a social explosion: the riots on the Rue Transnonain and at Saint-Merry Cloister in 1834 were followed by revolutionary uprisings in May 1839 and February and June 1848. The social transformation brought about by the Industrial Revolution was changing the city. The east-west division was unmistakably under way, and the exodus of the working class to the hills of Belleville and Ménilmontant went hand in hand with the destruction of the old center. Hygiene was no longer the only imperative; security became critical. Military leaders were aware of this, and added instruction on guerrilla warfare to the curriculum at Fontainebleau; taking the example of the siege of Saragossa in 1809, instructors described the tactics of urban warfare in great detail. The social situation was explosive; the army had to be prepared for the "war of the have-nots."

Indisputably, the new city belonged to those who could afford to live in it. At the end of Louis-Philippe's reign, the deterioration of the old central neighborhoods where workers lived became unbearable to public opinion. The transformation of the Halles answered the double necessity of loosening a very congested structure and cleaning up the center. The Second Empire attempted to find a more permanent solution, since bursting the abscess was not enough. The new urban order had to satisfy the needs of the entire population, that is, it had to be expanded to include the entire city. That is what Haussmann did, advised by the emperor himself, whose social visions may have been utopian, but were most certainly not lacking in compassion and generosity. Faced with a deteriorating city, the Second Empire set out to restore urban unity as a way of strengthening social unity.[33] Haussmann was to learn much from Rambuteau's earlier attempts to transform the city.

NOTES

1. S. Mercier, *Tableau de Paris*, vol. 1, p. 222, and vol. 8, p. 190, quoted in Michel Gallet, *Demeures parisiennes à l'époque de Louis XVI* (Paris: Le Temps, 1964), p. 17.

2. See Daniel Rabreau and Monika Steinhauser, "Le Théâtre de l'Odéon de Charles de Wailly et Marie-Joseph Peyre, 1767-1782, in *Revue de l'art*, no. 19 (1973), pp. 9-49, which provides a fascinating analysis of the district and its relation to the architecture of the theater and to social and cultural life in the late eighteenth century.

3. Since the C.R.H.A.M.'s study on the Halles (F. Bourdon, A. Chastel, H. Couzy, F. Hamon, *Système de l'architecture urbaine. Le quartier des Halles à Paris*, 2 vols. [Paris: C.N.R.S., 1977])—which expands on an earlier publication ("Urbanisme et spéculation à Paris au XVIIIᵉ siècle: le terrain de l'hôtel de Soissons" in *Journal of the Society of Architectural Historians*, vol. 32 [1973], pp. 355-64)—a new study has appeared by Mark K. Deming, *La Halle au blé de Paris, 1762-1813* (Brussels: A.A.M., 1984), in which the fifth chapter is devoted to the development of the area around the edifice.

4. Jean-Marc Léri, "Aspect administratif de la construction des marchés de la Ville de Paris (1800-1850)," in *Bulletin de la Société de l'Histoire de Paris et de l'Ile-de-France*, 1976-77 (Paris, 1978), pp. 170-90.

5. Paolo Morachiello and Georges Teyssot, "Città di Stato, la colonizzazione del territorio nel primo impero," in *Lotus international*, Milan, no. 24 (1979), pp. 24-39, and François Loyer, "L'Urbanisme napoléonien à Pontivy," in *Mémoires de la Société d'Histoire et d'Archéologie de Bretagne*, Rennes, vol. 57 (1980), pp. 5-30.

6. Bernard Rouleau, *Le Tracé des rues de Paris. Formation, typologie, fonctions* (Paris: C.N.R.S., 1967), p. 98, n. 123, referring the reader to A. Morizet, *Du vieux Paris au Paris moderne, Haussmann et ses prédécesseurs*, Paris, 1932. Further discussion can be found in Jeanne Pronteau, "Construction et aménagement des nouveaux quartiers de Paris (1820-1826)," in *Histoire des entreprises*, Paris, no. 2 (Nov. 1958), pp. 1-32; and Pierre Debofle, *Les Travaux de Paris sous la Restauration*, thesis at the Ecole des Chartes (summary in *Positions*, 1974).

7. The district's name comes from the magnificent villa designed in the Francis I style by the architect Constantin. Its owner, M. de Brock, had bought a sixteenth-century house in Moret-sur-Loing in 1822. The gallery façade of that house was dismantled, modified to look more Venetian, and used as the façade of the Paris villa. (The latter has since been demolished, and the gallery returned to Moret-sur-Loing.)

8. Rouleau, *Le Tracé*, pp. 92 ff. Our remarks are largely based on Rouleau's.

9. Laura Wodka, "Les Passages couverts dans Paris," in *Paris-Projet*, Paris, Mairie de Paris, no. 15-16 (1976), pp. 110-51; and François Loyer, "A propos des passages," idem, no. 17 (1977), pp. 108-19. For a more general approach, see Johann Friedrich Geist, *Passagen. Ein Bautyp des 19. Jahrhundert*, "Neunzehntes Jahrhundert" series (Munich: Prestel Verlag, 1969).

10. Excerpt from the *Mémoires* of Lamothe-Langon, attributed to the Marquise de Créquy. Quoted by Michel Gallet, "Ledoux et Paris," *Cahiers de la Rotonde*, Paris, Commission du Vieux Paris, no. 3 (1979), p. 108.

11. In *Système de l'architecture urbaine*, F. Bourdon tends to emphasize parceling rather than how buildings are grouped together. She does, however, refer to the problem (notably on p. 96, in connection with the composition of façades).

12. Recently it has been fashionable for architects to criticize the emphasis on lot structure found in the work of certain theorists of the 1970s—especially Jean Castex and Philippe Panerai in *Formes urbaines: de l'îlot à la barre*, Aspects de l'Urbanisme (Paris: Dunod, 1977), and in their subsequent works such as *Versailles. Lecture d'une ville* (Versailles: ADROS—UP 3, 1978), as well as in their courses. Personally, I continue to believe in the primordial importance of lot structure in the urban typology, even if I also emphasize other parameters such as a building's height and the organization of its façade. In any case, I shall never accept the free plan that modernists have called for: the spaces that this practice has generated are the biggest disasters in urban history, nor will the current return to a 1950s mentality keep me from saying so!

13. The inseparable link between layout and window openings is an excellent expression of the rationalism underlying the medieval approach to building. I have often used the example of the Louis XII wing at Blois, as opposed to the Gaston d'Orléans wing across from it, as proof of this.

14. On this point, see Bernard Rouleau's recent study *Villages et faubourgs de l'ancien Paris* (Paris: Le Seuil, 1985). The author examines the evolution of lot patterns in the outlying areas down to the present day.

15. Johannes Peter Franck's work, *System einer vollständigen medezinischen Polizei*, published in 1789, was the first big synthesis of hygiene theory. Franck was a professor of international renown. The considerable stir caused by his book led to the creation of three chairs in public hygiene in French universities (Paris, Montpellier, Strasbourg). The next generation concentrated on the deterioration of the inner city after 1830. The study by the English lawyer Elwin Chadwick dates from 1842, and those by Ducpétiaux in Brussels and Toulmouche in Rennes from 1844 and 1848, respectively. Statistical studies on urban poverty brought about a real awareness of the need to restructure the industrial cities.

16. Official report on the ravages of cholera in Paris in 1832, quoted in *Le Parisien chez lui*, Paris, catalogue for the National Archives exhibit, 1976, p. 49, entry no. 102. On this subject, the classic study remains Louis Chevalier, *Classes laborieuses et classes dangereuses à Paris pendant la première moitié du XIXe siècle* (Paris, 1958, 1969).

17. The first sidewalks in Paris appeared around 1825, following the example of England. Baron Haussmann claimed, a bit hastily, that they were "nearly unknown before 1845": Georges-Eugène Haussmann, *Mémoires* (Paris: Victor-Havard, 1890-93), vol. 3, p. 145. The law of June 7, 1845, required their installation, the cost being split fifty-fifty by the city and the owners of the buildings on a street.

18. Malls, initially installed for the game of pall-mall, were flat strips with a packed surface between two rows of trees; traffic was confined to lanes on either side. The bowling green was planted with grass, but was otherwise comparable.

19. By penetrating deep into the ground, the roots of big trees were meant to strengthen the embankments against the concentrated fire of enemy cannons trying to make a breach. In the event of hostilities, the trees were to be cut down to open up visibility. Their presence embellished the promenade on the ramparts considerably. This explains the shift in meaning of the term *boulevard*, purely military in origin, to its current use, which has nothing to do with siege warfare.

20. The planting of rows of trees on the river's lower and upper quays dates from the time when Rambuteau was prefect and contributed greatly to the quays' beautification.

21. The first big projects to move the building line back, after fairly modest operations during the reign of Louis XVI, date from the Empire—a law of September 16, 1807, ordered the widening of the Rue Saint-Denis and the Rue Saint-Martin. Fifty years later, a report by Haussmann attempted to show the futility of such operations (Haussmann, *Mémoires*, vol. 3, pp. 52-53). Most operations of this kind date from the reign of Louis-Philippe. Between 1831 and 1836, decrees were issued right and left to implement projects for changing the building lines. More often than not, these projects had first been formulated during the reign of Louis XVI.

22. The same year that Chadwick published his study in London, Henri Bayard published his *Mémoire sur la topographie médicale du IVe arrondissement de Paris. Recherches historiques et statistiques sur les conditions hygiéniques des quartiers qui composent cet arrondissement* (Paris, 1842). This work was directly related to the plans being drawn up to transform the Halles, which were put into effect starting in 1851.

23. On the history of building regulations, see Jean-Louis Subileau's remarkable study "Le Règlement du P.O.S. et le paysage urbain," in *Paris-Projet*, Paris, Mairie de Paris, no. 13-14 (1975), pp. 4-89. I have echoed his remarks in several publications on building regulations, which I too feel to be of utmost importance: François Loyer, "Les Immeubles parisiens du XIXe siècle," in *L'Art urbain à travers l'histoire de l'architecture parisienne*, Paris, Centre de Recherches et d'Etudes sur Paris et l'Ile-deFrance, no. 1

(April 1983), pp. 172-79; and "Paris du XVIe au XIXe siècle: l'espace urbain, espace public," in *Conservation du patrimoine et création contemporaine: complémentarité ou alternative?*, Paris, Rencontres de l'Ecole du Louvre, May 12-22, 1981, pp. 210-17.

24. Quoted in Louis Hautecœur, *Histoire de l'architecture classique en France*, vol. 6 (Paris: A. & J. Picard, 1955), p. 65. Like Françoise Boudon (with whom I have discussed this subject at great length, with regard to Hector Horeau), I am quite convinced of the influence of Hippolyte Meynadier's ideas on the projects of the Haussmann era.

25. *Formes urbaines: de l'îlot à la barre*, by J. Castex, J.-C. Depaule, and P. Panerai, was the first work (1977) to focus on block planning, as found in Amsterdam and also in public housing developments in Paris, reflecting their teaching and following trips we took, under the leadership of Jean Dethier, to Belgium and Holland. My remarks on the transition from a scale based on the individual lot to one based on the block as a whole draw on their ideas.

26. Common courtyards were the exception to the rule. Examples include, in Rennes, the buildings on the corner of the Rue Saint-Georges and the Place du Palais, and those on the Rue Saint-Sauveur. In both cases, the buildings were thought of as prototypes.

27. This regulation, reaffirmed on many occasions in the city's history, set up each building as a closed unit isolated from its neighbors. No communications were allowed between courtyards (fences and walls being required) or cellars, and chimneys were to be built so as to separate the roofs of adjacent buildings. This made the job of law enforcement easier when offenders were being pursued, as well as in the case of riots.

28. The late sixteenth century played on the "transparency" created by rooms with windows on their front and back walls. This effect was based on the principle of the medieval "gallery," with window openings directly opposite each other rather than in staggered rows, the latter arrangement being reserved for rooms in the building proper. The château of Courances is an admirable example of this.

29. Its traditionally lower height was abandoned. To use the standard two-thirds proportion between the height of the top story and that of the lower floors, it would have been necessary to limit the top floor to a ceiling height of 1.94 meters! Conversely, to attain the minimum of 2.30 meters, the floor above the basement would have had to be raised to a ceiling height of 3.45 meters.

30. It is remarkable that French architects have always been so attached—in Paris, at least—to coherent groups of façades. The power of nineteenth-century building officials is certainly not unrelated to this. In any case, this French tradition has long been admired abroad. When I was working in Greece, many architects mentioned it to me, regretting that their own country was not so architecturally refined.

31. A graph of the quantities of stone used in Paris between 1810 and 1850, according to the records of the city toll, was presented by Jean Blécon in the context of the 1976 exhibit *Le Parisien chez lui*; see the catalogue, p. 35, entry no. 35.

32. I pointed this out in my article "Le Paradoxe de la rénovation," *Revue de l'art*, Paris, C.N.R.S., no. 29 (1975), p. 75.

33. There is nothing paradoxical about such a point of view. For all too long, an oversimplified vision of nineteenth-century urban history has seen the bourgeoisie as the conscious and determined author of working-class suffering. This sentimental approach to the problem ignores the economic realities of nascent capitalism, just as it ignores the profound anxiety felt by leaders faced with a socioeconomic evolution that they could not control. Haussmann's *Mémoires* are quite explicit on this point. Moreover, the emperor's own point of view can be read in every line Haussmann wrote. Napoleon III was guided by a desire to unify French society and help the underprivileged. The beautification of the city with squares and tree-lined avenues was one way of doing so. Had Haussmann and Napoleon III been able to, they would have struck the suburbs off the map; for that matter, they tried to by means of the 1860 annexation. But their reasoning was doubtless more aesthetic or humanitarian than economic. Haussmann put his finger on the problem when he

pointed out that the industrial suburbs had reformed outside the city limits because coal was exempt from the city toll there, which inevitably led industrialists to move their factories out of town. All this in no way diminishes the value of the urban plan conceived by the generation of 1830 and implemented in the second half of the century.

Chapter III

The Beauties of Technology

A Technological Transformation

The Industrial Revolution brought about a major transformation in the way buildings were built. Art historians pointed out the importance of that transformation some years back; however, more recent investigation has shown the shortcomings of their emphasis on the pioneers of modernism. Indeed, over the last few years there has even been a tendency among scholars to emphasize instead the importance of tradition in nineteenth-century art and architecture. But it is time to leave such limited interpretations behind and to recognize that the nineteenth century was both incredibly inventive and indebted to a rich cultural tradition. The need for such a dual perspective is strikingly confirmed, if we look at the evolution of apartment buildings in nineteenth-century Paris. There we will find neither neo-Gothic extravagance nor cast-iron columns and impressive arches. Technological hyperbole had no place in the fundamentally classical vocabulary of the nineteenth-century apartment building, yet the technical and formal inventiveness of the age was truly extraordinary. Even Viollet-le-Duc recognized that the Parisian buildings of his day were a marked improvement over equivalent residences from earlier centuries. He conceded that rental buildings offered tenants "healthier places to live with better floor plans than in the past" and that they were "reasonably well fitted to current needs."[1] Coming from such a critic, this was no small compliment and may be taken as a valuable indication of how greatly technological progress affected the design and construction of apartment houses during the Second Empire.

Facing page: the construction of the Sacré-Cœur basilica. Photos: Durandelle, March 1882.

161

The Shell

The Rambuteau building foreshadowed the Haussmann building, or, put differently, the Second Empire apartment building was the logical outcome of an evolution that began during the July Monarchy. We have already seen how closely architectural typology and social class were related in the nineteenth century. Now we will consider how technological progress radically affected the construction of apartment buildings in the Second Empire. The Haussmann building can be said to be a faithful reflection of nineteenth-century industrial technologies—not so much in the materials, which remained traditional, but in the way they were used.[2] Technological progress—for example, the development of stonecutting equipment—first affected the apartment building's shell, then all its trim and interior fittings, which changed radically with the birth of such modern conveniences as running water and heating.[3]

Masonry

Most of the stone used in Paris at the beginning of the nineteenth century came from the old quarries on the Left Bank. Though "Paris stone" had not actually been quarried in the Chartreux quarries (beneath the Luxembourg Gardens) or in the old quarries at the Observatory and Val-de-Grâce for many years, it did come from the nearby village of Montrouge, just outside the Farmers-General Wall (in the present fourteenth arrondissement). Even after the annexation of 1860, stone from Montrouge and Clamart continued to be used in Paris. However, shipping by canal and then by rail led to a greater diversity of origin. The railroad, in particular, lowered the cost of transporting hard rock,[4] indispensable for the basements of tall buildings, from Chantilly, Verdun, and even Burgundy. The nineteenth-century Paris building was above all a fine stone construction. With the triumph of the use of stone, the tradition of wood-and-plaster architecture came to an end, and brick and rubblestone became synonymous with lower-class constructions.

The use of buhrstone became widespread after the invention of hydraulic cement, which began to replace lime for heavy construction during the Second Empire. Buhrstone and cement created a particularly sturdy combination, first used to construct the city's sewers (it was strong enough to prevent them from cracking in shifting ground), and then for the foundations and sidewalls of buildings. The use of buhrstone and cement much improved the stability of buildings, especially those built on clayey or spongy ground.

But the most significant change was the mechanical cutting of stone. Once stone could be cut exactly to size with a saw, it became considerably easier to dress a stone wall. Moreover, as stone was becoming easier to cut, it also became easier to handle; as new machines were designed to hoist stone, blocks were cut larger and larger. Since this entailed increasingly expensive equipment on the construction site, builders needed more and more capital.[5] By the end

Classical stereotomy.
1. The Louvre: Cour Carrée. 2. The Louvre: Petite
Galerie. 3. The Louvre: Colonnade. 4 and 5. The
Institut de France. 6. The Conseil d'Etat.

1. Rue Rampal, examples of rubblestone sidewalls.
2. Corner of the Rue La Fontaine and the Avenue du Recteur-Poincaré. The lower part of the wall was built of buhrstone, the upper part of rubblestone.

of the nineteenth century, blocks a meter high and two to three meters long were commonplace, whereas the old blocks had seldom been over thirty-three centimeters high and sixty-six centimeters long.

The building's stereotomy, then, in many cases became quite beautiful; the perfectly regular courses of huge stone blocks with wide cement joints created graphic patterns that rivaled in beauty the building's ornament proper. In the early twentieth century stonecutting reached its zenith: the most complex forms could be realized with utmost perfection. Most of the preparation was done right at the quarry. The only thing to be done on the construction site was to clean the surface and add decorative sculptures, many of which were prefabricated.[6]

The remarkable precision of nineteenth-century stonework is more understandable when one considers the spectacular progress in draftsmanship that had taken place since the eighteenth century and the general use of scale drawings. The industrial use of stone involved much more than just quarrying; it determined the division of labor and architectural design, which evolved together with stonecutting techniques. Precision was the stonecutter's ideal and was attained during the art nouveau period, one of the great epochs in the history of stereotomy. Finally, the stone façades encouraged fine ornament. The use of a soft and very fine-grained stone made extremely subtle nuances possible in the treatment of the surface.

Whereas the façades were built of perfectly cut stone, sidewalls were usually made of rubblestone at first. With the use of hydraulic cement, rubblestone was replaced, as has been noted, by buhrstone—quite resistant to crumbling and cracking—forming extremely strong sidewalls to which the rest of the building, the floors as well as the front

Nineteenth-century stereotomy was based on very long, high courses. **1.** Corner of the Chaussée de la Muette and the Avenue Mozart. **2.** 18 Rue des Ecoles. **3.** Corner of the Rue François-Ponsard and the Rue Gustave-Nadaud. **4.** Corner of the Rue Octave-Feuillet and the Rue Alfred-Dehodencq. **5.** 12 Rue de la Pompe. **6.** 9 Boulevard Saint-Michel.

165

The metamorphoses of the sidewall.
1. Rue Saint-Dominique, even numbers, between the Avenue Bosquet and the Boulevard de la Tour-Maubourg. Plaster chimney flues. **2.** Rue Daviel. Flues made of interlocking clay pipes. **3.** 43 Rue La Fontaine and 2 Avenue Boudon. Flues covered by a brick facing. **4.** 28 bis Rue La Fontaine. An air well.

and back walls, was attached. The carefully laid foundations provided an extremely solid base; numerous precautions were taken to avoid structural shifts (notably, cramps between sidewalls and between sections of sidewalls broken by an air shaft). Metal joists strengthened the solidity of structures. At the end of the century, reinforced-concrete floors replaced metal joists and further increased structural solidity.

The industrialization of components also greatly affected less visible parts than the façades of buildings: for example, chimney flues, made of interlocking clay pipes that form strange patterns on certain exposed gables, and courtyards, which were more and more frequently constructed with a brick facing. Only the air shaft—with its plaster walls, and sills and cordons protected by zinc bibs—remained technically outmoded. As industrialization spread, fibrocement tiles, zinc, and sheet metal were increasingly used, and the old plaster walls looked more and more out of place. Early modernism was marked by a pronounced taste for neatness and durability.

An indirect consequence of the technical and economic evolution of construction was to render the use of salvaged materials obsolete. If the old French saying that a torn-down building is already halfway rebuilt remained true down to the end of the eighteenth century, it became less and less exact as the nineteenth century progressed. Because of its high quality and relatively moderate cost, cut stone was increasingly preferred to traditional rubblework (where walls were filled with a mixture of lime mortar and rubblestone salvaged from demolished buildings). In new constructions, moreover, cut stone was no longer used as a facing but in perpends—that is, in single blocks that formed the entire thickness of the wall.[7]

The materials left after buildings were torn down became waste. Beginning with the end of the eighteenth century, they were used for landfills in the old quarries on the Left Bank. Rubble not thus employed was used for working-class constructions, which still adhered to traditional building methods because of their moderate cost and ease of execution.

The transformation of stonecutting marked the end of preindustrial society and at the same time significantly influenced the birth of the Haussmann style. Socially and architecturally, the turning point came at midcentury.

The Frame

Most houses constructed in Paris prior to the nineteenth century had façades and back walls of wood.[8] This allowed great freedom in the placing of window openings, whence the fact that there were more voids than solids in traditional construction. On the other hand, a building's sidewalls were built of heavy masonry, excellent for soundproofing and convenient for flues. Inside the traditional shell, floors and walls were also built of wood. This system continued to be used well into the nineteenth century, in spite of the new materials that industry had begun to produce. In the Rambuteau building only the façade was built of freestone; the back wall and the interior walls were still made of wood. Little by little, as has been seen, rubblestone began to be used for the rear wall, and then for the load-bearing walls inside.

The invention of hollow brick (laid edgewise with plaster joints) revolutionized the construction and the role of partition walls. Inside the shell, partition walls were distinguished from load-bearing walls and were no longer used to support anything. This allowed relatively important differences in the way each floor was partitioned into rooms. (The only requirement was that the partition walls be in line with the floor joists.) Thus a greater variety of apartment layouts became possible.

When hollow brick began to be produced industrially, construction entered a semi-industrial stage, and materials underwent elaborate processing before they arrived on a construction site. This was totally new in construction and played an increasingly important role in the years that followed. The decline in the use of wood went hand in hand with the rationalist approach to construction, as building materials were cut to size in order to save time and to reduce the waste of building material on the construction site.

The use of wood for floors had been an absolute necessity down to the nineteenth century, owing to its unique bending strength.[9] Rationalization of its use was already under way during the reign of Louis-Philippe, when builders attempted to decrease the use of wood by using a light filler made of flower pots turned upside down. Later, hollow brick replaced this rather simplistic system. The way floors were built was transformed by an accident, a carpenters' strike during the July Monarchy.[10] A contractor whose construction sites had come to a standstill because of the strike hit on the idea of replacing wooden joists with railroad track, and the iron joist was born.[11] Its use in combination with hollow brick soon became widespread in Paris buildings. But the strength of certain habits becomes obvious when one considers that iron floors were, at least in a few cases, still being used with wooden façades at the end of the nineteenth century—for example, in the Square Le Coin, in the sixteenth arrondissement, in 1894. That example (limited to air shafts) is the exception to the rule, but it is indicative of how inconsistent the transformations that affected construction were, and shows the link between that inconsistency and cost.

Iron and Cast Iron

Iron, the material that most strongly marked the architecture of the early industrial era, was used very little in Paris apartment buildings, since prior to 1870, only cast iron could be used at a reasonable cost.[12] Steel had made the birth of the railroad possible as of 1825. But the lamination process was far from perfect; in fact, the only way to cast steel satisfactorily was in the form of ingots. Moreover, the process used to convert pig iron into steel by lowering its carbon level (puddling) was out of date. Steel did not become marketable at a low price until the Bessemer converter and then the Martin oven were invented (i.e., not before the third quarter of the nineteenth century).

Thus in nineteenth-century Paris the metal almost always used was cast iron. Stone pillars and columns were replaced by thin cast-iron columns, which made it possible to use hollow masonry walls. But all attempts to use metal beams for big spans were bound to fail for lack of a better material than cast iron. When Labrouste, boldly imitating the experiments in cast-iron construction carried out by Lamendé for the Iéna and Austerlitz bridges during the First Empire, used cast-iron arches for the Bibliothèque Sainte-Geneviève in 1843, he did so inside a masonry envelope.[13] The combination of cast iron and iron to build the floors in certain constructions created serious problems when the floor expanded and caused the cast-iron pieces to crack. When cast iron alone was used (by Alavoine for the spire in Rouen and the Bastille column, and by James Bogardus in the United States), its rigidity made it particularly fragile. Thus one of the first buildings built completely out of cast iron, the Halles, dates only from 1853, and the fragile structure of cast-iron posts and crossbeams was cleverly strengthened with steel tie beams.[14]

In ordinary construction, where such marvels were obviously unthinkable, one found the oddest combinations of materials imaginable. Thus the strain on wooden beams was sometimes relieved with cast-iron pillars, as in the Passage des Panoramas, built during the First Empire. Such combinations, easy in wooden constructions, were also extended to stone architecture: numerous stone perpend façades

Two examples of riveted metal lintels.
1. 31 Rue d'Alésia. **2.** Castel Béranger.

built between 1830 and 1850 rest on wooden lintels, the strain on which is relieved by cast-iron posts. Steel girders did not really appear until the Second Empire, and were largely due to Rohault de Fleury.[15] Fleury, a supporter of the classical tradition, designed the famous metal greenhouses built in the Jardin des Plantes during the Restoration. During the Second Empire, for the façades on the Place de l'Opéra he used metal lintels, placed just under the third-floor balconies, with cast-iron pillars. An intelligent strengthening of the sidewalls and the load-bearing walls inside the shell allowed façades to be built with the first two stories (reserved for shops) entirely in glass, the freestone elevation really starting only on the third floor. That system, first seen about 1860-65, continued in use down to the eve of World War I.

It may seem surprising that sheet iron, the industrial equivalent of traditional wood siding, was not more widely used. This was doubtless because of its cost (unlike cast iron, laminated iron remained an expensive and even luxurious item throughout the nineteenth century), and because of the desire to avoid mixing different construction materials too much. Also, for façades and load-bearing walls, builders clearly preferred masonry, which they were sure of, to the newfangled sheet iron.

For iron as for wood, the law of good construction is to enclose neither in masonry, in order to avoid rotting and rusting respectively. Of course wood construction could hardly be said to have followed this principle—one other reason why it eventually faded out. Jules Saulnier did use exposed iron sheeting for his famous Menier factory in Noisiel, and Viollet-le-Duc proposed its use for bourgeois housing.[16] But city ordinances and public opinion remained resolutely attached to freestone construction: Sauvage's L'Argentine and Chédanne's *Parisien libéré* building are just about the only examples of sheet-iron construction in Paris.[17] It should be remembered that metal construction, not being very isothermal, was not really appropriate for residences.

All-steel construction, as noted, was exceedingly rare. This was doubtless because it was not altogether perfected until about the time reinforced concrete was patented in 1893. The considerably lower cost of this new material, and the fact that it could be combined with classic masonry much more easily, led to its quick success. Although buildings with reinforced-concrete skeletons (or, to be more exact, reinforced mortar until 1920) were exceedingly rare, concrete lintels, floors, and roofs did start to become widespread about 1905-10.

Roofs   Little has been said as yet about the way roofs were built. In the traditional mixed structure of load-bearing masonry walls and wooden cross beams, a wooden frame was used. The evolution that the construction of roof frames underwent was initially due less to a change in materials (though pine did replace oak[18]) than to a modification in the way they were used. Mechanical sawing transformed the shape of boards. Whereas boards had traditionally been almost square in cross section, very different-looking long, rectangular sections began to be used. They were much stronger and also allowed a savings in raw material.

The evolution of the shape of boards led to a change in the way they were assembled: the mortise-and-tenon joint, the classic technique of interlocking, was replaced by a new system in which two boards hugged a thicker one, to which they were attached with bolts. Nailing was also used more frequently, although Parisian architects did not go so far as to adopt the American balloon frame of the 1870s, which was really nothing but a giant fruit crate.[19]

The evolution of the way boards were cut and jointed in the nineteenth century could have taken place only in an industrial society. The use of nails, nuts, and bolts was a real luxury before then (the purchase of nails by the Sieur de Gouberville to build his Norman manor in the sixteenth century had represented a large part of the budget).[20] Thus, prior to the industrialization of building supplies, interlocking joints and pegs had been preferred. As soon as low-cost industrial products became available, the situation changed completely: what was expensive was not the supplies but labor, which made it necessary to find rapid construction techniques.

In Paris this evolution became obvious during the reign of Louis-Philippe. Light roofs with board frames were all the more attractive because they made it easier to erect a mansard roof, a relatively inexpensive way of increasing floor space. Iron roofs, which had been recommended since the late eighteenth century (especially for theaters, as a fire-prevention measure), were seldom used for residential buildings. This was no doubt because they were more costly and, not being visible, were not considered as appealing to potential tenants as, for example, stone façades. In spite of Viollet-le-Duc's theoretical projects,[21] and the rationalist school's pronounced attachment to solid construction, the roof was unquestionably the most mediocre part of the Parisian building. The only merit of most roofs—often little more than crude, makeshift structures—was that they were easy to build.

Industrial Materials

If the use of iron and especially cast iron to construct certain prestigious monuments—train stations, exhibition halls—can be said to symbolize one aspect of nineteenth-century architecture, terra-cotta played the fundamental role in the technical and formal renewal of housing.[22] Terra-cotta, including brick, pipes, and glazed ceramic, greatly simplified the construction of chimneys, floors, and partition walls.

Solid brick, the dimensions of which had not changed since antiquity (5.5 by 11 by 22 centimeters), would not at first glance seem to have played a particularly important role. Although brick had always

Following pages:
1. 7 Rue de Provence **2.** 46 Rue de Provence. Cast-iron posts supporting a wooden beam. **3.** Rue Auber. The cast-iron posts continue up to the mezzanine floor and are supported by a metal frame (hidden by the modern shop front). **4.** The last plate in Viollet-le-Duc's *Entretiens*. The perfect theoretical example of an exposed iron framework.

PANS-DE-FER DE FACE EN ENCORBELLEMENT AVEC REVETEMENT DE FAYENCE.

Ve A. MOREL & Cie Editeurs

been made in Paris with clay from Vaugirard, its architectural uses had been limited.[23]

Traditionally, brick had been used only edgewise as a filler in wooden walls, because of its inertia and the fact that it was easy to cut. (Vaugirard brick was badly fired and brittle.) But it was just a filler and was never exposed, as in Normandy (where it was later replaced by smaller tiles). Chimneys were never built of brick, but rather of plaster of Paris, which was shaped with a trowel, using techniques that closely resembled those employed by Nubian masons to construct clay vaults.[24] Brick reappeared as a construction material in Paris during the second half of the eighteenth century in the quaint structures used to decorate gardens—a use later echoed in the numerous pavilions Davioud built for the parks and promenades of Paris during the Second Empire.

The rather marginal use of brick was suddenly expanded by a radical transformation in the way it was manufactured, when, about 1840-50, charcoal firing was replaced by coal firing, generally with coke, which made higher temperatures possible. The resulting brick was better fired and less porous, and thus had greater resistance to erosion. As a result, brick became an excellent surface for façades and had the advantage of being relatively inexpensive—much cheaper than stone. However the aesthetic qualities of brick had changed: firing with coke blackened it and gave it a more opaque look. The problem worsened when cement was added to strengthen the clay; the resulting grayishness required the addition of artificial coloring that is still employed today.

Used to build factories and warehouses, bricks were often placed edgewise, as in the big Batignolles depots, the twin warehouses that could still be seen several years ago, apparently built in the 1840s, at the same time as the western railroad line. Facings of edgewise brick were eventually replaced by iron sheets[25] and then concrete, as in the Perret and Freyssinet warehouses.

The uses of brick were more varied than one might imagine. It was, of course, used for facings, but in that case the material served only to

cover a masonry core. It could also be used as the core of the construction. The bonding varied, depending on whether the bricks were laid in courses of stretchers or in courses of alternating stretchers and headers. This morphological difference reflected a big difference in quality. In the first case, there was a single thickness of brick (the wall was eleven centimeters thick). In the second case, there were two rows linked by brick perpends; if the wall was twice as thick, the quantity of brick needed was doubled, too. Finally, bricks laid flat could be combined with bricks laid edgewise (which was more economical) in one or several thicknesses, even if that meant leaving a void inside a wall.[26]

These variations, which at first seem purely technical or decorative, reflect a qualitative hierarchy ranging from the simple outer facing to load-bearing walls of various strengths. There were many qualities of brick construction in Paris. The thickness of the outer walls was reduced as much as possible in the construction of warehouses and lower-class housing, and greatly increased in more prestigious constructions. This detail is particularly important for working-class constructions in Paris, since, toward the end of the Second Empire, brick replaced wood there more and more. The exhaustion of salvageable materials, after the intense period of renovation under Napoleon III, doubtless had something to do with this, as did the dwindling number of carpenters. Being economical, regular, and relatively easy to transport and use, brick became the ideal material for do-it-yourself builders and all forms of inexpensive construction.

An Implicit Hierarchy

Little by little, a socioarchitectural hierarchy emerged. For buildings of equal size, quality changed—according to a neighborhood's status and its distance from the center—on the following scale:

1. Freestone construction using large blocks and ornamental sculpture.
2. Freestone construction using large blocks, but limiting sculpture to the cornice or stereotyped decorative motifs.
3. Large stone blocks for corners and frames, but small stones for the rest, with industrial ceramic ornament or no ornament at all.
4. Polychrome brick construction, sometimes with exposed metal elements (for schools and hospitals, fiefs of the proponents of rationalism).[27]
5. Stone corners and frames with brick facing—preferably yellow

Brick was the preferred material of nineteenth-century industrial architecture. The plates in J. Lacroux's *La Brique ordinaire* illustrate the rich possibilities of ornamental brickwork created by the interaction of crisscross patterns on the fillers between bays with the architectonics of the window frame.

brick, to blend in with the stone and create an illusion of all-stone construction.

6. Brick corners and frames with rubblestone walls, covered with painted plaster.

7. Thin brick walls with exposed iron lintels and no emphasis on frames.

8. Metal sheets with brick filler—solid brick for dwellings, and usually hollow brick for workshops and warehouses.

9. Brick corners and frames with cinder-block walls covered by cement roughcast. (In the twentieth century, this system was used to build suburban houses resulting from the Loucheur law. The nineteenth century ignored this technique, if we except several precursory experiments in concrete construction, such as the Coignet and Saint-Denis projects, 1853, and the Daumesnil housing development, 1867. These constructions, though, were made of molded cement, cinder block not having been invented yet.)

The hierarchy existed down to World War II, iron being replaced by reinforced concrete. It reflected the extremely rigid class system of nineteenth- and early-twentieth-century bourgeois society, ranging from the moneyed aristocracy down to the working class, with all the nuances of the upper, middle, and lower middle classes in between. The architectural hierarchy was also closely related to the geographical distribution of the various social classes in Paris—each neighborhood had its rank in the overall scheme—which proves the coherence of the French social hierarchy and its relative stability throughout the Second Empire and the Third Republic. Even in late examples, such as the government housing developments built near the old fortifications between 1925 and 1935, there were striking differences from one section to another. These differences were less a reflection of architectural originality than of a hierarchy of quality and location; the Suchet, Pershing, and Poniatowski boulevards, for example, required certain types of construction.

Inside a single construction there were also noticeable differences in quality: one treated the main façade differently from the service façade (between street and courtyard), and the courtyard façade differently from the air well. The Lavirotte building at 29 Avenue Rapp is very typical: the main façade was covered with a richly ornamented sandstone facing, while the courtyard façade was given a light brick facing with no ornament.

Brick—which had traditionally not been used for buildings—can be said to have established the socioarchitectural hierarchy in nineteenth-century Paris. It was in itself a sign of thrift, and the way it was used created further distinctions. In comparison, the differences in stone construction, depending on the originality of ornament and the size of the stone blocks, were much more discreet. It is as if the bourgeoisie as a whole wanted to assert its unity, autonomy, and superiority to the working class.

1

2

3

4

5

6

Freestone façades with limited sculpture and relief.
1. 9 and 11 Boulevard Saint-Michel. **2.** 35 bis Rue La Fontaine. **3.** 1-5 Rue de Cluny. **4.** 23-29 bis Rue Monge. **5.** 9-1 Rue Monge. **6.** 12 bis-18 Rue du Sommerard.

Facing page: A fine freestone façade with ornamental sculptures. 16 Boulevard Saint-Michel.

Combinations of yellow brick, red brick, and stone (or cement).
1. Rue Dangeau. **2.** 7 Rue Lekain. **3.** 68-70 Rue La Fontaine. **4.** Corner of the Rue La Fontaine and the Rue des Perchamps. **5.** Rue La Fontaine and Villa Jeanne d'Arc. **6.** 1-7 Avenue Mozart.

Comfort and Convenience

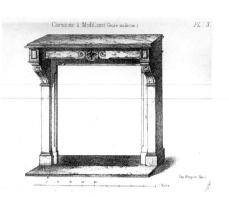

Fireplaces

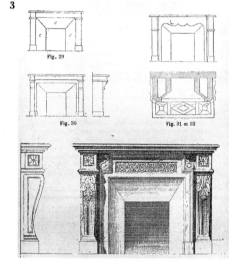

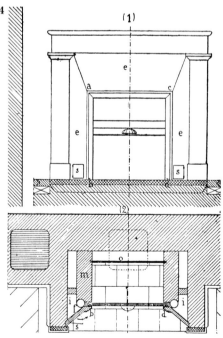

The transformation of the Paris apartment building during the industrial age concerned the infrastructure—all the pipes and shafts, as well as fittings linked to comfort and sanitation—as much as it did the masonry.[28] In that infrastructure the "modern conveniences" were born.[29]

Flues have already been mentioned. Industrial clay pipes began to be used at the very beginning of the Second Empire. The pipes were approximately thirty-three centimeters tall and three centimeters thick. Those dimensions remained unchanged until 1914, after which date the building code required an increase in thickness. (Since then, a width of five centimeters and a height of twenty-five centimeters have been standard.) The clay pipe entirely transformed the way flues were built and moreover made it possible to repair sections without redoing the whole; the old plaster flues had had to be totally rebuilt once they started cracking. As a result of the use of clay pipes, the space taken up by flues was considerably reduced, and smaller, lower fireplaces could be built.

The new fireplaces were industrially produced early on. During the reign of Louis-Philippe, marble mantelpieces—cut to imitate the standard neoclassical combination of pilasters and entablature—began to replace the traditional wood mantelpieces even in modest buildings. Complementary elements were soon added. The opening was lined with terra-cotta that was enameled white, and the hearth was given a brass frame, with a metal register that was opened and closed by a chain and counterweights. By the end of Louis-Philippe's reign, all these elements were commonplace.[30]

A new kind of fireplace, directly related to the use of coal, also appeared—the Prussian fireplace, which, flush with the wall, was a great improvement over the small curved grates used to burn coal in open fireplaces of the classic type. The closed cast-iron hearth drew well, thus eliminating the danger of carbon monoxide poisoning, while also cutting down on coal consumption. The front of the closed fireplace, in enameled clay, was equipped with vents that ensured the circulation and heating of the surrounding air by simple conduction. In addition, a brass door opened onto a small dish warmer, which was very practical in dining rooms.[31]

1

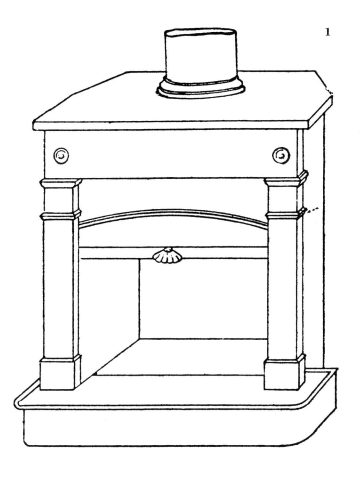

2

3

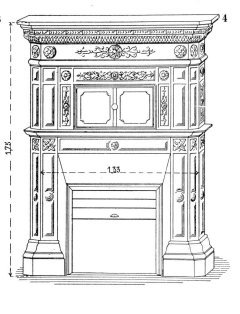

4

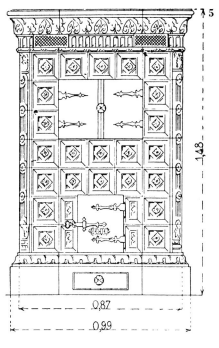

5

1.75

1.33

1.48

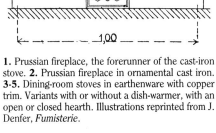

1.00

0.87

0.99

1. Prussian fireplace, the forerunner of the cast-iron stove. **2.** Prussian fireplace in ornamental cast iron. **3-5.** Dining-room stoves in earthenware with copper trim. Variants with or without a dish-warmer, with an open or closed hearth. Illustrations reprinted from J. Denfer, *Fumisterie*.

183

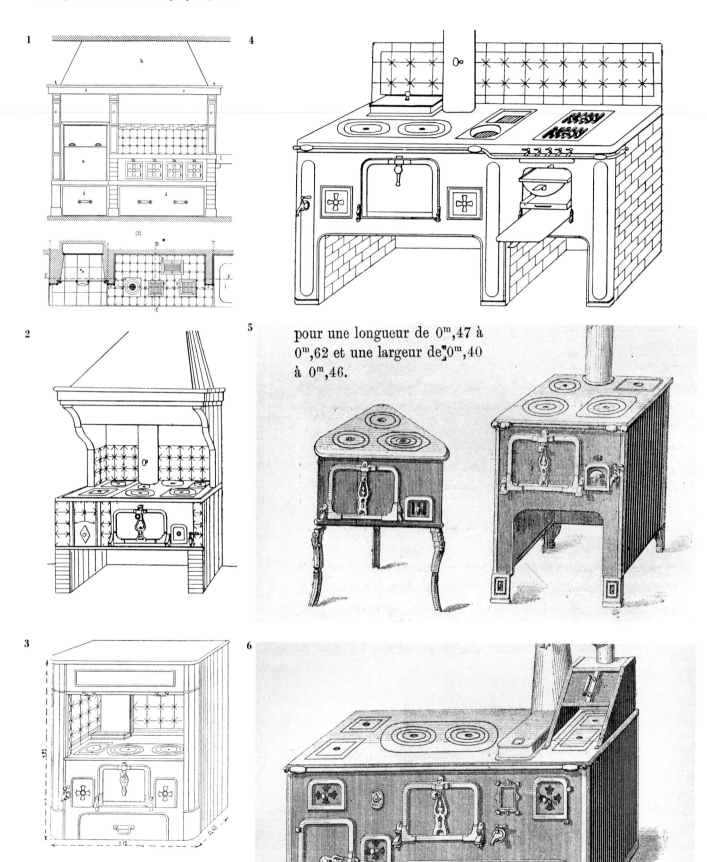

1. Kitchen stove with oven and hood. **2.** A stove for small kitchens. **3.** A simple stove for a concierge's lodge. **4.** A combination wood/gas stove. Illustration reprinted from J. Denfer, *Fumisterie*. **5.** Small cast-iron stoves. **6.** Big kitchen stove with grill. Illustrations reprinted from *La Petite Encyclopédie*, no. 9.

pour une longueur de 0ᵐ,47 à 0ᵐ,62 et une largeur de 0ᵐ,40 à 0ᵐ,46.

Another improvement in heating was the cast-iron kitchen stove. It appeared at the beginning of industrialization, about 1840-45. Usually consuming coal, it allowed food to be cooked on burners or in an oven, water to be warmed in a tank on the side, and the room to be heated. A century before it spread to rural areas, the cast-iron stove became the center of the Parisian kitchen. However, stoves of fired clay covered in ceramic tile—traditionally white with a lattice or flower motif in blue—were still used for cooking in warm weather.

Heating stoves were also very popular in the nineteenth century. These were a smaller version of the terra-cotta stoves of Alsace, whose big size reflected the harsh climate and the use of wood for fuel there. They became a standard and very useful feature of the Parisian apartment. It was not yet customary to heat bedrooms—indeed, a heated bedroom was thought to be very unhealthy—but the stove could be used in a sick person's room or in other rooms that lacked a permanent source of heat. Like the Prussian fireplace, which was in fact a built-in version of the stove, the heating stove was more economical and much more efficient than open wood-burning fireplaces.

Paris was heated with separate coal-burning hearths, which required as many flues as there were heated rooms in a building. Expensive though it was to build, this system prevailed until the midnineteenth century.[32] Nevertheless, a completely different method could be found in some buildings where a "central" heating system, the *calorifère*, linked various individual rooms to a single source of heat. Based on a technique worked out in ancient Rome and "modernized" in the early eighteenth century (in the Craon château in Lorraine, ducts installed by Boffrand about 1730 are still used today for heat), this system was employed throughout the nineteenth century. Hidden under the floor or in partition walls, big terra-cotta pipes connected the central unit to a hot-air vent in each room. As in the case of the Prussian fireplace, rooms were heated by conduction, the heated air tending to rise through the ducts to the rooms to be heated. An improvement in the system was obtained by installing outflow vents near the ceiling, thereby increasing the natural upward draw. Thus, on the façades of certain luxury buildings, one can see small ornamental cast-iron grates above the windows, an external sign that the apartments were centrally heated in the nineteenth century.[33] The architectural hierarchy was such that, as a general rule, only the prestigious apartments above the basement had central heating; indeed, sometimes only the third floor was so heated. Moreover, even when there was central heating, it affected only the living, dining, and reception rooms.

Stoves

Central Heating

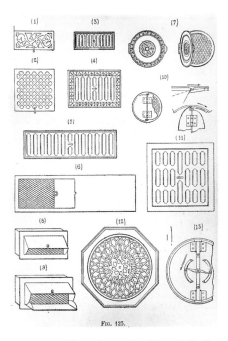

Hot-air vents. Illustration reprinted from J. Denfer, *Fumisterie*.

185

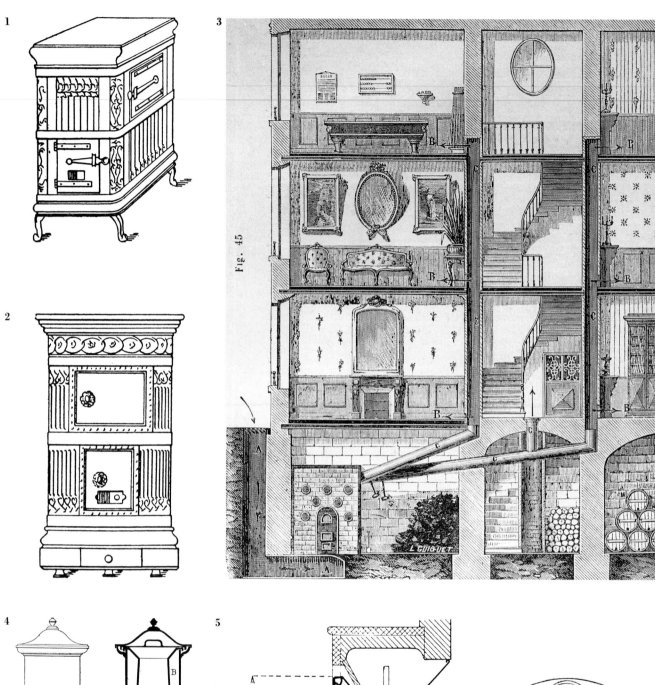

1 and **2.** Earthenware stoves for wood and coal. **3.** Cross section of a central heating system (hot air). Illustration reprinted from *La Petite Encyclopédie,* no. 9. **4.** Coal stove (Compagnie Parisienne du Gaz). **5.** Movable slow-combustion stove. Illustrations reprinted from J. Denfer, *Fumisterie.*

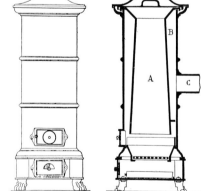

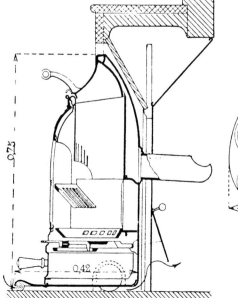

The improvement in living conditions brought by heating was accompanied by a real effort to improve sanitary conditions. After the 1832 cholera epidemic, it was decided to place raised sidewalks on either side of the roadway. Even then, however, the gutters were still used not only to collect rainwater but also as an open sewer line. Not even the law of 1844, which multiplied the public fountains in Paris and thus produced an almost permanent stream of water in the gutters, was enough, for sewers remained a rarity. Haussmann and his engineer, Eugène Belgrand, were responsible for the creation of an underground sewer system serving the whole city. Their huge undertaking took twenty years to complete and totally transformed hygienic conditions in Paris.

The sewer lines were constructed under the roadway in parabolic sections. They were built of buhrstone and coated with cement to make them watertight. The system was designed so as to prevent clogging in the case of a rupture in the circuit. Automatic flushing devices, ensuring the hourly cleaning of the mains, maintained perfect sanitary conditions.

The construction of the sewers was combined with that of a water conveyance system with two mains, one carrying drinking water for household consumption and the other water for cleaning the streets. Each building had two water mains, with a distinction between drinking water and washing water.[34] Because of the construction of huge reservoirs on the highest points in the city, there was enough water pressure to provide every floor with running water—a radical break with the past. However, until the end of the nineteenth century, only rainwater and a household's wash water were carried off in the sewers. The principle of dumping everything into sewers was established late. Until it was, each building had its own septic tank, or, a worse alternative, wastes were dumped into pits that, once full, had to be emptied. The wastes were taken to a foul-smelling port at La Villette, put onto a barge, and shipped out to the vegetable gardens in the suburbs. The fact that a building's sewage pit and well were both located in the courtyard was the cause of many mishaps.

The city water mains and sewers built during the Second Empire completely transformed sanitary installations in Parisian apartment buildings. Traditionally, kitchens and lavatories had been separated as best they could be from the rest of the apartment, to exclude odors from the reception rooms and bedrooms. A building's latrines and the big funnels used to pour waste water down the drainpipe were cleaned with water drawn from the well in the courtyard. The latrines were usually located off landings between floors in order to cut down on the number of installations. As social standing went down, so did the latrines—into the courtyard. When, thanks to Haussmann, running water became available on every floor, latrines were much easier to

Sewers and Water Mains

Sanitary Installations

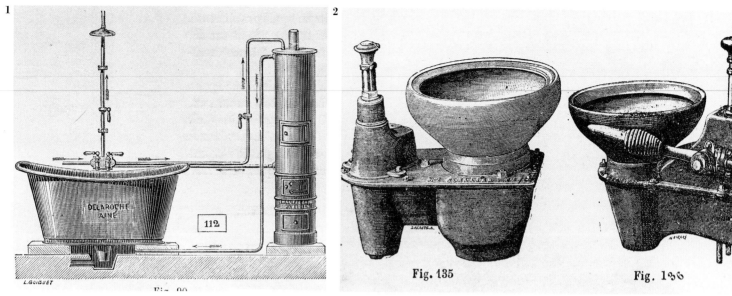

Fig. 135   Fig. 136

Different kinds of faucets.
1. Screw faucet. **2.** Push-button faucet. **3.** "Smooth faucet" (eliminating sudden spurts). Illustrations reprinted from *La Petite Encyclopédie*, no. 10.

clean (cast-iron tanks fitted with a flushing device were soon installed against the walls), and they could be introduced into the apartment itself.[35] In addition, an apartment could, to use the legal terminology of the day, have running water "on the sink"—a flat sandstone sink placed near the kitchen window.

The introduction of running water into the kitchen can be explained by the fact that kitchens were tiled and thus could withstand humidity; the floor was generally covered with hexagonal red tiles. When running water was introduced, tiles were also used for the walls, to protect them from splashing. Cooking fumes and steam from the boiling water used to wash clothes were evacuated through a big plaster hood.

On the other hand, there was a great deal of hesitation before running water was introduced into the bathroom. Since cold tile floors were deemed unhealthy, Parisians thought it better not to put a permanent source of water there. Bathrooms generally had a white wood parquet floor, washed with bleach, and walls covered with varnished wallpaper. The room's main piece of furniture was a wood-and-marble washstand with a pitcher, a basin, and a bucket for waste water.

A quite astonishing contraption was frequently found toward the end of the century: a glazed terra-cotta wall tank with separate reservoirs for hot and cold water.[36] Water had to be poured in by pitcher. One then had a certain quantity of water available, which flowed out of two faucets located at the bottom of the tank, just above the washstand basin. In the most sophisticated installations, the basin pivoted, thus making it possible to empty waste water directly into the bucket. The first real bathrooms—that is, with hot and cold running water—did not appear until the turn of the century and constituted a bravura achievement of the art nouveau period. The basic model was in fact an old one, since similar installations had existed in all châteaus and aristocratic houses since the Middle Ages. They were such a luxury

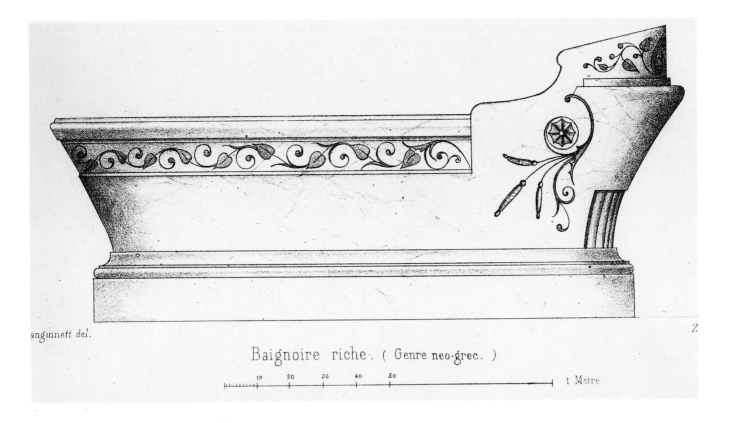

anguineti del.

Baignoire riche. (Genre neo-grec.)

10 20 30 40 50   1 Metre

that they were sometimes even housed in special bathing pavilions. In the early twentieth century the modern bathroom appeared, with its white enamel components—terra-cotta sinks and bidets, and cast-iron bathtubs—with tile walls and floors, and chrome-plated faucets.[37]

Modern convenience did not mean sanitary installations alone. Other nineteenth-century inventions revolutionized lighting, energy, and communications, and each new invention made it necessary to install yet another network under the city's streets. The earliest of these developments was gas, which was used for streetlights in the First Empire, then for indoor lighting during the reign of Louis-Philippe (the incandescent Welsbach burner). Gas being dirty, it was generally found only in kitchens, where it was first used for lighting but then, when the gas stove was invented early in the twentieth century, for heating as well. It was also used in other places where it was indispensable: entryways, staircases, corridors, and rooms without windows. One of the indirect consequences of gas lighting was to make buildings "thicker"; in the Second Empire, artificial light made it possible to place a windowless core in constructions. The core was initially used for hallways and walk-in closets; later, the lavatory was placed there, too.

Electricity appeared at the end of the nineteenth century, the essential invention being Thomas Edison's incandescent lamp in 1878. By the 1890s, electric lighting was already relatively common. At first, electrical wiring was installed under wood strips nailed to a room's moldings. But a little later a building's wiring was concealed in sheaths embedded in the masonry. The earliest examples are twentieth-century bathrooms, where wires were concealed for safety reasons.

The development of modern conveniences made the builder's job much harder. This can still be seen on old constructions where water

Gas

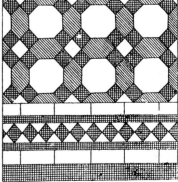

Examples of enameled tiles used for fireplaces and stoves. Illustrations reprinted from *La Petite Encyclopédie*, no. 8.

189

Fig. 82   Fig. 83

La figure 83 est une cheminée à gaz à incandescence, avec amiante.

Fig. 84   Fig. 85

La figure 84 est une bûche à gaz en terre réfractaire avec touffes d'amiante (rendues incandescentes quand les becs sont allumés).

Examples of gas fireplaces. Illustration reprinted from *La Petite Encyclopédie*, no. 9.

and gas mains, electrical wiring, and later telephone lines (not to mention television cables) were added on the outside, covering the façade in an astonishing pattern. Traditional architecture had known only vertical constraints. The masonry had to be level and the chimney flues straight, and even those requirements could be got around easily, especially with the cantilever.

Since water mains had to be vertical, it became necessary to place rooms with running water directly above one another. That led to the birth of various technical shafts: rising mains and drainpipes in kitchens, lavatories, and bathrooms, and gas and electricity mains in the stairwell. Drainpipes, hooked directly into the sewer, were placed on the façade. The architectural treatment of new technology was a constant preoccupation during the first phase of the industrial age, and many problems were never really resolved. The history of the relationship between ornament and technology shows a perpetual wavering between concealing technical elements and emphasizing them: to show or not to show?

The Elevator

Technological transformation affected not only the structure of the nineteenth-century building—symbolized by the use of iron—but also internal organization and consequently everyday life. The most eloquent example is the elevator. The first elevator was Elisha Otis's, at the 1853 Crystal Palace exhibition in New York.[38] It would seem to have been a steam elevator. The hydraulic elevator was developed in France for the 1867 fair but was not used in residential buildings until the 1880s. Hydraulic elevators were powered by the pressure in the mains conducting the city's nondrinking water. The water entered a telescopic cylinder whose gradual expansion pushed the elevator up. Two notched rails on the sides guided the elevator. These rails were equipped with a safety device that prevented the elevator from falling in the case of a leak in the hydraulic mechanism or a sudden decrease in water pressure. The replacement of hydraulic pressure by pneumatic pressure, toward the end of the century, represented a considerable improvement. Hydropneumatic elevators and then oleopneumatic elevators were common after 1900. Their operation was made possible by a special network of compressed air that covered practically the whole city. A private company got the concession by coming up with a clever proposition: regular impulses in the network that would make it possible to operate pneumatic clocks at major intersections, a number of which still exist today. But the clocks alone did not justify the creation of such an infrastructure. The compressed air was sold to industrial plants, craftsmen, and of course buildings with elevators.

The invention of the elevator turned the old hierarchy of floors upside down. Shrewd observers had pointed out fairly early that the most sought-after floors—those that were easiest to walk up to—were

also the most unhealthy, owing to noise, pollution, and insufficient light.[39] As the elevator became popular, the top floors with their sun-drenched terraces became the most sought-after place to live. This change came about in the early twentieth century. The new prestige of the uppermost floors transformed building façades. It led to the superposition of recessed stories on the sixth *and* seventh levels, then to the creation of the loggias so characteristic of art nouveau, and finally to Henri Sauvage's cherished "tiered" building of 1908.

Indoor Trim

Compared to the technological changes just discussed, the transformation of the interior woodwork and ornament seems much more modest. However, it too was closely linked to advances in technology and indeed drew on the stylistic possibilities created by those advances with great intelligence and subtlety. Moreover, the stylistic issue is certainly what interested the nineteenth century the most. If new technology and its applications to daily life somehow seemed normal, stylistic renewal based on the technical possibilities of the machine was highly controversial. The main aesthetic movements in the second half of the nineteenth century, from Viollet-le-Duc's rationalism to William Morris's Arts and Crafts in England, gave priority to everything in artistic production that allowed economies of means and tools. Though aesthetic leaders rejected the machine for symbolic reasons, their basic desire to simplify artistic production was fundamentally compatible with mechanical forms of production (e.g., William Morris's wallpaper). Parisian builders, of course, were oblivious to such lofty considerations; their goal was to replace the costly work of craftsmen with simplified—that is, cheaper—procedures creating a similar formal result.

Woodwork

The first element of interior trim to be systematized and produced in a simpler way was the woodwork.[40] During the Second Empire, doors and windows began to be manufactured industrially in a small but significant way. Promoted in part by the law of competition, such manufacture became the norm. This was a response to a particular business problem. Workshops could of course fill orders with custom-made items, but in order to survive, it became increasingly necessary to fill in the gaps between special orders by making standardized items that could be sold to any customer. The mechanization of woodworking required the purchase of new machines and an increase in manpower, and thus was very expensive. There could be no periods of inactivity in production, if a business wanted to survive. The items produced to keep workers busy between custom orders had to fit the needs of anonymous customers; this meant products that could be

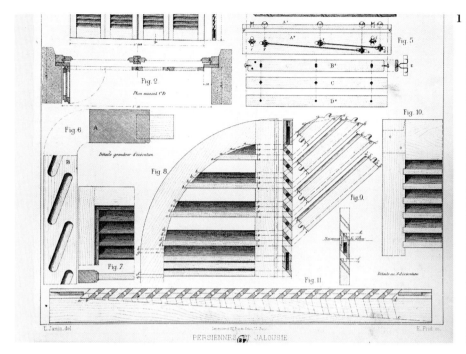

easily adapted to fill any order. As a result, woodwork gradually became less original as standard sizes and designs were developed to correspond to the new state of the market. Standardization was under way.

Nevertheless, industrial woodwork did remain very similar to the old craftwork: mortise and tenon joints were still used for frames, and rebates for door panels. From a technical point of view, the only thing that really changed was the way moldings were made. The plane, which had traditionally been used to cut moldings, was replaced by the lathe, which allowed beading and other types of molding, even when complex, to be cut very quickly, so long as the grooves were not to be too deep. The lathe was responsible for the abundance of moldings, highly decorative, yet relatively inexpensive, in the second half of the nineteenth century. Indeed, builders were eager to use lathed moldings, not only on windows and doors, where the frame and rebates were considerably enriched, but also for wainscoting.

On the lower section of walls, real wood wainscoting—that is, panels with molded frames—was replaced by a mock wainscoting of beading nailed directly to the wall. This was far less costly, but the result was quite similar and gave an air of prestige to the most modest interiors. Consequently, imitation wainscoting appeared in the smallest room. In a world of industrial objects, mock wainscoting represented a kind of nostalgia for the old craftwork that was dying out. It owed its commercial success to the prestige always associated with fine craftsmanship.

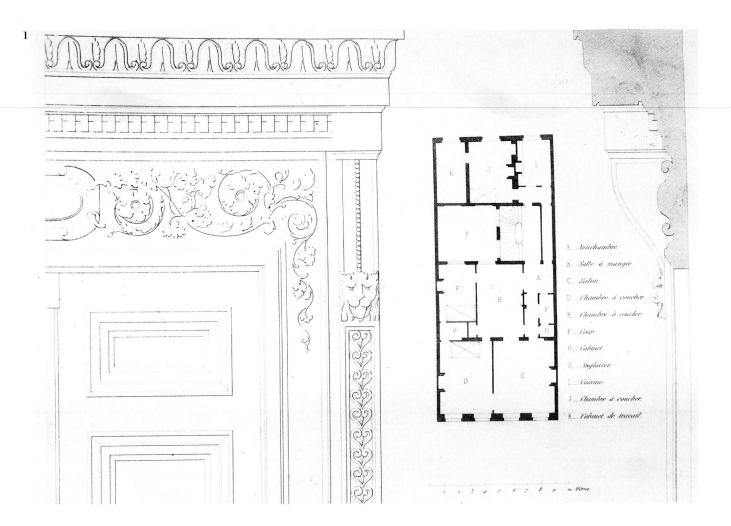

A. _Antichambre._

B. _Salle à manger._

C. _Salon._

D. _Chambre à coucher._

E. _Chambre à coucher._

F. _Cour._

G. _Cabinet._

H. _Anglaises._

I. _Cuisine._

J. _Chambre à coucher._

K. _Cabinet de travail._

Staff Moldings

1. Detail of an apartment door, 82 Boulevard Beau-marchais, 1849. **2.** Diagram explaining how to make plaster cornices. Illustration reprinted from _La Petite Encyclopédie_, no. 8.

Another kind of machine-made trim appeared at about the same time as mock wainscoting: the staff cornice molding. Cornice moldings, which date back to the Restoration, had originally been made of wood. Wooden moldings were simply nailed around the edges of the ceiling. However, compared to the infinite variety of plaster moldings, the possibilities offered by wood moldings were disappointing. Early in the reign of Louis XVI, moldings in staff (a mixture of fiber, glue, and fine plaster) began to enjoy considerable popularity—a popularity that continued into the middle of our own century. Ceiling moldings were introduced to conceal imperfections that made it difficult to put wallpaper or fabric on walls. In fairly low rooms, furthermore, cornice moldings made the ceiling look higher by "pushing" it up (which is contrary to the popular notion that the cornice weighs down on a room). Yet if these reasons were related to the success of the molded cornice, the most important reason was certainly the phenomenal variety of decorative possibilities.

A veritable industry sprang up in the old Plaisance district,[41] almost completely demolished today. Wood cornices and ceiling roses were made by craftsmen in the east of the city, especially in the Faubourg Saint-Antoine. Decorations of staff were the work of Italian craftsmen who had settled in France during the Restoration. The new fashion

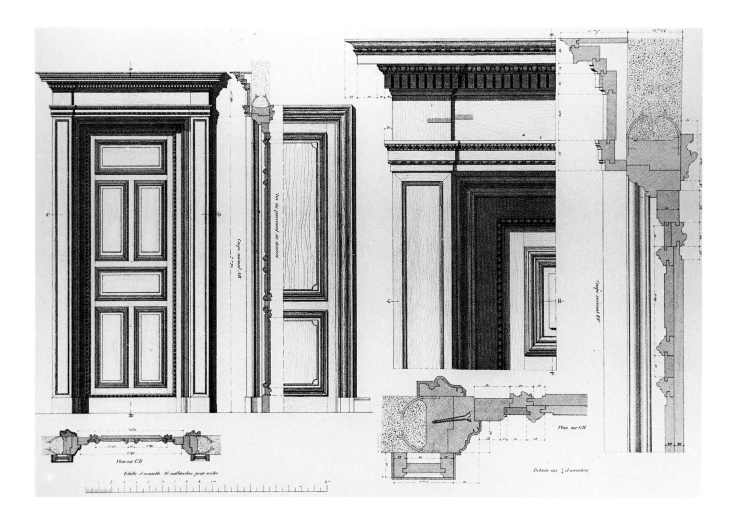

Detail of a door whose two sides are treated differently. Illustration reprinted from Léon Jamin, *L'Enseignement professionnel du menuisier.*

would seem to have been aristocratic in origin, as shown by the many staff decorations that Venetian craftsmen produced during the Restoration for the Duke of Padua's castle in Courson, near Paris.[42] Indeed, it might even be necessary to go back to the reign of Louis XVI and the fashionable gypsum door piers of Paris mansions to find the real origin of this decorative element.[43]

The bourgeois apartment started to be embellished during the reign of Louis-Philippe. A room's bare walls and corners, plain chimneys, and rough floors were transformed with wainscoting, cornices, ceiling roses, parquet, and marble mantelpieces with big mirrors above them. All this was made possible by industry. One of the first consequences of the mechanization of woodworking was the production of tongue-and-groove parquet at a low price. Later, mechanical procedures were found for cutting stone and marble, which lowered the cost of marble mantelpieces considerably. Mass-produced sculpture was created by the well-known pantographic process,[44] which made it possible to carve several pieces simultaneously and explains the proliferation of richly sculpted white marble mantelpieces. Moreover, during the Restoration the lamination process gave the glass industry such a boost that windows containing

The Enrichment of Interior Ornament

195

an abundance of little panes were soon replaced by larger panes, and then, in the most prestigious constructions, by big plates of glass. And once the bourgeoisie could afford the kind of big mirrors that had hung above the fireplaces of the aristocracy in the eighteenth century, the bourgeois living room[45] was turned into a replica of the reception rooms in the homes of the aristocracy under Louis XV—symbolized, as it were, by the combination of mantelpiece, mirror, and chandelier.

The existence of a model to imitate greatly conditioned the evolution of the techniques for decorating apartments in the nineteenth century. First, it seems fairly obvious that a large mirror (though prices had come down, mirrors were still expensive) was less effective at making a room lighter than wider window openings and thinner window frames would have been. But windows were transformed by the use of metal frames only in the most sumptuous constructions, such as the Louvre palace and Fontainebleau. Similarly, cast iron and terra-cotta were seldom used for mantelpieces, since marble was synonymous with luxury and (because of the "carving") with originality. Only the Prussian fireplace, relegated to a private part of the house—the dining room, the center of family life—was molded, which is highly significant. If cornices and ceiling roses were molded, it was because the art of stucco had established its pedigree (as in the sumptuous cornices of the Soubise palace), and the public did not see any difference between stucco and staff—that is, between an ornament directly modeled in stucco, therefore original and unique, and a mass-produced molded ornament. Or, to be more exact, as is today the case for ready-to-wear clothing, the general public did not *want* to see the difference, since it was synonymous with a difference in cost and hence social standing.

Outdoor Trim

The same confusion affected the outdoor trim of buildings. There, too, industrial techniques lowered the cost of ornament dramatically. Though one might not realize this today, some stone ornaments like cornices and balcony consoles were machine-made or at least rough-hewn mechanically, then finished along with the surface of the façade. The market was flooded with zinc, iron, and ceramic products.

Roof Ornament

Isolated in 1805 by Abbé Dony, who had the concession for the Vieille Montagne mines near Aix-la-Chapelle, zinc was first used to roof the houses on the Rue de Rivoli. But the nineteenth century was to place the greatest emphasis on zinc's ornamental uses. Indeed, building regulations had traditionally favored slate roofs, and slate was required even on the upper slopes of mansard roofs. Consequently, zinc was relegated to the terrace strip at the top of the roof, while at the same time replacing lead on the roof's edges, which lent themselves to decoration. After 1830, decorative zinc played an important role in the development of the neo-Gothic style: the Angers architect René Hodé frequently decorated his châteaus with zinc finials and ridges, in contrast to the lead ones found in flamboyant and rococo architecture.[46] In Second Empire architecture the use of zinc was limited at first. Instead of zinc, there were cast-iron gutters (as in Hittorf's mansions on the Place de l'Etoile, Garnier's Paris Opera House, and Rohault de Fleury's buildings on the Place de l'Opéra) and cast-iron ridge ornaments on the edges of the roof's upper slopes (Lefuel, Louvre palace; Davioud, Place Saint-Michel; Denfer, intersection of the Rue du Bac and the Boulevard Raspail). Most of these roof ornaments have disappeared today. They were usually made of cast iron, not because of its inherent qualities, but because it could substitute for stone and copper. Though never imitated, Vaudremer's church of Saint-Pierre-de-Montrouge was an interesting experiment: all the façades were trimmed with heavy red terra-cotta gutters that contrast sharply with the white stone walls. In 1897 Guimard returned to the cast-iron gutter, which had gone out of fashion, and decorated the gutters on his Castel Béranger building with Japanese-inspired masks.

All these attempts were the result of a city regulation requiring rainwater to be channeled directly into the sewers. The old system of a small projection above the cornice was replaced by wooden gutters clad in lead that carried rainwater from the roof to a drainpipe leading to the sewers. The technique had already been used at Versailles toward the end of the seventeenth century, with the gutters installed behind the façade's balustrade. The same principle was used for the big neoclassical mansions, which often had terrace roofs. In time, the building code required all constructions to have gutters, which were rendered all the more necessary when the development of the recessed top story made it even harder to recover rainwater.

Lead gutters being fragile, cast iron and terra-cotta were tried, but these brittle materials broke too easily during winter freezes. The only really effective material was zinc, which came into widespread use during the Restoration. Lighter and stronger, zinc gutters were adopted throughout Paris. As a result, a new interplay of materials emerged in the 1860s to create a style that could be said to symbolize French and above all Parisian architecture: the combination, and contrast in value, of bluish gray zinc and deep blue slate, highlighted by the orange touch provided by brick chimneys. The attractive harmony of the three primary colors—yellow façades, blue roofs, and red chimneys—was an old discovery (medieval "brick and stone"); however, despite the architecture's apparent severity, it was interpreted with particular refinement in the nineteenth century. When lead and Burgundy tile were replaced by zinc and slate during the last years of Louis-Philippe's reign, a new aesthetic was born. The Second Empire gradually discovered the possibilities of zinc in such stimulating experiments as (to give just one example) Henri Labrouste's Fould mansion.[47] Zinc ornament then became

Terra-cotta gutters on the church of Saint-Pierre-de-Montrouge.

Following pages: **1.** Zinc ridge, 1 Villa Montmorency. **2.** Ornament designs. Illustrations reprinted from *Ornements pour le bâtiment et l'architecture en zinc, cuivre, tôle et plomb* (Paris: Maison Javon et Rivière, Javon et Trocmé successeurs, n.d.). **3.** Castel Béranger, 14 Rue La Fontaine.

197

1

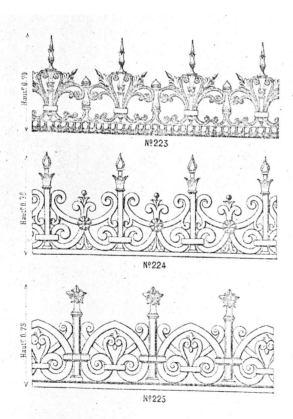

2

Haut⁰ 0.70

N°223

Haut⁰ 0.78

N°224

Haut⁰ 0.73

N°225

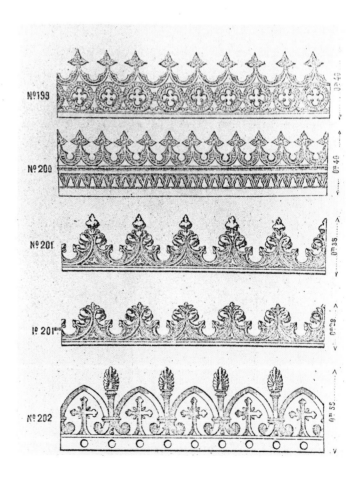

N°199

N° 200

N° 201

I° 201ᵇⁱˢ

N° 202

Façades with decorative brickwork.
1. 35 Avenue de Villiers. **2.** 9 Rue Fortuny.

widespread, culminating at the century's end in an explosion of bull's-eyes, dormer windows, gutters, bibs and balustrades, roof ridges and corners, pinnacles, finials, and air vents.[48]

Decorative Ceramic

Decorative ceramic might seem to have been less popular than it actually was. Indeed, it was so closely associated with brickwork that it tended to blend into it. Polychrome enameled brick was often used to create geometrical patterns on brick façades, emphasizing window openings or sections of the wall. But purely decorative motifs, usually floral designs, were also used to decorate walls and friezes with what look like big petrified flowers. The relationship between the type of glazed ceramic ornament that came into fashion toward the end of the Second Empire and the polychrome neoclassical architecture of, for example, Hittorff cannot be overemphasized.[49] The coloring of the component parts of classical architecture that characterized the early romantic period would seem to have indirectly influenced the industrial production of decorative elements with architectonic uses. This kinship is particularly striking in coffered ceilings and cornice friezes.

Cast Ironwork

If ceramic ornament did not, in the final analysis, enjoy the success it might have, largely because building regulations favored "nobler" materials like stone and slate, the situation was completely different for cast iron. Cast ironwork, which could replace wrought iron at a considerably lower price, enjoyed an extraordinary success throughout the nineteenth century.[50]

Wrought iron was not really used to decorate the plaster façades of Old Paris until the eighteenth century. Before that, a solid parapet appeared under windows. The use of bigger window frames, the popularity of tall windows, and the desire to eliminate the break between inside and out created by such parapets led to the introduction of metal balustrades—transparent screens that ensured people's safety when they leaned out the window while also making larger window openings possible and creating a look of elegance. Rather than French windows on a balcony, which were expensive—a stone balcony had to be built with a watertight seal between the balcony slab and the apartment's parquet floor—a kind of mock French windows became widespread. The opening descended to a little above the baseboard (thirty to forty centimeters above the floor), and outside, a metal balustrade was added to protect the opening.[51] A great help in the dating of buildings, balcony ironwork changed with fashion over the centuries. There were symmetrical volutes of flat iron bars and repoussé metal during the rococo period; powerful square bars with moldings that make them look rather like woodwork during the reign of Louis XVI; and thin graphic lines forming geometrical patterns during the neoclassical period.

Although available since the late eighteenth century, cast iron was not really used in tectonic decoration until the reign of Louis-Philippe. The Arab-style balconies of the prestigious Maison Dorée (Lemaire, 1839) would seem to have established its pedigree.[52] Widespread use of cast-iron ornament brought about a dramatic increase in compositional possibilities. As costs came down, an abundance of new designs appeared. Furnished in posts and sheets, cast-iron elements, which could be combined in a variety of ways, were initially attached to forged frames. The greatest architects—Duc and Labrouste, among others—experimented a good deal with this approach. However, ornamental cast iron really came into its own only with the development of complete moldings in relief. During the reign of Louis-Philippe, these moldings were designed with rich arabesques (foliage and weave patterns) and sometimes included elements in high relief, the most common being a figure in medallion. Ornamental cast iron then eventually spread from the balcony to other parts of the building and was used for stoves, air vents, and doors.

Despite—or perhaps because of—the popularity of cast iron, there was a renewal of interest in wrought ironwork during the Second Empire, and cast-iron elements were again attached to forged iron frames. Repetitive motifs were molded and combined to create a graphic effect resembling wrought iron. It became fairly hard to tell wrought iron and cast iron apart, for the increasingly slender cast-iron designs looked more and more like classic wrought ironwork. The only thing that gave cast iron away was the design's systematic repetitiveness and the absence of any variation.

With the rebirth of architectural grandeur and the monument-alization of the apartment building at the end of the Second Empire, cast-iron ornament did, however, come to look a bit less repetitive.

1

2

3

4

5

6

Ornamental wrought ironwork.

1. 22 Rue de Richelieu. Square bars in the seventeenth-century tradition.

2. 14 Rue de Richelieu. Flat bars in a typically eighteenth-century volute design.

3. 36 Rue de Richelieu. A neoclassical design based on thin bars forming a geometrical pattern.

4. 8 Rue de la Pompe. A Louis-Philippe balcony with a rich volute design inspired by ornamental cast iron.

5. 159-161 Rue Saint-Honoré. A late example (Second Empire) of neoclassical wrought iron on structures modeled after the Rue de Rivoli.

6. 3 Rue de Provence. The cast-iron pieces that make up the balcony of this Restoration building have been replaced by an art nouveau motif in front of the window.

Ornamental cast ironwork

1. 41 Rue de Richelieu. A cast-iron sheet assembled with other elements (shield, edges, balusters), 1840s.

2. 38 Rue de Richelieu. A cast-iron sheet of mediocre quality, around 1840.

3. 75 Rue Madame. A combination of iron bars and cast-iron sheets.

4. 75 Rue Madame. A panel in relief.

5. 38 Rue de Richelieu. Door panels with foliation. The central medallion could be replaced by a high-relief bust of Louis XII or Anne de Bretagne. A typical example of catalogue ornament.

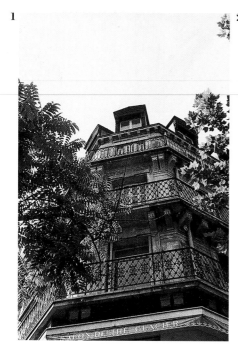

Second Empire balconies.

1. 20 Boulevard Saint-Michel. Continuous balconies with latticework designs.

2. 4 Place Edmond-Rostand. A combination of partial and continuous balconies, made of assembled filigree panels typical of late Haussmann architecture.

3. 16 Boulevard Saint-Michel. The uniform repetition of a symmetrical vertical design.

4. 32 Boulevard Saint-Michel. A rich, if repetitive, design of Louis XIV inspiration.

5. 7-11 Rue Bosio. Balconies and window balconies made of big cast-iron sheets.

6. 43 Rue de Richelieu. A repetitive design on sheets of molded cast iron.

7. 10 Rue de Richelieu. **8.** 77 Rue Madame. **9** and **10.** 2-6 Avenue de l'Opéra. Compositions based on the alternation of filigree sections and motifs in high relief, characteristic of the late Second Empire.

Ornamental ironwork from the 1880s and 1890s.
1. 10 Rue de la Pompe.
2. 5 Place du Théâtre-Français.
3 and **4.** 4 Rue Robert-le-Coin (third and sixth stories).
5. 31 Rue d'Alésia.
6. 65 Rue du Ranelagh.
In the late nineteenth century, cast-iron ornament was of fairly mediocre quality and often had a rather doughy look. Variations on seventeenth-century designs were created by riveting small cast-iron pieces together—another example of the strange nineteenth-century dialogue between craft and industry.

Ornamental cast-iron elements were designed with complementary motifs, so that variants could be created according to how they were combined. Molded pilasters, panels, and center motifs were arranged in highly architectonic ways to reflect the main divisions of the façade, the latter's spacing of solids and voids, and the decorative accents. Detail was often heavier: the thick cast-iron sheets were enriched with shields and medallions in high relief, recalling the style of the 1840s, and purely graphic geometrical patterns were often replaced by stylized floral compositions inspired by classical foliage motifs.

Eventually, cast iron was transformed into a kind of ersatz wrought iron. Since, over the years, wrought iron had continued to be equated with luxury, and since the rationalist school, inspired by medieval wrought ironwork, had designed sectional components that could be assembled to form floral compositions, builders turned to using molded sections and assembling them with rivets and screws—techniques derived from traditional wrought ironwork.

The use of molded sections that could be screwed together in a variety of ways led, in the 1880s, to a jigsaw-puzzle composition. The big molded sheet as such disappeared. All the components were made of cast iron, including the frame. The rigidity of the whole was created by the way the components were assembled into a grid, which created a visual counterpoint to the motif. Thus big molded cast-iron sheets gave way to assemblies of cast-iron sections.

At that point it became practically impossible to tell a wrought-iron from a cast-iron balcony.[53] Only an attentive observer will notice that the cast-iron components are thicker and have not been forged. Forging would have left tool dents and created the kind of slight surface irregularities that traditional craftsmen often exploited for their aesthetic qualities.

At the very end of the nineteenth century, technological progress again transformed the situation. For the same price as cast-iron pieces, one could find steel sections of forgeable quality, which led to a revival of the ironworker's craft. In the early twentieth century, Emile Robert and Victor Prouvé in Nancy, along with Brandt and several others in Paris, exemplified this renaissance of wrought ironwork with some of the most beautiful art nouveau buildings in Paris.[54]

Early-twentieth-century ironwork.
1. 3 Villa Patrice-Boudard. Big Spanish-style balconies molded in a single piece (1914).
2. 1-5, Avenue Mozart. Art nouveau balconies made by assembling cast-iron pieces and iron bars.

1. Rue Alfred-Dehodencq. The curving balconies were created by using flat industrial sections that were then shaped by craftsmen. Art nouveau artists saw this as an updated form of wrought ironwork. **2.** 4 Villa Patrice-Boudard. **3.** 3 Rue Marietta-Martin.

Advances in industrial ironwork were not unrelated to the appearance of big metal-and-glass doors during the post-Haussmann era. **4.** Rue Agar. The influence of art nouveau after 1910.

The Triumph of Typology

The triple evolution in apartment-building construction—the evolution in how the apartment building's shell was built (stone construction modifying the morphology of the façade); the evolution of indoor fittings (with important innovations in sanitary installations, heating, and lighting, plus the advent of the elevator); and the evolution of decoration and trim (transforming both the interior and the exterior physiognomy of constructions)—was accompanied by a fundamental reorganization in apartment layout.[55]

Since the late eighteenth century, buildings had been designed less and less as individual houses; instead, they were divided up to create apartment buildings in which every floor was laid out in nearly the same way. The decisive change came when lots were widened, which, as has been shown, made it possible to build more than one apartment facing the street on each floor. When that happened, the main staircase provided access to two apartments per floor, on either side of a central axis. Toward the end of the nineteenth century, façade width increased still more, along with the depth of buildings; hallways, storage areas, and lavatories were then inserted in the core of the construction. The adoption of an L-shaped building made it possible to place up to three apartments on a single landing. The staircase was then placed in the reentrant angle and was lighted indirectly from the courtyard.

Tradition had established a social and economic hierarchy between apartments facing the street and those built at the back of the courtyard. In the nicest buildings a service staircase behind the main staircase provided access to the less prestigious apartments at the back of the courtyard. Little by little this system led to the development of successive buildings of decreasing prestige in the depth of the lot.

Another important transformation also took place: during the reign of Napoleon III, the number of floors began to increase. An 1859 regulation authorizing an additional main floor on streets over twenty meters wide cleared the way for the classic Haussmann building: five main stories with a basement and a mansard roof. But as things turned out, that was just a beginning. The 1884 and 1902 building codes made it possible to fit two or even three floors into the attic, thanks to the generous volume authorized for roofs. Within a century, the number of floors inside a shell increased by half, but without significantly altering the façade.

Thus the history of the Parisian apartment building is one of an amazing increase in floor space that did not transform the buildings'

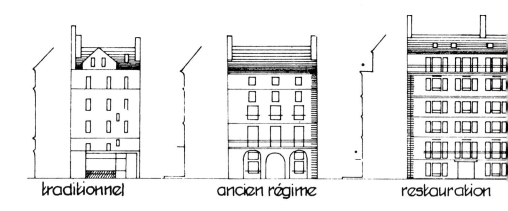

appearance in a shocking or spectacular way. Lots were widened, land filled fuller, and more floors built, but the façades—still governed by the traditional proportions of classical architecture—looked about the same.

The Bottom and the Top

Behind the basically unchanging façades of Paris, there was a major evolution in the inner organization of buildings. Most important, the hierarchy of floors and the use of depth were modified.

Traditionally, a building's third floor had been the most prestigious. The ground floor was for shops, and the mezzanine for the shopkeeper's residence. The third story, some forty or forty-five steps above street level, was the prestige floor—just high enough to be well lighted even in winter, and low enough to be reached without too exhausting a climb. Higher up, tenants paid lower rents, in proportion to the number of steps they had to climb to reach their apartment. Even when it had a large terrace, the sixth floor was far from popular, being too long a climb. Moreover, it was too hot in summer and too cold in winter, and too close to the servants' quarters in the attic, from which it was separated by a fairly thin floor. The last floor, reached only by a service staircase, was partitioned off into tiny, bare rooms seven to nine square meters in size, the servants' floor being treated with an inordinate sense of economy.

Perfected in the 1860s, the elevator eventually made the top of the building the prestigious place to live and thus turned the old hierarchy upside down. Nevertheless, it was a long time before the servants' quarters were moved down to the second floor, so that an apartment could be built on the roof. Henri Sauvage was the first to do so, in the

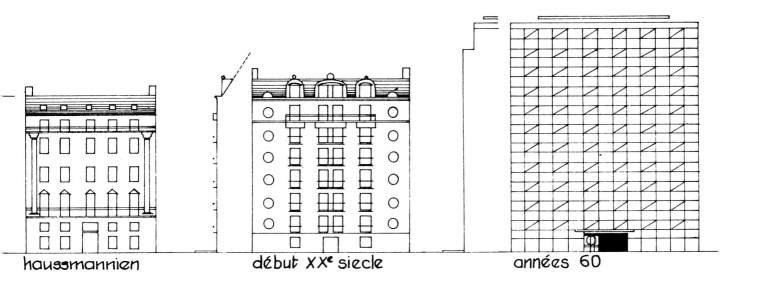

haussmannien   début XXᵉ siecle   années 60

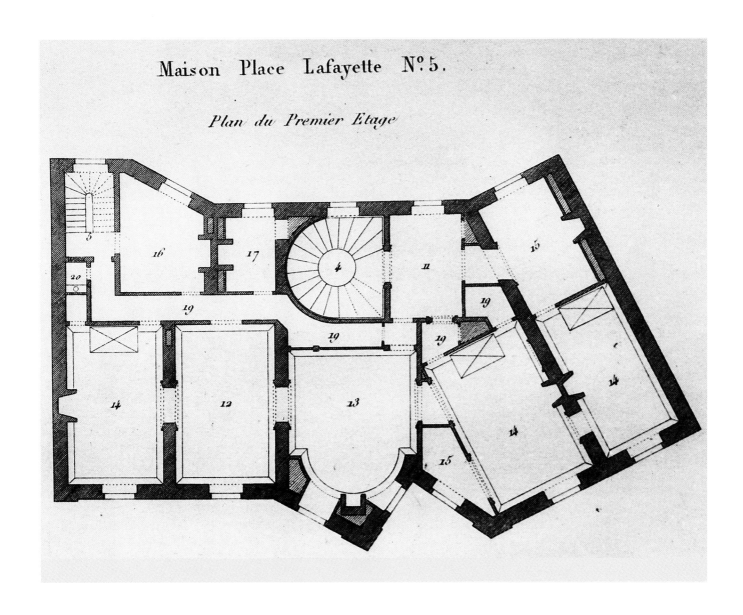

Maison Place Lafayette Nᵒ 5.

Plan du Premier Etage

29 Rue de l'Université. Plan for a third-floor apartment. An early example of a windowless core between an apartment's front and back rooms.

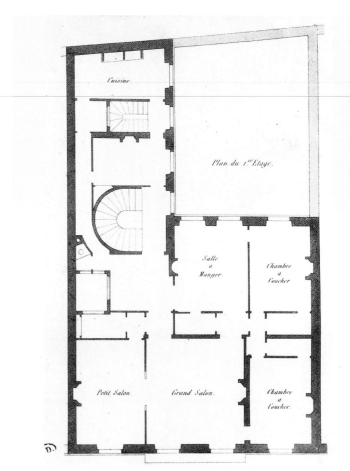

Rue Théodore-de-Banville and Rue Gustave-Flaubert. Plan for the main floors with an enlarged central core, lighted by air wells in the building's sidewalls.

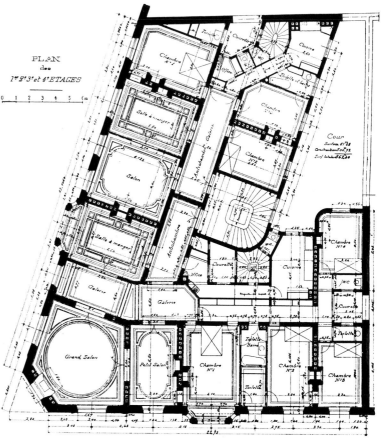

Rue Théodore de Banville

1920s. The elevator was but one influence in this evolution. The growth of automobile traffic, which filled the lower floors with exhaust fumes and noise, was also important. The use of terrace roofs built of reinforced concrete also played a role in modifying the status of the roof, which came to be interpreted as a roof garden. But it took a long time for the old hierarchy to be overturned. For over half a century the third floor's traditional prestige won out over the appeal of the roof terrace, which architects like Hector Horeau had been dreaming of since the Second Empire.[56]

Street and Courtyard

After the Second Empire, a comparable evolution affected the way the depth of lots was used. Traditionally, prestigious apartments had looked out on the street, and only rooms of secondary importance had faced the courtyard. But in the late nineteenth century, while reception rooms continued to be placed on the street, bedrooms and service spaces were moved to the back of the apartment. Increased traffic—in particular, heavy, noisy modes of public transport like the streetcar—explains this move toward the inside of the lot. As a result, the courtyard was architecturally embellished and then adorned with greenery, gradually being transformed into a garden. The inversion of the outside/inside hierarchy is one of the most important aspects of twentieth-century urban architecture. It has lowered the street's status and transformed it into an unwanted space, unworthy of architectural attention.

The Front Rooms

Inextricably linked to the architecture of the building as a whole, apartment layout evolved slowly throughout the nineteenth century. When the apartment appeared in the eighteenth century, it represented a clear break with the traditional house that had prevailed since medieval times. Indeed, its original layout was based not on the bourgeois house but on an aristocratic model. It ignored the traditional combination of an all-purpose common room and a chamber in favor of a row of rooms—a salon, an anteroom, and a bedroom—across the façade.

From Anteroom to Boudoir

Highly influenced by Palladio, the symmetrical floor plans that were used into the midnineteenth century placed a square salon and a square master bedroom of equivalent volume at the front of the apartment, on either side of a narrower anteroom running the depth of the building. When an apartment had a central core, which was used for storage, the "public" rooms were isolated from the domestic functions carried out at the back of the apartment. A very slow evolution—perfectly in keeping with the neoclassical emphasis on a layout's flexibility and practicality—continued through the end of the

213

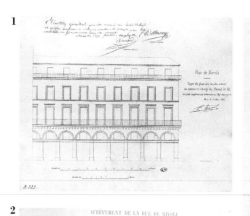

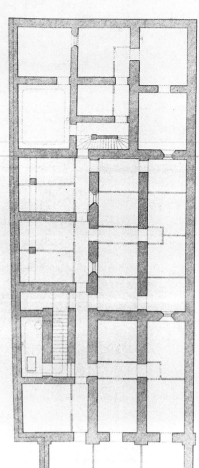

30 Rue de Rivoli, 1823.
1 and **2.** Façade plan for the Rue de Rivoli. From left to right, starting with the upper row: the plans of the building's eight levels, from the cellar to the attic.

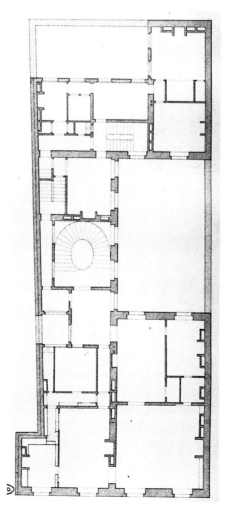

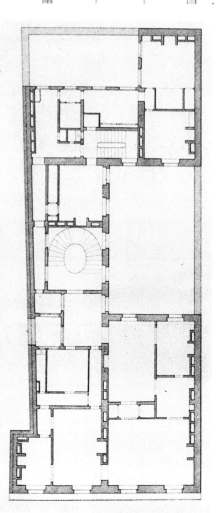

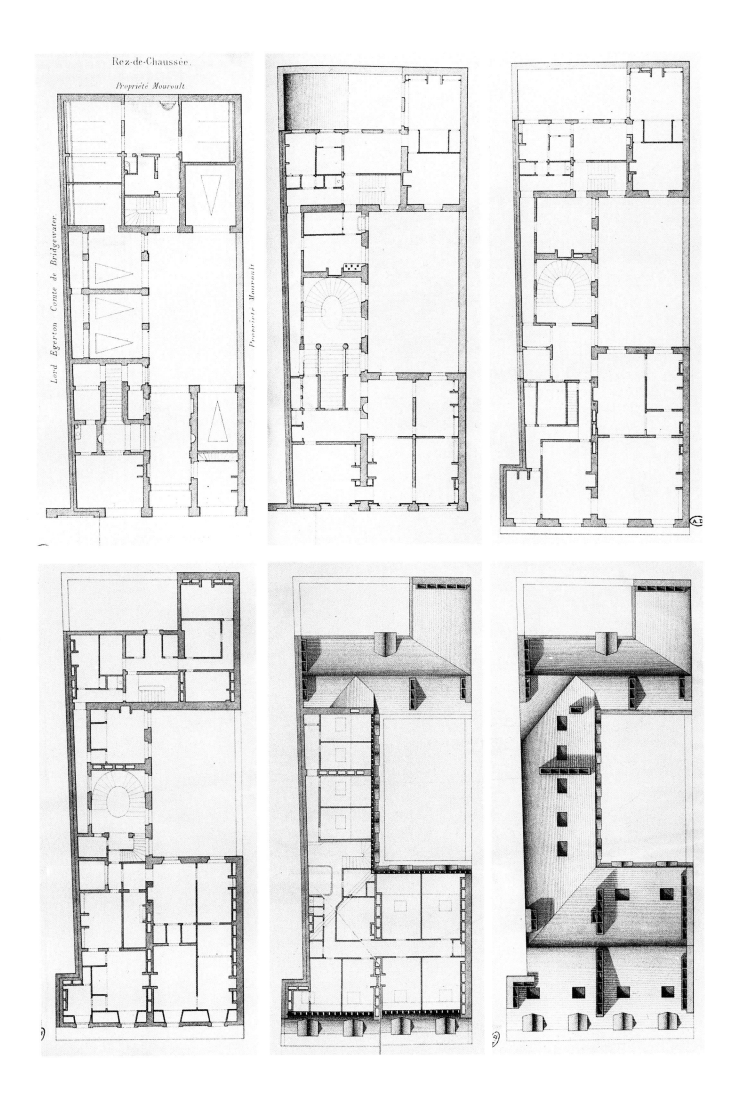

Rez-de-Chaussée.

Propriété Mouroult

Lord Egerton Comte de Bridgewater

Propriété Mouroult

Propriété Mouroult

72 Boulevard de Sébastopol. Plans for the third floor
and the attic (with the servants' rooms).

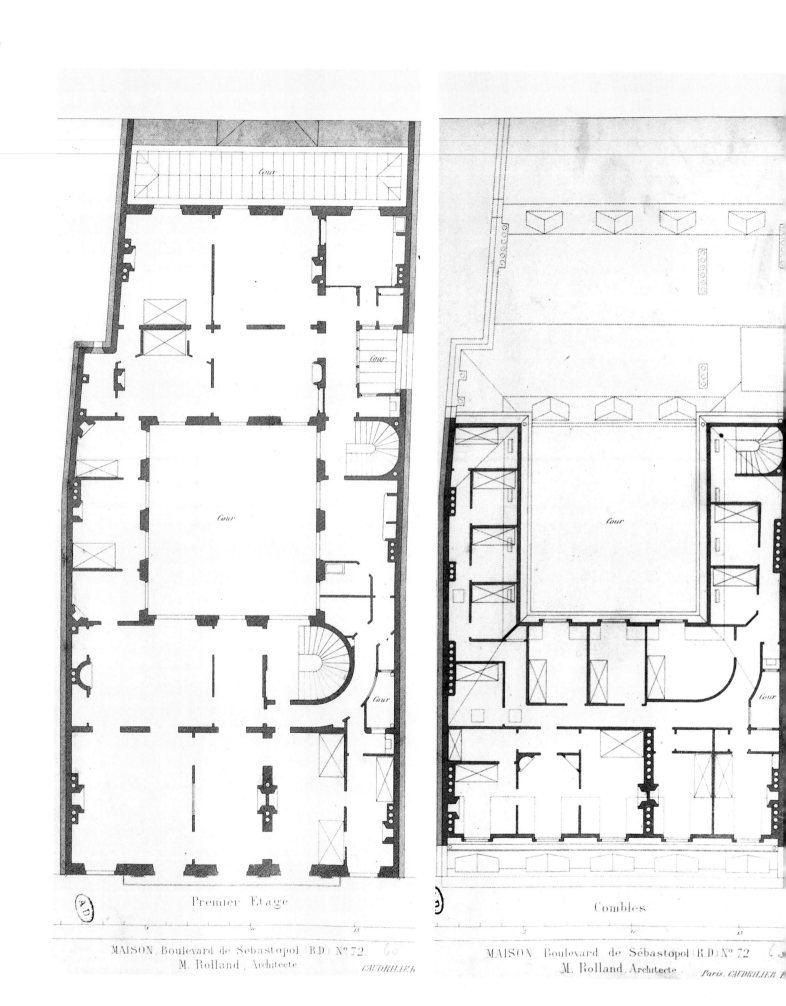

Premier Etage

Combles

MAISON, Boulevard de Sébastopol (R.D.) Nº 72.
M. Rolland, Architecte   CAUDRILIER

MAISON, Boulevard de Sébastopol (R.D.) Nº 72.
M. Rolland, Architecte.   Paris. CAUDRILIER

Second Empire. The floor plan's symmetry lost much of its importance; asymmetrical plans, designed with remarkable talent to create visual sequences and functional zones were used more and more. First seen during the reign of Louis XVI, this approach became widespread toward the end of Louis-Philippe's reign. As a result, the anteroom was replaced by a room that was rather vaguely termed a *cabinet* and that was used in two ways. Since the old custom of having visitors wait in an anteroom to be introduced had fallen out of use, the *cabinet* took on the traditional role of the old dressing rooms—indeed, the washstand and dressing table became the most elaborately decorated furniture in the room. But the *cabinet* was also used as a boudoir, a small sitting room where close friends could be entertained more comfortably than in the big, poorly heated salon.

The Dining Room

When the anteroom as such disappeared, apartment layout became less rigid. The old axes were broken, and the rooms tended to become part of a subtle hierarchy of public and private spaces. The dining room, which had existed in a very ambiguous way since the second half of the seventeenth century, became the center of the layout. For reasons that were initially technical, it was used as both a room and a corridor, especially since its stone or tiled floor—like the entrance hall's—could withstand dirt. Connected to the entrance hall by a large double door, the dining room provided access to the kitchen and pantry and also to the more private reception rooms—the master bedroom and boudoir. Thus it was possible to move about in an apartment without having to go through the main reception rooms.

In the 1840s the relationship between the dining room and the salon began to change. This slow evolution was closely linked to the transformation that removed everyday household concerns (the responsibility of the servants) further and further from family life. An apartment's kitchen and pantry were cut off from the reception rooms, and the dining room became the center of family life. The salon—reserved for official occasions, which were rare in the middle class—was practically abandoned, and its furnishings were protected with dustcovers. Thus, without anyone's really noticing, the old medieval all-purpose room was brought back, though it was no longer used for sleeping or cooking. In the 1880s the salon and dining room faced each other on either side of an entrance hall—the salon on the street, and the dining room on the courtyard; the kitchen was then moved to the very back of the rear wing.

The final stage in the evolution of apartment layout can be understood only in sociological terms. When the bourgeois model became available to the lower middle classes during the late nineteenth century, the dining room was moved from the courtyard again to the façade. The salon opened directly onto the dining room to form a small reception suite (seldom more than about forty square meters) isolated from the bedrooms and kitchen. In families without servants the kitchen, though the tiniest and least decorated room in the apartment, then became the center of family life; paradoxically, the whole family crowded into ten square meters while nearly half of the apartment was reserved for rare special occasions. Even today we are bound by this way of thinking, which, among other things, reveals the importance of the medieval model in our use of interior space.[57]

Day and Night

When the dining room was moved to the front of the apartment and turned into a reception room, the master bedroom was eliminated. During the Second Empire, bedrooms began to be grouped together in a single block. At the far end of the dining room, a discreet small door opened into a hall leading to the bedrooms on the street and the courtyard. There could also be a dressing room, a walk-in closet, or a toilet, all lighted by a well in the party wall. Used as a room and a corridor, the dining room was again given a mixed function. However, there were also layouts with a separate corridor totally independent of the rooms. Although an apartment's bedrooms were still poorly connected to its vestibule, the idea of a totally private night area, as opposed to the daytime area used for social and family interaction, was emerging.

During the Third Republic the block of bedrooms was linked to the entrance hall and was totally cut off from the reception rooms; at best, a little door was left between the dining room and the front bedroom. Then bedrooms were removed from the front of the apartment and put in the wing leading back to the kitchen, the boudoir often being replaced by a dressing room, which was soon fitted out as a bathroom. Finally, the old hierarchy of bedrooms—big and small, for parents and children—disappeared completely. All the bedrooms resembled one another in a humdrum way. The identical treatment of bedrooms shows that the idea of a master, or ceremonial, bedroom had totally disappeared from the French mentality.

Servants' Quarters

The grouping together of bedrooms at the back of the apartment went hand in hand with the transformation of the attic into servants' quarters. That custom began about 1860 in the apartment buildings constructed on the new boulevards (with the twenty-meter height authorized by the 1859 building code). Up to then, a servant's place had been close to his master.[58] Though they often lived in cramped, dark rooms, servants had been in direct contact with family life. Systematic construction of service staircases separated servants and masters into two distinct worlds: one of ceremony, ostentation, and show, and another of hard work and small recompense. The traditional practice of placing a secondary staircase on the courtyard—leading to the kitchens of the big apartments and to the less prestigious residences located behind them—then disappeared completely.[59] Taking up a minimum of space, the service staircase, with iron banisters and white wood steps, became purely utilitarian. It was used by an isolated and enslaved class of servants, delivery boys, and workmen who were allowed to enter only through the back door. Conversely, the main staircase was carpeted and then heated. Later, elevators were installed—for bourgeois tenants and their guests, not for servants or workmen.

The appearance of the servants' floor paralleled the creation of a separate service staircase and at times a service entry. The strict segregation of master and servant in the bourgeois apartment building created an enormous architectural problem. The two traffic networks were completely separate, socially as well as visually—dirty/clean, undecorated/decorated. Outside working hours, the two worlds could not meet. This led to some very odd solutions such as the interpolation, common toward the end of the nineteenth century, of the service staircase between the main staircase and the courtyard. The main staircase was then indirectly lighted through a frosted-glass partition separating it from the service staircase; behind the partitions, servants and workmen were only ghostly shadows.

A building's place in the socioarchitectural hierarchy depended on how the master/servant relationship was manifested in staircase design. In the most prestigious buildings, there were two completely separate staircases. Slightly lower in the hierarchy, the two staircases were built in a common well but were separated by a partition. Lower still, there was only one staircase, but it was decorated to resemble a master's staircase. In the poor man's building all pretense was dropped, and the staircase was treated in a purely functional way.

As the introduction of such modern conveniences as running water, gas, and central heating were making manual work objectively easier, the barriers between social groups were strengthened to the utmost. The servant was pushed out of the master's apartment into a Spartanly furnished room in a poorly insulated attic—a clear indication, were it needed, of the degradation of his social status.[60] The servant's proletarianization, which Emile Zola describes so well, led to the creation of a social microcosm on the servants' floor of Parisian apartment buildings, where small communities lived cut off from the rest of society.

Functionality and Rigidity

The most striking thing about apartment layout, from the late Second Empire until the end of the nineteenth century and beyond, was its rigidity. Whereas space had traditionally been designed so that each volume could be used in a variety of ways, the late nineteenth century turned to a highly monovalent approach: one space, one function. Earlier, a main door and a smaller door had been placed on a landing, for the masters and the servants respectively,[61] or for the main tenant and a secondary tenant; that hierarchy had always been coded in decorative detail, as for instance the quality of the workmanship and the relative richness of the moldings. As each space's function became specialized, such polyvalence was replaced by a uniform treatment for each type of room (dining room, salon, bedroom, etc.): a room's function determined its form, and that form could not be modified.[62]

Nothing could better exemplify the functional transformation of the bourgeois apartment at the end of the Second Empire than the treatment of traffic patterns. Whereas apartments from the 1830s and 1840s had many doors, of various size and design, opening directly from one room into another, the corridor layout gave each room only one door. An apartment's traffic pattern was designed like a tree diagram: each branch was connected to the trunk, but the branches could not be connected to each other. In other words, there was no possibility of adapting a layout to needs other than those provided for initially. Before the advent of the corridor layout, rooms had been arranged in rows and had opened into each other. Thus an apartment could easily be reduced in size or otherwise modified. To make a later reorganization possible, as many rooms as possible had opened directly onto the landing.[63]

From the Second Empire on, certain rooms like the kitchen, the lavatory, and the dressing room/bathroom were fitted out with specialized installations that made it impossible to transform them; moreover, technical constraints like water and gas mains made it impossible to move them. The other rooms were specialized in a rather similar way, their decoration and trim being designed to reflect each room's specific function; one can immediately tell a bedroom, a dining room, and a salon apart. This systematization of floor plan was closely related to the technical standardization imposed by industrial society. In the critical 1870s period, the Haussmann apartment was turned into a completely compartmentalized space. Whereas apartment layout had long allowed the evolution of a tenant's life-style, the rigid plan of the bourgeois apartment began to dictate how tenants could, and should, live. In the end, tenants were simply forced to make do with spaces that no longer corresponded to their way of life. When industrial society began to treat layout and function in a "rational" way, the apartment was turned into a constraining system of architectural and decorative signs, further strengthened by furnishings, fabrics, and even knickknacks.

Floor Space   An ever broader range of apartment sizes appeared in nineteenth-century Paris: the apartments of the rich got bigger and bigger as the apartments of the poor shrank to minuscule proportions. In Charles Garnier's building at 197 Boulevard Saint-Germain, apartments had 423 square meters of floor space, and in Charles Plumet's building at 40 Avenue Victor Hugo, 410 square meters. But in Guimard's building on the Rue Greuze and in Sauvage's on the Rue Hippolyte-Maindron, apartments were respectively only 33 and 32 square meters in size (the Sauvage building was public housing).[64] In the highly vertical society of the early nineteenth century, there was great typological variation: the poor worker's night shelter, the bourgeois apartment, the rich man's mansion. From the Second Empire on, there was obviously much less typological variation; the apartment system prevailed. The expanding middle class advertised its unity by adopting the collective building almost unanimously, even though marked differences in income existed within the bourgeoisie.

It is quite remarkable that the distinction between the various social groups was much less obvious on building façades than in apartment layout. The bourgeoisie wanted to *look* like a single, unified social body and, via public housing, even tried to annex the working-class population to its vision. This explains the decoration, layout, and furniture found in such housing, where residences were designed as miniature bourgeois apartments that in turn, as mentioned earlier, were miniatures of the aristocratic mansion.

From midcentury on, Parisian architects tried to conform to a single model that was seen as a symbol of prestige. In the 1850s the architecture of the apartment building underwent an extraordinary evolution. In one short decade, an entirely new conception emerged: the well-known Haussmann building, which was to dominate the Parisian cityscape from Napoleon III to Albert Lebrun.

NOTES

1. Eugène-Emmanuel Viollet-le-Duc, *Entretiens sur l'architecture* (Paris: V. A. Morel, 1872), vol. 2, p. 297.

2. The fascinating subject of nineteenth-century construction techniques has received little attention. With the exception of Jean Ache's rather superficial analysis in *Acier et architecture* (Paris: Arts et Métiers Graphiques, 1966), nothing resembling a serious study has been done. One can consult Viollet-le-Duc *Entretiens sur l'architecture*, 2 vols. plus an atlas (Paris: V. A. Morel, 1863-72) and the architectural reviews of the day (in particular, César Daly and the *Revue générale de l'architecture et des travaux publics*). My own information is primarily based on another source: a lengthy interview with the architect Jacques Robine, an expert on Paris buildings. This interview of June 21, 1967, made it possible for me to develop a more precise approach to construction in Paris. In many cases a close inspection of buildings has confirmed his valuable information. I wish to thank him here for sharing his knowledge.

3. Additional information on construction techniques can be found in the manuals used by the builders themselves: L. A. Barré, *Petite Encyclopédie pratique du bâtiment* (Paris: E. Besnard & Cie., 1898), as well as the famous series of manuals published by Roret.

4. Marble, in particular, benefited from the development of the transportation system. Charles Garnier, one of marble's greatest advocates, made an official government study on French marble and devoted a long chapter to the subject in *A travers les arts* (Paris: Hachette, 1869)—pp. 141-54 in the Picard edition, Paris, 1985.

5. Use of heavy construction equipment brought changes, but not until the early twentieth century. Henri Sauvage was one of the first Frenchmen to use construction machinery, for the Majorelle building on the Rue de Provence in 1910. The machines —cranes and jackhammers—came from the United States. For further information see F. Chanut, "Communication sur les conditions économiques et financières qui ont conduit les Américains à leurs procédés actuels de construction et sur les difficultés d'application de ces mêmes procédés aux conditions

européennes," in *Architecture*, Paris, vol. 42, no. 9 (1929), 293-309. But the industrialization of the construction site really took place after World War II, when prefabrication was developed in France and the Soviet Union.

6. Pierre Saddy, who like Henri Bresler is particularly interested in the history of nineteenth-century architecture in Paris, has studied the masonry companies in Paris and shown how the huge stonecutting workshops were organized to mass-produce the construction materials needed to build the façades of Paris. The concentration of labor was a key phase in the industrialization of the building trade and was already under way in the nineteenth century.

7. The blocks were so big and heavy that they were extremely difficult to transport. An eyewitness once told me that, during his youth, there were always horses for rent at the bottom of the Boulevard Saint-Michel, ready to help the heaviest loads make it up the slope. Viollet-le-Duc (*Entretiens*, vol. 2, p. 319) mentions the city requirement that stone walls be at least fifty centimeters thick, which is considerable for perpend construction. Less stone could have been used.

8. See Alain Michaud, "Les Maisons parisiennes dites de structure médiévale," in *Bulletin d'information*, nos. 33-34 (Nov.-Dec. 1974), published by the Association pour la Sauvegarde et la Mise en Valeur du Paris Historique.

9. The railroad radically transformed the way lumber was transported and used. Traditionally, logs had been floated into Paris. Cut in the springtime, wood arrived in Paris in the fall, and was left for two winters to dry before being used. Perceived as an advantage, the railroad's rapidity led to the abandonment of the old system. Builders then began to use green timber, which resulted in rotting and termite infestation. It took some thirty years for the disastrous consequences of rail transport to be perceived, then corrected by waiting for the sap to fall before cutting down trees. This development certainly hastened the elimination of wood as a structural material. Some of the wood buildings built between 1840 and 1870 are today in very poor condition.

10. During the Second Republic, accord-

ing to Jacques Robine. According to Jean Ache (*Acier et architecture*, p. 21), "in 1840, carpenters had the smart idea of going on strike, and a fearsome strike it was. A carpenter was no longer to be found anywhere. Up to that time, iron floors—made of extremely complicated and expensive components—had been used only in several public monuments. The need to get along without carpenters brought about a concerted effort to replace wood floors with iron ones. Builders pondered. They used iron girders placed edgewise (with plaster or a mixture of plaster and terra-cotta). Then several factories began manufacturing double T-girders, and the problem of the iron floor was momentarily solved. More expensive at first, metal floors soon cost no more than wooden ones, thanks to the savings they allowed on certain masonry elements and the rapidity with which they could be installed. Today, only iron floors are found in Paris."

11. They were almost immediately improved, as the thick shape of the railroad track, designed to carry very heavy loads, gave way to a thinner I-beam. Later, progress in laminating led to the birth of slender I-beams with wider "wings" on the top and bottom (made of steel rather than iron after 1900). Influenced by shipbuilding and the Chicago skyscrapers, builders then began using riveted steel frames.

12. Most historians of nineteenth-century architecture, notably Giedion and Francastel, seem, in their enthusiasm for metal construction, to have totally overlooked the economic problem that it created, as well as the problem of heat insulation. Even as late as 1872, Viollet-le-Duc wrote (*Entretiens*, vol. 2, pp. 323-24): "Iron construction is said to be expensive. That is debatable. It is expensive when builders, not knowing how to use it, overuse it, as is the case for more than one government building I can think of." Implicitly, Viollet-le-Duc here admits that iron construction *is* expensive. All-metal construction did not become competitive in price until the 1890s, just as reinforced concrete, much more economical, was on the verge of making metal construction obsolete.

13. The floors in the Bibliothèque Sainte-Geneviève (the successive projects were shown in the 1975 Henri Labrouste exhibi-

tion) are discussed by Pierre Saddy in "Labrouste, architecte-constructeur," *Revue des monuments historiques*, no. 6 (1975), pp. 10-17. Unfortunately, Saddy's modest contribution gives no technical details and does not discuss the role played by bridge construction, in relation to Bruyère's publications. The delicate problem of the rigidity of all-iron structures and the obvious problem of bracing them are implicitly evoked by Viollet-le-Duc for post-and-beam structures (*Entretiens*, vol. 2, p. 326). Indeed, this could be seen as the most important problem from 1840 to 1870, when either a heavy masonry envelope or steel bracing (e.g., in the Paris train stations and Baltard's Halles) had to be used.

14. The combination of cast-iron components with steel bracing to prevent beams and trusses from sagging was a specialty of French engineers. In other European countries rigid constructions made entirely out of cast iron were generally used. This was also the case for the huge spire Alavoine constructed on the Rouen cathedral in 1820. Viollet-le-Duc sarcastically predicted that one day it would begin to "rain rust" and "hail nuts and bolts" around the cathedral. That has not happened yet, but the structure is badly cracked. A parallel can be drawn between the combined use of cast iron and steel and the stonework of thirteenth-century cathedrals (revealed by Viollet-le-Duc); reinforced concrete could also be seen as an example of such a dialectical structure.

15. Closer study of Second Empire publications would shed additional light on this feature, which made it possible to open up the shops on the ground floor with big windows. Viollet-le-Duc devotes an interesting paragraph (*Entretiens*, vol. 2, p. 322) to the use of metal lintels, to replace the combination of a cast-iron beam and wooden posts.

16. Viollet-le-Duc, *Entretiens*, vol. 2, pp. 327-34 and plate XXXVI in the atlas. This text, published in 1872, was contemporary with the Noisiel factory (which is referred to on p. 334). Some critics have suspected that Viollet-le-Duc, taken by surprise by this new development, tried to take some of the credit. If we consider the examples in the text, the second volume seems to have been written just after 1870 (there are numerous

references to the 1867 fair, as well as various observations on the havoc wrought by the Communards—most notably, the destruction of the Tuileries and the Pavillon de Flore). Saulnier's building is mentioned in a note that seems to have been added to a text already finished.

This was a critical period, for progress in laminating had suddenly made sheet metal available at prices comparable to those of molded cast iron. Viollet-le-Duc writes (p. 327): "After early attempts, it was quickly noticed that cast iron has various drawbacks when combined with laminated iron, and that sheet metal, when used intelligently, is safer and makes much sturdier assemblies possible." This sentence contains the seeds of the principle of the steel frame. Plate XXXVI, the last in the volume, is the only illustration, while all the other projects (notably plates XXI and XXIV in the second volume, from 1872) show molded cast-iron components with laminated sheet metal elements (see in particular p. 72, based on the vaults of Saint-Denis de l'Estrée).

The project in Chapter 18 seems to have been forming in Viollet-le-Duc's mind at the same time as Saulnier's project for Noisiel. Both dramatically foreshadow the Chicago school.

17. For further information, see the catalogue for the Archives de l'Architecture Moderne exhibition on Henri Sauvage (Paris: S.A.D.G., 1976). The best general discussion of metal construction in Paris remains Bernard Marey and Paul Chemetov, *Architectures, Paris, 1848-1914* (Paris: C.N.M.H.S., n.d. [1976]).

18. The use of pine instead of oak was directly linked to the railroad. Northern pine, imported from Finland, could have been transported on the Seine. Before the railroad, however, it was much faster and easier to float wood into Paris from the Langres Plateau.

19. Siegfried Giedion analyzed this technology and its place in the history of industrial architecture very intelligently in *Space, Time and Architecture* (Cambridge, Mass.: Harvard University Press, 1941). The Delorme-style roof, rediscovered by Legrand and Molinos and used for the Halle au Blé during the reign of Louis XVI, did not enjoy

the success it might have. Though it considerably lightened the structure while also allowing much greater spans, there were corrosion problems in the train stations and industrial warehouses it seemed so perfect for. Mark K. Deming, *La Halle au blé de Paris, 1762-1813* (Brussels: A.A.M., 1985), pp. 175-97, is the most recent discussion.

20. To date, the cost of construction has received little attention from art historians. The subject is virgin ground and perhaps will one day tempt historians of science and industry.

21. Viollet-le-Duc, vol. 2, pp. 334 ff.

22. Terra-cotta, zinc, and staff were primarily responsible for the technological changes and resulting transformation of ornament (see Viollet-le-Duc, vol. 2, p. 334).

23. The Jacques Cœur house (early fifteenth century) seems to be the only medieval monument in Paris where this was used. The discovery of the house at 40 Rue des Archives greatly modified theories on the origins of "brick and stone." The current building is the result of a radical renovation in the eighteenth century; at that time, the old facing was concealed under a coating, and the window openings were moved.

A few rare edifices in Paris reflect the vogue of "brick and stone" in the eighteenth-century Ile-de-France: the Place Dauphine and the king's and queen's pavilions on the Place des Vosges are among the best examples. It is interesting to note that all the other houses on the Place des Vosges received mock stonework façades (coated wood), in order to cut down on costs.

24. The technique is explained by Hassan Fathy in *Construire avec le peuple* (Paris: Jérôme Martineau, 1970).

25. Like the studios that have been transformed into the Bourdelle Museum, Brancusi's studio near the Centre Beaubourg (renovated at great expense) is a typical example of a workshop with iron siding.

26. J. Lacroux's *La Brique ordinaire* (Paris: Ducher, 1878), with seventy-five color plates, is stunning proof of this fascination with brick.

27. *L'Ecole primaire à Paris, 1870-1914*, catalogue for the exhibition organized by the Délégation à l'Action Artistique de la Ville de Paris, edited by Anne-Marie de Châtelet, Paris, 1985.

28. The transformations that affected fittings and trim, which were even more spectacular than those affecting the shell, have scarcely been studied to date, with the exception of Henri Sauvage's attempt between World Wars I and II to do a brief history of contemporary technology (more on this later). Whereas the evolution of construction techniques for the shell has been studied, albeit often superficially, nothing of note has been done on how industry completely changed notions of hygiene, comfort, and convenience. That is unquestionably a vast subject and involves architectural history proper as well as the history of technology. R. H. Guerrand is now working in this area. We can only hope that more research will follow.

29. P. Ardenni, *Nouveau Manuel complet du poêlier fumiste ou traité complet de cet art indiquant les moyens d'empêcher les cheminées de fumer* (Paris: Roret, 1850). Technical progress in this area can be measured by comparing Ardenni with J. Denfer, *Fumisterie, chauffage et ventilation*, Encyclopédie des Travaux Publics (Paris: Baudry & Cie., 1896). Denfer's very complete work deals with apartment fireplaces, stoves, ovens, central heating, steam heat, and hot-water heat. The techniques Denfer describes concerning hot-water heat had not yet been fully worked out.

30. Louis Gilbert, *Le Marbrier* (Paris: A. Morel, 1860, 1886), and A. Sanguineti, *La Marbrerie au XIXe siècle. Cheminées, comptoirs, autels, bénitiers, tombeaux, etc.* (Paris: E. V. Camis, n.d. [1863?]), are important sources. But one should not overlook the marblers' catalogues, though these are extremely hard to procure.

31. The kitchen and dining room soon became the two heated rooms in the house, the former used by the servants and the latter by their masters. In early public housing the Prussian fireplace in the dining room was systematically dissociated from the cooking stove in the kitchen. This specialization of functions reflects the fact that the kitchen was no longer seen as a family gathering place (a traditional all-purpose common room, it had been used for a variety of functions).

32. Until the midtwentieth century, building regulations required a flue for every inhabitable room. The value of such a requirement became painfully obvious during the coal shortages of World War II, when modern, centrally heated buildings became uninhabitable, and stovepipes had to be stuck out windows. Heating on a room-by-room basis is much cheaper than central heating.

33. Emile Zola was very aware of the spectacular evolution of comfort and convenience in Paris apartment buildings and makes frequent reference to it in *Pot-Bouille*. Indeed, the novel starts with an evocation of central heating (p. 9 in the Livre de Poche edition, Paris, 1957):

> But what most struck Octave when he walked in was the greenhouse heat, warm air that a vent blew into his face.
>
> "How about that!" he said. "Is the staircase heated?"
>
> "Probably," Campardon answered. "Nowadays all self-respecting landlords lay out the money for it."

Real central heating appeared fairly late with the invention of steam heat, derived from the principle of the steam turbines used in shipbuilding. This was later replaced by less dangerous hot-water heat. But this evolution did not begin until the twentieth century. Hot-air vents were then replaced by cast-iron radiators.

34. In his *Mémoires*, Haussmann speaks about drinking water at some length. At the time there was a strong prejudice, shared by the medical profession, against spring water, which was thought to be bad for the digestive tract. River water was preferred. But industry and the city had so polluted the Seine that there had to be a change of attitude. Even so, Haussmann had a hard time getting Parisians to accept spring water.

35. Further details can be found in Roger-Henri Guerrand's brilliant study *Les Lieux. Histoire des commodités* (Paris: La Découverte, 1985; see note 28 above), and in his contribution to the catalogue for the Seventeenth Milan Triennial, *Il progetto domestico* (Milan: Electa, 1986), pp. 168-71 ("1883: la rivoluzione dello sciacquone in Francia").

36. This description is based on the installations in the apartment I lived in during the 1950s, at 16 Rue Nicolo in the sixteenth arrondissement. The building dated from 1893. All the bathrooms were identical. They were located in the building's core and were lighted indirectly through the bedroom, which opened onto the courtyard. They had wood floors, plaster ceilings, and papered walls. A ceramic tank on the wall provided water for a drainless washstand made of wood, marble, and earthenware.

37. Henri Sauvage presented a short history of bathroom technology in his article on the rental building, "Les Progrès de l'hygiène et du confort depuis le Moyen Age jusqu'à nos jours," *L'Illustration*, March 30, 1929, pp. 38-43. It is an extremely valuable document.

38. Giedion, *Space, Time and Architecture*.

39. Notably Hector Horeau, who mentions this several times, especially in *Edilite urbaine* (Paris: Morel, 1867).

40. The primary sources include, in particular, Buvy, *Modèles de menuiseries choisis parmi ce que Paris offre de plus nouveau, de plus remarquable* . . . (Paris: Bance, 1875), and Léon Jamin, *L'Enseignement professionnel du menuisier* (Dourdan: Henri Vial, 1897). On the subject of the carriage entrance, see Agnès-Dominique Pacaud's master's thesis, directed by Jean Laude, University of Paris I, 1982. The subject is vast; much work remains to be done. See also Jean-Charles Krafft's handsome album *Portes cochères, portes d'entrée, croisées, balcons, entablements et détails de menuiserie et de serrurerie* (Paris: J. L. Scharff, 1810) for the link between the Haussmann period and the neoclassical period.

41. Michel Vernhes, who teaches at the Ecole d'Architecture de Paris-La Villette, is working on this question, which has yet to be fully explored.

42. At Courson the wainscoting in the main salon was enriched. But the new decoration also overflowed onto the stone façades. Such exterior use on a stone construction was the exception to the rule; on the other hand, it was common on plastered façades. Unfortunately, the decoration of plaster façades was eliminated when the façades were replastered.

43. Although no historical study has been done, the methods used are described in Claude-Charles Toussaint, *Nouveau Manuel complet du maçon, du stuccateur, du carreleur et du paveur traitant de l'emploi des matières servant à la construction des bâtiments de ville et de campagne* (Paris: Roret, 1882), and in Théodore Chabeau, *Technologie du bâtiment ou étude complète des matériaux de toute espèce* (Paris: Ducher, 1882). The beginning of the Third Republic saw a rash of publications on the technical and artistic innovations of the Second Empire.

44. This supposition, though very likely, needs to be confirmed by a more detailed study of the reproduction techniques used by the sculptors who did the actual carving. Such artists as Falguière and Carpeaux created clay models but thought it beneath them to carve the stone themselves; the carving was done by specialists working under their supervision.

45. One of the best descriptions of interiors at the end of the Second Empire can be found in E. Daubourg, *L'Architecture intérieure, portes, vestibules, escaliers, antichambres, salons, salles à manger, etc.* (Paris: J. Baudry, 1876). Numerous illustrations can also be found in the architectural reviews of the day.

46. Christian Derouet, "Architecture d'hier: grandes demeures angevines au XIXe siècle. L'œuvre de René Hodé, 1840-1870," in *Les Monuments historiques de la France*, pp. 49-64. (The article served as the catalogue for an exhibition in Angers and Paris.) See also François Loyer, "René Hodé: le néo-gothique 'troubadour' en Anjou," in *Arts de l'ouest* 1 (1978) 37-44.

47. Does this mean that Labrouste and the Fould mansion were responsible for bringing stone and brick back into fashion? In any case, brick did come back into fashion at this time. Duban's restoration of Blois also helped renew interest in stone-and-brick architecture.

48. J. Miltgen, *Ornements estampés et repoussés. Zinc, cuivre, plomb* (Paris, 1886). Here, too, the manufacturers' catalogues are an invaluable source.

49. The use of color, as Hittorff conceived it, was tinged with rationalism (doubt-

less in a less systematic way than in Labrouste); see David Van Zanten, *The Architectural Polychromy of the 1830's* (New York, 1977).

This approach to color dominated French architecture for a long time. Color was not freed from structure until the art nouveau period and the use of enameled ceramic. However, Viollet-le-Duc had already evoked the possibility during the Second Empire (at Pierrefonds and in the article on "painting" in the *Dictionnaire raisonné de l'architecture*) when, based on an analysis of medieval edifices, he worked out the notion of decorative painting.

50. Fascinatingly rich, cast-iron decoration has been studied by the specialists. A bit superficial but abundantly illustrated, E. Graeme Robertson and Joan Robertson's *Cast Iron Decoration: A World Survey* (London: Thames & Hudson, 1977) was followed by François Chaslin's very complete *Les Fontes ornées ou l'architecture de catalogue* (Paris: E.N.S.B.A., C.E.R.A., 1978). In addition to the many manufacturers' catalogues, one can also consult François Husson, *L'Architecture ferronnière (grilles, balcons, ferrures, marquises d'après les travaux de Ballu, Duban, etc.)* (Paris: A. Lévy, 1873); *Les Métaux œuvrés (balcons, rampes d'escalier, marquises, grilles, portes, serrureries, etc.)* (Paris: Storck, 1885); and *Motifs de serrurerie extraits de publications diverses* (Paris: Morel, 1874).

51. This had a very positive effect indoors, for it made it possible to place the window opening far below the ceiling, thus creating a well-lighted lower area while eliminating the glare of sunlight on a white ceiling. (The use of plaster ceilings and lower window openings are closely related.) When a window was open, one enjoyed direct visual contact with the street even when seated, and could lean out the window without danger.

52. Cast iron of course had to be cast. All the ornament on the Maison Dorée was in cast iron; if not the prototype of cast-iron decoration, this edifice is certainly one of the most dazzling examples of it. Unfortunately, the renovation of the Maison Dorée has since turned it into a mere façade. As in all the architectural production of the day, a mixed technique was used to decorate the building. The frames were forged, and molded plates with cut-out motifs were screwed between the uprights. The front of each panel was in relief; the back was simply the negative of the front. To vary combinations, background panels were combined with various borders and center medallions. The pilaster theme was expressed by geminated uprights linked by a narrow panel, alternating with wide rectangular panels with axial motifs.

53. When molded sheets were abandoned for sections that could be joined together with bolts or rivets, it became possible to imitate all the forms of traditional ironwork, especially the skillfully wrought iron of the eighteenth century, of which many close copies can be found on the façades of late-nineteenth-century buildings. The only difference is that use of molded pieces allowed no individual variations; hence it is a different art.

54. While Parisian architects were turning steel into a marvelous decorative material (e.g., the balcony ironwork on the Boulevard Raspail), Americans were using it to build skyscrapers in Chicago. The comparison shows how totally separated the two cultures were and how different their respective outlooks—the French decorative, the American technical.

55. This issue could not be treated at great length in the present study, which focuses on the building as an element in the cityscape. Given the rich documentation found in architectural reviews, the question could be easily studied, which would doubtless increase our knowledge of the social structure and life-styles of nineteenth-century Paris. The pages that follow are closely based on my article "L'appartamento haussmanniano," in *Il progetto domestico*, catalogue for the Seventeenth Milan Triennial (Milan: Electa, 1986), vol. 1, pp. 120-27.

56. Hector Horeau has been mentioned in passing. His roof terrace is found in the 1868 Infiorata project (*Hector Horeau*, pp. 120-22).

57. The present-day trend toward what the French call an "American kitchen," which is none other than the traditional all-purpose common room, reveals how deeply the medieval model has influenced the entire

Western world. Today, the French are simply reimporting the model they exported to America.

58. The separation of the master's apartment and the servant's room seems to go back to the 1830s for buildings of middle standing. (In 1839 it already existed in the building at 44 Rue de Provence.) However, in luxurious Second Empire buildings, there was always a servant's room in the apartment itself. Doubtless there was more than one kind of servant's room: one in the garret for temporary help and servants of lower rank; one room in the apartment for chambermaids.

59. Though frequent before 1840, the custom of putting an office near the kitchen (i.e., on the back staircase, which implied that one received one's inferiors there) disappeared. Workplace and residence began to be separated from each other. The century's end saw the appearance of the office building, a specific construction given over entirely to work. Of the many dissociations that occurred in the nineteenth century, that of home and work is one of the most important.

60. The location of servants' rooms in the attic after 1860 reveals the evolution of the servant's status and the beginning of his autonomy as regards family life. However, it was at least another generation before the servant stopped being considered, at least a little, as part of the family.

61. One excellent example is the luxurious building—very narrow, because of the lot—located at 1 Rue de la Planche in the seventh arrondissement. Though built relatively late, about 1880, it is a fine example of the architectural hierarchy of entrances.

62. This effort at rationalization eventually led to functionalism, as an architectural and decorative system. The failure of functionalism can be attributed to the inadaptability of spaces designed in terms of specific functions. For industry, we know that a big, regularly lighted space (obstructed with as few posts as possible) is the most appropriate kind of construction. In housing, flexibility of layout and low functional specificity guarantee adaptation. On the other hand, movable partitions are totally useless. Experience has shown how deeply rooted traditional spatial models are. In Marcel Lode's experimental apartments at La Grand' Mare in Rouen, in the 1960s, tenants consistently arranged the movable partitions to form the most ordinary three- or four-room apartment.

63. Up to three doors opened onto the landing of a four-room apartment, making it possible to enter through the bedroom, the entrance hall, or the kitchen. In apartments with a core of rooms between the front and back rows of rooms, several traffic patterns existed: the corridor could be paralleled by doors linking the core rooms together, and those rooms in turn might contain one or more doors opening onto the corridor.

64. The examples quoted were studied by Claudette Guérin and Antoine Mistretta for their architecture diploma: "Essai sur le logement collectif parisien de 1875 à 1927," thesis, Paris, E.N.S.B.A., 1976.

Aerial photo of the Place des Ternes. Police photo.

Baron Haussmann.

Chapter IV

The Transformation of Paris during the Second Empire

The coup d'état of December 2, 1851, marked the beginning of a new era in the architectural and urban history of Paris. Napoleon III was determined to bring about the transformation of Paris that the city's residents wanted and the country's economic, technical, and social evolution necessitated. When he came to power, the president-prince was immediately faced with the urbanistic problems that his predecessors had left behind: the Rue de Rivoli, the Boulevard de Strasbourg, and the reorganization of the Halles. He began on two fronts. The "great crossroads of Paris" at the Place du Châtelet was to link the east-west axis formed by the Rue de Rivoli to the north-south axis formed by the Boulevard de Strasbourg and the Boulevard de Sébastopol. On the Left Bank, traffic was to be improved by building a new street halfway up the Sainte-Geneviève slopes, in the heart of the Latin Quarter. The emperor soon learned that the French think small: the Rue des Ecoles in no way corresponded to his great vision. He also discovered the thorny problems created by urban topography and, in particular, the insoluble question of how to level out the city's streets without destroying its vistas. Yet when Napoleon III asked Georges-Eugène Haussmann[1] to take charge of his great urban project, he was confident that Paris could and would be transformed.

A Great Urban Project

The man Napoleon III picked to carry out his plans was a man of action as loyal as he was efficient. The emperor counted on Haussmann to turn his vision of the city's future into concrete reality. That vision was unmistakably big, involving much more than a few new streets (most of them in the planning stage since the Revolution) or a few prestigious monuments like the wings joining the Louvre and the Tuileries. Inspired by the example of London, the emperor wanted to redo the city completely. Gardens, parks, and tree-lined streets were to be woven into the city's regular rows of façades, as done on English squares during the Georgian period.[2] Napoleon III saw this new typology as a way of solving the social problems of his day. The physical transformation of the city was unquestionably part of the emperor's project for social reform—indeed, it was its touchstone.

Over a period of twenty years—in two very different stages, one before and one after 1860, corresponding fairly closely to the political history of the regime—Napoleon III orchestrated the radical transformation that in so many ways created the city we know today. The crowning achievement of a flourishing industrial society, the Paris of the Second Empire attempted to reconcile social reform and economic growth within a single urban space. True to classical tradition, the city ignored zoning, struggled against the segregation of the social classes, and made a concerted effort to beautify public spaces. Rather than repudiate the new socioeconomic order or pretend it did not exist, the city endeavored to tame industrial society by integrating it into a broader cultural vision.

The City and Its Parts

Unlike the neoclassical vision, Napoleon III's vision of urban reorganization was not utopian but pragmatic. It was based on adapting to concrete situations and economic reality in order to find a "basic vocabulary" that could be repeated throughout the city. Thus Second-Empire Paris became one of the most coherent cities imaginable. The instruments used to transform the city were simple. The point of departure was a definite architectural type—the Haussmann apartment building—combined with very comprehensive building regulations that structured the city's component parts into a clear hierarchy. Individual buildings were always subservient to the public space they depended on. The strength of the Haussmann approach was to use the traditional elements of the urban hierarchy to create an extremely clear structure that informed people immediately of exactly where they were in the city. If Paris did not become sprawling and overgrown, it is because the vast, expanding city was structured by means of a hierarchy of edifices and a no less elaborate hierarchy of empty spaces (streets, avenues, intersections, and squares). The city was redesigned so that each of its parts would constantly refer back to the whole—the building to the street, the street to the neighborhood, and the neighborhood to the city.

Most cities, being the result of contradictory intentions and plans, wind up looking like unfinished projects. Guided by a clear and comprehensive urban system, Haussmann simply erased the incoherent city that Paris had become. While he destroyed much of Old Paris by gutting entire districts and leaving no more than stumps of the city's historical heritage (for which he was severely criticized in later years), he also eliminated the impression of incoherency created by the divergence of earlier projects and typologies and emphasized the city as a coherent whole. If Paris did, in some ways, remain a mosaic of urban fragments (the mosaic that classicism had fought against in vain), it also became the most coherent city in Europe. During the Haussmann era there was an astonishingly strong consensus about how the city should be organized. Haussmann reorganized Paris by reorganizing its component parts—its buildings, streets, and neighborhoods—at a time when industrial technology was drastically changing the way things had been done for centuries. An era of extraordinary technical, social, and urban change, the Second Empire was also a cultural epoch of great importance. Copied and admired, the Paris of Napoleon III remained the world's model capital for nearly a century.

A Style of Grandeur

The birth of the Haussmann building was so closely related to advances in technology and industry that the two issues must be treated simultaneously. The customary distinction between the Louis-Philippe building and the Haussmann building proper, as already noted, must be understood in technical rather than purely chronological terms. An expression of traditional building techniques, the plaster façade gradually disappeared; by the beginning of the Third Republic, it was being used only for the most modest constructions in outlying districts. In the course of this slow decline, the decoration of plaster façades became increasingly unoriginal; the delightfully exuberant neoclassical ornament used during Louis-Philippe's reign was replaced by depressingly trite moldings and window frames with fesses.

Conversely stone construction, still rare and prestigious at the beginning of the Restoration, became widespread, while its decoration, quite elementary at first, became more complicated and abundant. In retrospect, early stone façades—with their graphic moldings, big, bare walls, and overall simplicity—seem most austere; indeed, they rather remind one of the late plaster façades just described.

Thus there was a slow evolution from decorated to undecorated plaster façades, and from undecorated to decorated stone façades. At the beginning of Louis-Philippe's reign, plaster and stone façades were decorated in approximately the same way; indeed, when a façade has been painted over, it is hard to say whether one is looking at a stone or a plaster construction. Louis-Philippe architecture was a paradise of ornament. After a century of severity, decorative fancy burst forth, and the types of decoration that had been common for interiors since early neoclassicism were transposed onto façades. The real break between the Rambuteau building and the Haussmann building took place, as noted earlier, around 1840-42. Buildings from the end of Louis-Philippe's reign are hard to tell apart from early Second Empire buildings. As the new type emerged, and builders adopted industrial techniques, ornamental richness declined. Façades became more regular and severe. Simultaneously, new streets were being built. By the end of Louis-Philippe's reign, Paris was ready for Haussmann.

Chronology
of the Haussmann Era

Plaster façades in a poor neighborhood. Rue des Panoyaux. Postcard.

233

This spirit of regularity and unity was maintained throughout the Second Empire, but not without significant modifications. One need only compare the two halves of the old Boulevard de Sébastopol (the present-day Boulevard de Sébastopol and the Boulevard Saint-Michel,

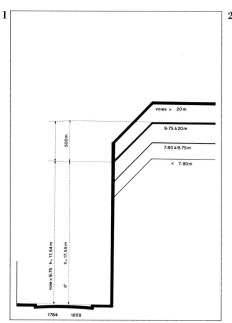

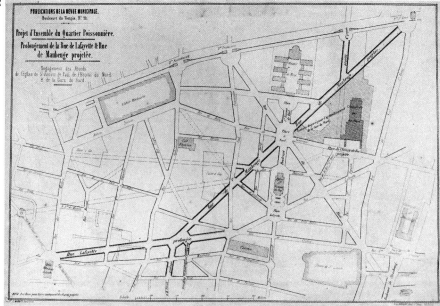

1. A diagram of the 1859 regulation on building height. Courtesy of the Atelier Parisien d'Urbanisme. On streets over twenty meters wide, cornice height was raised 2.5 meters, which made apartment buildings look much more monumental. **2.** Project for the Poissonnière district. Illustration reprinted from *Revue municipale*, no. 128, August 1, 1853.

built ten years later) to note a shift toward monumentality. The 1859 regulation[3] that authorized cornices to be raised from 17.54 to 20 meters on streets over twenty meters wide, was not unrelated to this shift. The recessed story then became a part of the stone structure, the "recess" being nothing but a very slight reduction in the thickness of the masonry on the top story.

The classic distinction between the Louis-Philippe building and the Haussmann building would seem to be somewhat misleading. The architectural evolution of the apartment building evidently took place in three, not two, stages: the Restoration and early Louis-Philippe building; the Haussmann building of 1840-60 (during the Rambuteau, Berger, and early Haussmann administrations); and finally the late Haussmann building, which emerged after 1860 (after the new regulation on cornice height and the annexation of the old suburban villages).

During the 1850s there had been a certain amount of wavering regarding building size, but after 1860, this wavering ceased. The role of city building officials (unclear, since the relevant documents were destroyed at the time of the Commune) would seem to have been essential. Haussmann gave them additional powers and thereby increased the impact of a regulation typology that, if not found in the building code per se, resulted from the more or less authoritarian "advice" given by these officials. As a result, the city's unity was strengthened with extraordinarily coherent rows of buildings, such as those on the Boulevard Voltaire and the Avenue de l'Opéra (which was

The effects of the 1859 regulation on building height.
1. 5-9 Rue Gay-Lussac. **2.** Corner of the Boulevard
Saint-Michel and the Boulevard Saint-Germain. **3.** 21
Boulevard Saint-Michel. **4.** Boulevard Malesherbes.
5. Place du 18-Juin-1840 and 171 Rue de Rennes. **6.**
27 Boulevard Saint-Michel. "Mock recesses" appear
(1,2,3). Five-story apartment houses begin to disappear (4); bigger roofs appear (5,6).

TOUT PARIS
945 - Le Boulevard Voltaire
au Carrefour du Boulevard Richard-Lenoir
(XIᵉ arrᵗ)

1905

COLLECTION E. FLEURY

New streets built by Haussmann.
Facing page: **1.** Boulevard Voltaire. Postcard. **2.** Rue
Portalis, in the Europe district (in the background,
the church of Saint-Augustin).

3

3. Avenue de l'Opéra.

built after 1870). The autonomy of individual façades disappeared
completely; not only were districts divided up into identical lots, but
buildings, all of the same height, were given the same structural lines
and ornament. The only variations that city building officials allowed
were infinitesimal: the design of a console, the frame around a window
opening, and so forth.

The transformation of the block into the basic architectural unit
deeply disturbed the traditional hierarchy of mass, volume, ornament,
and material characteristic of the classical system, which was based on
a very explicit opposition of vernacular and monumental architecture.
When apartment buildings became huge, richly ornamented stone
constructions, they took on the characteristics of the monument and
thus robbed the latter of its distinctive features. The old
distinctions—big/small, stone/wood, rich/poor—could no longer be
used to differentiate a monument from a house. To define a
monument, other criteria had to be invoked, such as isolation (as
opposed to the contiguity of apartment buildings) and verdure
(contrasting with the rest of the city's traditional mineral character).
The redefinition of the monument began in the late eighteenth
century, when small Palladian mansions were built in landscaped
environments. Eventually this led to a strict opposition between the
detached, four-sided public edifice and the private building, which was
always attached to other buildings. Traditionally, builders had carefully
matched a building's height to that of the nearby buildings and had
concealed the gables.[4] The architecture of the nineteenth-century

The Scope of Monumental Architecture

237

Boulevard Saint-Michel. **1.** Corner of the Rue des Ecoles. **2.** Corner of the Boulevard Saint-Germain.

apartment building, on the other hand, was characterized by the brutality of the walls between buildings, blind and summary, like severed limbs in search of tissue. Every change in size—from a big street to a small one, or from an apartment building to a townhouse—left strange vertical slices between buildings. The eye cannot fail to see them, especially in certain courtyards where they create abominable landscapes.

Such negligence might seem surprising, especially at a time when the architectural quality of the apartment building was advancing rapidly. The lack of any regulations concerning how buildings were to be attached does not really explain this, nor does the purely legal interpretation of the sidewall as an inviolable barrier. The real reason for the strong emphasis on the sidewalls between attached buildings is, in my opinion, structural. In a city whose absolute ideals were uniformity and regularity, the opposition between monument and house became less a question of material, scale, and decorative repertoire than strict antithesis between unity and plurality. A monument had to be an individual, separated from the group and singled out by its complex volumetrics (especially its top). On the other hand, an apartment building was defined as a standard vertical plane of regulation height that resembled its neighbors closely. What better way to show its absence of autonomy than to emphasize its common walls, thus demonstrating its link to an unbroken chain of façades? Apartment buildings came to resemble books lined up in a bookcase, or drawers in a piece of furniture. Monuments, to continue the metaphor, were more like curios—a vase, a clock, or a candelabra—which, though they can be seen from different angles, always retain their characteristic unity.[5]

3. Corner of the Place Edmond-Rostand. The individual buildings blend together to form a coherent row.

Deprived of its autonomy, the apartment building became a link in an unbroken chain. A façade's only function was to reflect the modulations of the urban space faithfully. The escalation of building heights that began with the 1859 regulation resulted in an explicit hierarchy of public spaces, from the street to the neighborhood, and from the neighborhood to the city. Each network was characterized by a particular façade typology, ranging from the most monumental down to the most ordinary. Thus the traditional signs of monumentality used in the architecture of apartment houses took on a key role in structuring the city. Although the sociological analysis of the displacement of the signs of monumentality from the aristocratic or religious monument to the public monument (in the late eighteenth century) and then to the private residence (in the midnineteenth) is not incorrect, it in no way explains how monumentality was used to structure the city. The varying degrees of monumentality of the city's apartment buildings structured the huge expanse of a city that had definitively broken with the old pedestrian scale, and created a hierarchy of major and minor streets—the outer crust and inside of each district. Thus when Haussmann built new citywide streets that formed the skeleton of a vast new space, those streets had to indicate their hierarchical superiority over the rest of the urban fabric.

The old system began to change when the monumental model traditionally reserved for public monuments was transposed—with great difficulty—to the architecture of the apartment building. Built with big, bare walls, fine stonework, graphic moldings, and a very restrained interplay of projections and volumes, Louis Duc's Palais de Justice, a severe construction of Florentine inspiration, and the handsome Lycée Saint-Louis, which Haussmann greatly admired, are classic examples of

The Need
for Hierarchy

239

1. South façade of the Palais de Justice, Quai des Orfèvres. **2.** Façade of the Lycée Saint-Louis, Boulevard Saint-Michel.

monumental public edifices. The tall stories, powerful stonework, and delicate, finely proportioned ornament identify these structures as monuments by opposing them to the more ordinary buildings around them.

Gabriel Davioud broke the traditional opposition between monumental and vernacular architecture when he introduced an astonishingly monumental compositional model for the apartment-building façades on the Place Saint-Michel and thereby changed the scale of residential architecture. The monumental apartment houses on the Place Saint-Michel were designed to echo the nearby Place du Châtelet, for which Davioud had designed two theaters in the form of Palladian basilicas. (Unfortunately, Rohault de Fleury's Chambre des Notaires and imperial fountain were too small for the vast square and its impressive vistas.) Thus the way opened by Visconti, who designed the Molière fountain on the Rue de Richelieu and the Saint-Sulpice fountain in front of the church, found its architectural fulfillment in the huge apartment buildings and wall fountain (a Frenchified version of Rome's Trevi fountain) on the Place Saint-Michel.

For the buildings on that square, Davioud adopted the curved roofs he had used for the theaters on the Place du Châtelet (which were simply variations on Debret's old Opera House and its Palladian volume). But the design also drew on the Rue de Rivoli, adapting and amplifying the structures found on that prestigious street. The extraordinary collage was further enriched by reintroducing classical proportion: Davioud took the monumental pilasters, basements, and rich window frames used for the Louis XIV façades on the Place Vendôme and stuck them onto pure neoclassical volumes reminiscent of Percier and Fontaine. The Place Saint-Michel was created by an inimitable architectural scrambling of historical models; in that respect, it is typical of nineteenth-century eclecticism. Practically every element in the monumental repertoire—mass, scale, ornament, theatricality—was exploited on the Place Saint-Michel—formulas that previously had been used only separately but that now were combined. Later the 1884 and especially the 1902 building regulations would draw heavily on this hierarchical structuring of mass and height, thus defining a type that was directly derived from the Saint-Michel model.

The theatrical, symphonic fullness that makes the Place Saint-Michel such an exemplary nineteenth-century achievement is not, however, found on the Boulevard Saint-Michel itself (a less important space). The boulevard was structured as a gradual return to uniform, less monumental buildings. On the block closest to the square, the basement arcades and colossal pilasters were eliminated and replaced by a more graphic pattern of stories and bays. In addition, the big curved roofs were clad in zinc instead of slate and were broken with more numerous window openings, thus further strengthening the graphic impression created by the block, as opposed to the impression of mass that characterizes the square. On the next block there was a return to regulation 45-degree roofs and an increase in individual

compositional variations (e.g., the dormer windows in the mansard roofs), the only monumental constant being the emphasis on the tall third floors with their balconies and pediments. Farther up the street the latter feature was eliminated: one had now left the world of monument and returned to everyday life.

Place Saint-Michel. Anon., 1905 (?).

Truly monumental architecture was reserved for crucial points in the urban space. But the Second Empire had many ways of indicating that its big new streets were important spaces. These were all derived from the classicism of, among others, Palladio and Hardouin-Mansart. The difficulty of actually using them came from the building officials' constant desire *not* to overindividualize façades. Architects had a double task: to respect the inviolable law that a building's façade and story levels match those of the nearby buildings, yet also to find a way to individualize composition.

The solution was largely decorative, nor were the constraints set by the city unrelated to a particularly exuberant use of the decorative repertoires of the past. But a new style did crystallize around two motifs based on models invented during the reign of Louis-Philippe.

Two Motifs

241

7 Place Saint-Michel and 1-3 Boulevard Saint-Michel. The transition from a big curved roof in slate or zinc to an ordinary roof.

Ordered façades on and around the Place Saint-Michel.
1 and **2.** Corner of the Rue de la Huchette and the Place Saint-Michel. **3.** Place Saint-Michel. **4.** 19-29 Quai Saint-Michel. **5.** Saint-Michel fountain. **6.** 9-13 Place Saint-Michel.

Place du Châtelet, 1860. The fountain is being constructed. The Chambre des Notaires is already built,
but not the theaters.

The first was the salon. The model of the Venetian palace, which had greatly inspired neoclassical architects, retained its vitality. Bedrooms were moved to the side of the apartment to make room for a spacious square salon in the center with big windows opening onto the street. Few windows were placed on the sides, but the middle was opened up with three big windows that flooded the main salon with light. An extraordinarily clever architectural feature was also used. The window-fireplace, a paradoxical combination introduced in the eighteenth century, became enormously popular and was eventually combined with the triple window. A small fireplace was built beneath the central window, while on either side French doors opened onto a balcony. Owing to the presence of the fireplace, the outside seemed inaccessible, but to go out onto the balcony, one had only to use one of the French doors flanking the fireplace.

13 Boulevard Saint-Michel. The triple windows of the living rooms.

The second motif was the building entrance: simple doors became impressive portals, and doorframes were turned into elaborate sculptures. The compositional possibilities were virtually limitless, and the Second Empire took obvious pleasure in using—and abusing—them. Mannerist pediments, urns, and vine branches decorated lintels, and huge frames often encompassed the two stories of the basement. Within the portal frame, the introduction of a window on the mezzanine floor created a paradoxical play on solids and voids. Finally, the fascinating caryatids appeared that were so popular from 1865 to 1875.

Though only somewhat secondary compositional elements, these two motifs were enough to individualize the monotonously similar façades of Second Empire Paris. The relative individuality of the first motif faded out toward the end of the 1860s, at which point the entrance door (inserted between the windows of the ground-floor shops) became the most individual feature of the Parisian apartment building.

Uniformity and Detail

The compositional uniformity of apartment houses was compensated for by an effort to individualize detail. Thus the stylistics of the Haussmann building was based on the repetition of an identical grid and, at the same time, on an astonishing prolixity of detail. The repetition was sometimes carried to an extreme: the lots on the new streets were of equal length, the only alteration occurring when a new street was not parallel to the old grid it was set in. Another cause of irregularity was the delicate question of how to treat corners, especially when two streets converged to form triangular lots. A lot's width was determined by the interior layout planned for a building. The basic formula was one staircase per building, regardless whether the width was twelve meters or twenty (meaning, respectively, one or two apartments on the façade). This formula also held when several buildings were grouped together: the spacing of the sidewalls corresponded to that of the

Fig.1.

Fig.2.

Fig.4.

Fig.3.

Tous les détails
sont au ¼ d'exécution

Plan sur E F   Plan sur D   Plan sur C

Echelle de 0°080 pour ⅖

Fig. 7.

0ᵐ 75

Fig.8.

0ᵐ 75

Models of apartment-building doors. Illustrations
reprinted from Léon Jamin, *L'Enseignement professionnel du menuisier.*

1. 61 Boulevard Saint-Michel. **2.** 34 Boulevard Saint-Michel. **3.** 14 Boulevard Saint-Michel. **4.** 12 Boulevard Saint-Michel. **5.** 60 Boulevard de Sébastopol. **6.** 32 Boulevard Saint-Michel. Doors were narrower than carriage entrances, but a bit wider than ordinary doors, and were sometimes topped by an arcade at mezzanine level (2, 5).

1. 15 Rue Clapeyron.
2 and 3. 20 Boulevard Saint-Michel.
4, 5, and 6. 33 Rue Leconte-de-Lisle.

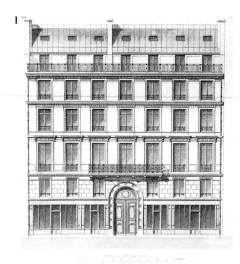

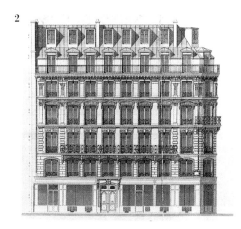

1. 39, rue Neuve-des-Mathurins, élévation, 1860.
2. 4, boulevard de Sébastopol, c. 1866. Paris, Bibliothèque des Arts décoratifs, fonds Maciet.

stairwells. The respect of the basic lot/staircase unit was thus absolute.

Buildings were so similar that they could be superposed on a single grid. From one building to the next, one always found an identical number of window openings of identical size (French doors that always measured 1.20 meters across), narrow piers that could not be as wide as the openings between them, and a systematic use of decorative compartmentalization (framed bays, and vertical motifs linking lintels to the windowsills above them).

The only dynamic interest in this rigorous framework was created by the difference in scale between horizontal and vertical motifs. The horizontal motifs were used to form a continuous link between buildings, in the form of balustrades and balconies whose visual impact was strengthened with ornamental cast iron. The vertical motifs took the form of rising voids linked with ornament. The graphic patterns and mass of the strong horizontals created a large-scale unity—the unity of the block. At closer range, the predominantly vertical window openings and sculpted decorative links created a dynamic interaction with the horizontals.

This approach to the treatment of horizontals and verticals is particularly subtle, for it is no simple feat to design a single form using two scales of distance. Once the balcony had taken on its dual role as projection and graphic motif, the decorative reorganization of the façade became possible, and the classical system was replaced by frame ornament on a reduced scale. The weak point in Louis-Philippe architecture was its lack of interest at close range; the use of graphic compartmentalization stabilized a form by linking it to the mass of the block, but created no visual interest closer up (other than the stereotyped detail of the frames). On the other hand, low relief—stylized vegetation on window frames—created a link between how a façade looked from a distance and how it looked at close range, and as a result made façades perpetually interesting.

Thus from far off one saw only a block's overall mass. At a middle distance the "packaging" formed by the balconies running along the third and sixth stories took over. A little closer up, the spacing of the heavy sidewalls and the groupings of window openings emerged; what counted was not so much the size of the openings, always equal, as the modulations of the piers and significant details like the typically Parisian use of ornamental balcony consoles and balustrades to create visual groups (usually one, two, or three consoles, depending on the size of the balcony). From still closer up, each building was individualized with sculpture and carving characteristic of the "Greek" style so popular during the Second Empire. Finally, for attentive observers balcony motifs created additional interest: the balustrade, a medium-gray blur at a distance, became a rich interplay of interlocking figures at close range. Indeed, it would hardly be an exaggeration to say that the ornamental cast-iron motifs on Parisian balconies were

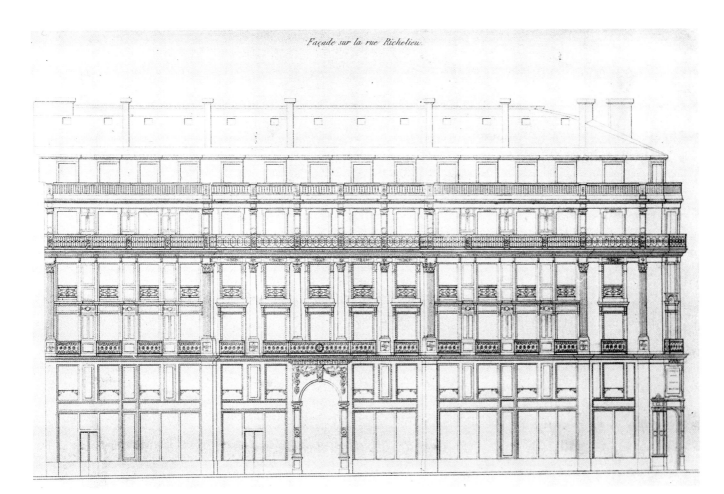

79 Rue de Richelieu, 1851. Paris, Bibliothèque des Arts Décoratifs, Maciet Collection.

meant to be a part of everyday life—to be constantly and unavoidably contemplated from the building across the street.

The subtle use of successive scales of perception was a defining characteristic of the Haussmann apartment building. Second Empire architecture has been criticized for the poverty of its mass effects and the boring uniformity created by buildings of identical size, which is to overlook the fact that the monotony of the general forms was compensated for by an extraordinary variety of visual detail. In this respect, the architecture of the Parisian apartment house continued the tradition of classical monumental architecture, whose refined contours were so perfectly adapted to the gentle light of Paris. (Indeed, the Louvre's Cour Carré was a kind of model for the treatment of detail.)

Eventually this compositional system, based on the total uniformity of voids, led to the disappearance of all strongly axial compositions; ternary compositions were replaced by binary ones (paired window openings), thus eliminating the impression that a building had a center. This resulted in quite monotonous compositions that, like the lines of the balconies, extended beyond the individual lot to strengthen the overall unity of the block. By the end of the Second Empire, binary composition was almost imperative, which made buildings seem extremely humdrum and so drew even greater attention to the infinite variety of decorative detail inscribed on the grids of their identical forms.

251

The Rhetoric of Ornament

While emphasizing the uniformity of the block as the highest priority (identical volumes and evenly spaced window openings), Second Empire architects devoted enormous energy to diversifying the treatment of window frames—both the frame itself and also ledges, consoles, and keystones. Louis-Philippe architects had already used projecting ledges (with consoles) above window openings and linked them with a single motif to the window ledges on the story above, thus emphasizing the vertical unity of the bays. When these "canopy ledges" were linked together with a cornice strip, the three separate motifs of the top of the window frame, the window ledge, and the cordon formed a perfect grid pattern. As a result, the alternation of solids and voids—the black holes of the windows in the pool of white formed by the façade plane—was totally neutralized. The wall lost all depth; windows seemed to be projected forward by the graphic interplay of their framing, while the wall itself was hollowed out by the decorative dynamism of the frames. The façade was no longer a mass but a plane—a purely graphic interplay of lines dividing up a flat surface.

Well before the appearance of glass-and-steel façades, the heavy sidewalls and metal floors of Parisian apartment houses made it possible to build diaphanous façades. A new formal vocabulary emerged, whose elaboration wooden construction certainly facilitated. A bit later, however, the new vocabulary of the transparent façade had to be transposed to stone architecture. The flattening out of relief was one way of doing so; but what really made it possible to destroy the stone façade's materiality was the use of window frames to create a skeletal structure in which only elements placed immediately around the windows were perceived as solids. The rest of a wall was perceived as a neutral void, as were the windows, whence the odd impression that

252

Following pages: 9 Rue du Conservatoire. **1.** Detail, third story. **2.** Detail, second story. **3.** Detail, fourth and fifth stories. Illustrations reprinted from César Daly, *L'Architecture privée au XIXᵉ siècle sous Napoléon III. Maison à loyers* (Paris: A. Morel, 1864).

1

2

3

1. 12 Boulevard Saint-Michel. **2.** Detail of façade ordonnance, Place Saint-Michel. **3.** Façade detail, Rue Ollivier (now the Rue de Châteaudun), 1866. Paris, Bibliothèque des Arts Décoratifs, Maciet Collection.

1

Coupe AB CD.

CROISÉES DU 1ᵉ ÉTAGE.

Coupe E.F.

2

Coupe sur A.B.

CROISÉE DE L'ENTRE-SOL

Coupe sur C.I

Échelle de 0.05ᵐᵉᵗ pᵉ Mètre

1 Mètre

Echelle de 0,05^{cent} p^r metre

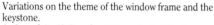

Variations on the theme of the window frame and the keystone.
1, 2, and **3.** 68 Rue des Vignes. **4.** Detail of a mansion, Rue de la Bienfaisance, 1866. Paris, Bibliothèque des Arts Décoratifs, Maciet Collection.

certain façades built of load-bearing masonry could have been constructed using cast-iron posts and beams.

As frames became the focal point of façades, decorative motif spread from the void to the solid. Through a transposition of wainscoting motifs, frames bordering window openings were used to break the masonry surfaces into more or less complex rectangular compartments. What would be perfectly understandable with wood—for example, the opposition of a door's panels and uprights—was more disconcerting on freestone façades, especially since the lines formed by the courses were totally unrelated to the decorative treatment of the façade surface.

This technical aberration (which rationalists violently attacked from the start) created yet another scale of perception. The complex decorative systems used inside apartments (where scales of perception are necessarily finer) were transferred to the façade, which sometimes included hierarchical subtleties based on scales of perception that differed but slightly. Viewed from close up and far off, big elements and tiny details constantly interacted in ever subtler ways.

In the context of eclecticism pervading the beginning of the Second Empire, the classical repertoire of ornament was called into question. The issue is well known to art historians, who have inflated it into one of the major themes in nineteenth-century art. Laborde's report on the London world's fair in 1851 (often invoked since Pierre Francastel's analysis of it) begot the widespread notion that the nineteenth century was incapable of creating a style of its own. Thus well before art nouveau, midnineteenth-century architects were trying to invent a style devoid of classical reminiscences. One of the odder examples of Second Empire "modernism" is provided by B. Tremblay's two buildings on the Boulevard Saint-Michel (on the corners of the Rue

Saint-Séverin, 1858). Influenced by Labrouste, Tremblay played on the opposition of graphic compartmentalization and supple relief—drapery and scroll ornaments—and thus created a repertoire of spirals, curves, and diagonals of naturalist inspiration. A similar stylization cropped up in the work of a good many other architects (particularly in England, as for instance Owen Jones) and culminated in the neo-Gothic trend of the third quarter of the nineteenth century.

Even in more classical vocabularies, a new stylization of detail emerged during the Second Empire. In some cases it was clearly of Romano-Gothic inspiration, but it could also impregnate the most rigorously academic forms, particularly in the use of monumental motifs for giant frames around portals and bays uniting several stories under a single arcature. The fact that architects ignored the proportions advocated by the Academy reveals the extent of the effort to renew and adjust motif and scale that began at midcentury, and may be seen as a statement of modernity.

5. Passage du Désir. 6. 9 Place Saint-Michel. 7. 73 Rue de Monceau. 8. Second and third stories of a house, Boulevard Haussmann, 1866. Paris, Bibliothèque des Arts Décoratifs, Maciet Collection.

The quest for a new ornamental vocabulary during the Second Empire.
1, 2, 3 and **4.** Boulevard Saint-Michel, corner of the Rue Saint-Séverin. **5.** 41 Boulevard Saint-Michel. **6.** Corner of the Rue de Constantinople and the Rue de Naples.

258

The Public Space

A component part of a new urban system, the Haussmann building was, architecturally as well as technically, a new development and at the same time the final expression of a long classical tradition. A similar duality also characterized the urban structure itself: though unquestionably new, it was perfectly in keeping with a long cultural tradition. Indeed, nineteenth-century Paris could be considered the last and the most dazzling of Europe's baroque cities. Some years back, Siegfried Giedion[6] compared the Paris of Napoleon III to sixteenth-century Rome. Indeed, the use of wide, straight streets leading to pivot-monuments characterized the whole classical tradition, which emphasized the urban void at the expense of monumental constructions proper.

In the Middle Ages monuments were carefully designed, autonomous objects that tended to clash violently with the rest of the urban environment. Between a monument and its context there was a relationship of complementarity and opposition. The city existed around the monument; the monument, though fundamentally a symbol of power, also structured the city by functioning as a visual marker in the tangle of streets.

In the classical conception, the monument continued to organize urban space. But matters were complicated by a new interest in the continuity of urban voids, which were designed to form big, empty spaces and create impressive vistas. The classical approach attained perfection in the eighteenth century. When Gabriel designed the Place de la Concorde and surrounded the square with nothing but tree-lined moats, he succeeded in structuring a huge space in a purely negative way. An even clearer example of the classical approach is provided by the transformation of the Place du Palais in Rennes. By tearing down the palace staircase, Gabriel integrated the monumental construction into the repetitive elevations of the façades on the square. The monument then yielded its power to the square, thus creating the model of the "European city"[7] that is still with us today.

The impact of the compositional systems used to design the great royal squares of the seventeenth and eighteenth centuries—from the Place Vendôme to the Concorde—was so great that they strongly influenced the city's building regulations. The model that grew out of the Desgodets code[8] conformed exactly to the proportions (basement, main floors, cornice, roof, etc.) used by Hardouin-Mansart, but adapted them to the six-story bourgeois apartment building. In practice, that model resulted in the rigorous alignment and repetitive composition of façades. As a result, the focus of visual interest shifted from the edifice to the varied types of urban void. The dilation and shrinking of spaces came into play; the city's uneven topography was used to create scenic effects; and diagonals were introduced into the cold rigor of the street network to reveal multiple and varied vistas. The eighteenth-century streets in the Invalides/Ecole Militaire area provided Haussmann with a model.[9]

Inside and Out

The model for apartment buildings with five main floors and two balconies emerged during the reign of Louis XVI. As it did so, the traditional principle of building up a lot around a central courtyard was weakened.[10] Then, too, buildings became more specialized. Parallel functions—shops, craft, and storage—were gradually eliminated from residential buildings, and the old ways of using the backs of lots (which Castex studied in the vernacular architecture of eighteenth-century Versailles[11]) started to disappear. When that happened, space was frozen into a single functional role, creating the model that urban planners have been using ever since. The specialization of buildings in the housing function led to the monumentalization of the courtyard as a second façade, if only to make the apartments there more appealing to prospective tenants. In point of fact, the "architecturalization" of the courtyard, though it did improve its appearance, impoverished the lot's interior. It turned the inside into another outside and eliminated the fundamental polyvalence that had defined the courtyard in the past.

Indeed, in older constructions a lot's outside—determined by the baroque interpretation of urban organization—had been counterbalanced by the nonappearance of its inside, which was the negative space of private life, work, and storage. The same contrast had been found in apartment layout (i.e., the reception/privacy opposition) ever since the disappearance of the medieval all-purpose room.

However, though the inside/outside opposition was weakened, a front/back distinction was architecturally maintained, since buildings with freestone façades usually had rubblestone or plastered wooden walls on the courtyard. This distinction usually meant a return to the front/back dialectic of Gothic architecture.

The regularization of courtyards that began in the eighteenth century led straight to twentieth-century block urbanism,[12] in which the inner façade is simply a close visual variant of the outside. Indeed, it is extremely easy to confuse the front and back of most modern buildings. The defects of twentieth-century apartment buildings —where there is absolutely no interplay between inside and out—help us to understand the specific qualities of the traditional opposition, which prevailed into the midnineteenth century. In the Haussmann era the traditional model began to be called into question; it disappeared completely in the twentieth century.

From Bedroom to Street

Apartment layout had traditionally been based on a weak specialization of functions; apartments could easily be adapted to meet the changing needs of tenants. Buildings were divided into private apartments and common areas, but the dividing line was fairly vague, first, because apartments were organized around the building corridors, and second, for reasons of a psychological nature. Each man's limit was the one he set for himself, or the one set for him by his neighbor. Makeshift constructions like closets and stalls often sprang up in a building's staircases, courtyards, and corridors, to the benefit of one resident or another. The upkeep of buildings varied, since it was up to each resident to do his fair share.

Inside Haussmann buildings, the outside/inside dialectic was as visible as in apartment layout. In addition to separate staircases for masters and servants, there was a sharp visual contrast between courtyard and entrance hall. The entrance and main staircase often received elaborate architectural attention, as did the salons in the apartments. On the other hand, the courtyard received little attention; being a service area where noisy and smelly activities were carried out, it was the place of the *unseen*. This arrangement had not been particularly obvious prior to the nineteenth century; the courtyard had been the center of everyday life and was not ashamed of its role (e.g., in certain courtyards, the emphasis on the latrines and the pump). But in the nineteenth century, representation and function came into open conflict. Whenever it was not necessary to maintain an appearance of bourgeois respectability, architectural refinement vanished. Thus the "decorated" part of the building stopped at the foot of the main staircase or at best at the end of the entrance hall, where a door in frosted glass hid the shabby courtyard. Behind that symbolic door, craftsmen could sometimes be found,[13] usually working in makeshift constructions (sheds with wood frames) could easily be built on or heightened.

Ground-floor shops were cut off from the rest of the building. It was rare to find a shop with a door opening into a building's entrance hall or onto its courtyard, and in a good many cases shop cellars did not communicate with the rest of a building either. Apartment houses and shops generally coexisted without too many problems. The craftsmen or manufacturers in a building's courtyard used the main entrance; when there was a lot of coming and going, the entrance hall became an annex of the street, thus pushing the break with the public domain back into the lot. In the transition from private (the bedroom and curtained bed) to public (the place of social interaction, i.e., the street), there were numerous subtle signs to express the status of each space. Every time one crossed a threshold, its presence was architecturally indicated by a specific framing motif, which varied according to the nature of the change. Every building was a perfectly coordinated and coded hierarchy of public and private spaces.

The public/private opposition can also be used to interpret the urban structure of Paris as a whole. Like the apartment building, the city was structured in progressive levels, ranging from the least to the most public—from direct relationships within a given neighborhood to distant or exceptional spaces reserved for public ceremonies and celebrations. I will proceed from outside to inside, so as to emphasize the progressive conquest of interiority in the urban structure.

Everyone who has visited Paris knows of several places that are meant to be contemplated from outside: the big monumental spaces used for celebrations and official ceremonies (the Foire du Trône, the Champs-Elysées) and such tourist attractions as the Eiffel Tower, the Louvre, and Beaubourg. The fact that these large forms are linked to monumental streets gives the city a very clear superstructure in which one always seems to find oneself on the same streets and at the same intersections. After this general (and superficial) view of the city's overall structure, which includes a number of monuments that orient one in the city, one notices the structure of specific zones or arrondissements. Inside a given area less imposing edifices like parish churches and town halls, as well as open-air markets and public gardens, indicate points of relative centrality; shopping and business activity is always clustered around these central points. In the outer arrondissements these subdivisions clearly reveal the role the old villages played in structuring the development of the neighborhoods. At the bottom of the city's hierarchical structure, we find secondary spaces grafted onto a district's busiest shopping streets. Oddly enough, as fewer shops are found, architectural coherence increases: indeed, on secondary streets there is a kind of dreariness produced by the similarity of the constructions. Our analysis of the main spaces in the urban hierarchy confirms the fact that the most prestigious areas contain identical façades, while less prestigious areas merely look repetitive.[14] I shall now examine the role of architectural appearance in the urban hierarchy of interior and exterior spaces.

At the top of the hierarchy, one finds collective spaces designed for the ceremonial processions of the baroque age. Their architecture forms the permanent ornament of a latent ceremony; certain nineteenth-century utopian architects[15] even dreamed of installing permanent garlands and Chinese lanterns to create an atmosphere of continual celebration. The major collective space is the monumental square with its identical façades, strongly symmetrical structure, and—on all the big royal squares—a statue of the prince on his horse. Linking these squares (which the nineteenth century took care to do: Châtelet, Saint-Michel, Etoile, Péreire) are tree-lined avenues and boulevards, spaces without any temporality of their own. Designed to facilitate rapid transportation, they form monumental parentheses between the squares. These avenues and boulevards

Place Péreire. Anon., 1899.

reveal a very specific hierarchy. Their façades are rigorously identical in height, and the spacing of the bays is monotonously regular. The only variation lies in ornamental detail, designed to make a building recognizable. The result is as impressive as it is boring: being nonspaces between the city's big, powerfully structured squares, the boulevards and avenues of Paris have the style of the squares but lack their personality. Thus the second degree in the monumental hierarchy is repetitiveness without identicalness. There are, however, two extraordinary exceptions to this rule: the Rue de Rivoli and the Quai de la Mégisserie, each with the kind of absolutely identical façades that are otherwise reserved for monumental squares. But in both cases only one side of the street is built up: visible from afar, the buildings on these streets look like an enormous palace integrated into the long urban façade running along the north bank of the Seine—the monumental center of Paris, the major space par excellence.

It is, however, rare for a meeting of major streets to form anything more than an intersection. Though often misunderstood, there is a reason for this: the weaker structuring of most of the intersections makes the monumental squares stand out even more. This becomes obvious when one compares the Cluny intersection (where the Boulevard Saint-Germain crosses the Boulevard Saint-Michel) to the nearby Place Saint-Michel: one of the two poles was intentionally downplayed in order to maintain and emphasize the preeminence of the other. The big Haussmann boulevards are, fundamentally, buffer spaces between the highly structured points where so much of the

city's architectural organization is concentrated. Corridors between major points, and trenches between zones, they cut the city into distinct areas (and usually form the administrative boundaries between different arrondissements and districts). In the center of the city the boulevards create great gaps completely out of proportion with the tight urban fabric, and are thus perceived as the border (if not the rampart) around each particular zone.

The trees along the city's boulevards also differentiate them from the hard mineral appearance of the rest of the city and thus further strengthen the boulevards' partitioning role. Boulevards were designed for special promenades (the Sunday stroll), not for daily walks. In the nineteenth century, the boulevard represented adventure, a break with the ordinary. Since a boulevard was perceived as a district's façade, the buildings that lined it had to look as respectable and coherent as possible. Thus even when neighboring buildings were not built at the same time, the most visible parts are in perfect keeping with each other: the basements form a regular row beneath the third-floor balconies and the foliage of the trees, and are further unified by the standard benches and kiosks that Haussmann lavished on the arteries of Paris.[16] Whenever a vista exists (as at an intersection), monumental architecture comes back to the fore (cut-off corners and, later, rotundas and domes that resemble certain medieval towers). Even in modern compositions the corner remains an architectural focal point and is treated as such.

Boulevard Magenta and the corner of the Rue Guy-Patin.

267

Boulevard Magenta.

On secondary streets, such grandeur would be unthinkable. The inside of a neighborhood is in total contrast with its outside: the former is the place of representation, regularity, and monumentality; the latter, the place of everyday life, good cheer, and disorder. The incoherent rows of buildings, heterogeneous materials, and chronological succession of styles found on secondary streets form a mosaic that deeply shocked the eighteenth century's spirit of unity, but whose picturesqueness we have learned to appreciate. Neighborhood architecture does not have a statement to make, or rather, it makes a number of unrelated statements. The general disorder is increased by the many little shops that tend to reestablish the space of the medieval continuum by spreading their wares outside on the sidewalks and even on the roadway itself (e.g., Saint-Antoine, Mouffetard).

The old neighborhoods of Paris are far from possessing the formal coherence of either the unified streets built by Haussmann or the big outlying developments. There is marked architectural variation: streets are lined by totally heterogeneous rows of constructions that are chronologically and architecturally foreign to each other, or by coherent architectural groups juxtaposed in an utterly anarchic way (thus revealing the multiplicity of real-estate operations that created the city's morphology).

The Spirit of a Neighborhood

1. Rue Madame. A plastically coherent row of buildings from different historical periods. **2.** Rue de Monceau. The use of corner buildings to structure major axes.

This analysis of the heterogeneousness of secondary streets must not make us forget the strong coordinating links that ensure a neighborhood's cohesion. Unity is primarily created by the shops on the ground floors of buildings: their colorful and lively presence robs the basements of their architectural identity. The only rule is that there be a clear break between the commercial basement and the residential floors above, or between animation and construction. The upper floors usually go unnoticed by passersby, who see only the shops. In the final analysis, the kaleidoscope of color, light, and movement at street level totally dissolves the static statements of the architecture (which no one even notices after a while). In the most extreme cases, the absence of architecture is perfectly possible, as at the city's flea market, a mere shantytown. (In such areas, the reappearance of architectural order usually signifies the death of commercial activity.)

Yet one architectural feature characterizes even the most chronologically incoherent groups of buildings. A single treatment of the vertical rows of solids and voids, emphasizing the bays, is enough to unify completely heterogeneous buildings, the strong graphic pattern concealing differences in material and form from one building to the next. Though abandoned by twentieth-century architects, that simple feature ensured the urban continuity of Old Paris. Finally, the very heterogeneousness of secondary streets can be seen as complementary to the homogeneousness and monumentalism that Haussmann introduced, because it codifies the limit between the outside and inside of specific neighborhoods and thus strengthens the clarity of the city's structure. No one can mistake a residential street for a shopping street, or a neighborhood's edges for its center. The outside and inside of a neighborhood are both contradictory and complementary in form and function. It would, however, be an oversimplification to define a neighborhood only in terms of this general opposition; many intermediate degrees are just as important.

3. Boulevard de Courcelles.

Situated between outside and inside, they are the city's flesh. What is most striking here is the city's overall coherence, produced by a regularity and identicalness that have nothing to do with any particular architectural or decorative effort.

Nuances do exist from one street to the next, depending on the age and style of the buildings and on the degree of formal elaboration. It is these nuances that individualize each neighborhood. The buildings in rich and poor neighborhoods form a contrast in architectural appearance, age, and size. The expansion of Paris to the north and then to the west gave the city's various zones very different appearances. Generally speaking, the Left Bank—largely because of the quarries that hollowed out the substratum—looks much less built up than the Right Bank. The contrasts between the city's historical center and the outlying arrondissements, and between the east and west sides of the city, further nuance the morphology of Paris. What Bernard Rouleau calls the city's mosaic aspect[17] can be attributed to the diversity of models found within it. This diversity explains why some of the city's neighborhoods are so fragile.

The center of Paris has always been easily recognizable because of its small, densely built-up lots and the mediocre architectural appearance created by the modest building materials and the dearth of decoration. The paucity of voids in the center (apart from the destruction wrought by Haussmann), and the near total absence of reserves of land in the middle of blocks, accentuate the city's minerality. Around the city's historical center, the old suburban fabric of the faubourgs can still be detected in the fifth, seventh, and eighth arrondissements. The main characteristic of these formerly outlying areas is their diversity, resulting from the successive operations that shaped them zone by zone. Thus the seventh arrondissement is a tight intertwining of working-class buildings with mansions from the seventeenth and eighteenth centuries and

Landscape of rich districts in the west of Paris. **1.** Rue de Monceau. **2.** Rue de Téhéran.

apartment houses from the nineteenth and early twentieth. The whole—whose coherence is, to say the least, fragile—is made up of autonomous sequences that are all interesting in themselves, but that seldom come together to form a large homogeneous unit. The very diverse intermediate fabrics between the old center and the outlying arrondissements contrast sharply with the monolithic developments built during the reign of Louis-Philippe (Saint-Georges, Saint-Vincent-de-Paul) and the Second Empire (Ternes, Europe, Magenta). Indeed, in those areas the high density and minerality that characterize the old center reappear, emphasized by the unmistakable monumentality of the architecture.

That monumentality becomes obvious when we compare the districts just mentioned to the old sections outside the Farmers-General Wall, which were always suburban in style, characterized by small mansions and detached houses never over four stories high, including the attic, with private gardens (e.g., Batignolles, Epinette, François Ier). They can also be contrasted with the poor districts in eastern Paris (La Chapelle, La Villette, Belleville, Ménilmontant), whose working-class identity grew as the nineteenth century progressed, and with the lower-middle-class districts in the south of Paris (Beaugrenelle, Plaisance). During the Third Republic a uniform architectural model was introduced in the outer arrondissements, which were built up with surprisingly similar apartment houses. By that time the Haussmann model had conquered the entire metropolitan area, including the new suburbs that sprang up outside the city limits established by the annexation of 1860. Thus the "central" model of the big freestone apartment building was automatically used for the northern part of the sixteenth arrondissement, the fifteenth and seventeenth arrondissements, and sometimes even the big avenues in the east of the city.

The architecture of working-class faubourg —chaotic but alive. **1.** Rue Julien-Lacroix. **2.** The bend in the Rue de Belleville, before the church of Saint-Jean-Baptiste. **3.** Place Etienne-Pernet.

273

Corner of the Rue du Vieux-Colombier and the Rue de Rennes. The new façade (Rue de Rennes) continues the eighteenth-century façade.

The Role
of the Boundary

Haussmann cut through Old Paris with wide new streets and lined them with tall, monumental buildings. Morphologically speaking, the joining of old and new fabrics created very visible frontiers and thus largely determined the way many districts came to look. Often improvised, the joining of old and new was sometimes appalling, especially when there was a brutal juxtaposition of buildings of different heights. But Haussmann generally made an effort to smooth the transition between juxtaposed types by reconstructing corner lots so as to create a gradation between the tall new buildings on the boulevards and the smaller buildings on secondary streets. In this respect, however, much remains to be done. The city would seem to have had trouble imposing a coherent morphology, for only large operations really succeeded in creating a smooth transition between a district's monumental outer crust and its vernacular interior.

The most successful junctions are those that form a kind of square between boulevard and street. Widened near the boulevard, the secondary street was transformed into an intermediate space—a sort of estuary at the junction of two urban networks. This type of space—a "landing," so to speak, between one of the city's big inter-neighborhood structures and a given neighborhood's internal structure—often favored the development of commerce. The linearity of Haussmann boulevards precluded commercial activity, whereas the dilations around intersections became busy commercial areas.

In other cases, juxtaposition of heterogeneous fabrics resulted in a complete degradation of preexisting structures, if the latter were not strong enough to resist. This was the case on the Rue Jean-Lantier (behind the Châtelet) and around the Halles, as for instance on the Rue Berger. But those are examples of residual fabrics left after a large-scale operation had destroyed the old neighborhood's coherence.

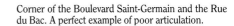
Corner of the Boulevard Saint-Germain and the Rue du Bac. A perfect example of poor articulation.

The most noticeable confrontations between fabrics occur at corners. The problem was handled with considerable care during the Second Empire, as seen in the corner of the Rue de Rennes and the Rue du Vieux Colombier, where Second Empire architecture tried to pastiche the eighteenth-century façades on the secondary street; but it was done more bluntly afterward. The confrontation of different heights has often left extremely unattractive exposed walls, and the confrontation of different building materials and architectural styles has often been handled clumsily.

However, the corner is not just a problem of juxtaposition. In many cases the new architecture used on the boulevards was extended to their tributaries and joined to the old fabric in a fairly acceptable way. Nineteenth-century building regulations required that buildings be lower on narrower streets; though not always successful architecturally, this did facilitate coordination. The most interesting thing about this is the obvious desire to maintain a hierarchy between streets of unequal size and importance. The most striking expression of the implicit code that governed Parisian architecture in the nineteenth century can be seen in the different treatment of the façades of certain corner buildings. Thus for buildings with one façade on a major artery and the other on a dead-end street, one finds a very obvious difference in appearance, owing to the use of poorer materials (brick, plaster) and less ornament (simplification of moldings, frames, and sculpture) on the less important street. There is an obvious continuity in the principal compositional lines, but also a clear desire to simplify the façade on the smaller street. This distinction, which is most perceptible when two very different kinds of street intersect, can also be found, albeit to a lesser degree, at intersections formed by medium and large streets.

45-51 Rue du Ranelagh. The main façade is built of stone, while the secondary façade (facing the entrance to the Boulainvilliers hamlet) is built of brick.

275

Monumental Corners

Designed to be viewed frontally, with a row of façades receding behind them, cut-off corners and corner rotundas attract one's attention by virtue of their opacity and volumetric power. These short monumental sequences are either surface planes rising up like pylons (which, for better or worse, have often been "decorated" with signs and billboards) or cylinders contrasting with the flat parallelepiped structures behind them. Most important, they signal a transition from one space to another, from the outside to the inside of a neighborhood. The message is, however, ambivalent. A monumental corner signals a difference between two spaces, but it is also part of a block whose architectural organization it cannot disrupt. Thus overindividualization of a building's corner (e.g., a marked opposition between the tower theme and the repetitiveness of the façades) has never been acceptable. It must be emphasized that the monumental corner is not autonomous; it is a part of the space that it structures. This is why cordons continue from a building's main façades onto the corner with no break; they downplay the corner volume by linking it to the façades on the intersecting streets.

In addition to the monumental treatment of corners, which played an essential role in the hierarchical structuring of Paris, Haussmann, as has been noted, attached a great deal of importance to the transition between old and new fabrics. He sought to integrate new streets into their environment by cutting yet more deeply into the old fabric than his predecessors had done. Indeed, Haussmann criticized his predecessors for being too timid and limiting their operations to the immediate vicinity of a new street. To smooth the transition between new streets and old, Haussmann rebuilt entire blocks or redid them so they would blend with the new constructions. The quest for a smooth transition led to the architectural hierarchization of buildings. On streets that intersect with a Haussmann boulevard, one first notices that windows are spaced farther apart than on the boulevard. Farther away from the boulevard, one notices a simplification in the silhouettes of the balconies (multiple balconies, then the third-floor balcony, and finally even the recessed story disappear). One sometimes also finds a gradual change in building materials—from large stones to small, from stone to brick, from brick to plaster—and a simplification of architectonic decoration (elimination of sculptures, simplification of moldings). All these attenuations of boulevard monumentality help create a smooth transition back to vernacular architecture. Almost imperceptibly, one passes from the vertiginous horizontal organization of the continuous balconies on the boulevards back to the traditional vertical style.

Unfinished Fabrics

More than a historical period, the name Haussmann evokes a kind of urban planning. The nineteenth-century transformation of Paris left many unfinished fabrics. How were they to be completed? Two attitudes are possible: to try to conceal any alterations in the earlier approach in order to reestablish urban continuity, or else to exploit such alterations as new structuring elements. Contradictory in theory, these attitudes can sometimes prove complementary.

The old villages on the outskirts are a good example of an unfinished fabric. Their concentric growth resulted in their running together without ever really being joined. The areas where the old villages ran together were characterized by a weak road network, big lots occupied by industry, and very irregular alignments of buildings. Contemporary construction has developed mainly in these areas and gradually filled up most of the voids. The introduction of autonomous structures that are in no way joined to the city's preexisting major spaces has only aggravated the problems of these areas and hindered the actual joining of the old fabrics.[18]

A second example is provided by certain boulevards. A vast landscaped space that subdivides the urban network into different areas, the boulevard requires the formation of coherent façades based on a single typological model synthesizing the morphological features found in a given part of the city. On boulevards that were built up slowly, one finds a great diversity of buildings based on quite heterogeneous typological models; consequently, the façades on those boulevards are morphologically incoherent. This is particularly true for the boulevards near the old Farmers-General Wall, where vestiges of the former suburbs are still perceptible in the variety of ways the lots are used and the markedly irregular heights and styles of the buildings. These areas clearly need to be renovated, in order to eliminate underoccupied lots and regularize building heights.

Corner of the Avenue Mozart and the Rue de l'Assomption. The last houses in Passy.

Corner of the Avenue Mozart and the Rue de la Cure. A few dozen meters from the point where Passy and Auteuil meet.

Boulevard de la Villette. An irregular row on the outer side of the old Farmers-General Wall.

One of the greatest qualities of Haussmann's Paris was a great flexibility that favored the evolution of the urban environment. The unity of the public space, based on a minimum stylistic consensus, was not unrelated to the city's amazing ability to adapt. It was precisely when we started interfering with the general stylistic unity of the public space that the city began to fall apart.

The Street

Haussmann's Paris was characterized not only by the hierarchy of streets (and institutions) that structured it, but also by the conformity of its streets, despite their extreme architectural variety, to an astonishingly uniform model.

A Haussmann street is above all a proportion: that of the height of the buildings to the width of the street. Paris was long characterized by the fact that, while street width varied, building height remained constant, at 17.54 meters on streets ten or more meters wide. The city remained faithful to that height—first stipulated in the 1784 building code—for nearly two centuries. The only alterations—which, coming between Louis XVI and the Third Republic, did allow an increase of almost ten meters—affected the roof but did not modify façades. The latter were always structured in the same way—basement and main floors—without any significant change in the relative proportions of their parts. The great wisdom of later regulations was that they progressively modified one part of the edifice—the roof—while maintaining an identical height for the more visible stone façade.

Paradoxically, the rule that the cornice be placed at the top of the sixth story resulted in a great variety of spaces. Unlike the modern equation of height and width, based on a theoretical inclination of the sun at 45 degrees and a standard proportional model (size counting less than proportion), the use of a set cornice line resulted in highly variable width/height ratios that changed relative to a street's width. Following tradition, the 1784 regulations provided for two basic cases.

For streets under eight meters wide, cornice height was set at twelve meters, thus limiting buildings to four stories (or two stories over a ground floor and mezzanine). For streets of about ten meters in width, the same harmonious two-thirds proportion was maintained; there was a change of scale but not of proportion. Thus the open "trench" between the two sides of a street was given a harmonious rectangular cross section whose height equaled the diagonal of the hypothetical square formed by using the width of the street. The larger scale was used for central areas, while the smaller one determined the fabric of ordinary neighborhoods. Finally, variations in street width—most streets were between ten and fourteen meters wide—modified the standard two-thirds proportion, creating a visual relationship between a street's width and the volume of the void between the buildings on

Scale and Proportion

279

Facing page: Rue Saint-Louis-en-l'Ile. The narrow width of a major street in Old Paris.

Boulevard Henri IV and Rue Saint-Paul. The intersection of a narrow old street and a wide Haussmann street.

From the traditional street to the wide street (with building height equal to street width). **1.** Rue de la Bienfaisance. **2.** Rue de Monceau. **3.** Rue Cervetto.

either side. As building height remained unchanged, the variation in proportion became all the more perceptible.

Haussmann continued this tradition, but also introduced a new element: the square cross section between buildings on streets of eighteen meters in width. A bit strange, and clearly more massive in appearance than the two-thirds ratio, the height-equals-width proportion distinguished Haussmann streets from the rest of the city's streets while also strengthening their role as boundaries between districts. The problem was to maintain this new proportion on wider streets. This led to the 1859 regulation authorizing an extra story to be added on streets over twenty meters wide (thus reestablishing a square cross section), and to the use of trees to create the illusion that the void had a square cross section. Moreover, on very wide streets one notices that double rows of trees were used. Extremely wide streets like the Avenue Foch are the exception; they play a structural role comparable to that of the big urban void created by the river. Obviously, such volumes could not be repeated without endangering the unity and clearness of the city's structure. Paris was fundamentally organized using a combination of the traditional two-thirds proportion and the more recent square cross section. Systematic use of those two proportions made it possible to give the city a highly unified appearance, despite the astonishing disparity of its initial component parts.

A Monotonous Landscape

Other elements were also used to strengthen the city's unity, giving rise to an indispensable monotony. Beyond the rich diversity of individual forms in the city, a minimum of coherence had to be maintained. The necessary monotony was primarily created by using granite curbs, gray asphalt sidewalks, and beautiful cobblestone streets

4. Place de l'Europe.

to form a uniform gray ground[19] that takes on a bluish cast when it rains. Several dark brown details were also used: metal grids at the bases of trees, gutter drains, and ornamental cast-iron drainpipes. As the city grew, benches, pillar-shaped billboards, and kiosks appeared to complete this harmony of blue and bister (the very combination Patout so wisely used in the 1930s to design polished aluminum kiosks and the shop fronts of the Nicolas wine stores).

These elements combine magnificently with the golden glow of the city's stone façades and the light-dappled foliage of the tall trees that line its avenues and boulevards. In winter the leafless trees stand out against the ocherous white buildings and warm them with reddish reflections, and one can then see the midnight-blue slate roofs above. Since the Impressionists, French painters have often captured this atmosphere beautifully, using various shades of gray and subtle changes of palette to represent the city's seasons and neighborhoods, the raw white of Montmartre's plaster walls contrasting with the buttery shades of stone façades, which look warmer when combined with ocherous brown Burgundy tiles, and colder when combined with zinc and slate. The painters have understood what many contemporary architects have not: harmonious nuances of gray are the very essence of Paris. Some architects have tried to re-create those nuances with stone facing. In point of fact, painted plaster can and has produced similar results at considerably less expense. In industrial architecture, brick and ceramic can be used without endangering the city's traditional color harmony.

1. Place Pereire and the Courcelles-Levallois station. Anon., 1903. **2.** Pont Saint-Michel and Boulevard du Palais.

Structuring Space

The Parisian landscape is a neutral, uniform element—an endlessly repeated cadence that forms a background for major urban moments. Neither more nor less than a basso continuo, it sets off the monumental melody of the big edifices. To construct a monument is, more than anything else, to compose a city around it. Regardless of the ideology that it represents, a monumental edifice always contrasts with the general proportions of other constructions and, by virtue of its morphological particularities, can be identified from near and afar. How true it is that the French cannot conceive of a village without a steeple! Needless to say, a steeple without a village is just as inconceivable.

In Western civilization, monuments have always been designed to be seen from afar and marked with specific features such as towers, spires, and steeples. In the Middle Ages, monuments were designed first with refined vertical silhouettes and later with domes; but the volumetric richness of masses was always less important than the contour, the only thing perceptible at a distance. That rule held throughout the Middle Ages, as seen in the massive silhouette of the tower of Notre-Dame, the overly elegant spire of the Sainte-Chapelle, the domes of the Visitation and the Val-de-Grâce, the Censier tower, and the cube on the Rue du Banquier. Even for smaller monumental constructions (today dwarfed by the modern buildings around them), the same principle applied: the short spire on the Passy church must have stood out with elegance when the Rue de l'Annonciation was a two-story street and the Delessert park still overlooked the Seine.

Medieval monuments were not, however, designed to be seen from a middle distance: a monument's silhouette dominated the cityscape when seen from afar, but disappeared as one drew closer to it. Turning a corner, one would suddenly find oneself at the foot of a monument, surprised by its huge scale. On the other hand classicism, with its pronounced taste for continuity, correlated perception from afar, at a middle distance, and close up. Then, in the nineteenth century, the monument became a "target" situated at the end of a long approach. The drawback of the nineteenth-century conception was that the approach to the monument became uninteresting; the structure could be seen in its entirety from the start and could scarcely change as one drew closer to it. To compensate for this, "target monuments" were given complex compositions based on different scales of perception (e.g., Baltard's Saint-Augustin), and an impression of depth was created to make up for the lack of surprise in the approach (e.g., the

1

2

Interaction of the city and its monuments.
Facing page: **1.** Notre-Dame. **2.** The Panthéon and
Maine-Montparnasse.

3

3. Church of Saint-Paul and Montmartre.

sides of Garnier's Opera House, the bays on the sides of Saint-Augustin).

The nineteenth century often renounced harmonious structure and created complex architectural organisms whose different elements were designed to be perceived on different scales of distance, but that are not really interconnected. The Sainte-Chapelle spire, which Lassus reestablished during the July Monarchy, is a good example; it is scarcely linked to Louis Duc's palace visually, but this lack of relationship is compensated for by the interest of the vista that Haussmann created from the Boulevard Saint-Michel. Similarly, the Tribunal de Commerce is an astonishing edifice because its dome was designed to be seen only from the Boulevard de Strasbourg, while the façades can be seen from the quays and the Boulevard du Palais. The two elements seem to be completely unrelated, until one discovers that the odd-looking bulb tops the staircase and forms the building's architectural center of interest. As the nineteenth century progressed, the taste for autonomous silhouetted elements (which seem unrelated to the façades supporting them) grew steadily and resulted in an intentional disequilibrium between monumental silhouettes and unimposing façades that scarcely stand out from the buildings around them (e.g., Vaudremer's Eglise des Quatre-Vingts). Such incongruous monuments might be seen as microcosms of the city's structure, for they combine intentional monotony with monumental accents. This way of inserting the monument into the urban landscape—so typical of the Haussmann era—is not without medieval precedents; in any case, it is worlds removed from the frontal style of baroque architecture. In the nineteenth century, the coherence of the urban form as a whole

287

The odd appearance of certain nineteenth-century monuments is created by the juxtaposition of different scales.
1. The medieval steeple of Saint-Séverin inspired several Second Empire and Third Republic steeples.
2. The steeple of Passy. **3.** The spire of the Sainte-Chapelle, photographed from the Boulevard Saint-Michel. **4.** The steeple of Quinze-Vingts, Avenue Ledru-Rollin. **5.** Façade of Saint-Augustin. **6.** Side of the Opera House.

Nineteenth- and Twentieth-Century Paris

A Cartographic Study

Based on François Loyer's research, the Atelier Parisien d'Urbanisme was able to map the entire city, dating each lot and assessing the quality of the construction found on it. In addition, the maps indicate the quality of the city's streets and public spaces. The plates in this supplement present several examples of the meticulous and complete analysis that was carried out.

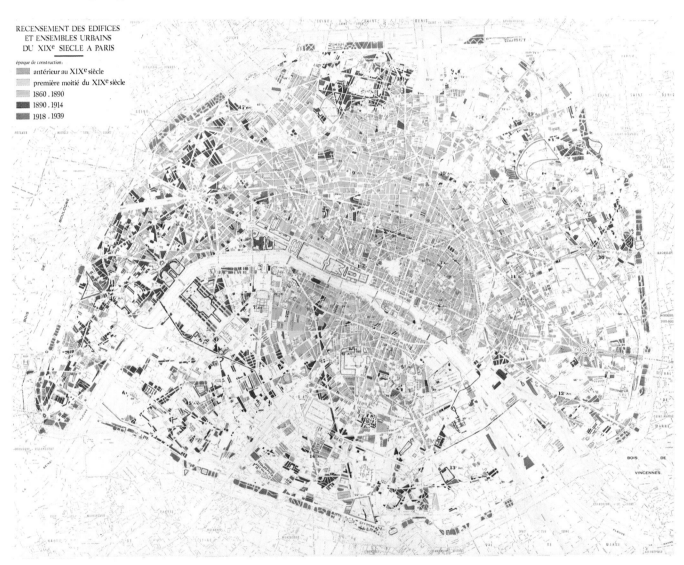

RECENSEMENT DES EDIFICES
ET ENSEMBLES URBAINS
DU XIXe SIECLE A PARIS

époque de construction:

antérieur au XIXe siècle
première moitié du XIXe siècle
1860 . 1890
1890 . 1914
1918 . 1939

Eighteenth-century Paris (green) never expanded beyond the medieval ramparts. During the Restoration and the July Monarchy (light yellow), the city expanded northward. Then the urban organism split in two, creating a contrast between the bourgeois districts to the west and the working-class sections to the east; despite Second Empire efforts to rebalance the cityscape, that split still characterizes Paris today. The city's expansion in the nineteenth century took place on the Right Bank. Much of the Left Bank was not built up until the twentieth century. In the 1920s and 1930s the city was given a coherent border (in blue, along the outer boulevards).

Legend:
Inventory of Nineteenth-Century Constructions in Paris
period of construction:
— prior to the nineteenth century
— first half of the nineteenth century
— 1860-90
— 1890-1914
— 1918-39

I

North of the Halles, the location of the medieval rampart (Rue de Cléry and Rue d'Aboukir) is shown by the the light-gray diagonal rising from the far left. Many traces of Old Paris can still be found in this area. The Haussmann network (Boulevard de Sébastopol, in dark gray, rising from the bottom right) was superimposed on the old urban structure. On either side of the big boulevards (gray horizontals), one finds the Bourse and SaintVincent-de-Paul sections (orange-yellow), constructed during the First Empire and the Restoration. The fabric of the central districts is a mosaic of successive interventions.

INTERESTING FAÇADE
ALIGNMENT
URBAN SPACE
COHERENT
EXCEPTIONAL

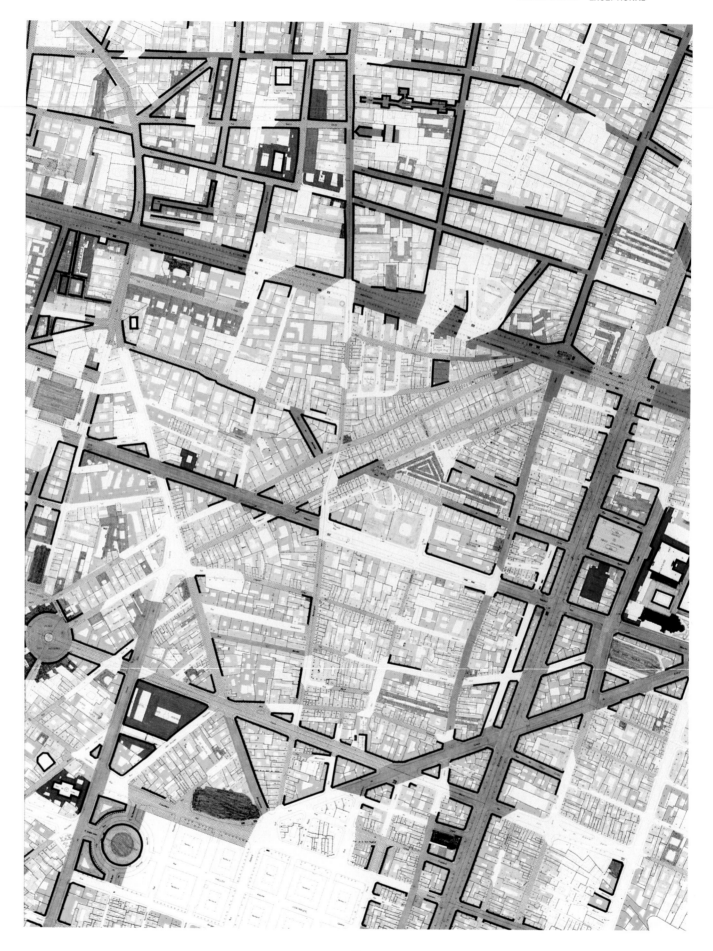

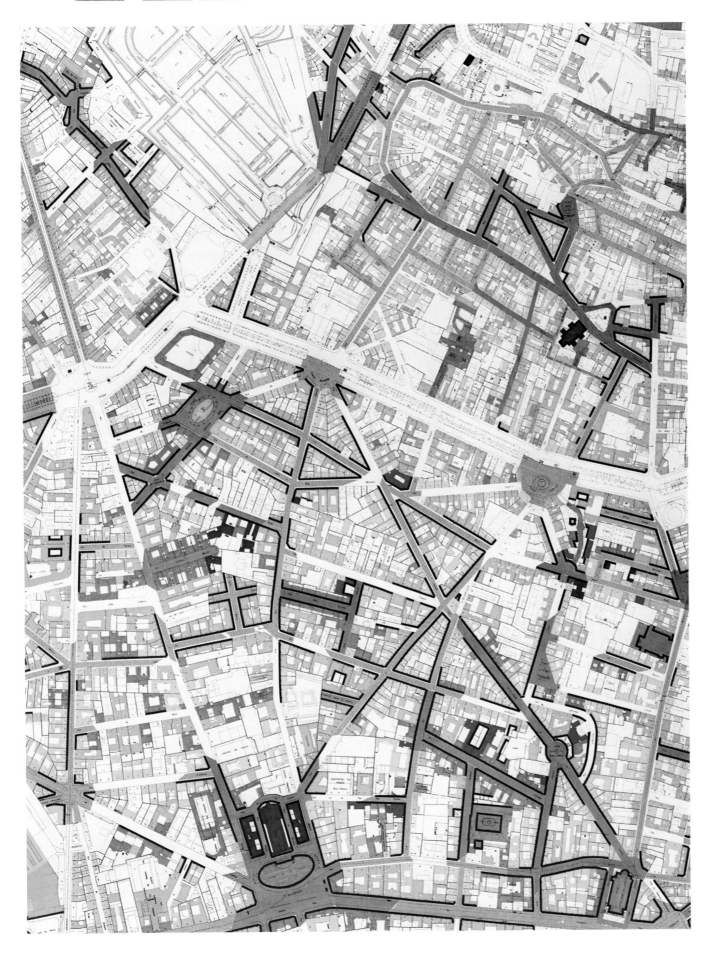

Situated between Trinité church (bottom) and Montmartre Cemetery, the Saint-Georges or Nouvelle Athènes section was the most beautiful ensemble in Louis-Philippe's Paris. The farmers-general boulevard did not prevent expansion onto the slopes of Montmartre, where working-class housing was built.

III

PARIS XIXe SIECLE
L'IMMEUBLE ET L'ESPACE
URBAIN.

ESPACES URBAINS (1)
d'intérêt exceptionnel
d'intérêt élevé

EDIFICES DU XIXe SIECLE 1790-1920
de qualité exceptionnelle
de qualité élevée

de qualité moyenne, riverains des espaces
urbains intéressants.

(1) sans distinction d'époque

0   90   250   500m

Atelier Parisien d'Urbanisme

IV

Street layout and design is every bit as important as the architecture of apartment buildings. The streets that Haussmann built, which had been foreshadowed by the 1793 Artists' Map, are the skeleton of Paris. They clearly structure the city; indeed, their structural role is even greater than the one played by the great monuments with which they articulate.

On this map, urban spaces of exceptional interest are colored brick red, and those of high interest are yellow. Edifices of exceptional quality are colored black, and those of high quality are brown. Edifices of average quality on interesting streets are shown in cream.

Legend :
URBAN SPACE[1]
--- of exceptional interest
--- of high interest

19th-CENTURY EDIFICES 1790-1920
--- of exceptional quality
--- of high quality
--- of average quality, on interesting streets

[1] regardless of date

V

The Péreire development has the most complicated
street layout in Paris. Exemplifying the Haussmann
approach, the streets delimit many triangular blocks,
which puts greater emphasis on corner buildings and
creates interesting vistas. The district as a whole is
structured by several big landscaped squares with
ordered architecture (Péreire, Wagram, du Brésil).

INTERESTING FAÇADE

ALIGNMENT

URBAN SPACE

COHERENT

EXCEPTIONAL

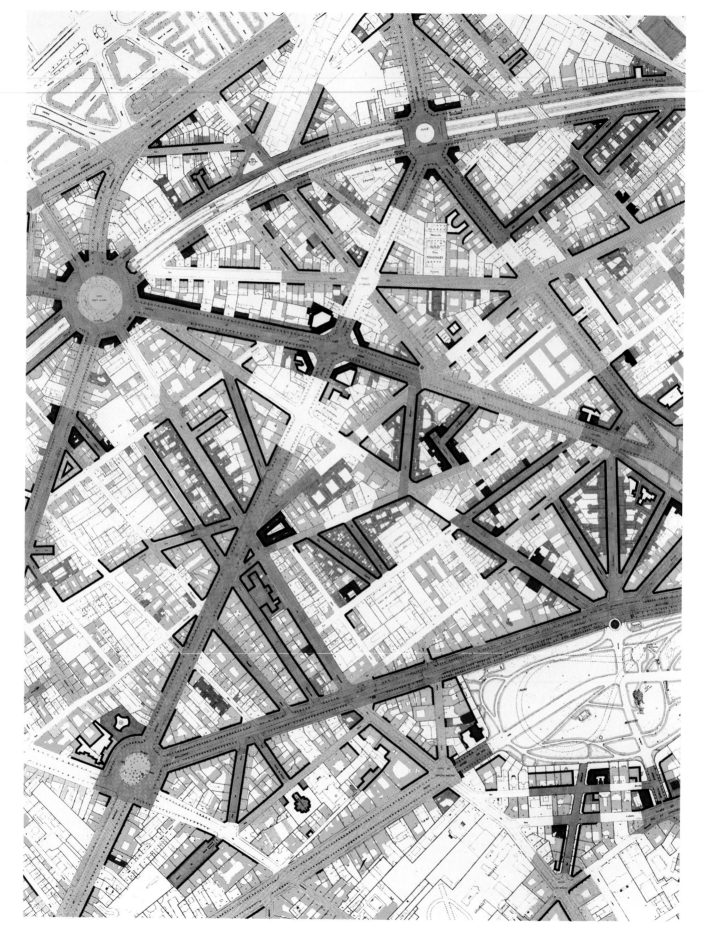

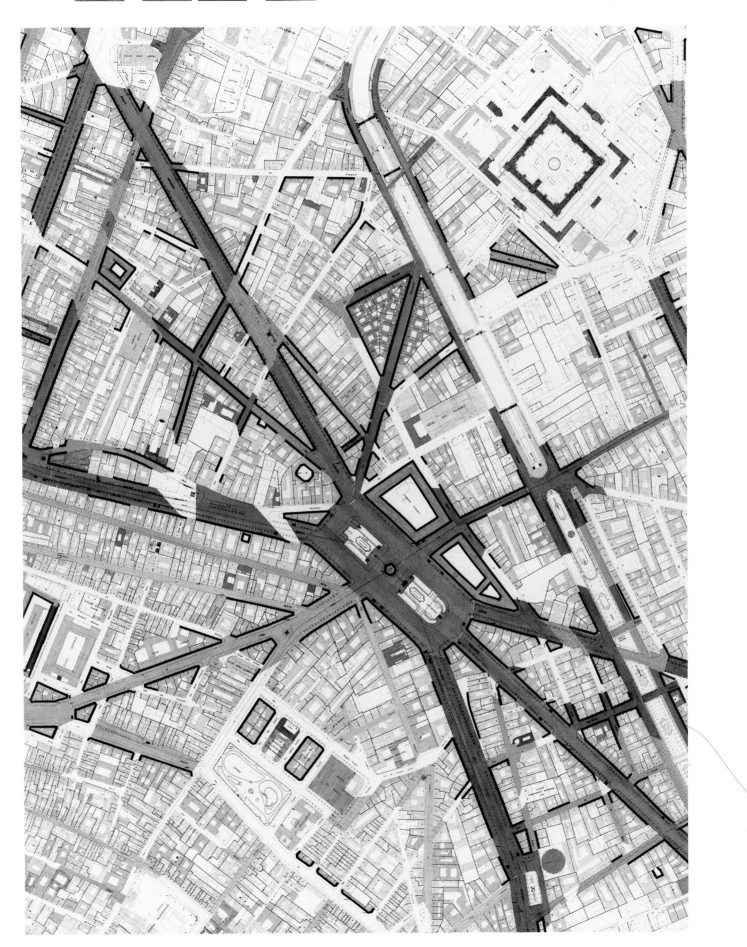

QUALITY:

AVERAGE OR MEDIOCRE
HIGH
EXCEPTIONAL

20th cent.   1st half 19th cent. 2nd half   18th cent.

Haussmann superimposed the Place de la République on the layout of a suburb that was still quite recent. He cut into the existing buildings and stuck the uniform ordonnance of the square onto a section that he otherwise ignored.

Above Père-Lachaise Cemetery, Ménilmontant and Belleville were devastated by urban renewal in the 1960s. Nevertheless, one does find traces of the working-class environment that emerged as the area was built up during the Second Empire. In this hilly area one finds few traces of the Haussmann approach, with the exception of the handsome buildings on the Place Gambetta (bottom right).

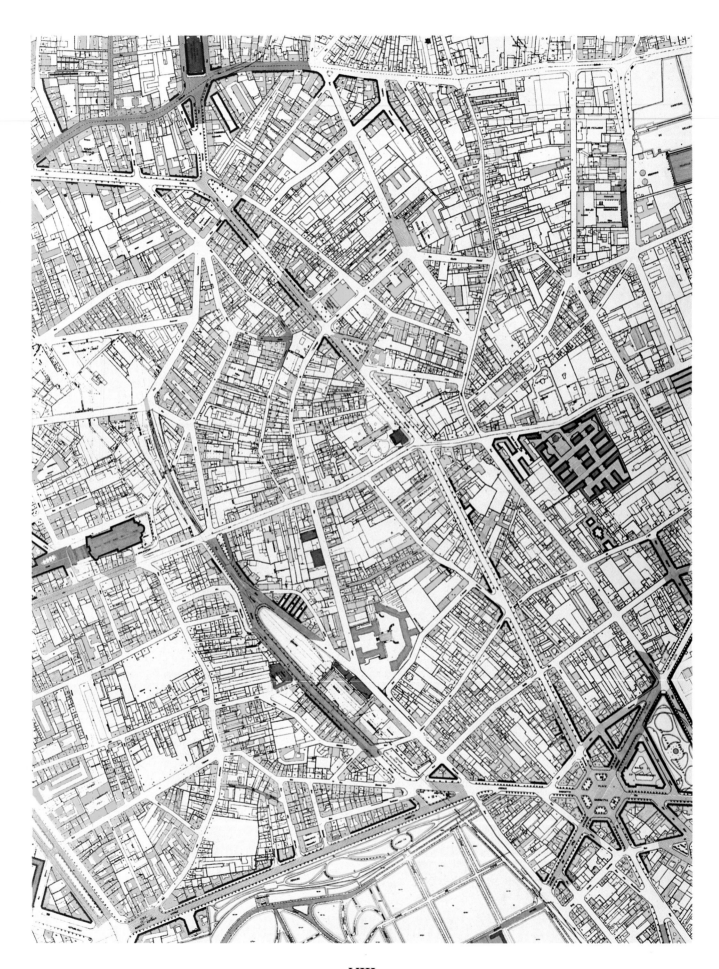

The dome above the Tribunal de Commerce, photographed from the Pont Saint-Michel.

Saint-Augustin, photographed from the Rue du Général-Foy.

291

triumphed over the clear structuring of individual edifices. The city became a tightly spun web—so tightly spun, in fact, that not even a monument could wholly break free from it.

A Difficult Dialogue

Monuments tend to be rather ambiguous. They do more than fulfill the symbolic and institutional role that is their raison d'être, for they are also landmarks, major points in a city's spatial organization. It is no accident that road signs in France always give the distance to Notre-Dame, the capital's main cathedral and geographic center. Because of its exceptional character, a monument crystallizes and clarifies the urban structure around it.

A monument is inherently and fundamentally an "object"—isolated, heterogeneous, autonomous, and self-contained. Some historical periods have attempted to create a coherent urban structure by subordinating monuments to large voids used as structural elements, but even they did not eliminate the monument as such. Rome's Piazza Navona would be nothing without Sant'Agnese; big as they are, Bernini's fountains would be utterly meaningless without the cathedral. When one does find a major space without a convincing monumental landmark—like the Place du Châtelet, where Davioud's two big theaters and the old imperial fountain called for something more than Rohault de Fleury's Chambre des Notaires—the absence is painfully obvious. It took all the skill the eighteenth century could muster to make the centrifugal Place de la Concorde a stable space by treating the environment in a purely negative way (the palatial buildings, pool of water, sentry boxes, escarpments, and dry moats). Even then, the Madeleine church was eventually built to anchor the space. The oversimplified geometry of that edifice is not really suitable for the vista from the Place de la Concorde, which called for a considerably stronger treatment of depth and mass to counterbalance the imposing square, the gardens, and the river. Constant d'Ivry's initial project would have worked perfectly. The dramatic increase in scale that Vignon attempted for his Greek-style temple could have been successful only in close proximity to, and formal confrontation with, the city's vernacular scale—as is sometimes the case for cathedrals and skyscrapers.

The Monument as Exception

Monumental form is by definition the opposite of ordinary form. The two are complementary, but the monument always emerges triumphant. There has recently been a good deal of talk about "companion architecture": the expression can be understood only as designating architecture designed to make a monument stand out.

To achieve this, a number of compositional recipes have been used. When viewing a monument from a distance, we are struck by the rising silhouette that dominates the constructions around it—or in rural areas by the trees, since a church can always be identified by its steeple rising not only above the roofs but also above the treetops. Close up, we are struck by the incomparable scale, the heterogeneousness of matter and color, and the rich and subtle treatment of detail.

At the end of the Rue Laffitte, Notre-Dame de Lorette can be understood only in terms of its colossal portal—five stories high—and its four heavy Corinthian columns. The cylindrical volumetrics and curve of the columns, the absence of windows, the marked confrontation of plane and sculpture, and the very height of the courses used for the drums and the walls make this severe form stand out sharply against the graphic spirit, small scale, and interplay of voids that characterize the architecture of the buildings around it. But the contrast is governed by one major opposition: that of the rich and unusual mass of the four big cylindrical columns rising against the dark façade, and the purely graphic treatment of the façades of the nearby buildings.

Throughout the Second Empire, the definition of the monument in terms of gigantic scale continued to thrive, but the opposition of the stylistic vocabularies of monumental and vernacular architecture became less pronounced. A single style was used for apartment buildings and monuments, whether Garnier's Opera House or Ballu's Trinité; monumental and vernacular masses were given a similar density, a sort of weight or heaviness that prevents any clear volumetric structure from emerging. However, in the urban jungle that at first glance might seem to have grown over them, monuments continued to stand out in two ways: the height (and variety) of their tops, and the size of their voids. The Trinité's tower and the Opera House's curved dome are unusual shapes and easily orient one in the city. Moreover, the church's archways and the openings in the Opera House's colonnade form giant black shapes that have nothing to do with the window openings of the surrounding buildings.

During the Haussmann era the traditional structuring of city and monument began to undergo profound modifications, owing to the "shrinking" of urban space that had been under way since the birth of mechanical transportation. As streets and boulevards were modified, and new scales of perception emerged, the size and location of monuments had to be reexamined.

The palatial apartment house was a new element in the urban organization and defined the major routes used to give the city a clear skeletal structure. To tower over palatial buildings, monuments had to be absolutely gigantic in scale. What, indeed, distinguishes the Louvre and the real palaces on the Place de la Concorde from the palatial apartment buildings on the Rue de Rivoli? Thus immense constructions were designed to dominate the entire cityscape. Montmartre's eighty-three-meter dome, higher than the towers of Notre-Dame, was built on a hill that is 104 meters higher than the Seine. And after years of debating and dreaming, Eiffel's thousand-foot

Rue de la Chausée-d'Antin, looking toward Trinité.

293

tower was finally built, dwarfing the hundred-foot arches that had been the pride of Saint Sophia's in Constantinople and Saint Peter's in Rome!

The Invention of Relative Scales

Needless to say, such gigantic exploits could not be repeated too often without giving the city's skyline a confused and unstructured look. The Seine, Montmartre, and the Eiffel Tower were quite enough to structure the geography of Paris at the end of the nineteenth century. For the landmarks needed to identify the city's important points and their place in the urban hierarchy, intermediate scales were established.

Thus the Gare du Nord, the Louvre, and the Hôtel de Ville, for example, had to be more monumental than an arrondissement's town hall or a parish church, the latter in turn being hierarchically superior to a hospital, a secondary school, or a fire station—and a secondary school superior to a grade school, a parish church to a chapel, and a hospital to a community clinic. Discovering the architectural equivalent of the extraordinarily complex hierarchy of functions and services found in a major capital city was all the more difficult, because the architecture of the apartment house tended toward hyperbole. Between 1830 and 1870, nineteenth-century architecture crystallized around this issue. The norms established during those years were used until the collapse of the Haussmann system itself.

A construction's place in the hierarchy depended on its silhouette, the void around it, its lines and openings, matter, color, ornament, and detail. The top of the hierarchy was represented by totally isolated constructions, gigantic in scale and unique in form (the Opera House, Sacré-Cœur). A notch below, big monuments were given dramatic roofs to dominate the rows of buildings around them (the Louvre and the Gare d'Orsay). In addition, stylistic detail was used to create a strong contrast with nearby façades and to emphasize a monument's exceptional scale at close range. A notch below that, monuments were less isolated and were sometimes even attached to other buildings. Roof volumes, treated in a much less dramatic way, were sometimes accentuated by nothing more than ridge and cornice pieces. In short, the monument was flattened out, became rather commonplace, and blended into the buildings around it.

In some cases only one part of a monument's mass stood out—a pinnacle, an unusual spacing of the voids in a big monumental arcade, or a large decorative motif—while the rest blended in with the other buildings on the block. The loggias of the Gaîté-Lyrique and Saint-Charles de Monceau and the pinnacle of the town hall in the eleventh arrondissement are good examples of how local monuments were defined with very localized monumental elements. Descending another rung in the ladder of monumentality, one finds the arcade of the "Gagne-Petit" on the Avenue de l'Opéra and the corner rotundas

294

of the Printemps department store on the Boulevard Haussmann, where monumentality is limited to the rich treatment of a bay—an approach that Garnier had already used in the Second Empire for the Cercle de la Librairie on the Boulevard Saint-Germain, to create a break in the smooth continuity of the façades.

Finally, the treatment of detail at close range was also an important issue. Ornament was used, and abused, to mark a monument's place in the hierarchy; the results ranged from overdecoration to the stark aggressiveness of certain self-infatuated edifices. As it began to be used on apartment buildings, the traditional repertory had trouble maintaining its specificity in monumental architecture per se. The nineteenth century loved ornament: to contrast with apartment houses, monuments were given a formal sobriety synonymous with grandeur. Hector Lefuel's exceptional attempt to give the façade of the new Louvre, on the Rue de Rivoli, a decorative richness that would equal Philibert Delorme's Tuileries façade ended in failure. Though extremely refined, the façade is not strong enough for its location. The delicate ornament quickly fades from view as one moves away from the façade, and fails to produce the impression of mass needed to balance the impressive vistas.

Following Lefuel's experiment, Haussmann and post-Haussmann architects generally preferred to limit ornamental detail to those parts of monumental edifices most visible at close range, such as ground floors and basements. The silhouetting and individualization of detail to create breaks in the façade plane were used—to the exclusion of practically everything else—to indicate the presence of a monument to passersby.

Throughout the Haussmann era there was an astonishing complementarity between the apartment house and the monument. That complementarity was, however, seriously disturbed by real-estate promoters in the late nineteenth century, so that the apartment house and the monument became open rivals.

Saint-Charles-de-Monceau.

Public Buildings

One of the biggest quandaries of nineteenth-century architects was how to make the various new types of public buildings—lying outside the old church/château/palace trilogy—formally identifiable. If the "public monument" (town hall and law courts) quickly found an appropriate form (based, respectively, on the Italian palazzo and the Greek temple), the situation was more problematic for churches, which often wound up looking like an expression more of political power than of religion; in the end, an appropriate, religious-looking form was provided by the neo-Gothic style. Finally, schools, train stations, and hospitals, now promoted to the rank of monument, also had to be given an appropriate form, so as to counterbalance the industrial and commercial invasion of the city by offices, factories, and stores.

Ornamental details and unusual structures: small-scale monumentality.
1. Pinnacle of the town hall in the eleventh arrondissement. **2.** Rue Portalis, photographed from the Rue du Rocher bridge. **3.** Gare du Nord, photographed from the Rue de Dunkerque. **4.** Elevated railway, Boulevard de la Chapelle, photographed from the Rue de Chartres. **5.** Closed bridge over the Rue de Maubeuge.

297

Printemps department store, corner of the Rue du Havre and the Boulevard Haussmann.

Facing page: Gaîté-Lyrique theater, photographed from the Square des Arts-et-Métiers.

The monumental types used for public buildings reveal a great deal about early industrial society, socially as well as politically. If town halls were distinguished from apartment houses by their stronger architectural lines, slightly smaller size, clearer volume, monumental roof with dormer windows, and big stone chimneys (elements more suggestive of the château than the city mansion), it was because the community monument was clearly being identified with the traditional architectural signs of aristocracy. The city mansion—so typically Parisian—could have been taken as a model, but it was not spectacular enough to satisfy the bourgeoisie's thirst for respectability. Symbol par excellence of bourgeois power, the town hall could be treated only with themes from palace and château architecture.

In church architecture the debate opposed the fashionable forms of pure ostentation—the Renaissance-style Trinité, the Gothic-style Sainte-Clotilde, and the Romanesque-style Saint-Augustin—to the powerfully austere style of Chartres Gothic, used by Lassus for Saint-Jean-Baptiste in Belleville. Was a church to look like a theater or a frivolous demimondaine's townhouse? Or was it to express the Christian vision with architectural dignity? From Lefébure-Vély's musical improvisations at Saint-Sulpice to the severe charms of "industrial" Gothic, nineteenth-century church architecture reflected the uncertain place of Christianity in French society. Eventually, the brutal monumental forms of the "archaeological-rationalist" style created an antithesis to the frivolous, ostentatious churches that were the pride of wealthy parishes.

299

A protest against the neutral regularity of classical façades: the neo-Gothic and rationalist styles.
1. Saint-Jean-Baptiste, Boulevard de Belleville. **2.** Collège Chaptal, Rue de Rome. **3.** Lycée Molière, Rue du Ranelagh. **4.** Paris photographed from Saint-Gervais. Anon., ca. 1867.

Facing page: Sainte-Clotilde, Rue Las-Cases. Postcard.

Being neither palace nor château, what should a hospital look like? And above all a school, the key nineteenth-century monument, erected to knowledge as the only means of social advancement? Rather by accident, the rationalist architects created a repetitive, economical, and efficient model not unrelated to the fire station and the factory: a construction with vast, well-lighted floors, built of cheap, sturdy materials. It somehow seemed wrong to turn hospitals, a place of refuge for the sick and lonely, and schools, a world of minors, into monuments in the accepted sense of the term. By emphasizing values linked to rationality—economy, efficiency, hygiene—architects endowed schools and hospitals with a new kind of symbolic power, as seen in Train's Collège Chaptal and Vaudremer's Lycée Buffon and Lycée Molière. The Third Republic continued this tradition in unforgettable red-and-white brick edifices and made them the standard-bearer of its political values.

961   La Rue Las-Cases et l'Église Sainte-Clotilde

ND Phot

Town hall in the tenth arrondissement, Rue du
Faubourg-Saint-Martin.

Outdoor Installations

Second Empire Paris was, essentially, an undifferentiated fabric of apartment buildings structured by a hierarchy of monuments. But the public space was also given a number of intermediate architectural elements. It would be a mistake to overlook the role played by outdoor installations such as fountains, grillwork fences, and streetlamps.

Fountains

The fountain's traditional function was hygienic and utilitarian. Flowing onto the pavement, its waters carried off various kinds of waste. Before sewers, fountains emptying into a well-designed gutter network were indispensable to city hygiene. Moreover, they supplied many city residents with their drinking water at a time when running water was still unheard of. Before Haussmann, the fountain remained an essential meeting place for everyone who did not have access to a private well. Even more important than shops selling basic provisions, a neighborhood's public fountain determined its geographic and social boundaries, and community life revolved around it.

Fountains thus played a major role in the formation of neighborhoods. Like all public structures, throughout the entire classical age they were designed and perceived as a tribute to the nation and its glory. Even when the fountain's utilitarian function became obsolete, its monumental and institutional role was maintained; the handsome series of fountains Visconti designed at the end of the July Monarchy—the Molière and Saint-Sulpice fountains—are striking proof of this. One might even conjecture that as the fountain's utilitarian and social functions decreased, its institutional role was strengthened as a form of compensation. Indeed, the most beautiful fountains in Paris—Saint-Michel, Observatoire, Square Louvois, Théâtre-Français, Châtelet, République, Daumesnil—were built during the Second Empire.

Over the years the traditional form of the wall fountain was maintained because it was best adapted to the cramped lot pattern in the center of the city and allowed easy access to residents, passersby, and horses. In less built-up areas, isolated monumental constructions were sometimes built (Visconti's Saint-Sulpice fountain). Fountains with basins, like Hittorf's design for the Place de la Concorde, had limited success, being purely ornamental constructions more appropriate for gardens than for city streets. Thus wall fountains and their variants, ranging from the sculpted monument to the triumphal arch, were used to create and identify a neighborhood's central meeting place. Fountains were always designed to be seen close up. A number of miniature architectural effects were used to emphasize their monumental status, even when they were quite small—which is, of course, the case for the city's famous "Wallace fountains."

1. Square Louvois. 2. Champs-Elysées gardens.

Fountain with naiads, 91 Rue du Faubourg-Saint-Martin. On the left, the entrance to the Passage du Désir. Photo: Marville, ca. 1870.

1. Omnibus ticket office, Place de la Bourse. Photo: Marville, 1866.
2. Wallace fountain, Place de Passy.
3. Kiosk, Place de la Bourse. Photo: Marville, 1870.

305

Wallace fountains served to "furnish" the city in the same way as did benches, streetlamps, and kiosks. All these elements were designed to make the city a safer, more pleasant place and thereby encourage people to take advantage of its streets at a time when traffic problems were intensifying. The quest for a certain coziness in the urban space corresponded to the city's explosion in scale. As the city outgrew its old pedestrian scale, it was humanized with little fountains, benches, and streetlamps.

Grillwork Fences and Streetlamps

At once identical and monumental, grillwork fences and streetlamps played an essential role in Second Empire Paris. This is particularly noteworthy, because modern urban planners have waged open war against both of them. The history of the grillwork fence is a history of variants—with or without pillars, flush with the ground or built on a wall, high or low, open or covered with sheet metal. The different variants separated contiguous spaces to varying degrees. Nothing could be more different than the tall, light fence around the Tuileries, and the low fences covered with sheet metal and hidden by bushes that Hittorf used on the the Avenue Foch. The former separates two spaces in a very transparent way; the latter completely block visual contact between the street and the private gardens behind them. In classical architecture, grillwork fences played a key role in structuring spaces (e.g., Jean Lamour's admirable fences in Nancy). The Second Empire refined the classical approach and used such fences to create monotonous borders. Haussmann tells[20] how he made Ballu, the architect who designed the Square Saint-Jacques, set his fences directly on the ground rather than on a low wall. The fence thus became totally subservient to the public space and was as neutral as the asphalt sidewalks and cobblestone streets. The fact that city regulations required one repetitive model to be used on certain streets contributed to the neutralization of the grillwork fence and thus to the standardization of public areas.

The Second Empire also made the streetlamp a major theme. Haussmann, who obviously did not like heavy bases, removed the ones that Hittorff had used on the Champs-Elysées.[21] Streetlamps rising directly out of the ground were installed throughout the city to form an appealingly abstract, graphic landscape. At night this forest of cast-iron trees created a low layer of light. Lampposts were relatively short not only for technical reasons (turning the lamps on) but also for aesthetic ones. The light they gave off just reached the top of the ground floor; the stories above were no more than shadows. Baltard, who clearly understood the aesthetic interest of this approach, used it even indoors, lighting the Halles and the church of Saint-Augustin with

306

Rue d'Alsace. In the background, the Gare de Strasbourg, today the Gare de l'Est. Photo: Marville, ca. 1874.

Streetlamp on pedestal, Square des Arts-et-Métiers.
Photo: Marville, n.d.

Two-branched streetlamp on the Champ-de-Mars esplanade, near the Avenue La Bourdonnais. Photo: Marville, ca. 1870.

Streetlamp at the end of a balustrade in front of
Saint-Vincent-de-Paul. Photo: Marville, ca. 1870.

an arrangement of relatively low lamps to create an effect similar to the admirable lighting provided by the big coronas in Ottoman mosques.

"A gaslamp that is placed too high up," Haussmann wrote,

> will project its light farther, but will not give adequate light to the immediate area around it. Obviously, that was not our goal.
>
> The higher a lamp, the greater the unlighted area at its base. By reducing the height of streetlamps and the distance between them, and decreasing the intensity of the flame in each lamp so as not to use more gas, we were able to light the city's streets better.
>
> Extremely bright lights are useless; they blind people more than they light their way.

Haussmann's technical motives cannot be separated from purely stylistic considerations. Haussmann gave Second Empire Paris a very special quality that has totally disappeared today, because of the widespread use of lamps better suited to highways than to a big city's streets. In Haussmann's Paris there were three types of streetlamps, the last of which had three variants. The generic models established a perfectly clear hierarchy of streets. At the very bottom of the hierarchy was the wall fixture, used on little streets whose narrow sidewalks made it practically impossible to use lampposts. On midsize streets, single lampposts were used. Finally, along the city's major arteries one found big posts topped by one, two, or more lamps. A large number of secondary variants were used for individual streets and contributed to defining particularly prestigious places.

In all, there were seventy-eight stylistic variants of the generic models. Systematic use of brown cast iron, sometimes trimmed in gold, provided a strong common denominator to unify the streetlamp network. Rare exceptions, the bronze streetlamps around the Louvre and the Opera House identified two of the city's most monumental sites. It is a shame that the marvelously refined hierarchy of streetlamps found in Second Empire Paris has in large part disappeared. (The streetlamp Hittorff designed for the Champs-Elysées has been used in a number of more or less prestigious places, which in no way makes up for the drastic reduction of the initial range of models and the destruction of the old hierarchy.)

My analysis would not be complete without a word or two about how green spaces were used to structure the cityscape. It might be a good idea to start by recalling the history of green space in the urban organism. Verdure can be used to structure a city only after all ties between city and country have been broken, that is, only after a city has so grown that the rural landscape is no longer perceptible or directly accessible from it. In the Middle Ages this break was very pronounced. A city's ramparts limited usable space, so all reserves of land gradually disappeared. Later this situation was modified when, after the invention of artillery, medieval walls were replaced by embankments topped by boulevards that, for purely military reasons, had to be lined with trees. The military boulevards gradually became a popular place to go for a stroll. In the cool shade of the trees one could contemplate the countryside around the city or chat with friends, while also enjoying the fresh air. Though the boulevards' military function eventually disappeared, they were left standing and remained popular promenades. When cities overflowed beyond the embankments, strips of verdure were left between the old town and the new.

If the boulevard began as a boundary between city and country, the avenue is of purely rural origin. Avenues were lined with tall trees[22] to distinguish them from the surrounding landscape of leafy forests, low hedges, and fields of crops. To contrast with the flowing lines of the rural landscape (where lot pattern is determined by the lay of the land), they were made abstract and straight, and thus may be considered a forerunner of land art. Leading to a farm, a manor, a castle, or a village, avenues always prepared one for an important event in the rural landscape. Eventually built just outside cities, they announced that something exceptional was nearby and foreshadowed the city's geometrical organization.

Seventeenth-century engineers often used rows of trees along roads and around towns to structure vast landscapes. Their efforts eventually resulted in the invention of suburban areas, where organized verdure and nature constantly interact.

The eighteenth century "urbanized" the avenue and used it to build new districts. The tree-lined streets preceded the buildings: they defined urban compartments and, when necessary, hid an unfinished section's disorder. The urbanization of Versailles clearly shows how avenues could be used to divide a town into a series of autonomous neighborhoods (reflecting purely sociological zoning criteria). Avenues split the town up into fragments, while also giving each fragment the autonomy it required.

Cities made up of autonomous towns reveal the initial status of the tree-lined street: at once a boundary and a place of social interaction, it is also a frontier. Tree-lined streets had no permanent function of their

Landscaping

The Hierarchy
of Green Spaces

1. Boulevard Haussmann, looking from the corner of the Avenue de Messine toward the Avenue Friedland. Photo: Marville, ca. 1876. **2.** Avenue Mozart. **3.** Rue La Fontaine.

Facing page: **1.** Boulevard de Sébastopol, looking toward the Gare de l'Est. **2.** Avenue Ledru-Rollin.

Place de Vintimille, today the Place Adolphe-Max, looking toward the Rue de Bruxelles. Photo: Marville, ca. 1874.

own, but took on a variety of temporary functions, ranging from the seasonal stroll to fairs, open-air markets, demonstrations, parades, and public ceremonies. In short, they replaced the polyvalent spaces outside the medieval city's ramparts (e.g., lists, fairgrounds, military esplanades).

In the nineteenth century, when new streets absolutely had to be built through the extremely dense center of Paris, the avenue was brought into the city. The avenue model was first used for the second of the big new streets that prepared the way for Haussmann. The extension of the Rue de Rivoli had been built without trees; the Boulevard de Sébastopol, on the other hand, created a stately corridor of verdure through the center. This did not lessen the city's unity (indeed, Paris has never had the specialized fabric of the London parks). But the Boulevard de Sébastopol was the first new street to subdivide the urban continuum of central Paris by using a model previously found only on the outskirts (the Louis XIV boulevards and the big suburban avenues that accompany them).

Every Parisian boulevard provides some district with a border and a showcase. Seen from the middle, the city's boulevards look like nothing but tree-lined roads. But from a little farther off, their monumental power emerges. The opposite sides of each boulevard merge to form a single landscape, a bit like the banks of a river. And to continue the metaphor, the flow of traffic is so great on certain streets that they are as impassable as a river.

The avenues and boulevards of Paris are one of the mainsprings of the city's spatial organization. They are the city's skeleton, and the yardstick by which all the other streets are judged. By virtue of their vastness, their verdure, and their architectural regularity, they are at the top of the hierarchy of intraurban areas. Beneath them are found, in descending order, those streets that lack verdure, width,

architecturally coherent façades, and finally regularity in the height, alignment, and materials of the buildings.

Parks and Gardens

Paris was also landscaped with woods, parks, and gardens, whose place in the hierarchy of green spaces depended on their size, their location, and the social class using them. The Second Empire structured woods as urban spaces by using benches and other items to contrast the "civilized" avenues and paths with the "wilderness" of copses and groves around them, and closely modeled the city's squares and gardens on the boulevard. Open spaces designed to loosen the tight urban fabric, the city's parks and gardens were usually framed with monumental avenues and façades. (The most striking examples are the avenues around the Monceau park and the façades that border the Square Montholon and the Square Maurice Gardette.) All the city's green spaces were structured strongly, but in different ways. In the city's various woods, the roads alone were responsible for organizing space and determining scale. For smaller green spaces, there was a striking increase in spatial markers such as sculptures, grillwork fences, and flower beds. Finally, when a green space was small enough to be easily identified as a whole, a very picturesque, irregular landscaping was used, since the regular lines of the buildings around small gardens provided an omnipresent structure. Squares containing public gardens became anti-intersections, just as the boulevard was an anti-street. Between the city's quiet, landscaped squares and its busy intersections, there was no lack of intermediate structures. Often underestimated, the Place de la République is a mixture of garden and intersection where leisure and commerce alternate. Though such combinations of antithetical functions have been seen as illegitimate

317

319

1. Square Berlioz. 2. Square Montholon.

hybrids, they can also be admired for their exceptional complementarity and their way of linking separate organisms.

Center and Outskirts

Another development in Second Empire Paris, the 1860 annexation, shows that Haussmann saw the city as a highly unified organism made up of a great diversity of component parts. The 1860 annexation of the old suburbs lying inside the Thiers fortifications of 1844 led to the creation of a number of new arrondissements (from the eleventh to the twentieth) and to a radical restructuring of the areas concerned. In particular, the new arrondissements were organized around centers, which in itself is most revealing of Haussmann's conception of urban space.

Haussmann is usually remembered as the man who demolished Old Paris, but what he actually did is quite another matter. Indeed, Haussmann's greatest and most brilliantly orchestrated project —though it did sometimes have disastrous social and economic consequences—was the reconquest of the suburbs that had sprung up around the Farmers-General Wall during the reign of Louis-Philippe. The 1860 annexation was an extraordinarily bold undertaking: "In 1859, when it was decided to eliminate the toll wall and annex the suburban Zone, the latter had a population of 331,593, according to the 1856 census; but in actual fact the number was closer to 400,000. Old Paris, which officially counted 1,174,246 inhabitants, most assuredly had a population of over 1,200,000, crowded onto 8,125 acres. After the suburban Zone was annexed on January 1, 1860, Paris had a population of some 1,600,000 and a total surface area of 17,515 acres."[23]

A very ambitious undertaking, the annexation was also a big gamble: would the city be able to deal with a doubled surface area and a 30 percent increase in population? The annexed area's infrastructure (apart from a few public-works projects already undertaken) was limited to some old suburban roads, and to some poorly organized housing developments built over the preceding twenty years. The development of the street system was an utter necessity, but certainly not the only one. Haussmann realized that each new district needed a center active and autonomous enough to attract the local population. The traditional way of creating such centers had been to build a church, weekly attendance ensuring the prosperity of tradesmen who set up shop nearby. (Indeed, a district's main shopping street could always be found in the vicinity of its church.) Since the First Empire, neighborhood life in the outlying areas had also revolved around big markets, which made it unnecessary to come into the center of Paris for provisions.[24] The combination of church and market characterized the big new Restoration developments (e.g., Beaugrenelle and

1

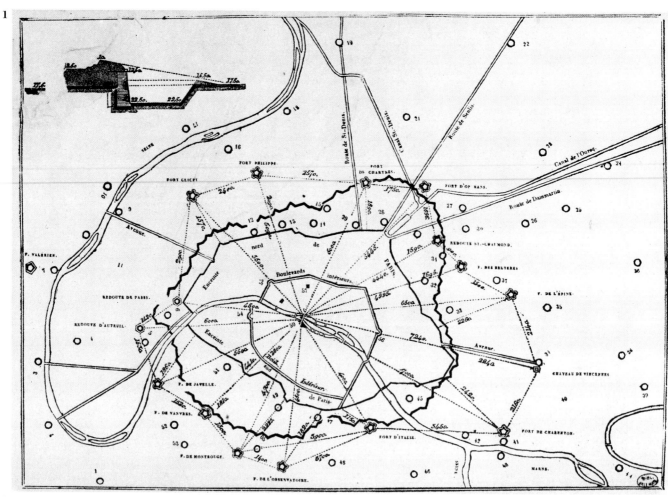

2

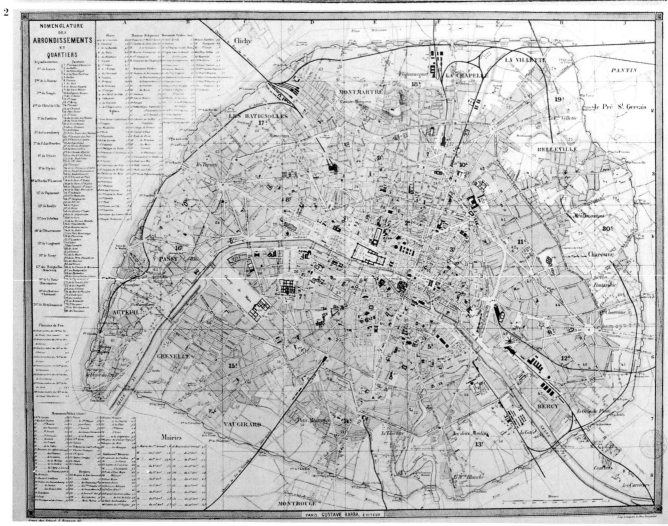

PARIS. GUSTAVE BARBA, ÉDITEUR.

Facing page: **1.** *Plan ministériel des fortifications autour de Paris*, ca. 1840. The initial project was slightly modified when the Thiers fortifications were built. For topographical and strategic reasons, the rampart was placed well outside the city. **2.** Twenty years later (1860) the city annexed the area between the Farmers-General Wall and the Thiers fortifications.
Below: the old town hall in the seventeenth arrondissement, 18 Rue des Batignolles (now destroyed).

A forerunner of Haussmann city planning: the new center of the La Villette district was set up down the canal from the old one.
1. Saint-Jacques-Saint-Christophe and the Square de Bitche. **2.** Place de Bitche, photographed from the canal.

Batignolles) and indeed was largely responsible for their popularity. In the La Villette district, the combination of a church, a school, and a fire station—with a public garden and market in front, and the town hall and a night shelter in back—is a perfect example of the nineteenth-century conception of a neighborhood center. Though the basic structure was set up prior to the Haussmann era (the church was built in 1841-44), La Villette can be seen as the prototype of the outlying centers built after 1860.

The Second Empire's main contribution was to add a public garden to the market and church—an addition certainly not unrelated to the emperor's desire to "elevate" the working classes and improve public health conditions. However, the most important single element in a new district's center was the town hall.[25] Since 1830, an original architectural interpretation had been developing in response to the town hall's expanding role in community life. Not only an administrative building, the town hall also served as a police station, a charity office, even an open university, and eventually became the community center and secular temple of today.

The Second Empire's goal was to destroy the old suburban structure by creating new centers on undeveloped ground. It was a risky decision to build the sixteenth arrondissement's town hall on a deserted boulevard between Passy and Chaillot, the nineteenth's halfway between Belleville and Ménilmontant, and the eighteenth's very far from Butte-aux-Cailles. But the town halls were accompanied by numerous structures and services, and the old suburban fabric was gradually restructured with new artificial centers.

None of the town halls in the ten outlying arrondissements was located in a preexisting center (with the exception of the town hall of the seventeenth arrondissement, which had been the town hall of Batignolles before the 1860 annexation). But if the new edifices were built far from the old suburban centers, they were always built near an old faubourg. Thus the eleventh arrondissement's town hall was admirably located at the intersection of the Rue de la Roquette and the Boulevard Voltaire (where it joins the important Avenue Parmentier). Similarly, the twelfth arrondissement's was built at the intersection of the Rue de Charenton and the Avenue Daumesnil—an intersection that has held its own, despite the construction of the railroad line that killed the rest of the area. In the thirteenth arrondissement the new Avenue des Gobelins, grafted onto the Avenue de l'Italie and the old boulevards, offered a perfect location that had the advantage of being close to Butte-aux-Cailles and the church of Sainte-Jeanne-d'Arc. In the fourteenth, the intersection of the Avenue du Maine and the Plaisance development was chosen; in the fifteenth, the intersection of Vaugirard and Grenelle. In the sixteenth arrondissement the site chosen was the intersection of the Rue de la Pompe and the Rue Henri-Martin. In the seventeenth, on the other hand, the standard approach was not used, which led to the Ternes neighborhood's being cut off from the rest of the arrondissement (just as Auteuil was later to be separated from Passy). But in the eighteenth the standard approach was used; the town hall was erected halfway between Abbesses and Goutte-d'Or, at the intersection of the Rue du Mont-Cenis and the new Rue Ordener, which let the arrondissement expand northward and fill the back of the hill. In the nineteenth arrondissement an artificial network of new streets was built around the Rue de Crimée and the Rue de Meaux, and the town hall was erected opposite the entrance to the Buttes-Chaumont park. Finally, in the twentieth, Charonne was joined to Belleville and Ménilmontant, and the weakness of the old network (Rue Orfila, Rue de la Chine, Rue Pelleport) was compensated for by building the town hall next to Tenon Hospital.

The monumental architecture of the town halls indicates that they were meant to play an important role in structuring the new arrondissements. Around those prestigious buildings a public garden, a market, a school, a police station, and a clinic were eventually built (during or after the Haussmann era, and even as late as the 1930s). Yet, as in the case of the city's big new streets, there was always a tendency to avoid overconcentration. Churches often kept the size of the old parish churches and formed secondary centers in the general hierarchy. When there was a heavy concentration of major edifices, it was because a particularly strong center was needed in places where there had been nothing before, as in the case of the town hall of the eighteenth arrondissement. Markets were usually distributed in an

Grafting the New Centers On

1. Town hall, nineteenth arrondissement, Place A.-Carrel.
2. Town hall, twentieth arrondissement, Place Gambetta.

The Structure of the New Arrondissements

arrondissement's various neighborhoods (e.g., in the nineteenth, the olive, Tanger, and Secrétan markets). A market always strengthened a new neighborhood. Temporary stands, which could be dismantled, were used at first. Though still sometimes found today, they were, to Haussmann's mind, just a preliminary stage to be replaced later by permanent, monumental edifices that would structure not only individual districts but also the city as a whole. (Similarly, a number of temporary town halls, churches, and even schools were built, supposedly to be replaced later by big, monumental edifices.)

In the early twentieth century, athletic facilities took on a comparable structural role. The monumental gymnasium on the Avenue Jean-Jaurès and Louis Bonnier's remarkable swimming pool in the Butte-aux-Cailles area are noteworthy examples. More recently, attempts to give the city's post offices a similar structural role have been much less successful.

In each of the new arrondissements, secondary centers clustered around the major center, and the Haussmann and pre-Haussmann networks became closely intertwined. In turn, each individual neighborhood had multiple nuclei that determined its unique flavor. In the sixteenth arrondissement's Passy district (where real-estate promoters have destroyed much of the historical center), the church and the market, at either end of the Rue de l'Annonciation (the main shopping street), formed the pivotal points in a neighborhood that spread on one side toward the Place de Passy and the Rue de Passy (a busy suburban route), and on the other side, via the Rue Duban and the Rue Lekain, onto the lower slopes of the hill (Vignes, Ranelagh). Passy was structured to form a coherent whole with various centers of secondary importance (the post office, the La Muette train station, the primary schools on the Rue des Bauches, and the Lycée Molière), and was clearly distinct from the neighboring area where the Rue de la Pompe intersects with the Rue de la Tour. Owing to the presence of the town hall and the big Lycée Janson-de-Sailly, and to its connection with the big monumental streets around the Arch of Triumph, the Trocadéro, and Alma, the Rue de la Pompe section became the center of the sixteenth arrondissement. Yet the arrondissement was given not just one focal point but a number of diverse elements. There is nothing exaggerated about the hierarchy Haussmann invented. It gave the city a rich and nuanced structure that made it possible to interpret every space on several levels.

Nineteenth-century city planning was based on a very concrete, progressive, and dynamic approach to urban structure. Haussmann used a modular approach, but he never lost sight of the city's overall unity. His policies are all the more praiseworthy because, during the real-estate boom of the Second Empire, they provided developers with clear guidelines concerning what they could and could not do.

The use of coherent and coordinated models to channel building activity seems particularly admirable today; despite their training and dedication, modern city planners lack the pragmatic expertise that characterized the Haussmann era. What is particularly remarkable is that Haussmann's approach was worked out in the field and was never given any theoretical underpinnings.[26] Yet his approach strongly reflected a global vision of the city and city life that was deeply embedded in French and European culture.

Mansion or Apartment Building?

While the apartment house triumphed in the central districts of Paris, the mansion, as various eye-witnesses of the day were quick to point out,[27] underwent a veritable renascence during the Second Empire. Directly related to the city's expansion, this renascence was made possible by the very flexible conception of urban space that characterized the Haussmann era. The mansion became one of the terms in the hierarchy of spaces and constructions to which the Haussmann era was so attached.

The sumptuous apartment houses on the new avenues in the central districts represented the top of a hierarchy that remained faithful to the center/outskirts distinction handed down from the eighteenth century. Façade ornament decreased as one moved away from the major streets. And when one crossed the boundaries of the city's traditional core (circumscribed by the Louis XIV wall, which still functioned as a frontier), one found a gradual alteration in other elements structuring the city's appearance. Building height decreased; the visual separation of a building's main floors from its basement and roof was weakened; and continuous balconies were diminished or eliminated.

Indeed, the absence of a third-floor balcony is a fairly sure sign of a building's noncentral location. The elimination of the balcony was often accompanied by the disappearance of shops on the ground floor. Thus the development of the residential function in outlying districts was marked by a weakening of the separation between basement and main floors. (In the central districts, there was always a strong break between the shops and the shopkeepers' residences at basement level and the bourgeois apartments above.)

Similarly, as one moved away from the center, there was a gradual transition from apartment buildings to big houses. Apartment buildings commonly lost a floor, and the zone separating the main floors from the roof was weakened. In some cases, the recessed top story and the continuous upper balcony were eliminated altogether. In others, the roof was brought down to where the recessed story had been; the lower slope of the mansard roof and the dormer windows merged with the top story and sometimes resulted in an original new approach, as on the big squares in the seventeenth arrondissement's Péreire section. The windows on the top floor were then treated as

Small apartment buildings in the new arrondissements. **1.** Rue Lekain. **2.** Corner of the Rue Duban and the Rue Lekain. **3.** Rue Guichard. **4.** Rue Gavarni.

dormer windows barely projecting from the base of the roof; the pediments recall those above the third-floor windows, but are in a more contrasted position since they stand out against the lower slope of the roof. In the seventeenth arrondissement the merging of a building's roof and recessed story was carried even farther: the slate covering of the lower slope continued down to the balcony slab.

The centers of the new arrondissements were indicated by a return to six-story apartment buildings with a recessed story and continuous balcony at the top. Rich ornament reappeared. But the centers of the new arrondissements were generally distinguished from the city's center by the absence of third-floor balconies, the use of a standard ceiling height for every floor, and the reduction of the basement to a simple ground floor (even when used for shops). The new centers, like the arrondissements around them, were predominantly residential. As soon as one left them, one found a mixture of architectural types and sizes; mansions and private houses reappeared, creating variation from one lot to the next. In some areas a clear structure was found from the start and was respected in later years. In others the evolution of urban policy has created more or less incoherent mixtures of architectural types, especially on the edges of the old villages.

Small Apartment Buildings

The Europe district reveals the beginnings of a conflict between hierarchical structure and typological uniformity. The initial model for the Boulevard Malesherbes was the five-story apartment building: a two-floor basement; two main floors, of which the lower was given a more prestigious treatment; a recessed top story; and a mansard roof. Later on, a certain number of six-story buildings were introduced, which caused breaks in the alignment. These six-story buildings,

328

5. Place Wagram.

scattered throughout the surrounding neighborhood, indicate an important change in urban policy. The originality of the Europe-Monceau area had been based specifically on the slightly lower height of its buildings; comparison with the area around the Arch of Triumph is proof enough that such a distinction was not without interest.

Nevertheless, the "small apartment building" persisted throughout the Second Empire. The architectural regularity of the boulevards, even when buildings lost a story, showed that they were hierarchically superior to the rest of a neighborhood. Moreover, on secondary streets basements were usually treated as a simple ground floor, and there was no important separation between a building's basement and its upper stories. (Often there was no balcony, and elaborate pediments were sometimes placed even on the second floor.) In addition, an identical ceiling height was used for each of the three main floors. The roof cornice retained an unmistakable visible impact, and the use of a continuous balcony was far from systematic. All these elements bring us back to the traditional model of the private house.

But such typological nuances were eliminated in the big blocks of flats built in the outlying developments during the Haussmann era. An "economical" version of the central model appeared. While the quality of ornament declined, neither the size nor the shape of buildings was touched. The big, uniform apartment buildings constructed on the new streets clearly reflected the fact that the east of Paris was less prestigious than the west. The apartment houses on the Rue Monge, the Boulevard Morland, and the Avenue Laumière, for example, were simplified versions of the sumptuous bourgeois constructions on the Avenue Victor-Hugo and the Boulevard Saint-Germain. The stonework was retained, but builders skimped on sculpture, cast iron, room size, insulation, and the decoration of entrance halls, staircases, and living rooms.

In poorer neighborhoods the central model was realized with cheaper building materials. In the 1860s poor versions of the big bourgeois apartment buildings were built with coated rubblework façades, but they conformed to the bourgeois model in shape and size (e.g., Ménilmontant). Lower-class architecture as such began to die out. Whether developers were building for the rich or the poor, they used the same economic and financial methods. The result was very similar architecture, the poor man's building being distinguished only by the flatness of its façade, based on a simple opposition of cordons and bays, whereas the rich man's building was adorned with elaborate window frames and sills, balconies, cast ironwork, and various projections and recesses. Thus did industrial standardization transform and impoverish culture. In the traditional hierarchy a certain number of interesting architectural elements had been unique to each social class. Henceforth there was one cultural type for everyone, but only the rich could realize it fully. In other words, one group could afford to be elegant, while everybody else had to settle for mediocre copies of the bourgeois model.

Aristocratic Mansions

As typological variation disappeared in the construction of apartment houses, the mansion was reinvigorated with an updated approach combining features from the apartment building and the bourgeois house.[28] In the age of classicism, sumptuous mansions had been built between a courtyard and a garden, particularly in the Marais (e.g., Rohan) and the Faubourg Saint-Germain. In the nineteenth century, mansion architecture moved away from the earlier models, which took up too much space and were really only suited to the suburban setting of the old faubourgs. Nineteenth-century mansions,

3. Rue de Monceau and Rue de Lisbonne.
4. Rue de Monceau and Rue de Vézelay.

like the century that produced them, were fundamentally urban. They were designed for smaller lots and attached to adjacent buildings so as to disturb a block's homogeneity as little as possible. Compact designs based on three or four stories were created, skillfully combining the volumetrics of an apartment building with the layout of a mansion.[29]

On the edges of the Monceau park, a small number of mansions were built between a courtyard and a garden (their garden being, in fact, the park itself). They had the traditional carriage entrance, with the mansion at the back of the lot and a courtyard (for the stables) on the side. Somewhat reminiscent of the neoclassical mansion/villa (e.g., Rue de Trévise), these mansions resemble isolated monumental sculptures. The eighteenth-century treatment of the lot—the transition from public to private—was abandoned. Indeed, the most surprising thing about these constructions is that the lots have no interior. Visible from all sides, these mansions, like monuments, are entirely public. The Menier mansion on the Avenue Van-Dyck can be seen from all sides; despite its size, it resembles a suburban house more than a city mansion. Though mansions sometimes included a winter garden, a caretaker's lodge, or a shed at a right angle to the main building, there was little taste for annexes: masses were to be dense and unified.

At the beginning of the Third Republic, mansions moved even further away from the classical tradition. Inspired by Blois, Jules Février's huge neo-Gothic construction on the Place Malesherbes (1879) is based on extremely dense, compact volumes, and was built right on the street with cut-off corners. The only open space inside the lot is a narrow courtyard accessible through a carriage entrance. At once a house and a monument, the mansion is compositionally far removed from the eighteenth-century conception of the city mansion.

Finally, in the transition from mansion to apartment house, one

Following pages:
1. Fould mansion, Rue de Berri, 1858.
2. Mansion, Avenue du Bois-de-Boulogne.
3. Basilewsky mansion, initial project, 1864.
4. Camondo mansion, Rue de Monceau. Paris, Bibliothèque des Arts Décoratifs, Maciet Collection.

1

2

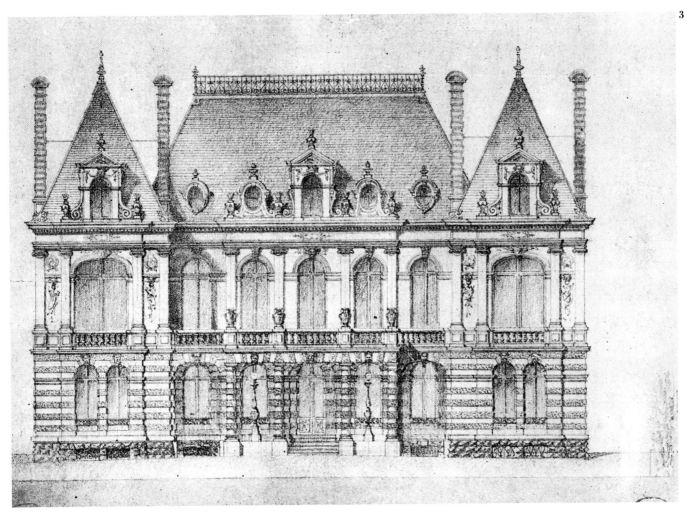

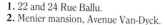
1. 22 and 24 Rue Ballu.
2. Menier mansion, Avenue Van-Dyck.

finds the four- or five-story mansion/building, which differs from the bourgeois apartment building only in interior layout (invisible from the street), size (two stories less), and façade ornament (often exuberant). Being miniature apartment buildings, these constructions were not particularly suitable for use as private houses, as seen in their superposition of identical stories. (The architecture of the last quarter of the nineteenth century often played on the opposition between a building's regular appearance outdoors and the functional reality of the residence within.) On some avenues like the Boulevard La Tour-Maubourg, one finds heterogeneous rows of bourgeois apartment houses, classical-style mansions, mansion/buildings (for residential or mixed use), and luxurious private houses on narrow lots.

Small Mansions

Rows of small attached mansions set back from the street behind grillwork fences appeared in the eighteenth century and remained popular through the end of the Second Empire. Interest crystallized much more on punctuating the row—with multiple little repetitive stops—than on the mansion itself. Quickly altered by the individual evolution of each lot, attached mansions can be considered one of the most original developments in the neoclassical tradition.

Other small edifices, set back slightly from the building line behind a low grillwork fence and a little garden, were also popular during the Second Empire. Unlike the English, the French never adopted the principle of a cellar kitchen lighted by a trench (made possible by setting a building back from the street). The little gardens existed not to provide light, but to modify a street's status by bringing it a little verdure. Thus the residential character of these low constructions —usually two floors and an attic—tended to be combined with the typically suburban idea of verdure.

Certain mansions are hard to tell apart from apartment houses. **1.** 32 Rue de Prony. **2.** 8 Rue de Prony. **3.** 14 Rue de Prony. **4** and **5.** 1 Place Malesherbes. **6.** 2 Place Malesherbes.

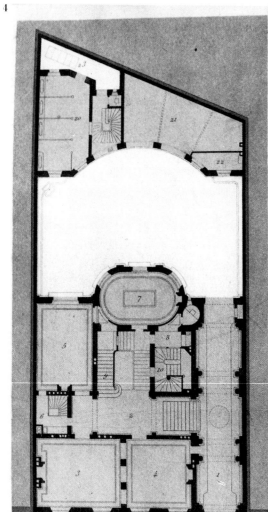

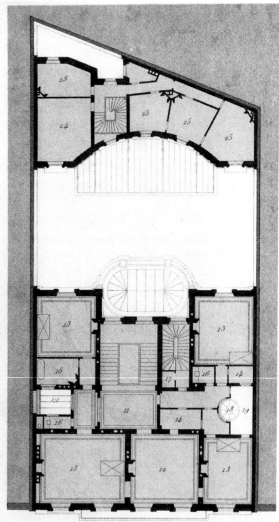

Rez-de-Chaussée

1er Etage

Mansion, 12 Rue de Prony, 1883. **1.** The façade today. **2.** Street façade. **3.** Courtyard façade. **4.** Plans of the first and second floors. Bibliothèque des Arts Décoratifs, Maciet Collection.

Though groups of small mansions were seldom built in a single operation (indeed, the mansions in a single row can date anywhere from 1850 to 1910), they formed a coherent landscape, primarily because the building line was unanimously respected (even when that line was moved back from the official line). When a mansion was not actually attached to the side of the building next to it, a wall was built to hide the gap; while each edifice was treated as an autonomous individual unit, it also had to be linked to the continuous plane of façades on a street.[30]

One might think that an unbroken row of highly contrasting façades would create a deep break in urban composition. In fact, the traditional compositional grouping of similar detached mansions is no more unified than a composition that, while emphasizing individualized façades, requires those façades to form an unbroken row. Urban unity is as strong in the second case as in the first, despite the great diversity of façades.

It is striking that private houses became increasingly diversified expressions of their occupants' personalities during the Second Empire, just as apartment buildings were all coming to resemble one another. Neighborhoods of private houses became mosaic spaces that in a way were rivals. Nothing could be more indicative of the disintegration of the social body that began with the advent of the industrial world.

As a rule of thumb, rows of small mansions with identical façades date from the beginning of the Haussmann era. On the other hand, rows with highly varied façades were usually built in the Third Republic—from the 1870s to the 1890s—and reflect the new cult of bourgeois individualism: a dialectical relationship between social conformity and the development of individual personality.

Private Houses

Neighborhoods of two- and three-story private houses enjoyed great popularity during the Second Empire. Although these neighborhoods are usually lumped together under a single heading, they can in fact be divided into two categories, for some are based on a suburban model, while others are fundamentally urban.

The suburban-style neighborhoods were made up of detached houses (or pairs of attached houses), linked together by verdant spaces quite visible behind the low, vine-covered grillwork fences on the street. Unlike the big avenues in the center, the streets in these sections did not have to be lined with trees to be considered green spaces; the abundance of plants around the houses was quite enough. Streets could be quite narrow, since their only function was to provide access to the houses on them (which also explains the many dead ends). The unity of these neighborhoods was created by the picturesque architecture of the houses and the abundant verdure.

Small mansions. **1.** 1 Villa Montmorency. **2.** Rue de Prony, between the Rue Médéric and the Rue de Courcelles. **3.** 19 and 21 Rue Fortuny. **4.** Rue Fortuny, photographed from the Rue de Prony.

Quite opposed to this approach were essentially urban neighborhoods with continuous or nearly continuous rows of identical façades, rigid landscaping (lawns, low grillwork fences), and strongly structured arrangements of forms. In some cases, trees were planted along the streets; significantly, some of these streets were called avenues (like the Avenue Jules-Janin in the sixteenth arrondissement).

No real distinction has been made as yet between the kinds of individual houses in these neighborhoods. In spite of their common properties (low constructions meant to be used as individual houses, small lots and streets, structural use of verdure), important nuances separated suburban-style and urban-style neighborhoods. Just as apartment buildings varied according to whether they were located on a square, an avenue, or a secondary street, so too did individual houses vary according to their location.

The neighborhoods concerned have changed greatly since the Second Empire, rendering the original suburban/urban distinction considerably less obvious. Yet many of the outlying sections in the west of Paris deserve study, for they are far richer than the models of urban organization—based on the strict opposition of collective buildings and private houses, and by extension, of mineral and verdant environments—in use today. Midnineteenth-century architecture proves that such simplistic oppositions can be greatly nuanced, for there exist a number of possibilities between the two extremes of the collective-mineral and the individual-vegetal. Just as several sizes of building are possible, so also are several types of relationship to the vegetal, regardless of whether individual houses or apartment buildings are involved.

8-18, Place Malesherbes.

Antiurban Styles

In the 1860s the suburban characteristics of the private houses in the outlying districts were accentuated, and a tight intertwining of verdure and construction triumphed. Because of their monumentality, the apartment houses of the day were not suitable for the city's outlying areas. There emerged instead a rustic style based on picturesqueness and exoticism and diametrically opposed to monumental architecture. Exposed brick and plaster replaced stone, and picturesque shutters, glazed tiles, and ceramic ornament decorated façades.

Exemplified by brick houses with intricate wood trim, and directly derived from neoclassical garden architecture, the chalet style dominated. Color and tectonic detail triumphed, in a style that did not hesitate to draw on neo-Gothic and neo-Romanesque modernity—indeed, on anything opposed to classicism. Everything about the new style was opposed to the sobriety of freestone construction and the graphic luxury of cast ironwork.

1. 17 Avenue des Tilleuls, in the Villa Montmorency.
2. Artist's house, 32 Rue de Boulogne, 1868. Paris, Bibliothèque des Arts Décoratifs, Maciet Collection.
3. 30 Avenue des Tilleuls.

The nearly systematic absence of cast iron is, moreover, quite significant: intricate wood trim similar to a chalet's was preferred. Similarly, French-style wood shutters were used, rather than retractable metal ones. Yet despite their rustic look, these elements were all machine-made.

The chalet style—which first appeared in the 1840s, but really caught on after 1870—was not inevitable. The delightful Ionic style of wooden houses with abundant ornamental latticework, like the houses in the Hameau Montmorency, would have served just as well. Similarly, the odd isbas in the Villa Beauséjour would have made an excellent model (especially after the publication of Viollet-le-Duc's book on Russian art). But as fate would have it, the chalet style triumphed. In the early twentieth century, to be sure, the Normandy sea-resort style returned in houses with half-timbering and big picture windows. Yet whatever the style, all these houses were designed in a resolutely antiurban spirit.

A New Dialectic

The center/outskirts opposition, as expressed in the contrasting urban and antiurban styles, became so pronounced that it could be considered the key structural feature of Paris at the end of the Second Empire. On the other hand, apartment houses became so monumental that the old opposition between monumental and vernacular architecture practically disappeared. The public monument was no longer defined in opposition to the apartment house, but simply as the highest degree in a hierarchy that also included the grandiose apartment buildings on the city's big boulevards and squares and, lower still, the more modest buildings on secondary streets.

4. 8 Rue La Fontaine. 5. Avenue Jules-Janin. 6. 16 Hameau Boileau. 7 and 8. 8 Villa Beauséjour. 9. Corners of the Rue du Ranelagh and the Rue de Boulainvilliers.

1. 1 Villa Montmorency. **2.** 40 Rue du Ranelagh and
26 Rue de Boulainvilliers.

Avenue des Chalets.

The ambiguity of the public monument's status is clearly revealed by the contrast between the Gare du Nord and the nearby Opera House, two edifices of enormous scale and monumentality. The train station is based on an austere, very solemn style that creates a striking stylistic break with the buildings around it. From the colossal pilasters to the immense windows, everything is of truly gigantic scale; the verticality of Hittorff's station (e.g., the tight fluting) contradicts the insistent horizontals of the neighboring blocks of flats, as its "diaphanous" quality contradicts their compact masses. Conversely, for the Opera House Charles Garnier drew on all the characteristic features of the apartment houses around the site: the power and denseness of their mass, the insistence on horizontality, and the regular spacing of solids and voids. Consequently, the Opera House is in total keeping with the buildings around it, even though they were designed by two different architects using rigorously opposed ornamental repertoires. The only thing that individualizes Garnier's edifice is the richness of its ornament and coloring. The Opera House is, so to speak, an embellished apartment building.

Interestingly enough, an identical tendency to make the monumental edifice commonplace had appeared in the eighteenth century, characterizing two of the most prestigious realizations of the day: the Grand Théâtre in Bordeaux and the Théâtre-Français in Paris. In fact, the integration of the individual monument into a global

343

Avenue de l'Opéra, photographed from the Rue Louis-le-Grand. Photo: Marville (?), 1871.

monumental hierarchy is one of the key features of the modern style. That hierarchy calls the very notion of monumentality into question by shattering the monument's dialectical relationship to its environment. Working in a very old tradition (symbolized by Vitruvius), neoclassical architects did their best to maintain the contrast between the individual monument and its environment for nearly a century, but urban standardization eventually won out. This change coincided in a most obvious way with the appearance of antiurban morphological types. Thus did the dialectic of the detached suburban-style house and the hard monumentality of the center replace the traditional dialectic of the monument and its context. Unlike the old faubourgs, the new suburban-style developments were not even fragments of the city, being resolutely antiurban spaces.

By disturbing the old hierarchy of architectural typologies, this new dialectic eventually led to the disappearance of an entire range of edifices and to systematic use of the two contradictory models of the apartment building and the suburban house. During the Second Empire there was still some variety. In some parts of the city there was even a fairly lively reaction to the typological simplification of the urban space, the small mansions discussed earlier being a case in point. However, all the signs of a profound alteration of the urban order were already present. The mechanisms that would determine the city's subsequent evolution had been set up; the first results, positive as well as negative, were beginning to be felt.

The Crisis of the Haussmann Approach

Paradoxically enough, the hierarchy that formed the very foundation of the Haussmann approach was responsible for this deterioration. In the first phase of the city's transformation, that hierarchy made it possible to restructure an urban landscape on the verge of bursting at the seams. But inevitably, there was a sort of monumental escalation, the indirect consequence of which was to lower the value accorded other urban types. Furthermore, regulation architecture, based on a uniform model of urban space, began to reveal its shortcomings.

The need for a hierarchy cannot be contested. The key problem that Haussmann and his contemporaries ran up against was how to clarify a system that, having grown beyond the old pedestrian scale, had become confusingly complex. The city's seemingly infinite expansion, lamented by all late-eighteenth-century observers, had enlarged and beautified the city; now it was necessary to bring order to the chaos. Given the city's huge scale, the old opposition between urban and suburban was no longer enough; different structural levels had to be introduced into the city itself. In the 1840s the method of "architecturalization," derived from the traditional antithesis between the monumental and the vernacular, appeared spontaneously. During the reign of Louis-Philippe, the forms of monumental and vernacular architecture were codified in large units—the compositional grouping of buildings constructed by different landowners. The goal was to unify new developments and give them a look of coherence by emphasizing unity and monumentality, as opposed to the dense and often incoherent fabric of eighteenth-century buildings. The new architecture triumphed all the more easily in that it let the bourgeoisie express its power and at the same time make money by fueling the real-estate market. The guiding principle of apartment-house architecture was modernity; each new generation elaborated increasingly bombastic models to express its superiority over the previous generation. As already noted, the evolution of the apartment house was closely linked to the city's geographic expansion. Thus one finds a linear progression from east to west: Faubourg Saint-Denis, Faubourg Montmartre, Boulevard Malesherbes, Avenue Victor-Hugo, Avenue Henri-Martin.

The typological evolution of the apartment house strongly reflected the city's historical and sociological evolution, and defined the particular atmosphere of every section of Paris, from the working-class areas on the hills in the east to the bourgeois developments of huge post-Haussmann buildings (early twentieth-century) in the west. Between these two extremes (geographical, chronological, architectural, and social), one finds in turn the bourgeois apartment

The Need for a Hierarchy

Following pages: **1.** Demolition of the Butte des Moulins to build the Avenue de l'Opéra. Place du Théâtre-Français and Rue de l'Echelle. Photo: P. Emonts, January 16, 1877. **2.** Between the Rue de l'Echelle and the Rue Saint-Augustin. In the background, the Rue d'Argenteuil. Photo: Marville, 1877. **3.** The lower end of the Avenue de l'Opéra. On the left, the Rue d'Argenteuil. Photo: Marville (?), 1877. **4.** Building the Rue Réaumur. Anon., June 1895.

347

buildings of the last quarter of the nineteenth century; those of the Second Empire, the reign of Louis-Philippe, and the Restoration; lower-middle-class constructions from the same periods; and the tightly packed streets of the preindustrial period.

These very different fabrics usually form coherent wholes, juxtaposed to each other in the city's overall structure. Different typological models were seldom mixed together except in transition zones, those borders where a neighborhood's character begins to be defined. Indeed, a mixture of types almost always marks a frontier. Thus one finds a mixed "fringe" in the sixteenth arrondissement where Auteuil joins Passy; in the seventeenth, around the Batignolles trenches; in the eighteenth, on the Rue Vauvenargues; and in the seventh, behind the Champ-de-Mars. Clear breaks in architectural typology also create frontiers, as seen in the southern edge of Auteuil and the houses on the the Poterne des Peupliers and the Rue de Mouzaïa. But the clearness of the city's structure, based on typological and chronological distinctions, also depends on the presence of shopping streets. If a clear typology is not combined with a strong shopping axis, a neighborhood will seem weak and confused, as for instance certain poorly elaborated zones in the twelfth, fifteenth, and nineteenth arrondissements. On the other hand, the combination of different chronological models in districts whose centrality had been long established was not a problem in Paris. The Haussmann streets that disemboweled the République area were easily assimilated, as was the meeting of Haussmann and post-Haussmann architecture between the Arch of Triumph and the Trocadéro. In the latter case, the two types of buildings resemble each other in mass and cornice height. The rest—the size of the roofs, the materials, the architectural ornament—forms a secondary variant that establishes a hierarchy within the neighborhood; the larger post-Haussmann buildings allow one to identify the major streets.

Monumental Hypertrophy

The "escalation" in the height of Paris buildings after 1859 strengthened the frontier character of the wide streets built through the city's traditional fabric. Unity was maintained by retaining a traditional elevation up to cornice height (basement and upper floors), and also, though this would not seem to have been obligatory, the third- and sixth-floor balconies. In the early twentieth century an important evolution in the treatment of the roof made it possible for a building to have nine or even more floors. The full and most elegant volumetrics of the roofs along the city's big avenues create powerful urban façades that clearly delimit neighborhoods. (The most obvious of these borders is formed by the imposing wall of public housing built on the old Thiers fortifications.) When Haussmann modified recent fabrics, as in certain Louis-Philippe sections of the ninth and eleventh

arrondissements, he relied on the use of higher buildings to indicate the preeminence of the new streets. The difference between streets built prior to 1859 (e.g., the Boulevard de Sébastopol and the Rue de Rivoli) and those built afterward is quite perceptible; the hierarchy is considerably stronger in the newer streets, which are like monumental valleys cutting through the undifferentiated fabric of the old neighborhoods. In the late nineteenth century new building regulations resulted in the creation of a new hierarchy in certain Haussmann neighborhoods weakened by systematic repetition of the earlier monumental model. Thus on the Boulevard Raspail, Bonnier's big curved roofs easily triumphed over the rather flat mansard roofs of the Haussmann buildings. (One cannot overemphasize the importance of the transition from the 45-degree slope still being used at the beginning of the Second Empire to the big curved roofs of the twentieth century.)

In the 1860s and 1870s another crop of big new streets was built through the center—most notably, the Avenue de l'Opéra and the Rue Réaumur. The relatively modest scale of Haussmann and pre-

351

The monumentalization of the apartment building in the late Second Empire. 65 Rue de Turbigo, corner of the Rue Volta. Photo: Marville (?), ca. 1870.

1. 8-4 Quai du Marché-Neuf. 2. Rue de Phalsbourg.
3. 6-8 Boulevard Saint-Germain.

Haussmann architecture was then replaced by a much more monumental approach. Based on the formal model provided by the Boulevard Saint-Michel and especially Davioud's Place Saint-Michel, a very dense, unified typology tended to be used for all buildings, regardless of their location. This seriously threatened the old hierarchy. To put it simply, the capitalists were stronger than the building code. In the Europe and Monceau districts, all building activity was concentrated in the hands of a few investors. For better or worse, the modern real-estate developer was born. It did not take long for the architectural consequences of this to be felt. Buildings were standardized beyond the city government's wildest dreams, creating monotonous, unimaginative blocks whose only quality is their extreme minerality—gray stone pavement and yellow stone façades. The Rue de Rennes and the Rue des Ecoles are good examples of this new taste for architectural sobriety and power, which also reigned supreme on the western edge of the city. One might see this change in style as a transition from a shopkeeper's architecture of signs and advertisements meant to catch the eye of passersby, to a capitalist architecture based on efficiency and profitability, and perhaps intended as a moral critique of the vulgar presumptuousness of the parvenus of the early Second Empire.

The transparent façades fashionable around 1860 gave way, ten years later, to a strong return to monumentality. Solids took on new importance, ornament was simplified, and moldings were eliminated in favor of a classical architectonic ornament. The wall as wall—powerful big stone blocks stripped of ornament—came back into fashion. The rationalists, whose ideological hold on architects was now complete, demoted the decorative style of the previous decade to the rank of "bad taste." In the course of a fairly slow formal transformation (from 1865-

353

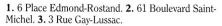
1. 6 Place Edmond-Rostand. 2. 61 Boulevard Saint-Michel. 3. 3 Rue Gay-Lussac.

70 into the 1890s), an architectural style based on mass and solids reappeared. Apartment houses were now systematically modeled on the big imperial squares—Saint-Michel, but also Europe and Opéra.

Multiple Balconies

The most visible modification—and also the easiest to interpret, thanks to its immediate sociological implications—was the appearance of a balcony on every floor. For tenants, this indicated that all a building's floors were of equal prestige, the third floor losing its hierarchical superiority. At the same time, identical ceiling heights were used on every floor. This dual transformation implied that the social distinctions between a building's tenants—however limited—no longer existed, and at the same time reflected the accelerated segregation of the various social groups in distinct neighborhoods. The architectural consequences of this were enormous. Façades were invaded by balconies, and while a subtle hierarchy was introduced between continuous balconies, partial balconies, and shallow balconies for individual window openings, refinement of detail tended to be destroyed. Comparison of both ends of the Boulevard Saint-Michel reveals this eloquently. The late Haussmann building lost much of its charm when it lost its refined ornament. Of course it gained in sobriety what it lost in subtlety, but it is hard for systematic solemnity not to lead to banality. At the end of the Second Empire a uniform architecture began to spread throughout the many sections of Paris; the break with the classic hierarchy was complete.

Multiple balconies were the most revealing sign of this new architectural banality. The heavy cast-iron balconies and repetitive architectonic detail on the Rue Gay-Lussac had nothing to do with the elegance of the first buildings on the Boulevard Saint-Michel. But

Two-floor attics.
9-11 Rue de l'Echelle.

there were also other modifications that, foreshadowing the 1884 regulation, mainly affected the shape of roofs.

A third slope, slanted 45 degrees, was placed between a roof's lower, almost vertical slope and its top slope, and two floors were built under the new roof. The lower floor was used for a bourgeois apartment that opened, via big dormers with French doors, onto a continuous balcony. The upper floor, lighted with skylights, was used for servants' quarters. This model first appeared at either end of the Avenue de l'Opéra, on the Place du Théâtre-Français, and on the Place de l'Opéra.

By the end of the Second Empire, building shells were being stuffed with as many floors as possible. Whereas apartment houses had initially included only a ground floor and mezzanine with two or at most three main floors and an attic, late Second Empire buildings had three additional floors of apartments. The mezzanine began to be used for a bourgeois apartment (as a result, the term itself has fallen into disuse). In addition, a recessed story was created between the main floors and the attic, and the attic itself was enlarged and divided into two floors. Thus on the Avenue de l'Opéra, apartment buildings contain seven floors over a basement, and their roofs have a much more powerful mass than do the neoclassical roofs built a generation earlier.

355

From Corner to Rotunda

As the scale of real-estate development changed, the individual apartment house became a very subordinate element in the composition of the block, whence the birth of special corner treatments.[31] Of course the fact that cut-off corners were needed to ensure visibility at intersections was not unrelated to this, nor was the widespread use of diagonal streets, which created triangular lots. But the main reason that corners were enhanced during the Haussmann era was the increase in compositional scale that occurred at that time. On the other hand, the special corner treatments used toward the end of Louis-Philippe's reign—notably, the coupling of window openings on the narrow bay of the cut-off corner—were just a way of strengthening a building's ornamental structure.

It is hard to say exactly when corner rotundas appeared, for various classical antecedents can be found (e.g., the marvelous Pavillon de Hanovre that once stood on the Boulevard des Italiens, and the Deshayes mansion on the Boulevard de la Madeleine). Rohault de Fleury and Henri used corner rotundas on the Place de l'Opéra as early as 1858, and Charles Garnier used the idea for the Cercle de la Librairie on the Boulevard Saint-Germain. These two prestigious models would seem to have launched the fashion of corner rotundas, which were used on more ordinary buildings at the bottom of the Rue de Rome in 1870.[32] A bit later, Paul Sédille adopted them for the new Printemps department store, turning them into one of the most prestigious motifs of late-nineteenth-century architecture. The corner rotunda characterized the second phase of the Haussmann era and enjoyed great popularity into the 1890s.[33] This continued popularity is, among other things, proof that the real architectural break between Haussmann and post-Haussmann archi-tecture did not occur at the end of the Second Empire, but rather in the 1890s and above all following the building codes of 1893 and 1902. Fundamental modifications brought about by those codes coincided with a total change in aesthetic ideals that owed in large part to the influence of art nouveau.

69 Boulevard Saint-Michel and 2 Rue Gay-Lussac.

A Style of Grandeur

Since neoclassicism, façade ornament had played a purely graphic role even when used in relief. Though discreet at first, over the years that graphism had become increasingly intrusive. On certain streets like the Rue La Fayette and the Rue de Maubeuge, façades were covered with tight systems of clashing horizontals and verticals that totally concealed the materiality of walls. The grid patterns were usually combined with an increased number of window openings separated by narrow piers. Such abuses provoked a reaction toward the end of the 1860s, when window openings were set farther apart and ornament was reduced in order to make façades look more powerful and monumental. At the beginning of the Second Empire, façades had tended toward transparency; indeed, some of them could almost have been built of cast iron rather than stone. Use of decorative grids was so pronounced that even solid panels were enriched with a frame that, more often than not, clashed with the window frames and the lines of the bays and cordons. The only thing that brought a little order to this proliferation of detail was the use of elements in relief. The buildings of the second phase of the Haussmann era, on the other hand, were characterized by an evolution in decorative approach that tended to reestablish classical order. The unexpected counterattack of colossal pilasters, columns, and entablatures must be understood in terms of scale—as an effort to put ornament into proportion with mass. Thus the colossal orders took on new vigor and replaced the delicate but monotonous relief of cordons and window frames repeated from one story to the next.

Dome, Quai Henri-IV.

After 1880, during the period leading to the highly monumental constructions of the fin de siècle (a transition that could almost be considered the third phase of the Haussmann era), the elimination of graphic proliferation and the colossal treatment of elevations reflected an important change in compositional scale. It was no accident that the apartment houses built by the big insurance companies and financial institutions were the most characteristic expressions of the new style, which can be seen as directly related to the concentration of building activity in the hands of a relatively small number of capitalists. As blocks of apartment houses became increasingly monumental, domes and pavilions were used to create large-scale symmetries, which made blocks look extremely unified when seen from a distance. The huge façades formed a single high wall crowned by the buildings' complicated tops.

The monumental vocabulary elaborated during the second phase of the Haussmann era[34] brought a change in architectural detail. There was an obvious return to the classical style, which was adapted to the particularities of the apartment building and modified with numerous mannerist and even Louis XIV features. The abundance of styles that had characterized the beginning of the Second Empire was replaced by stereotyped detail—to be blunt, a sort of "basic classic"—on a backdrop of pilasters, consoles, and pediments that, though vaguely reminiscent of Michelangelo, were "improved" with elegant Louis XIV touches. Widespread use of colossal pilasters and cornice entablatures was directly related to the renewal of interest in the wall that began at this time. However, the buildings themselves would not have been very interesting, had there not also been an extremely rapid renewal of cast-iron ornament, based on heavy models that were usually Louis XIV in inspiration. Facilitated by the use of assembled cast-iron sections instead of big molded sheets, there was a return to the traditional stylistics of wrought ironwork. But powerful elements in relief, even in high relief, were added to the traditional designs.

The interesting thing about this approach is the close relationship between stylistic detail and the treatment of mass. Indeed, that relationship defined the second phase of the Haussmann era more

357

Corner rotundas.
1. Rue des Pyramides, corner of the Rue d'Argenteuil. **2.** Corner of the Avenue de l'Opéra and the Rue de l'Echelle. **3.** Boulevard Saint-Germain, photographed from the Concorde bridge. **4.** Corner of the Rue de Lisbonne and the Rue du Général-Foy. **5.** Rue de la Chaussée-d'Antin, photographed from the Square de la Trinité. **6.** Rue de Maubeuge. The strong graphic grids of late Haussmann façades.

358

4

5

6

than anything else. At first glance one might think that, in a sort of return to academicism, the official architecture of the imperial regime had triumphed over the whims and fancies of the previous decade. In actual fact, the somewhat schematic new plastic approach won out because it was better adapted to large-scale real-estate development; industrial capitalism was finding its vocabulary. It was no accident that sculpted detail became banal as molded detail was revived. The abandoning of the grid treatment of façades in favor of a vertical patterning of voids was the logical consequence of the heavy new emphasis on cast-iron ornament, for the graphic network of continuous and discontinuous horizontal strips formed by the balconies in front of façade planes required a powerful vertical background for balance. The opposition of the diaphanous plane of cast-iron ornament and the sculptural treatment of the solid that acted as its background gradually replaced the structuring of scale that had fascinated the previous generation. The heavy emphasis on cast-iron ornament—to the exclusion of just about everything else—made it necessary to treat walls as elementary masses with clear lines but no useless detail. Though it may not seem obvious, there was a total break with the subtlety and refinement of the architecture of the 1850s.

The Garnier Style

The monumentalization of apartment buildings, which were increasingly designed and built in groups after 1860-65, was sometimes accompanied by a particular kind of ornamental enrichment: figurative sculptures in the form of keystone masks, which had also been used in the eighteenth century, then caryatids and atlantes supporting balconies. Of course this race of stone figures had monumental precedents, including the Opera House with its famous bronze caryatid lamps, and various classical models, not the least of which was the Louvre's Pavillon de l'Horloge. Generally speaking, and as Garnier himself recognized, the style of the late Second Empire was "close to the Louis XIV style in the harmonious arrangement of mass" (and also, increasingly, in the use of a decorative repertoire of baroque origin).[35] Nevertheless, one of Garnier's major contributions to Parisian architecture, which he strongly helped to revitalize, was to bring back polychromy—not as painted elements (which Hittorff had wanted, and Haussmann refused, for the church of Saint-Vincent-de-Paul), but as polychrome combinations of materials—marble, stone, and slate—in the fashion of a Philibert Delorme. With it came the use of mosaics on a gold background, as in Sédille's masterly design for the Printemps department store.

"I dream of the day," Charles Garnier wrote in *A travers les arts,*

when tawny shades of gold will spangle our city's monuments and buildings. We will then stop building big straight streets that, although beautiful, are as cold and stiff as a dowager. Our streets will become less rigid and, without hurting anyone, a man will be able to build his house as he pleases, without worrying about whether or not it fits in with his neighbor's. Cornices will shine with the colors of eternity; gold friezes will sparkle on façades. Monuments will be decorated in marble and enamel, and mosaics will make the city vibrate with color. This will not be meretricious. It will be true opulence. Once people have become accustomed to the city's marvelous, dazzling nuances, they will demand that our clothes be redesigned and brightened up as well, and the entire city will be harmoniously bathed in silks and gold. But alas! I look around and see a somber gray sky, renovated houses, and dark shadows trudging along the endless boulevards. In short, I see Paris as it really is! And my artist's dream comes to an end as I am thrown back into bourgeois reality.[36]

This beautiful text indirectly reveals the tyranny of city building officials during the Haussmann era, as well as the deep aesthetic reaction against the Haussmann approach that, after twenty years of authoritarian city planning, developed in artistic circles. Garnier, who was the head of modern academicism and Haussmann's leading critic, never saw his dream realized, but he did exert a major influence on fin de siècle architects. Jules Broussard, in particular, was influenced by Garnier (Place des Ternes, Rue Ribéra, Avenue Mozart, Rue du Louvre), and his work is most appealing. Nevertheless, the Garnier style was long stunted by city building officials hostile to anything and everything resembling nonconformity. The imperious rule that buildings form coherent rows allowed for very little individual initiative. Corner treatments, discreet decorative mosaics (mainly for lintels or on the parapets beneath windows), and sculpted figures would seem to have been the only means that architects could use to individualize façades.

The Destruction of the Hierarchy

The golden rule of Haussmann architecture, the systematic ordering of residential buildings, eventually came to be deemed unacceptable. Around the middle of the Second Empire, numerous artists began to protest against the monotonous spaces produced by the Haussmann approach. Their reaction would not have been as vehement as it was, nor echoed so widely in other circles, had it not revealed a fundamental economic evolution in the urban organism. Industrial capitalism was radically disturbing the baroque order. The municipal government's old dream of beautifying the city with a strong ordonnance of façades began to be realized through repetitive series of buildings, eliminating the diversity of the traditional style. The effects of this radical change of approach did not really begin to be felt until after 1860. Gradually, however, the regulation typology was systematized, and its reproduction throughout the city led to a growing neutralization of space. The typology was destroying the very hierarchy on which it had initially been based!

A Single Type

As apartment houses were constructed around the city, they came to resemble one another more and more. The many models of the neoclassical period gave way to a single type—the Parisian apartment building—which spread from the central districts to the new arrondissements, and then to the outer belt of suburbs that sprang up in the 1880s. Indeed, the central type's impact was such that, by century's end, certain seaside resorts and provincial towns contained perfect rows of Haussmann buildings—chunks of Paris exported to the provinces. Unlike during the Second Empire, when Haussmann-style streets were adapted to a town's scale (Lyons, Brussels, Marseilles, Poitiers), the apartment houses built in provincial towns at the end of the nineteenth century retained all the typological features elaborated for the central districts of Paris.

Exactly the same thing happened in the capital's outlying districts. The central model won out, eliminating all the hierarchical subtlety described in the preceding pages. The five-story building disappeared from the Monceau district, and small mansions and houses were pushed out to the Thiers fortifications and then devoured by the central model. In the new sections, as big rows of identical façades became commonplace on secondary streets, the contrast between the inside and outside of a neighborhood disappeared.

This evolution, to be sure, met much resistance. Big operations —involving a street, a block, or an entire neighborhood—remained relatively rare and tended to introduce a certain amount of diversity, as when the ordonnance of the apartment-building façades on the Rue de Phalsbourg was combined with English-style terraces on the Rue de Prony and picturesque little houses on the Rue Henri-Rochefort. Most apartment houses were still being built one at a time, but by now the evolution of the real-estate market toward the construction of identical groups of apartment houses was ineluctable. To compensate, it would have been necessary to draft a building code that encouraged modulations in height and type—the only measure that might have maintained the diversity needed to structure the city into distinct areas. An exceptional moment in the city's history, the early Haussmann era had made the baroque dream reality. But all too quickly, the aesthetic ideal was overruled by economic considerations. The city's perfect balance became increasingly precarious. In the 1860s an important change in the urban system began. As mansions (which now included several rental units under their roofs) came to resemble apartment buildings more and more, the outlying neighborhoods of houses strongly asserted their diversity. What nobody really noticed at the time was that the geographic segregation of the two remaining typologies was growing stronger and stronger. In the end, that segregation became systematic, and the urban hierarchy was completely destroyed.

Divergent Aims

The Haussmann era was a transition between a traditional approach to urban hierarchy and the use of an extremely rigid model to build huge groups of practically identical buildings throughout the city. As such, it constituted a brief moment of equilibrium in the city's urbanistic history. However, the unity of Haussmann's Paris was threatened from the start. This is particularly striking in the way public spaces were designed, for there was obviously a dual approach. One of the major problems of the Haussmann era turned out to be the functional ambiguity of the big new streets. The city planners were obviously thinking in terms of traffic flow, yet the models they used and continued to believe in were still essentially baroque. This conflict between intentions and formal vocabulary was personified by Haussmann and Napoleon III. The emperor saw things in terms more of prestige than of efficiency—the great crossroads of Paris, the joining of the Louvre and the Tuileries, his rejection of diagonal bridges over the Seine. His prefect's aims were sometimes just as monumental, as witnessed by the Louvre/Hôtel de Ville axis and the Sébastopol, Saint-Michel, and Henri IV vistas, but when necessary, they became purely practical: the rather jagged route chosen for the Boulevard Saint-Germain; the filling of the Concorde moats; the decision to build the Rue Médicis and the Caulaincourt viaduct. Furthermore, over the years Haussmann became increasingly functionalistic in approach and less and less interested in the great urban composition that he had initially hoped to realize.

Rambuteau and Berger had followed a timid policy of building new streets of modest scale like the Rue Rambuteau and the Rue des Ecoles. Even the first really big new streets—the Boulevard de Strasbourg and the Rue du Pont-Neuf—were rather petty and awkward operations. When Haussmann took office, things changed dramatically. His streets project was far vaster and far more rigorous in design than his predecessors', and its effect on the city's neighborhoods was much greater. But in later years Haussmann's monumental tastes became much less pronounced. Streets built for purely utilitarian reasons—La Fayette, Turbigo, Rome—outnumbered monumental routes, doubtless in part because, once the early projects had been completed, there were enough monumental streets to organize the city. Be that as it may, a street like the Rue de Caulaincourt, which was used to organize the entire northern zone, clearly no longer had the impressive fullness of earlier Haussmann streets. In projects such as that one, the hierarchy of streets and spaces faded out. A street's size began to be determined by practical necessities, not the least of them financial. One need only compare Haussmann's later streets with the truly magnificent Boulevard Voltaire to realize that, after the splendor of the initial projects, a much less elaborate approach prevailed. This was largely because the city gave in to the wishes of speculative developers, as in the Villiers/Monceau area, where private interests clearly reigned supreme. The big imperial roads leading out to Saint-Cloud (the Avenue Victor-Hugo and the surrounding area) were, in a way, Haussmann's revenge. There, reasons of state justified a return to coherence and a structuring of scales. In retrospect, the Haussmann era can be seen as a desperate struggle between economic efficiency—in an unregulated free-market economy—and the cultural values of a civilization steeped in classical tradition. Later, the emperor's great project having disappeared with his Empire, no architectural determination whatsoever was expressed in urban composition, which is one reason why the new streets built at the beginning of the Third Republic are of so little interest. (One exception is the Avenue de l'Opéra, which was given the monumental force of an early Haussmann street, but after what a battle!)

Nineteenth-century industrial society was plagued by the absence of a model to succeed the obsolete baroque model. Despite the keen awareness of the city's problems in artistic circles, Paris began to come apart at the end of the Second Empire. The disintegration started with the anarchic development of the suburbs—a phenomenon that only worsened in later years. It then affected the unity of the city proper: the typology was impoverished, the hierarchies abandoned, and the interior/exterior dialectic destroyed. Finally it spread to the urban organism itself, with the systematic segregation of social classes and the strict zoning of activities.

Twentieth-century attempts to reshape the city—in particular, Le Corbusier's 1922 plan for a city with a population of three million, which makes explicit reference to Paris—have only aggravated things by emphasizing the opposition and dissociation of functions. In practice, such attempts to redo the classical city have been even more negative than the suburban illusion. Never has such a concentration of economic means resulted in such a waste of space and loss of scale.

1906

58. — PARIS — Boulevard Saint-Germain, pris de la place Saint-Germain-des-Prés

P. Marmuse, Paris

Boulevard Saint-Germain. Postcard.

Today more than ever, the traditional urban model—that of the European city in the eighteenth and nineteenth centuries—is the most stimulating. The order and urban mixture on which it was based have been so lacking in recent realizations that its faults—a certain rigidity, overemphasis on appearance alone, and excessive density—seem relatively minor. That is why the last great models of classical composition—Berlage in Amsterdam, Speer in Berlin—are again being praised and taken as references. There has even been a modest renewal of interest in Haussmann and the streets he built.[37]

365

NOTES

1. Georges-Eugène Haussmann (1809-1891) wrote three volumes of *Mémoires* (Paris: Victor-Havard, 1890-93) that are essential reading. In addition, there have been a number of biographical studies, the most noteworthy of which are Louis Réau and Pierre Lavedan, *L'Oeuvre du Baron Haussmann* (Paris: P.U.F., 1954), and G. N. Lameyre, *Haussmann, préfet de Paris* (Paris: Flammarion, 1958). Yet to date there have been no major studies of the city's contemporary urbanistic history, with the exception of Norma Evenson's survey *Paris: A Century of Change, 1878-1978* (New Haven: Yale University Press, 1979). Evenson's book is more a review of other research than a new contribution, and its chronological framework is too vast for a study of any thoroughness.

2. In the wake of Siegfried Giedion, Philippe Gresset studies the theme of the English square in *Le Fragment de ville. Une unité d'architecture urbaine de l'époque géorgienne (1715-1815)*, CORDA research report (Paris: M.U.L.T., S.R.A., 1982). My own interpretation differs somewhat from earlier ones, which insist on crowd control and analyze the new boulevards in purely military terms. Such a point of view must be approached with caution, though it does contain a grain of truth. Haussmann himself is candid on the subject when he discusses lowering the level of the Saint-Martin Canal at the Boulevard Voltaire to make it possible, "if need be, to take the whole Faubourg Saint-Antoine from the rear," (*Mémoires*, vol. 2, p. 318). The emperor himself promoted the often costly creation of gardens and parks in Paris. Haussmann reminds his readers of this, while also emphasizing that he did not entirely share his "master's noble and generous illusions" (vol. 3, p. 240). With the passing of time we have become aware less of these military considerations than of the merits of the many promenades in the center of Paris. The failure of modern city planning, founded on a purely intellectual theory of zoning that experience has shown to destroy the city's structure and alienate its population, leads me to be much less critical of Haussmann than my predecessors have often been. How can one not realize that Haussmann's Paris is one of the greatest successes in urban history? The "dark intentions" of the men responsible in no way lessen the value of the city they created.

3. It would be interesting to determine exactly when this new system appeared —probably with Haussmann's first project, the Rue des Ecoles. Although the actual decision to build the street was made before he took office, many of the extant buildings were built at a later date. A closer analysis would be needed to determine which buildings were built at the same time as the street, and thus determine the original typological characteristics. We would then have a clear model of Haussmann planning at the beginning of the Second Empire. The Rue Monge and the Rue de Rome, precisely dated, reveal the model that was used later.

4. Jean-Pierre Babelon pointed out to me how, in the case of the Bony mansion on the Rue de Trévise, the neighboring buildings built at the same time as the mansion form a smooth veneer around the edifice and its garden, while the newer buildings on the Rue de Trévise (built two years later, in 1832) have big windowless gables. Thus the traditional system of ordonnance was replaced by a new typology emphasizing boundaries between buildings. The correlation of neighboring façades was inversely proportional to that of the sidewalls.

5. The rule of contrast between frontality and spatiality can also be used to analyze the different degrees of relative independence of objects in interior decoration. The design of the space above mantelpieces, with a clock and wall chandeliers, is in itself a fascinating subject, as is the dialectic between a room's armchair or table and its wardrobe, chest of drawers, or bed.

6. Giedion, *Space, Time and Architecture.*

7. The expression is Léon Krier's, in *La Reconstruction de la ville européenne. Architecture rationnelle* (Brussels: Archives d'Architecture Moderne, 1978). A symposium on this topic was organized by the Commission Française de la Culture de l'Agglomération de Bruxelles in 1979.

8. This is the volume of regulations (Royal Edicts and Customaries of Paris) put together by Antoine Desgodets (1653-1728), a member of the French Academy, and Louis XIV's superintendent of buildings. Desgodets's norms were used by all builders for nearly a century.

9. To the best of my knowledge, there exists no comprehensive study of the use of diagonal routes in eighteenth-century city planning, or of their influence on Haussmann.

10. This system, which became the rule in the nineteenth century, was tested when the Halle au Blé was rebuilt. But the idea was already in gestation during the early years of Louis XV's reign. A number of examples date back to the reconstruction of Rennes, which began in 1720. It would be worthwhile to study the emergence of this new interest in dressing up courtyard façades in the architectural literature of the day (treatises, reviews, pamphlets, etc.). In the case of Rennes, fairly precise dating is possible, since the two neighboring buildings at the bottom of the Place du Palais (the earlier building built by Robelin, an engineer working from plans sent by Gabriel, and the later one built after Gabriel's visit to Rennes) are entirely different in courtyard design. The earlier courtyard has a light façade in wood and glass, which contrasts with the stone façade on the street. The later one, on the other hand, resembles the great models in Nantes (Ile Feydeau), because of its handsome courtyard walls with cut-off corners. Moreover, the later building shares its courtyard with the adjacent building, whereas the earlier one is still closed in on itself. Very tentatively, I would date the new approach around 1725. My friend Henri Bresler is currently working on this question.

11. Jean Castex has shed new light on the urbanization of Versailles in Katherine Burlen, Jean Castex, Patrick Céleste, Céleste Furet, Philippe Panerai, *Versailles: Lecture d'une ville*, research report, Ministère de la Culture et de l'Environnement, CORDA, 1978. His findings were presented at the Brussels symposium on the European city (see n. 7).

12. Jean Castex, Philippe Panerai, *De l'îlot à la barre* (Paris: Dunod, 1973).

13. Today there is mounting interest in how the backs of lots were used. Jean Castex gives a fine analysis in *Versailles: Lecture d'une ville.*

14. The distinction between ordonnance

and order was first formulated by Jean-Louis Subileau in *Paris-Projet*, no. 13-14 (1974). The drafting of that project was inextricably linked to the present study. Indeed, I sometimes have trouble recalling who originally formulated certain ideas, so closely did we work in symbiosis with all the members of the Atelier Parisien d'Urbanisme.

15. I am obviously thinking of Hector Horeau.

16. Jules Ferry, the author of *Comptes fantastiques d'Haussmann* (1867), deplored the fact that the city's new benches, kiosks, streetlamps, etc., in no way reduced the hugeness of the voids created by the prefect's big new streets. Haussmann's contemporaries and critics were unable to get used to the gigantic scale of the latter.

17. Bernard Rouleau, *Le Tracé des rues de Paris*.

18. In such cases it is a good idea to require strong alignments, while architecturally marking breaks between spaces. Breaks can be marked by differences in style or by using cut-off corners, setting a building back from the building line, enlarging the public space, varying size and form, or introducing an architectural object (which is how fountains, stelae, and statues were once used).

19. Haussmann was unable to get the emperor to agree to pave the city's macadam arteries. Though quieter and easier on horses, the macadam arteries were quite expensive to keep up and moreover were very dirty. The roads had to be watered down several times a day and gone over with a roller to keep the city from disappearing in a cloud of dust or, in rainy weather, turning into a cesspool. After the fall of the Second Empire, paved arteries became widespread.

20. Haussmann, *Mémoires*, vol. 3, p. 516.

21. *Ibid.*, pp. 493-94.

22. *Ibid.*, pp. 254-55.

23. *Ibid.*, vol. 2, pp. 446-47.

24. The restructuring of the Halles market is analyzed in detail in the C.R.H.A.M.'s study of the district (ch. 2, n. 3), as well as in J. M. Léri's article (ch. 2, n. 4).

25. Dominique Perrault, "Les Vingt Mairies de Paris. Insertion dans le tissu urbain, adaptation d'un plan type," thesis, University of Paris 6, Paris, E.N.S.B.A., 1978; summary in *Architecture d'aujourd'hui*, 1979.

26. It is indeed remarkable that Haussmann's city planning was essentially carried out in the field. The destruction of the city's archives in 1871 does not fully account for the dearth of primary sources on the Hauss-

mann era; the role of building officials was so strong and clear that numerous regulations were as unnecessary as artificial theoretical publications. In the final analysis, the proof of what Haussmann did lies in the city itself that he and his contemporaries left us.

27. Viollet-le-Duc analyzes the popularity that small mansions enjoyed in the late Second Empire. His explanation is financial: "Many people thought it better to build a small mansion that, including the price of the lot, would cost about 500,000 francs, than to keep the money in the bank and spend the interest without controlling their capital. That is why so many little mansions were built in Paris, filling up the empty ground in Chaillot, La Muette, Neuilly, Passy, Auteuil, etc. The habit of owning a mansion or a little house gradually caught on, even among people of more modest means. Everyone who had the available capital preferred to use it to build a house rather than to spend the interest to rent an apartment in a banal building" (*Entretiens*, vol. 2, pp. 298-299).

28. The emergence of the hybrid mansion/building—something between a small apartment building and a mansion—gave certain residential districts in the west of Paris a rather particular typology that compensates for the banal model used for the façades. Oddly enough, the reduction in a building's size tended less and less to modify the proportions of the basement. Thus one often sees three- or four-story houses with the balcony on the third floor (rather than the second, which would have been logical in such cases). Can such hybrid structures be called mansions? In fact, they were usually small apartment houses (one residence to a floor) or combinations of a two-floor "mansion" at basement level with apartments on the floors above. Used as small apartment houses, these structures began to look their part. A building's number of floors was reduced in proportion to its distance from the center. The result is so disconcerting that one sometimes wonders whether these edifices were not designed to be heightened at a later date.

29. They might have been inspired by various seventeenth-century examples of a flexible approach to small lots (most notably on the Ile Saint-Louis). These examples include terrace gardens above street level, so as not to break the alignment at ground level; constructions built at right angles with the alignment, so as to create a courtyard on the street (which, thanks to its fine façades,

pavement, and grillwork fences, has a status comparable to that of public squares); successive buildings with a rental building on the street and a mansion at the back of the lot; and mansion/buildings with a dual use (e.g., the old Le Vau mansion on the corner of the Quai d'Anjou).

30. When strongly structured masses were used, they were always limited to the tops of buildings. Belvederes, pavilions, domes, and big dormer windows were clearly individualized but did not break the alignment. From the end of the Second Empire on, many compositions—this was almost a rule—played on dynamic asymmetries juxtaposing a symmetrical main section (generally three bays) and a narrower side section that formed a façade's focal point, owing to the dominance of voids and the projection of the top. This formal system created a contrast between stable and unstable form. A composition was at once reassuring and disturbing (as is often the case when there is a conflict between volume and surface, between façade and depth, or between the apparent clearness of a composition and the reality of its interior layout). There was a continual dialectic between respecting the rules and getting around them.

31. In his *Mémoires* Haussmann explains how Deschamps thought of using corner buildings to establish the alignment on new streets. Builders could simply take those buildings as references, with a very small risk of error.

32. Viollet-le-Duc has some interesting things to say about the corner rotunda in the eighteenth of his *Entretiens*, vol. 2, p. 320.

33. City regulations long hindered the development of the corner rotunda by requiring that it be inscribed inside the cut-off corner (i.e., with no projection over the building line), and by limiting the size of a rotunda's dome. However, fashion proved stronger than the law: domes gradually emerged—at first timidly and then with greater fullness—from the mass of buildings. This formal escalation peaked thirty years later (1898-99) with the domes that L. Dauvergne built on the slopes of Passy (Rue de l'Alboni).

34. Haussmann's dismissal in 1870 did not mean the end of his conception of city planning, which continued unchanged until the new wave of regulation-making of 1893-1902. (The 1884 building code simply generalized a practice that had been in limited use since the 1860s on major sites

like the Place Saint-Michel and the Avenue de l'Opéra.)

35. Charles Garnier, "Le Style actuel," in *A Travers les arts* (Paris: Hachette, 1869)—p. 100 in the Picard edition (Paris, 1985).

36. Ibid., "Les Mosaïques," pp. 159-60. Though Garnier built relatively little, he influenced his contemporaries considerably.

37. Long scorned, Haussmann began to attract new interest in the 1960s but at that time was not taken as a model. More recently, the rehabilitation of the nineteenth century would sometimes seem to have passed Haussmann by. The current vogue of the 1950s has brought functionalism back. As the only thing a functionalist approach can do is destroy what remains of the urban organism, I advocate a neo-Haussmann approach, the greatest advantage of which would be to reestablish the link between the classical conception of urban space and contemporary industrial structures. The superiority of the Haussmann approach to all others is shown by the fact that, in Second Empire Paris, that approach harnessed (if only partially) the powers of industrial production without losing sight of the unity and hierarchy inherent in classical form. If I have my doubts about the chances of success of a hard-line neoclassical approach like Léon Krier's, I do strongly believe that a neo-Haussmann approach is the way to go in the future. In my opinion, the neo-Haussmann approach is the only one capable of organizing and neutralizing the incoherent juxtaposition of architectural objects with which the 1960s has graced the city of Paris.

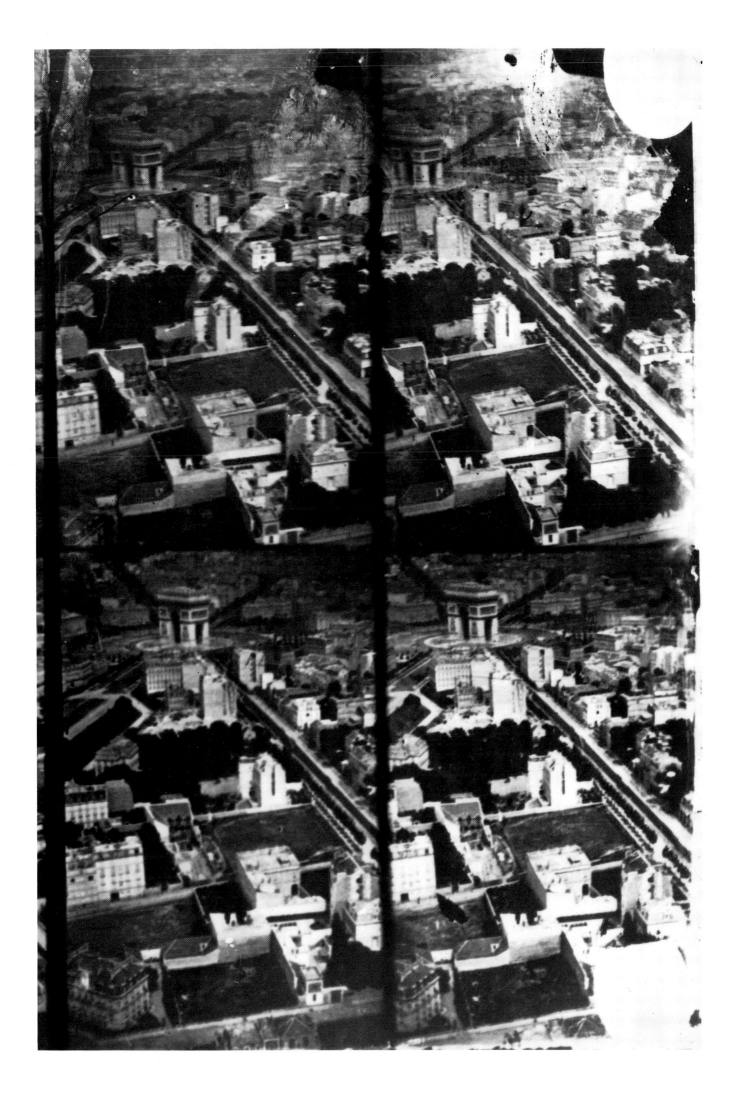

Boulevard Delessert, corner
of the Avenue Camoëns.

371

1. Apartment building, Boulevard du Prince-Eugène (now the Boulevard Voltaire). Photo: A. Liebert, May 25, 1871. **2, 3,** and **4.** Buildings at the intersection of the Rue Saint-Martin and the Rue de Rivoli. Destroyed during the Commune, these buildings were rebuilt in almost identical style.

1 Boulevard du Prince Eugène (10ᵉ). 25 mai 1871 – A. Liebert, Photo.

Chapter V

Post-Haussmann Paris during the Third Republic

The fall of the Second Empire in 1870, and the tragic incidents that followed during the siege of Paris and the Commune, were not as critically important in the urban and architectural history of Paris as one might think. Despite the bloodshed (and, one might add, the irreversible damage done to the capital's monuments), the end of the Second Empire was not the end of the architectural and urban approach of the Haussmann era. The three apartment houses located on the corner of the Rue de Rivoli and the Rue Saint-Martin are a striking case in point. To cover their retreat before the advancing Versailles troops, the Communards blew the buildings up. With the return of peace, the buildings were reconstructed practically identical to how they had been before. (Indeed, only a trained eye will notice that they are aesthetically closer to the 1870s than to the 1850s.) In fact, the generation of the 1860s, taking over from the elite of the 1830s, kept the Haussmann approach alive for almost twenty years after the fall of the Empire. The really critical changes did not come until the 1890s. Following the collapse of the Union Générale in 1882, the economic crisis of 1884 announced a decade of great instability. During that period France's second industrial revolution took place, less than half a century after the first. The violence of the fin de siècle anarchists is one sign of how painful a period this was in the social history of France.

The 1880s were a decade of uncertainty and protest. The ideology of the Second Empire was demolished. New trends appeared but did not reach maturity until the very end of the century. Stylistically speaking, art nouveau was in gestation. On the level of city planning, its equivalent was the post-Haussmann approach, which was not given concrete expression until after the 1893 and above all the 1902 building codes.

Amplifying a reaction that had first been voiced around the middle of the Second Empire, the fin de siècle generation violently attacked the Haussmann approach. Above all else, the monotonous alignments on imperial streets were singled out and condemned as a symbol of autocratic power. The attacks on Haussmann's Paris were echoed by rather bombastic declarations on art and individualism. Artistic and individual freedom came to be seen as one and the same; refusals to

Facing page: **1.** *The Pont de l'Europe.* Gustave Caille-botte, oil on canvas, 1876. Musée du Petit-Palais, Lausanne.
2. *A Street in Paris on a Rainy Day.* Gustave Caille-botte, oil on canvas, 1877. Art Institute of Chicago.

respect norms and regulations were applauded as courageous expressions of artistic individualism and thus of liberty itself.[1] Rejecting what it saw as Haussmann's systematization, the fin de siècle was characterized by the proliferating inventiveness of a particularly diversified architectural repertoire or, to be more exact, by the gap between the protean richness of one part of production and the absolute systematization of the rest. The gap between art and mass production, which previous generations had not known, grew ever wider in the years that followed. The history of modernity is essentially the history of that widening gap.

Loyalty to a System

The intensity of the artistic debate must not blind us to the fact that the city's reference structures did not change. The artists' inflammatory proclamations were accompanied by an extraordinary durability of principles and modes of production. Odd as it may seem, the anti-Haussmann period of the 1880s constantly referred back to the Haussmann model. While the artists loudly attacked Second Empire Paris, neither the typology of the apartment house nor the structure of urban space underwent any significant transformation. What the fin de siècle contested in Second Empire art was its poverty of expression, its uniformity, and its monotony. The reaction was all the stronger because the conflict between artistic tradition and industrial production was intensifying. At the time of the 1889 world's fair, the city's more "refined" artists, led by Joris-Karl Huysmans, joined forces to campaign against what they saw as a skinny monster: the Eiffel Tower. Others, however, began to champion anything and everything connected with machines; in architecture, the steel girder was to become the symbol of modernity. But this trend was still very weak; the vast majority of fin de siècle artists were guided by a rich cultural tradition. They simply wanted to increase and diversify expressions of that tradition—in a word, to express tradition in as new and independent a way as possible.

It is thus not so surprising that the Haussmann system survived. Rigid applications of the system were called into question, but its basic correctness was not, which explains why some of the most beautiful Haussmann buildings date from the 1880s. (The most famous architects of the time were, after all, Garnier, Davioud, Ballu, Abadie, and Corroyer.) Indeed, the heyday of the Haussmann approach could be said to have come *after* Haussmann. The vast plan that the emperor and his prefect had conceived twenty years earlier became reality. The new streets were finished; apartment buildings were rising throughout the city; and trees were growing along the asphalt sidewalks. The Paris of Zola and Caillebotte was the worthy heir of the Second Empire. Not only did the city fathers expand and complete the public-works projects begun before 1870, they also began new ones. The Third Republic is responsible for the Rue Caulaincourt viaduct around

Montmartre and for the Place Gambetta, which gave the twentieth arrondissement its center.

Even the early twentieth century remained loyal to the Haussmann conception of urban form. Though the architecture changed, post-Haussmann Paris was—as the expression implies—still guided by Haussmann's approach to city planning.

In Search of a New Style

The Issue of Ornament   This loyalty to the architectural typology and city planning of the Haussmann era did not, however, prevent the ornamental repertoire from being radically transformed. The 1880s saw the triumph of a picturesque eclecticism that would not have displeased Camillo Sitte.[2] At first glance the new use of architectural ornament, which greatly changed the way the city looked, might seem rather ambiguous. In fact, there were two contradictory approaches: one was a very dry, severe interpretation of the Haussmann style; the other, an exuberant eclecticism whose raison d'être was above all to oppose the other approach. (A similar duality also characterized art nouveau, in an even more striking way.) The reason that one part of production was so austere, cold, and boring was above all ideological, indeed moral. The 1870 defeat and the social unrest that followed were felt by many to be a kind of punishment for the careless ostentation of the Second Empire: some Catholics even went so far as to see these calamities as God's message to a heathen capital. Amends were made for Garnier's much-admired Opera House by building the nineteenth century's starkest monument, Sacré-Cœur. During this period, ornament was a very hot issue: one was either fascinated or repelled by it. Toward the end of the 1880s the divorce between the picturesque style and the philosophy of rationalism was finalized; there could be no in-betweens.

Thus, though the architectural typology stayed the same, ornament changed completely. One was either a citizen of the republic of rationalism (sometimes classical, sometimes not) or a dedicated lover of art for art's sake. No dialogue was possible between the two camps: the rhetoric of constraint had no common ground with the rhetoric of liberty. As it was well nigh impossible not to choose sides, the academic architects joined forces with rationalists to combat the ornamental proliferation and incredible liberties of formal eclecticism. But the struggle proved to be too much for the generation of 1830. Soon the philosophy of dignified restraint that the "Gothic" and classical

376

movements had shared became totally outmoded. The new generation had won the right to dare to be different.

The Rigors of Rationalism

Rationalism's hour of glory came in the early 1880s. Architects followed the lessons of Viollet-le-Duc, Baudot, and Corroyer but usually transposed them into the official classical style. The stylistic references were, however, discreet, for any ostentation would have detracted from the clarity of the rationalist approach.

The rationalists placed particular importance on masonry, emphasizing a building's monumental stonework to the detriment of almost everything else. (The joints were sometimes colored so as to make the lines of the bonding the only dynamic interest of the big, flat façades.) Rationalist architects also liked to mix building materials so as to create a permanent polychromy. White or gray stone from Burgundy was combined with yellow Paris limestone and brick. The hard Burgundy stone was used for the lower floors, which bore the building's whole weight and required big window openings, while limestone was used for the main floors, including the recessed story. As a rule, all a building's projecting elements—cordons, cornices, consoles—were also built of hard stone, as were balcony slabs; directly exposed to the rain, these elements needed to be stronger than the rest of the masonry. Finally, ornament was added in those places where, according to the logic of Gothic architecture, it would most strongly emphasize a building's structure, for rationalism was more structural than functional. The reestablishing of stringcourses (indicating internal floor levels or linking window ledges) was one consequence of this structural approach to form, as was the emphasis on bays and consoles. When such traditional ornamental features as pilasters and pediments were maintained, the pilasters were always simplified to the utmost and used only to underscore—discreetly—the size of a building's main stories, while the pediments were restricted to the third story. (On the fourth story, windows were topped by ledges supported by consoles; above that, simple frames were used.) As the rationalists were basically uninterested in the academic treatment of ornamental hierarchy, the system became increasingly stereotyped.

The last years of the Haussmann approach favored flat façades and a strong graphic interplay between the lines of a building's stonework, cast-iron motifs, and frames. As in all modern art in the nineteenth century, there was a pronounced taste for strong oppositions, especially those involving scale; the contrast between the scale of the mass (e.g., the big pilasters encompassing several stories) and the scale of a story (e.g., the frames around window openings) was heavily emphasized. Similarly, the plastics of elements in relief tended to be altered. They were given a simplified volumetrics that accentuated their silhouette so that, when seen in perspective, they formed successive screens. The struggle between a wall and the silhouettes of its ornament was sometimes violent.

131 Boulevard Malesherbes.

377

1. Corner of the Rue La Fontaine and the Avenue de l'Abbé-Roussel. **2.** 35 bis Rue La Fontaine. **3.** Corner of the Rue d'Assas and the Rue Joseph-Bara.

Facing page: 4-6 and 8, Villa Michel-Ange.

The Petit Bourgeois Building

The simplification of ornament was not brought about by an aesthetic ideal alone. It was also closely related to the new way that buildings were being built—not one at a time, but in ever larger groups. In the late eighteenth century there had been investors with enough money to build part of a row, or even an entire street, of apartment houses. With the growth of banking, it became possible to design and build entire developments of apartment buildings at the same time (the Péreire Bank setting the example around the Monceau park). Even private parties sometimes had the money it took to build a street of buildings (quite a few streets in Paris were named after their developer). The concentration of capital made it commonplace to develop several blocks in a single operation. They were generally completed in two or three years, which implies that the lots were developed simultaneously and not in staggered sections, since it took a good two years to construct an apartment house.[3]

Architecturally, the apartment houses in the new developments all resembled one another, owing to their systematized façades and the simplification of ornament. They courted a different clientèle. Built on the edge of town in the arrondissements annexed in 1860, they were meant for middle-class employees with modest salaries and people with small private incomes. Outside, the buildings were a somewhat simpler version of the big bourgeois apartment houses on the boulevards in the center; inside, the apartments had considerably less floor space. Thus the model was more compact. The service staircase was made smaller or eliminated; more doors were placed on each landing; rooms were reduced in size (to bedrooms of under ten square meters and living rooms of about fifteen); and apartment floor plans were more economical, with a central hall opening into all the main rooms. One commonly found three-room apartments of under sixty square meters and four- or

Rue Faraday.

five-room apartments of between eighty and one hundred square meters. The petit bourgeois apartment house was born. Later, the model slowly spread eastward from the sixteenth and seventeenth arrondissements.

Formally speaking, there was no hesitation to repeat the same façade on every building in a row. But to attract potential tenants, there was an increased effort to vary each façade's appearance by modifying the ornament. Cast-iron ornament was best adapted to such variations, which were in fact quite modest. The Rue Pierre-Guérin (Auteuil), Rue de Sfax, Rue de Sontay, and Place Victor-Hugo, which were all built up at this time, reveal their developers' concern with diversifying ornament.

On the ornamental level, "mass production" of buildings brought a radical transformation in decor, since all the stonecutting was mechanized, which made deeply carved ornament and high relief impossible. Not only did ornamental sculpture (figures and foliage) disappear, but the classical architectonic motifs were simplified. The tendency to silhouette was strengthened by a technical necessity: only one side of a stone element could be shaped. The sawing technique that was used allowed only distinct planes to be cut; otherwise, moldings were lathed. The results of this simplified method are particularly visible on consoles (supporting balconies, cornices, pediments, and ledges above windows), where one finds molded ornament on the front but nothing on the sides. Ornament could exist in slices, but not as a volume.

Mechanically cut ornament characterized petit bourgeois architecture. (For more prestigious constructions, where rough-cut pieces were finished off by a sculptor, there was still a volumetric treatment of form.) Contractors who specialized in petit bourgeois apartment houses concentrated all their efforts on adapting classical ornament to the possibilities of the machine, which no doubt partly explains the graphic appearance of the forms (relief was now a luxury) and the pronounced taste for consoles and ledges projecting from the façade plane to create a tight, cadenced patterning of shadow and light. The petit bourgeois style, which took its formal repertoire from the great neoclassical architects of the reign of Louis XVI (Wailly, Jacques-Denis Antoine, and Ledoux) exploited only heavy shadows, abandoning the classical tradition's refined use of light and halftones.

Eventually, a further simplification of the façade model transformed the traditional architecture of working-class apartment buildings in the east. Technically speaking, working-class buildings were built in about the same way as petit bourgeois buildings, but as an even more elementary version of the bourgeois model. Traditional building methods—heightening houses, filling up the back of the lot—gave way to rigid constructions that could not be modified.

Similarly the practice of salvaging, which had long provided the poor man with affordable building materials, disappeared. Regardless

Apart from variations in detail (rotundas, cut-off corners, groupings of windows, frames above window openings), whole blocks of the developments in the new outlying districts looked alike. This was largely due to a change in the scale of building operations from individual lots to entire blocks.
1. Intersection of the Rue Poussin, the Rue Pierre-Guérin, and the Rue La Fontaine. **2.** 17-21 Rue Pierre-Guérin. **3.** 11-13 bis Rue Pierre-Guérin. **4.** 2-6 Rue Poussin. **5.** 5-13 Rue Bosio. **6.** Rue Bastien-Lepage.

383

1. 4 Rue de la Pompe. 2. Corner of the Rue d'Alésia and the Rue Vercingétorix. 3. Rue Rampal. 4. 33 Rue Leconte-de-Lisle.

The Backlash

of the social class an apartment house was meant for, stone perpends were used. In working-class developments that meant economizing elsewhere—with cramped layouts, poor façades, and inferior fittings. Working-class buildings thus became poor imitations of a great bourgeois art. On façades the austere frames (formed by a single plane), the simplified consoles (spaced too far apart), the dreary lines of the stonework, and the cubical modillions of the upper balcony were, if nothing else, sober. Unlike the sculptural riches of bourgeois architecture, however, this was most assuredly not the result of an aesthetic choice.

The transition from a severe style of grandeur to the simplified façades found in the outlying developments had certainly not been foreseen by the emulators of rationalism. Reacting to the ornamental ostentation of the decorative style popular during the Second Empire, they had proposed a "purified" version whose apparent simplicity was based on great intellectual sophistication. When the rationalist style was diverted to the outlying petit bourgeois developments, the most advanced artists of the day, such as Anatole de Baudot, reacted with brilliance and began designing mass-produced ornament made of stoneware and opaque glass (which was combined with concrete as soon as it became available). The avant-garde's radicalism began as a form of protest and ended up being popularized. The most austere builders in the early 1860s—Viollet-le-Duc on the Rue Chauchat, Baudot on the Rue Saint-Lazare—were only fifteen years later championing a lively decorative style based on the very special vocabulary of industrial mass production (e.g., Viollet-le-Duc's project for a metal apartment building with a polychrome earthenware ornament in the *Entretiens*, and Baudot on the Rue de Pomereu).[4]

524

Façade detail. Project by Anatole de Baudot, 1894.
Paris, Musée des Arts Décoratifs, Maciet Collection.

A.D.

1891

524. BAUDOT (Joseph-Eugène-Anatole de). *Projet d'habitation parisienne.* Composition basée sur l'emploi de procédés nouveaux de construction et de décoration. (Chauffage par les murs creux.) Détail d'une baie avec encadrements creux perforés en ciment et céramique renfermant des tuyaux de chauffage destinés à combattre le refroidissement des vitres.

Latent since the 1860s, the crisis of the Haussmann approach became unavoidable. The powerful uniformity that it required was no longer bearable. The regulations concerning building height and façade ordonnance were challenged, and animated surfaces were introduced to compensate for the rigid monotony of the city's perfectly aligned buildings. What had been a goal came to be seen as a defect. An aesthetics of variety waged war on the old aesthetics of uniformity. The 1884 building code[5] was the first step in dismantling the Haussmann vocabulary. Continuing in the direction announced by the 1859 increase in building height, it created a real break in the Parisian landscape. The new increase in height concerned only the roof above the cornice line. Henceforth a building's roof was no longer governed by the imperious 45-degree slope,[6] but by a circular arc with a radius of six meters. The aim was unquestionably to make roofs stand out with imposing volumes (whereas the old requirement that a roof's lower slope be slanted at a 45-degree angle had made it all but impossible to give a roof any dramatic interest). But, practically speaking, the result was to increase a building's height by a story.

The raising of the roof created a new volumetric scale. Though the traditional organization of a building's main levels was respected, the size of the mass was considerably increased. As entire blocks of buildings were built at the same time, the new apartment houses ensured the hierarchical superiority of new streets over the earlier Haussmann fabric. There was no modulation in building size from one area to the next. The new seven-story buildings—powerful masses of stone, glass, and slate—were organized in rows or blocks that clashed with the traditional plaster constructions, the horizontal structures of the July Monarchy, and the six-story Haussmann buildings. Yet the coexistence of buildings of diverse historical origins was not necessarily harmful. Such highly coherent streets as the Rue du Louvre, Rue Etienne-Marcel, Avenue Kléber, Avenue Simon-Bolivar, and Rue Marbeuf played an important role in structuring the neighborhoods around them.

Eclecticism did not fundamentally contest Haussmann's conception of urban structure, but rather the uniformity produced by it. The architects of the last two decades of the nineteenth century aimed at the controlled reintroduction of variety into the urban structure. As the unity of mass and of compositional lines was not called into question (indeed, it was growing stronger), the only way to create variety was through detail—secondary lines and ornamental motifs. Even so Haussmann, a firm believer in rigorous ordonnance, would never have tolerated the liberties taken by fin de siècle architects.

This regulatory retreat marked the beginning of the anti-Haussmann reaction that continued down to the beginning of the twentieth century. Apartment buildings tended to be as individualized as possible, though they respected the old compositional stereotypes.

The Regulations Challenged

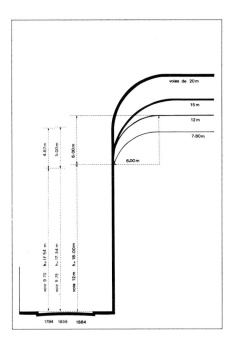

A diagram showing how the 1884 regulation affected building height.
By authorizing roofs that fit under an arc with a radius of six meters, the 1884 regulation resulted in larger roof volumes; cornice height, however, did not change. Diagram courtesy of the Atelier Parisien d'Urbanisme.

1. Rue de Viarmes. The apartment buildings around the Commodity Market curve with the street, thus creating an odd volumetrics. Their big roofs are the result of the 1884 regulation. **2.** Avenue La Bourdonnais and Place du Général-Gouraud. The successive regulations on building height are materialized from left to right: on the left, a Second Empire building; in the middle, buildings heightened in accordance with the 1884 regulation; on the far right, a product of the 1902 building code. Cornice height is the same for all the buildings.

3. 26 and 26 bis Rue La Fontaine. Built on a winding street (once a rural road), the façade of this apartment house has a bent look; the Second Empire would never have allowed such an irregular structure.

Individualization was first seen when the regularity of window openings was altered. The phenomenon had been latent since the Second Empire, but city officials would seem to have long curbed the trend toward irregularity. True to the classical conception, the apartment houses of the Haussmann era were designed with rigorously spaced pairs or triplets of window openings in a symmetrical overall structure. The piers were irregular in width, but not the window openings; the irregularity of the piers was used to express interior layout (presence of a dining room or of a big salon) without disturbing a façade's formal regularity. At the beginning of the Third Republic, larger windows (with three or four panes of glass instead of two) suddenly appeared in reception rooms, which they identified to the outside world. Such windows had been common on courtyard façades for twenty years or so, but had never been used on street façades. They created a visual break in the regular succession of window openings—a break that was much more visible than the old irregularity of a façade's piers, which the big frames around them minimized. The pairing of window openings and the resultant widening of bays called for a form of emphasis that did not take long to develop: partial balconies on every floor soon defined vertical projections on a façade's horizontal system of decorative lines, turning the façade into a colossal grid.

Another step away from Haussmann's conception of ordonnance was taken when metal bay windows were introduced. The bay windows were, in fact, closed balconies that were initially constructed in light materials. Brought back by picturesque architecture, they made a rather timid appearance in Paris around 1885-90.[7] Of English origin, they were used in that humid country to help heat houses. They had characterized the whole rural tradition, with its roots in the architecture of the Gothic manor, before reappearing in cottage architecture and the various forms of the picturesque style. Their transposition to the apartment house can be understood only in terms of sea-resort architecture, which adapted the cottage style to bourgeois houses and imperceptibly transformed the bay window into a conservatory. The first bay windows in Paris were found in big aristocratic mansions whose winter gardens remained fashionable throughout the Second Empire. At the end of this long evolution, the bay window became a glass cage whose metal frame was integrated onto the balcony outside an apartment's dining room. Stone balconies were constructed on every floor, and structures with cast-iron frames, sheet-metal parapets, and glass panels were interpolated between the balconies. As the building code did not allow such projections, architects (like the owners of today's cafés with sidewalk terraces) claimed that the shallow appendages were temporary and could be dismantled. But the popularity of bay windows was so great that they were increasingly designed as part of the structure—even if, in deference to the building code, they were built of materials that looked less permanent than stone (wood or iron). As a result, the bay of the windows corresponding to a building's dining rooms—the center of family life—was widened. Just as people were beginning to see home life as something natural and full of happiness and light, dining rooms were given very wide windows that opened onto a glassed-in balcony. As the reader will have guessed by now, the only thing English about the bay windows of nineteenth-century Paris was the name. They were, in fact, much closer to the oriel windows found on the Rhine (or, in a few extreme cases, to those found in Turkish and Balkan houses).

Use of bay windows expressed, first of all, a new interest in projecting apartment layout onto façades—a direct outgrowth of the rationalist movement. But, more important, bay windows made apartment interiors more pleasant (extra light, diagonal views of the street) and created a new type of façade based on powerful projections. Very light glass-and-steel boxes were placed in front of the façade plane, contrasting with the massiveness of the wall and breaking the absolute continuity of a row of façades with projections that structured it vertically by strengthening the bays. In the new vocabulary that was forming, the bay window was an important element of dynamic interest. Moreover, a building's decorative interest came to be focused on its bay windows. A symbol of modernity, the metal structures were given polychrome ornament (stained glass, mosaics, and tiles) that, together with the iron balcony railings located in the same plane, created focal points of great formal richness.

Bay windows caught on fast in Paris. First seen around 1880, they were officially recognized in the 1893 building code, which authorized their permanent construction.[8] But even before 1893, bay windows had already become a key theme in Parisian architecture. They linked a building's three main floors. Wedged between the third-floor balcony and the upper balcony of the recessed story, they were supported by enormous consoles on the basement and were sometimes enriched with rather wild decoration (stained-glass windows of Oriental inspiration combined with zinc on the Avenue de l'Observatoire and the Avenue de Tourville; small cast-iron columns, wood frames, and decorative brick parapets at 18 Rue de la Source). Generally speaking, however, early bay windows were relatively fragile; not properly kept up during the wars, many of them have had to be torn down over the past twenty years.

The 1893 building code made it possible to build bay windows of stone and thus to create the undulating façade planes that the post-Haussmann period so loved. The change of material led to a gradual transformation in form. Because of the weight of the cantilever, bay windows had to be supported by big consoles (a building's lower floors thus bearing the load), for the building code still forbade any break in alignment at basement level. The regulations also forbade projections beyond a roof's regulation curve; a row of bay windows had to stop at the balcony slab of the recessed story (though there was an attempt to conceal this break by topping the projection with a light metal parapet). But gradually the regulation constraint weakened, and projecting bays were reproduced, slightly recessed, on a building's top story. Then the 1902 building code authorized bay windows above the recessed story, continuing up onto the roof.

Stone or Iron?

In the final analysis, bay windows fit in fairly well with the Parisian tradition because, like shop signs and balconies, they were placed in front of the façade plane and thus did not destroy the alignment of façades on a street. The ribbon of stone was altered, but not broken. The strength of that ribbon cannot be explained by the Parisian builders' keen sense of solid construction alone. Indeed, it is somewhat surprising that metal skeletons—championed by no less a figure than Viollet-le-Duc, and constituting the major attraction at the 1889 world's fair—did not have a greater effect on the architecture of apartment houses.

Although riveted steel frames (based on the famous model of the Chicago skyscrapers) were used to construct two impressive groups of office buildings, on the Rue Réaumur and the Rue d'Azès, they were never adopted for residential buildings. When used for office buildings,

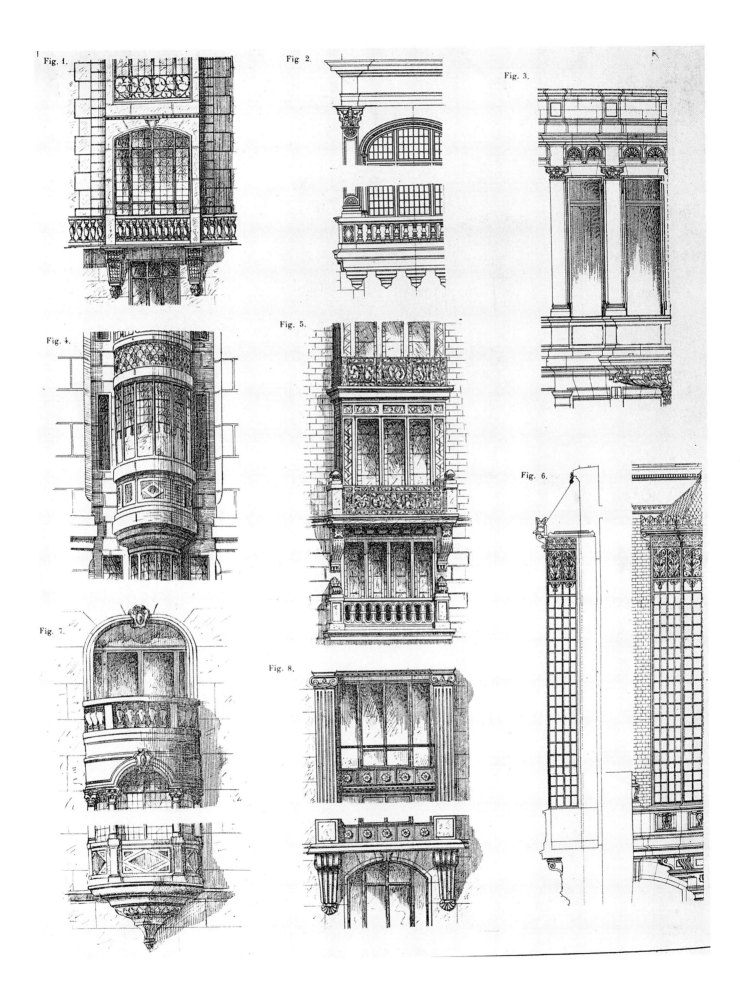

Examples of bay windows built of iron and glass or brick. Bibliothèque des Arts Décoratifs, Maciet Collection.

Fig. 1.

Fig 2.

Fig. 3.

Fig. 4.

Fig. 5.

Fig. 6.

Fig. 7.

Fig. 8.

1. 47-51 Rue du Ranelagh. **2.** 5 Avenue de l'Observatoire. **3.** 1-3 Rue Leneveux. **4.** 9 Rue Fortuny. **5.** 23 Rue de la Pompe. **6.** 1 Avenue de l'Observatoire and Rue Auguste-Comte. Iron-and-glass bay windows are often decorated with zinc cutouts and stained glass and come in a variety of forms: projecting turrets (4), glassed-in loggias alternating with open ones (6), and even semicircular towers descending onto the second floor, which clearly violated the building regulations of the day (facing page).

1. 5 and 7 Rue Donizetti. **2.** 51 Rue du Ranelagh. **3.** Rue Adolphe-Focillon. 4 and **5.** 7 Rue Lekain. **6.** 18 Rue de la Source.

they were still given cast-iron and stone façades, a combination known and accepted for half a century (whereas the steel frame represented an important technical innovation that could have inspired interesting formal transpositions). As is well known, late-nineteenth-century architects were often critical of the decorative cast-iron veneers of the city's steel bridges (Mirabeau and Alexandre III). As comparison of Chédanne's famous *Parisien libéré* building and its neighbors on the Rue Réaumur clearly shows, a similar criticism can be applied to buildings, for the pure exposed frame of Chédanne's building is completely out of keeping with the excessively rhetorical sculpted and molded ornament found on the buildings near it. The steel-and-glass edifice breaks with its environment and destroys the continuity of the façades. And what good is modernity, if it destroys the urban environment's necessary morphological coherence? Nineteenth-century Paris was above all *a stone city*—a fact that, until very recently, was not changed by the occasional attempt at polychrome architecture (Hittorff, Viollet-le-Duc, Horeau, Formigé, Baudot). Once the old rules had been discarded, we finally realized how essential they were for conserving the city's unity. Indeed, we have had to go back to the elementary rules of alignment, height, and structural coherence (strong bays and vertical windows). Perhaps one day soon we will also return to neutral walls of stone or plaster.

1. Réaumur department store, Rue Réaumur. 2. Rue d'Uzès. Examples of constructions with metal frameworks, stone piers, and huge windows.

The fact that nineteenth-century façades were built almost exclusively of big stone blocks did not prevent an evolution in façade design. Toward the end of the Second Empire, façades slowly began to change; eventually a new vocabulary emerged. The main modifications affected frames and ornament. The principle of the grid pattern, expressed in Second Empire architecture by cordons linking the ledges and the tops of windows, had been fading out for some time, as bays were given new emphasis. Indeed, there was an increasing tendency to emphasize verticality: either cordons were chopped into sections by the parapets in a building's window openings, which formed a strong vertical row, or window ledges were shortened to the width of the window opening, allowing piers to continue upward from one story to the next without interruption. The second tendency eventually won out and led to a new way of structuring façades: a building's bays were pushed inward, ornament and window openings both being set back from the façade plane, which was dominated by big piers stripped of all decorative elements.

The strengthening of the structural role of solids was accompanied by one of two decorative approaches. Either the solid panels were framed (but now each framed panel was several stories high), or colossal pilasters were used.

The reintroduction of bygone styles, generally associated with the idea of eclecticism, was in fact only one aspect of the evolution of

The Triumph of Eclecticism

façade design, for there was also a spectacular transformation of the classical vocabulary. Use of mannerist techniques allowed bold ornamental innovations, which were produced by enriching the classical vocabulary with new combinations (which, strictly speaking, constitutes eclecticism), but also by transforming that vocabulary's component parts.[9] The result was an odd impression of disorganization created by the choice of heterogeneous details and by the weak links between them. Façade decoration was executed in a systematically cold way that eliminated all surface vibration. The often excessive realism of sculpted detail created disruptive representational pockets; overall, façades began to look like chance clusters of separate, autonomous elements. Systematic use of strong contrasts emphasized the disturbances that affected the traditional scale and rhetoric of classical ornament. In short, façade unity was utterly destroyed.

The isolation of cold clusters of ornament on façades during the last quarter of the nineeenth century had some very odd results, such as what I have designated as "staple ornament," and Jacques de Caso calls "the ornament of separate motifs."[10] Indeed, the handsome façades that Duban, Visconti, and Lefuel designed in the 1850s (before the style flourished in the 1880s) sometimes look like superpositions of motifs that, despite a certain similarity and coherence, remain basically heterogeneous. The absence of visual links between the motifs and the stiff realism of their realization strengthen this impression of unrelatedness, which architects would almost seem to have taken as an aesthetic ideal. The influence of industry on the evolution of decorative systems should not be underestimated. The old aesthetics of stone ornament was modified by the aesthetics of cast iron.[11] The inherent precision and repetitiveness of cast-iron ornament influenced the emergence of a style based on perfectly executed, perfectly similar motifs that were endlessly and almost obsessively repeated. The nineteenth-century "manner" does, moreover, make one think of the gestural aesthetics that characterized artistic production in the mideighteenth century—an aesthetics that the late nineteenth century suddenly rediscovered in the powerful works of sculptors like Carpeaux and painters like Van Gogh.[12]

Details of 240 bis Boulevard Saint-Germain. Paris, Bibliothèque des Arts Décoratifs, Maciet Collection.

Unlike the stiff, repetitive style of façades from the 1860s to the 1880s, the antiacademic style that emerged in the 1890s created animated surfaces by bringing back such typically late-medieval devices as polychromy and dynamic asymmetries. All the resources of picturesque vocabulary were exploited to liberate style, resulting in extremely idiosyncratic façade ornament. Instead of composing regular, balanced façades, architects subordinated the whole of a composition to various focal points. Thus at 109 Avenue Mozart the dominant feature is verticality, which is emphasized by the building's triangular shape and narrow cut-off corner. The walls never rest: the brick fillers are locked in between the strong cornerstones and bays.

1. 18 Rue Gustave-Zédé. 2. 71 Avenue Mozart. 3. Boulevard Emile-Augier.

Beginning at basement level, the dynamic pattern continues up to the base of the roof, where it culminates in the undulation created by the pedimented dormer windows on the recessed story. At 14 Boulevard Emile-Augier, powerful stringcourses push the bays toward a deep hole created by a big corner loggia in the Louis XII style. Finally, at 76-78 Avenue Mozart, in a building whose façades draw heavily on the vocabulary of the French Renaissance, everything crystallizes on the huge, windowless cut-off corner and the oversized niche that adorns it.

These three examples could give a very negative picture of eclecticism. However, it should be remembered that, despite their formal diversity, eclectic façades were all governed by the law requiring that some feature or features should be focused on. In opposition to traditional classical composition, in which the balance of the various elements was the overriding consideration, the new compositional mode treated each work as a distinct, autonomous object contrasting sharply with its context. The new urban ideal, based on the notion of individuality, placed façades in direct competition with each other in order to create a more diversified urban landscape, and rejected anything tending to subordinate individual expression to a common rule.

1. 131 Boulevard de Sébastopol. **2.** 26 Rue de Boulainvilliers. **3.** 22 Rue de Téhéran. **4.** 8 ter Rue La Fontaine. **5.** 19 Rue des Pyramides. **6.** 10 Rue de la Pompe. Apartment-building doors tended to be wider than ordinary doors, but narrower than the old carriage entrances. They usually opened into a building's entrance hall and rarely allowed carriages access to the courtyard. An extraordinary number of variations on the main door can be found. While office buildings tended to use a single model (big double doors topped by an arcade at mezzanine level), residential architecture exhibited a great diversity of doors.

1. 45 Rue Ribéra. **2.** 5 Rue Dangeau. **3.** 75 Rue Madame. **4.** 10 Rue de la Pompe. **5.** 41 Rue Ribéra. Ornamental sculpture flourished during the last quarter of the nineteenth century. Whereas the Second Empire had used only frames (sometimes punctuated with keystones or medallions), the 1880s made heavy use of high and low relief: busts, caryatids, symbolic figures, and mythological scenes.

1. Corner of the Boulevard Emile-Augier and the Rue Gustave-Nadaud. **2** and **3.** Corner of the Avenue Mozart, the Rue Jasmin, and the Rue de l'Yvette. **4.** Avenue Kléber. **5.** 109 Avenue Mozart. Fin de siècle apartment buildings gradually moved away from the Haussmann standard, with the appearance of elements that were out of scale: niches, loggias, chimney stacks, dormers, etc.

401

The Picturesque City After 1880, Garnier's prophetic vision of the city as a permanent celebration of color and decoration—the opposite of industrial drabness—inspired more and more architects. There was a burst of creative energy that totally contradicted the rationalists' standardized brand of historicism. It did not really matter anymore whether the Gothic style was best for churches, the neoclassical style for courts of law, the Renaissance for mansions, or Louis XIII for châteaus. What counted henceforth was that each façade stand out. The flamboyant and Louis XIII styles of polychrome architecture were preferred because the brick and stone contrasted strongly with the uniform ocherous yellows and black window openings that characterized the rest of the city. But there was more than one way to create a contrast with Haussmann banality; numerous alterations made stone architecture stand out, too. Architects played greatly on the shape of windows (e.g., the reappearance of arched openings) as well as on their scale. There was a pronounced taste for variations in size, ranging from tiny squares to big double windows, and for unusual spacings like those formed by staggering windows in a building's staircase. Architects paid special attention to spacing solids and voids dynamically, sometimes using very tightly spaced window openings—separated by piers reduced to the width of a pillar—and expressive exceptions such as big double windows with four vertical panes. They did not hesitate to invent new ways of spacing windows (sometimes asymmetrically) in order to liven up façades while also expressing a building's interior layout.

The interest in dynamic façades led to an even more ambitious quest: the creation of dynamic volumes. City regulations on building height and alignment were challenged by numerous innovations. Thus recesses in a building's façade created an interplay between two façade planes; corner rotundas were strongly separated from the rest of the façade; and domes and big stone dormer windows began to stand out on roofs. In addition, the traditional levels became unrecognizable. Despite the presence of the big third-floor balcony, the basement was not clearly separated from the upper stories—a circumstance closely related to the mezzanine floor's being used for bourgeois apartments. The main floors—often increased from three to four—lost their clear structure owing to the building of balconies on every floor. And the roof, part of which was converted into apartment space, was given more window openings, spaced so as to continue the bays.

In certain projects, the alignment of façades was quite blatantly ignored. Curving and herringbone rows appeared (Boulevard Emile-Augier, Avenue d'Eylau), favoring the creation of unusual volumes that were completely unrelated to the rectilinear masses of Haussmann's Paris. The edges of volumes were rounded in order to strengthen the impression of mass by erasing the line where façade planes intersected (a technique that Louis XV architects had already used with beautiful results). Similarly, the inside/outside hierarchy of big and little streets,

1. Corner of the Rue Auguste-Comte and the Avenue de l'Observatoire. 2. Corner of the Rue Gustave-Zédé and the Rue Antoine-Arnauld.

1

2

Facing page: Rue Marbeau.

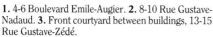

1. 4-6 Boulevard Emile-Augier. 2. 8-10 Rue Gustave-Nadaud. 3. Front courtyard between buildings, 13-15 Rue Gustave-Zédé.

and of courtyards and streets, was also eliminated; the systematization of the "second façade" gave courtyards and alleys an urban status. Although the hierarchy of materials and ornament was still respected, the window openings on this façade were spaced to form a composition rather than reflect interior layout, and even sought to recall the main composition of the street façade. Toward the end of the century, service courtyards were sometimes even placed at the front of lots that were hard to build on (e.g., Rue Gustave-Zédé); when that happened, there was absolutely no distinction left between courtyard and street (i.e., between a lot's inside and outside). However, the dynamic interest that the imperatives of plan and layout sometimes gave courtyard façades did create a typically fin de siècle picturesqueness. Is this eclecticism or art nouveau? The question is important, for it lets one better grasp the elaboration of the formal ideology of the post-Haussmann era.

The 1902 Building Code

How absurd it is to cut history up into arbitrary hundred-year slices that have nothing to do with reality. Socially as well as culturally, the early 1900s were still very much a part of the nineteenth century. The real watershed was World War I, for it marked the collapse of the socioeconomic system of nineteenth-century Europe. The early twentieth century, on the other hand, was the apogee of that system.

The slow evolution of the Paris apartment building after 1859 had led to a deep modification in façade ornament, resulting particularly from the appearance of bay windows, which were "officialized" in the 1893 building code. But the greatest changes were yet to come. In 1902 a new building code, drafted by the city planner Eugène Hénard and the architect Louis Bonnier, was enacted. It authorized architects to use the elements they had been clamoring for: in particular, strong silhouettes and dynamic relief. Head of the City Department of Streets, Louis Bonnier devoted himself to bringing about a renewal in the aesthetics of the apartment building. His first tool was an annual "façade contest" that brought the winning building's architect public recognition for his creativity, and its owner an attractive tax exemption. The façade contest greatly stimulated architectural innovation and at the same time provided builders with a constant supply of models to copy (which was exactly what Bonnier wanted). When the 1902 building code was published, it included an extraordinary series of models—in all styles, but always in keeping with the new code's spirit and letter.

Down to World War I, city building officials played an important role in controlling and encouraging use of the model defined in the official regulations (just as they had in the Second Empire). The run-ins that architects like Henri Sauvage had with them prove how autocratic they could be, when they suspected an architect of trying to get round the regulations.

The Composition of Masses

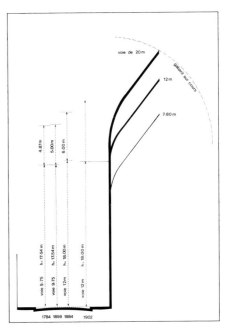

A diagram showing how the 1902 building code affected building height.
The 1902 regulation on building height was the most generous in the city's history. While cornice height remained the same, roof volume was determined by an arc whose radius, varying according to street width, was extended by a 45-degree diagonal. Maximum building height thus rose to 32 meters (compared to 22.41 meters in 1784). Diagram courtesy of the Atelier Parisien d'Urbanisme.

Enormous Roofs

Unlike the 1859 and 1884 building codes, the 1902 code marked a total stylistic break. A huge increase in the volumetrics of roofs was combined with a transformation of building alignment (foreshadowed in 1893). In theory, cornice height had remained unchanged since the eighteenth century, which had made it possible for new buildings to fit in with earlier constructions reasonably well. But in the 1902 building code roofs were dramatically transformed: the circular arc used to define roof volume in the 1884 regulations was henceforth set not on a horizontal (the top of the building), but on a 45-degree diagonal. As a result, deep buildings gained several extra stories, and roofs became so

1. 104 Boulevard Saint-Germain. 2. Rue Saint-Jacques and Rue Sommerard. A building based on the 1902 code rises above the Second Empire building in the foreground.

enormous that they crushed the façade vertical. Although the modification was simple enough, its consequences were enormous. Restoration and Louis-Philippe buildings were seemingly roofless constructions whose 45-degree slopes were almost never visible from the street. The use of mansard roofs on most big Second Empire streets (authorization for general use came in 1884) created roofs that could be seen by passersby; indeed, it could be argued that the skyline of mansard roofs is what most strongly characterized Haussmann's Paris. The 1902 building code raised a building's total height to thirty or thirty-two meters (eighteen meters for the façade, six for the radius of the curve, plus the additional height created by the diagonal). Thus while the height of the façade vertical had not really changed since 1784 (17.54 meters in 1784; 18 meters in 1902), ten to twelve meters had been added at roof level. Henceforth the roof represented over a third of a construction's height. It could contain up to four or even five floors—in many cases, as many levels as the elevation above the ground floor, and more than the elevation above the basement (which still grouped the first two floors together). The common distribution of floors became 2 + 3 + 3 or 2 + 3 + 4—which made buildings look extremely top-heavy. Since the 1880s, moreover, the availability of elevators had completely transformed the status of the top floors: now prestigious, they bloomed with terraces and gardens (e.g., Guadet's houses on the Rue Elisée-Reclus; the Perret brothers' apartment building on the Rue Franklin, 1903; Boileau's Lutétia Hotel on the Boulevard Raspail; Guadet on the Boulevard Murat). The transformation of the top floors was particularly facilitated by the invention of reinforced cement, which made it possible to build roof terraces. For his 1903 "hygienic housing" on the Rue Trétaigne, Sauvage was already using the kind of roof gardens generally associated with Le Corbusier.

FIG. II. — *Partie de rue de 20 mètres (largeur de la rue de Châteaudun) conforme au Décret du 22 juillet 1882.*

FIG. III. — *Partie de rue de 20 mètres de largeur, avec les saillies de windows tolérées actuellement et contrairement au Décret de 1882.*

FIG. IV. — *Partie de rue de 20 mètres de largeur et dont les saillies et les silhouettes seraient autorisées par le Décret projeté.*

FIG. V. — *Partie de la rue de 30 mètres (largeur de l'avenue de l'Opéra) et dont les saillies et les silhouettes seraient autorisées par le Décret projeté.*

1. 24-26 Rue Charles-Baudelaire, winner of the city's 1910 façade contest. **2.** 199-201 Rue de Charenton, winner of the 1911 façade contest. **3.** 11 Rue Réaumur, winner of the 1903 façade contest.

1

2

410

1. Comparison of the 1882-84 and 1902 regulations on façade projections (sketch by Louis Bonnier). **2** and **3.** Examples of projections from the roof authorized by the 1902 code, for street widths of 20 meters (left) and 30 meters (right).

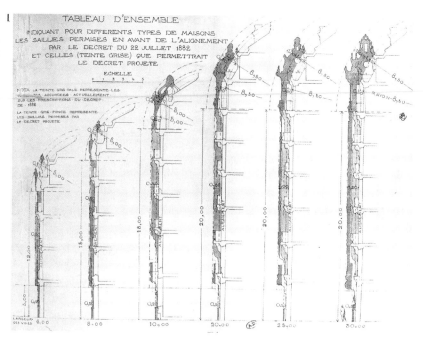

TABLEAU D'ENSEMBLE

INDIQUANT POUR DIFFERENTS TYPES DE MAISONS
LES SAILLIES PERMISES EN AVANT DE L'ALIGNEMENT
PAR LE DECRET DU 22 JUILLET 1882
ET CELLES (TEINTE GRISE) QUE PERMETTRAIT
LE DECRET PROJETE.

Fig. IX. — *Partie supérieure d'une maison de 20 mètres, sur voie de 20 mètres, vue du trottoir opposé et dont la silhouette serait autorisée par le Décret projeté.*

Fig. X. — *Partie supérieure d'une maison de 20 mètres sur voie de 30 mètres, vue de la rue et dont la silhouette serait autorisée par le Décret projeté.*

CROQUIS DE M. Louis BONNIER, ANNEXÉS A SON RAPPORT SUR LES TRAVAUX DE LA SOUS-COMMISSION TECHNIQUE DE REVISION DU DÉCRET DE 1882

Eugène Hénard's propositions for a new kind of boulevard. **1.** Street with a straight alignment. **2.** Boulevard lined by trees. **3.** The new type of indented boulevard, with alternating trees and buildings. **4.** A boulevard with triangular indentations. **5.** Plans of a boulevard with triangular indentations and a street with a broken alignment. Paris, Bibliothèque des Arts Décoratifs, Maciet Collection. Hénard's principle of the indented row was used to extend the Boulevard Raspail. The interesting thing about it is that it broke the rigidity of the Haussmann alignment and made courtyards an extension of the street. This approach did much to weaken the traditional opposition between a building's front façade (public) and the courtyard in the middle of the lot (private). In addition, it made more verdant streets possible, since the indented areas could be landscaped.

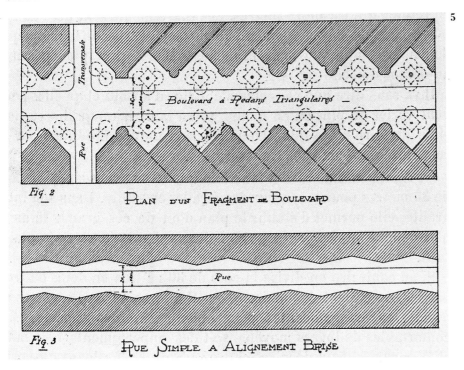

Fig. 2

PLAN D'UN FRAGMENT DE BOULEVARD

Fig. 3

RUE SIMPLE A ALIGNEMENT BRISE

413

The transformation of roof proportion was accompanied by the break in alignment that bay windows created. The new building code can thus be said to have brought about a major typological transformation. Moreover, by authorizing certain kinds of open courtyards (which break the continuity of the plane of façades on the street), the new regulations also defined a new type of urban space: the herringbone avenue, conceived by Eugène Hénard and first used to finish the Boulevard Raspail (from Sèvres-Babylone to Bac/Saint-Germain).

Plasticity of sculpture

Corner of the Rue des Perchamps and the Rue La Fontaine.

This typological evolution did not, however, fundamentally alter the traditional physiognomy of apartment buildings; it simply modified the component parts in order to adapt them to the new emphasis on the roof. Thus the balcony running across the third floor gradually disappeared, weakening the break between a building's basement and its main floors. Architects invented numerous ways of breaking the tyranny of the horizontal between the basement and the third floor. Thus bay windows were visually linked to the basement with gigantic consoles or squinches; or the traditional horizontal (expressing the functional break between commerce and residence) was lowered a floor; or multiple breaks and projections were used to destroy the line's continuity. The 1902 regulation on bay windows encouraged what the 1893 regulation had not yet even allowed: the proliferation of complex volumes at roof level—domes, pavilions, monumental dormer windows, and decorative sculptures—to complete the powerful rise of the masses with distinctive silhouettes. Traditional graphism was completely outmoded: art nouveau repudiated the dry, linear compositions that had still characterized the 1880s (e.g., in the use of frames on neutral grounds and of light, intricate cast ironwork in front of stone façades). A new taste for sculpturesque masses and rhythmic gradations won out over regularity and precision. A sculptor's architecture more than a draftsman's, art nouveau owed a great deal to baroque art. The bay window is an excellent example. As a result of the authorization to build bay windows of stone as permanent parts of the façade, they were blended into the façade so as to create an undulating flow.

This dynamic approach saw form in terms less of shape than of light, color, and movement; in that respect, it can be compared to quite a few other fin de siècle experiments. Architects were much less interested in ordonnance than in creating unexpected spaces. They wanted to emphasize the cityscape's mobility, accidents, and variety of atmospheres. Controlling form was not a priority, for architects did not want to risk thwarting the sculpturesque expansion of mass.

The 1902 building code was based on a remarkably efficacious approach that respected the traditional figures of façade organization, but it transformed façade dynamics. In this reworking of classical tradition, increasing the volumetrics of roofs and allowing a new

1. 77-81 Avenue Paul-Doumer. **2.** Corner of 99 Faubourg Saint-Antoine and 89-91 Avenue Ledru-Rollin. **3.** 1-5 Avenue Mozart. **4.** 113 Avenue Mozart. **5.** 24 Rue de la Source. **6.** Rue Duban.

Post-Haussmann architects had a passion for domes and corner pavilions. However limited their functional value, they are quite spectacular on a purely plastic level.

1. Rue La Fontaine, looking toward the Rue Georges-Sand and the Rue des Perchamps. **2.** Rue La Fontaine, between the Square La Fontaine and the Rue Gros.

element of dynamic interest on façades were enough to give traditional form a new meaning. The city planner Hénard and the architect Bonnier were responsible for the revolution in urban art that was the official embodiment of art nouveau. As the term "post-Haussmann" suggests, their approach was deeply anchored in tradition as well as totally original.

The variety that the urban composition of the early twentieth century sought in façades, it also sought in architectural masses. For new developments such as the Champ-de-Mars, a gradation in building size was used: intermediate four- and five-story models were combined with the big regulation size of seven or eight stories. A staggered or bleacher arrangement of building heights was found whenever a row of façades bordered a large open space. In a narrow space like a street, the difference between five stories and eight might hardly be visible. But for vaster spaces such as big squares and esplanades, such differences proved to have definite advantages. Clearly visible, they emphasized and nuanced the individual forms while giving the composition of the row a rather châteaulike ordonnance based on progressive volumes hierarchized in space. Used with great expertise on the Champ-de-Mars, gradations were also employed, albeit to a lesser extent, on the Esplanade des Invalides and the Rue de Tilsitt, near the Arch of Triumph. In the latter case, the two big mansions built on the corner of the Avenue Kléber and the corner of the Champs-Elysées (one of which unfortunately burned down several years ago) rose above the mansions built by Hittorff and corrected the disappointing disproportion of scale between the earlier edifices and the Arch. Even in less ambitious compositions (e.g., the beginning of

Gradations in Height

417

The Champs-de-Mars esplanade and the statue of Marshal Joffre.

the Avenue d'Eylau), gradations in height continued to be used throughout the first quarter of the twentieth century.

Return to Unity

The typological originality of post-Haussmann apartment houses distinguished them profoundly from earlier buildings. Organized as wholes, they created original and visually rich spaces, as seen in the famous Boulevard Raspail, but also the Avenue Frémiet and the Rue Raynouar. On the other hand, when not built in groups, post-Haussmann buildings always looked out of place because, given their volumetrics, they introduced an intolerable break at roof level and in the alignment. In point of fact, after 1884, apartment houses just about had to be designed and built in groups. Reconstruction of an empty lot in a row almost always created breaks in rhythm and scale as inevitable as the earlier confrontation of pre-Haussmann and Haussmann buildings with traditional construction. However, in Second Empire Paris such breaks had been carefully orchestrated to create a hierarchy of streets and spaces. What happened in the early twentieth century is an entirely different matter. For various reasons, a post-Haussmann building did not always look hierarchically superior to the Haussmann buildings that it happened to neighbor. Moreover, the successive changes brought by the 1884, 1893, and 1902 building codes came too fast not to create perpetual clashes between neighboring buildings, which were often quite different in size and morphology. The resulting incoherence did great damage to post-Haussmann Paris. Yet when applied to large groups, the 1902 building code created impressive landscapes as powerful as they were unified; the twofold principle of modulating the façade plane and the

418

1. Lutétia Hotel, Boulevard Raspail. 2. Rue Leneveux. 3. Rue Bosio. 4. Avenue Charles-Floquet. 5. Corner of the Rue Jasmin and the Rue de l'Yvette. 6. Rue Huysmans.

419

Square de l'Alboni.

building size generated full, undulating rhythms that can be preferred to the systematic horizontals formed by the cornices and continuous balconies of Haussmann façades. Indeed, the new approach resolved the compositional conflict between bays and continuous balconies that had troubled the entire history of the Haussmann era. In wholes as perfectly designed as the Champs-de-Mars esplanade, one cannot but admire the post-Haussmann approach, which, without contesting the foundations of Haussmann's approach to urban space, corrected certain weaknesses in architectural design.

Art Nouveau

The post-Haussmann building evolved as much on the decorative as on the plastic level. As already noted, the new stylistic phase began around 1885-90. After 1890, once the monumental vocabulary had been entirely assimilated, architects began to move away from the classical decorative commonplaces, and in particular from the orders (pilasters, columns, entablatures) that Garnier's emulators had used to decorate bourgeois apartment houses. From this point of view, the apartment houses that Dauvergne built on the Rue de l'Alboni in 1899 can be considered one of the last examples of strict classical ordonnance (e.g., the colossal order used for the corner rotundas). Henceforth strong masses and a rhythm of solids and voids were to form the essential vocabulary of the façade, with ornament serving only to bring out a building's main compositional lines. Thus isolated decorative medallions on the panels between a building's bays (a common recipe around 1850) gave way to bare panels and frieze motifs emphasizing the lines of the balconies (consoles, corbeling), of the arched window openings (arches, parapets, and even the inner edges of the opening), or of the successive cornices on the top stories. Although the repertoire was usually of eighteenth-century inspiration (a highly conventional Louis XV or Louis XVI), the way it was used had nothing classical about it, since the traditional orders and proportions had been totally abandoned. Their eclectic ornament notwithstanding, these buildings were "modern" in style.

It is important to realize how close this decorative system is to the neo-Gothic style[13] and its art nouveau derivatives. The only thing that distinguished an academic from an art nouveau building was the conventional or unconventional (classical or floral) ornament. The positioning and the plastic role of ornament were the same in both cases. The basic principle was to outline a façade's main forms, clearly marking the lines separating planes. Architects stopped emphasizing the stacking of superimposed levels in order to strengthen the mass: as ornament on window frames would have looked parasitical and blocked perception of the form as a whole, window frames were used only to demarcate openings, which is how frames had traditionally been used in Gothic architecture. What is surprising is that this approach was not combined with the stylistics of Gothic, but rather with classical motifs adapted to the new context. However, classical tectonic ornament (entablatures, pilasters, pediments, decorative medallions) was used far less than motifs transcribed from furniture and curios. The early-twentieth-century style has been criticized for turning façades into gargantuan teaspoons. Indeed, architects did usually prefer ornamental motifs originally designed for small objects, since they were easier to integrate into lines and proportions foreign to classical ordonnance.

The procedure was not in itself new: it had been used in ancient Rome and even more since the sixteenth century, when it had been necessary to adapt the ordonnance of the Greek temple to edifices completely different in form and scale. But the principle was modified. Baroque architecture had turned the façade into a veneer, either by emphasizing the imbalance between a building's actual mass and classical ordonnance, or by embedding one scale in another in order to conceal the difference in proportion between parts.[14] On the other hand the modern approach, which had been foreshadowed by the rococo style in the eighteenth century, tended to not only accept but even emphasize a building's real scale. Thus, starting in the 1880s and 1890s, a new monumental ordonnance emerged, freed from the traditional proportion of the story and from the impression of stacking that it tended to create. For this, the model of the baroque palace (via its French transposition on the Place Vendôme) provided something

447 · PARIS — Rue Alboni.   J. L. C.

1906

of a model. Thus, as the twentieth century got under way, one found a new plastic approach that rejected academicism even when a building's ornament seemed to bind it to academic architecture.

1. 10 Rue Leneveux. **2** and **3.** Corner of the Rue François-Ponsard and the Rue Gustave-Nadaud.

An essential aspect of the post-Haussmann era is revealed by the rather surprising renown of the sculptors who decorated apartment houses. On façades their names can commonly be found next to the architects'—proof that their contribution was considered to be of equal if not greater importance. Their prestige was closely related to the renaissance of the decorative arts in the late nineteenth century and in particular to that of sculpture and ironwork. The apartment houses on the Boulevard Raspail were illustrated and discussed in numerous publications, and their sculptors became famous. Indeed, some of those buildings must be considered key moments in the history of art nouveau in Europe.[15] It should not be forgotten that early-twentieth-century apartment houses had a privileged place in the hierarchy of constructions. Architects did not hesitate to mention their apartment houses in the same breath with their châteaus and mansions. At the beginning of the century the apartment building came to be seen as a monument comparable to other prestigious realizations in the public or private sector. Architectural criticism focused increasingly on residential construction; the apartment house was no longer viewed as common. Yet it is hard to distinguish the work of such great masters as Guimard and Lavirotte from that of their contemporaries. Despite the absolutely exceptional originality of their formal investigations (freed from eclecticism, though one can still easily identify the Gothic and Oriental sources), the typology they used was perfectly in keeping with their generation's attempts to give the city a new dynamic interest. Thus the "Guimard style," art nouveau, and the art of the bourgeois apartment house can be seen as branches of a single family: post-Haussmann architecture.

423

An Exceptional Success

The influence of Louis Bonnier's building code was such that, during a period of intense real-estate speculation, it affected the appearance of entire arrondissements in at least as significant a way as the Haussmann approach proper. Indeed, for many, Paris is as much a turn-of-the-century city as it is a Haussmann city. Bourgeois art was quick to adopt the new typology defined in the 1902 building code. A good example is provided by the two apartment houses that the architect Armand Sibien built across the street from each other on the Avenue Paul-Doumer (Place Possoz) for the La France insurance company. The earlier building, in brick and stone, is of an utterly rationalist coldness; the discreet bay windows are nothing but oversized window openings that project slightly from the façade. Built ten years later, the building across the street is a huge dynamic mass beneath a rich columned loggia and includes a fine roof pavilion. Comparison of the cut-off corners—the earlier ones thin and graphic, the later ones protuberant—sums up how totally different the two buildings are.

Early-twentieth-century architects used the conventions of past styles, but in an utterly new way. Domes and pavilions could be Louis XIV, Louis XV, neoclassical, or Renaissance, but, given the supple treatment of mass and detail, they were first and foremost art nouveau. A pronounced and somewhat bombastic taste for contrasts eliminated intermediate scales. Architects concentrated on extremes: the pathos of powerful masses and the daintiness of detail. The result was an almost Wagnerian force that gave the most ordinary apartment houses a striking monumentality, which the following generation attacked as the pompous grandiloquence of hacks trying to flatter the bourgeoisie. Such basically political judgments do not change the fact that the bourgeois architecture of the early twentieth century was an exceptional success.

A Significant Detail

Early-twentieth-century architects devoted particular attention to the question of how to support bay windows made of stone, and often treated the transition from the façade plane at street level to the plane of the bay windows (which started on the third story) with great originality. Corbeling was first of all a technical matter, for it had to support considerable cantilevers in stone masonry projecting beyond a building's foundations. But it was also a question of plastics: how were bay windows to be smoothly integrated into façades? Since the building code did not permit façade projections to descend to the ground, it was necessary to find a way to support bay windows rising from the third floor. Consoles, squinches, and pendentives were usually preferred, as they allowed sunlight to enter the second-floor window beneath the overhang of the bay window. Supports were given elegant silhouettes in order to link a building's corbeling to the rest of the façade. In addition, small window balconies were placed on the second floor so as

With the new roof designs encouraged by the 1902 building code came loggias built outside the most prestigious apartment (transferred from the third floor to the top of the façade). **1** and **2.** 77-81 Avenue Paul-Doumer. **3.** 97-95 Avenue Mozart. **4** and **5.** Rue d'Assas and Rue du Cherche-Midi. **6.** 1-5 Avenue Mozart.

425

1. Corner of the Rue Gustave-Zédé and the Rue du Ranelagh. **2.** Corner of the Chaussée de la Muette and the Rue de la Pompe. **3.** 4 Rue Verdi. **4.** Villa Patrice-Boudard. **5.** Liégeois mansion, Avenue René-Coty. **6.** Corner of the Rue Octave-Feuillet and the Rue Alfred-Dehodencq.

Following pages: **1.** 1-3 Rue Huysmans. **2.** Building entrance, 29 Avenue Rapp.

The Castel Béranger, 14 Rue La Fontaine, is generally considered the wildest art nouveau edifice in Paris. Yet this apartment building is but one manifestation (granted, the most original) of a type of architecture that was widespread at the time.

to link the lower openings to the bay windows above them. An interplay of arcades in the bays with bay windows further unified those bays, which contrasted with the rest of the façade. Finally, consoles and pendentives of gigantic scale (up to two or three meters high, for what should have been but a secondary detail in the architectural ordonnance) further emphasized the continuity of the verticals.[16]

The most classical solution was the console, of Venetian origin. Since the Second Empire, balcony consoles had played a major role in Parisian architecture. Architects had not hesitated to support balconies with consoles placed so close to one another that they resembled rows of giant modillions, and had sometimes even combined a console into the keystone of the window beneath it, thus creating the bivalent motif of the keystone-console, so characteristic of the Second Empire. When this tradition was adapted to the bay window, architects created a hierarchical structure of real and fake consoles, ranging from the huge load-bearing consoles of the bay windows to ornamental keystone-consoles, with balcony consoles in between. Consoles did not, however, lose any of their repetitiveness.

When seen from the street, these consoles gave a façade rhythm and depth. Moreover, because of their hierarchical structure (i.e., the gradation in size), they introduced a form of variety. Pendentives were often designed to stand out in profile like consoles, or to create powerful focal points. Indeed, the relative disproportion of these elements was entirely guided by a quest for compositional focal points that were positioned to be seen from the street (i.e., not frontally). Along with strong contrasts in scale, the emphasis on one or more focal points is a defining characteristic of the modern style popularized in the early twentieth century.

When, to make a building better fit its context, art nouveau tried to incorporate certain aspects of Haussmann ordonnance, the results were, to say the least, unconvincing. On buildings with no strong focal points (like the building at 114 Boulevard Saint-Germain, wedged between two late Haussmann buildings), the flatness and regularity of the façades created an impression of monotony and moreover made the detail look crude—out of scale and poorly integrated into the general grid pattern. The early-twentieth-century style was based on a system of "antiform": the grid created by a building's window openings and story levels was used as a background for a dynamic interplay of curves in relief. For the style to work, there had to be a strong dialectic, whereas the graphic Haussmann style existed in the façade plane itself.

A Lingering Influence

A movement of essentially decorative origin that valued originality above all else, art nouveau was the opposite of a unified art and therefore was destined to be very short-lived. But after the movement's demise, a whole circle of Parisian architects did continue to work in the spirit of art nouveau until the birth of art deco and even later. They

1. 9 and 13 Rue Gustave-Zédé. 2. 44 Rue du Rane-lagh. 3. Rue Alfred-Bruneau and Rue Singer. 4. 240 bis Boulevard Saint-Germain. Guadet designed this building to protest against art nouveau and encourage a return to the austere architecture of the Haussmann era. Paris, Bibliothèque des Arts Décoratifs, Maciet Collection.

created a subdued style—less personal, but more coherent—based on discreet references and elegant lines. This purified version of art nouveau earned its representatives—Guimard, Plumet, the early Sauvage, Herscher, Lucien Bechmann, and even Boileau, Jalabert, and Albert Vèque—great acclaim. The subdued style, which remained in perfect keeping with the 1902 building code, lasted quite a while (for example, as late as Landes's Place Félix-Eboué, 1926) and deeply influenced early public housing in Paris.

Around 1910, Lemaresquier and his generation opted for a middle road between academicism and art nouveau. The result was a very Parisian compromise between the geometrism then in fashion and the suppleness of art nouveau. Architects drew on the rigor of a powerfully architectonic Louis XVI style, but continued to show a pronounced taste for monumentality and dramatic contrasts. Oddly enough, architects turned to the mideighteenth century—Desforges, Desprez, Lequeu—in their search for unusual ways to use the classical repertoire, which had come back into fashion. The now-forgotten architects of this generation—Louis Marnez, Cadilhac, Henri Petit—attempted to fuse the classical approach they had been taught, in its most outmoded and bombastic forms (e.g., Laloux's Gare d'Orsay), with the innovative and refined reinterpretation of Gothic created by the last generation of the nineteenth century. Some of these architects had once espoused art nouveau—most notably Louis Marnez, who, with Majorelle, designed the famous decor of Chez Maxim's—and were reacting to what they saw as its facility. Some, like Sauvage, evolved toward an approach devoid of all classical references. Others never evolved at all and right down to World War II continued to use a stylistics based on the geometrism of the 1930s, as seen in L. Plousey's disappointing Rue Paul-Cézanne.[17] But whatever the style,

1. 65 Rue du Ranelagh. 2. 6 Rue Huysmans. 3. 20 Rue Gustave-Zédé. 4. 3 Rue Capitaine-Olchanski. 5. 4 Rue du Lunain. 6. 1-3 Rue Huysmans.

for a good thirty years architects continued to respect the architectural and urban approach set out in the 1902 building code, which is no doubt the main reason why late post-Haussmann architecture became the *bête noire* of the modern school. (In the 1920s Sauvage was already publishing virulent articles against the 1902 building code and its negative consequences for hygiene and the development of an industrial architecture.)

Housing the Poor

One is sometimes tempted to see post-Haussmann architecture as a bourgeois art, if for no other reason than the enormous success it met with in that social class. Nothing, however, could be further from the truth. The art nouveau approach was used—urbanistically, architecturally, and decoratively—for all kinds of construction. Although ornament changed when the social level was lower, and stone was replaced by brick, and apartments were reduced to handkerchief size, the basic typology of the apartment building remained unchanged from one end of the social spectrum to the other. Moreover, whatever the social class concerned, architects and contractors constructed for prospective tenants who were allowed less and less participation in the building process. The first public housing, financed by the big industrial companies, appeared during the post-Haussmann years. Ironically enough, luxury apartment buildings and public housing were often designed by the same architects, since the leaders of the Third Republic hired the architects they knew—those who had designed the sumptuous buildings where they lived—to come up with low-cost housing for the lower classes. A clear split took place in the field of building: architects were entrusted with the two ends of the scale (the residences of the rich and poor), while contractors, often

1. 15-17 Rue des Perchamps. **2.** 20 Chaussée de la Muette. **3.** Avenue Alphonse-XIII.

using more old-fashioned (or more conformist) aesthetic models, aimed at a middle-class clientele. But despite this specialization, the type of architecture used was totally unified. A building was simply designed with greater or lesser imagination, depending on the social class in mind—and with more or fewer concessions to that class's tastes, depending on whether the class could choose what it wanted, as the middle class could, or had to take what it could get, as in the case of workers being offered low-rent housing.

Trade-union and business leaders, politicians, and modernist architects worked together to create public housing in France. The buildings built between the two world wars were made possible by the technical and plastic innovations of the first decade of the twentieth century and in particular by the stimulating contributions of such architects as Sauvage, Provensal, and Ruté-Bassompierre. In its early public housing Paris possesses a veritable, if little-known, architectural treasure that, surprisingly, has never been studied in depth or benefited from the protective measures it deserves.[18] Early public housing is as remarkable for its technical innovativeness—use of reinforced concrete, brick façades with industrially manufactured ornament—as for the design of blocks from outside to inside (the individual lot now being a completely obsolete notion), and the use of radically new approaches to collective areas (green spaces and places meant to promote social interaction).

This might lead one to think that traditional working-class architecture disappeared completely at the beginning of the century. In fact, in both Paris and the suburbs the working class still had a little leeway. While building one's own home had practically disappeared (replaced by the housing development), one can find scattered examples of tiny houses built by workers—on lots sometimes

Elementary school, Rue des Bauches.
Typical of the Third Republic, this school, with its brick façades and concrete floors, is also an example of the modern style that Louis Bonnier and his colleagues advocated.

measuring less than fifty square meters. The poor man's version of the bourgeois house, such constructions had the merit of being independent, permanent residences of solid construction.

As the working class was pushed farther away from the mainstream of society, it reacted by coming up with solutions of its own. It was aided by the fact that certain areas of Paris had not been built up, being situated above the underground galleries of the old quarries. In such areas workers' cooperatives created neighborhoods of rudimentary houses on streets only three or four meters wide, like the Rue de la Mouzaïa, the Poterne des Peupliers (a more elaborate development), and the Rue Parent-de-Rosan. Two-story houses with simple lean-to roofs were built at the back of lots (against the back walls of the buildings on the adjoining lots), which left room for a little fenced-in garden in front. The houses were built with cement bricks (for walls eleven centimeters thick) and pine floors. Practically uninsulated, these houses also lacked modern conveniences; at best there was a toilet and a sink, not necessarily inside the house. As simple as possible, this architecture was completely unrelated to refined architecture. The evolution of building techniques led to the abandoning of rubblestone and plaster (craft materials) for brick (often coated, with quoins and simple ornament above the windows), and to the use of an elementary form of roofs whose low slopes were clad in zinc or machine-made tiles (the roof sticking out over the perpendicular façade, with no cornice and a simple round zinc gutter). Thus industrialization did modify the appearance of constructions, but the principal result was to make the poverty of workers' houses even more pronounced than in traditional working-class construction. The working class's only link to culture was found in the decoration of shops. Every bakery and bistro in Paris—covered with wainscoting,

RÉSUMÉ DES DÉPENSES (Rue Pelouze)

DÉSIGNATION		PAR CORPS D'ÉTAT	PAR MÈTRE SUPERF.	P. 1000 F DE DÉPENSE
Maçonnerie	115.000 »			
Stucs	1.080 »	118.380 »	369 93	351 55
Canalisation	2.300 »			
Charpente bois	4.000 »	10.250 »	32 03	30 43
Escaliers	6.250 »			
Serrurerie, quincaillerie	48.000 »	51.200 »	160 »	152 05
Persiennes en fer	3.200 »			
Couverture et plomberie	19.000 »	21.000 »	65 63	62 36
Appareils bains	2.000 »			
Menuiserie, parquets		43.000 »	134 38	127 70
Fumisterie	5.700 »	8.200 »	25 62	24 35
Calorifère	2.500 »			
Marbrerie		6.800 »	21 25	20 19
Peinture	20.000 »			
Tentures	1.700 »			
Vitraux	1.000 »	33.450 »	104 53	99 33
Vitrerie	2.500 »			
Miroiterie	7.650 »			
Sculpture		14.000 »	43 75	41 57
Monte-charges	1.500 »	10.200 »	31 88	30 29
Ascenseur	8.700 »			
Sonneries, électricité	4.030 »	4.230 »	13 22	12 56
Branchement gaz	200 »			
Ensemble		320.710 »	1.002 22	
Honoraires de l'architecte		16.035 »	50 11	47 62
Totaux		336.745 »	1 052 33	1.000

MAISON DE RAPPORT

RUE DE VAUGIRARD ET RUE DE LA GROTTE (XVe) A PARIS

M. Émile BERTRAND, ARCHITECTE

Répondant à « la demande », en ce quartier excentrique, l'immeuble ci-contre représenté, en son ensemble,

FIG. 100. — FAÇADE SUR LA RUE DE VAUGIRARD (A 0,004 P. M.).

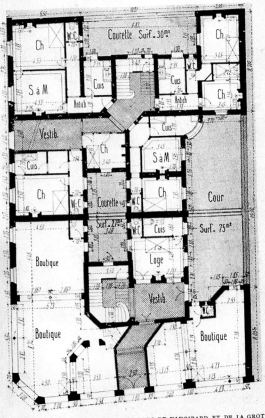

FIG. 101. — PLAN DU REZ-DE-CH., RUES DE VAUGIRARD ET DE LA GROTTE
(A 0,004 P. M.)

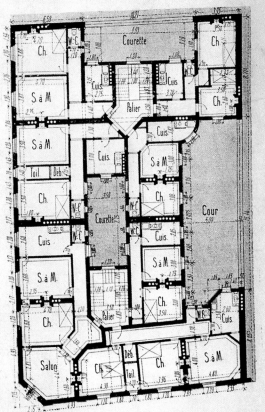

FIG. 102. — PLAN DES ÉTAGES, RUES DE VAUGIRARD ET DE LA GROTTE
(A 0,004 P. M.)

ceramics, and mirrors not without charm—became a workingman's palace. With the development of cinema, replacing the theaters on the boulevards, art nouveau entered another domain and showed the working class the delights of the Belle Epoque, from which it was otherwise excluded. Be that as it may, working-class architecture as such had disappeared; now there was only poor architecture. The working class was robbed of the culture that had once been theirs; the rare tidbits of culture they did get came from a distant world. Art nouveau's effort to create a "modern industrial decorative art" (the title of a famous review of the day) did not find rapid fulfillment and in any case never made its way into the extremely elementary neighborhoods of the working class. The situation did not begin to change until the period between the wars, when the evolution of the working class allowed it access to art deco via the architecture of suburban houses.

A Difficult Conversion

Rapid Technical Advances

As working-class production was being reduced to the construction of shantytowns, and the memory of the old craft culture was fading fast, industrial technology developed with the speed of lightning. The steel skeleton was soon supplanted by reinforced concrete, which was cheaper. Moreover, contractors began to organize construction work methodically; the outcome, starting in the 1920s, was prefabrication. A highly skilled work force was then replaced by unskilled workers, and improvisation disappeared from the construction site.

Technical progress affected Parisian apartment houses—not only experimental buildings, but also everyday construction—in many ways. Thus reinforced-concrete roofs were frequently adopted starting around 1905-10, and use of that material for floors became almost commonplace. Only appearances were saved, by keeping the freestone façade in front. Nevertheless, apartment houses with reinforced-concrete frames were fairly rare and experimental in character. In addition to the famous prototype[19] (a sort of publicity stunt to drum up business) realized by Hennebique for his offices on the Rue Danton in 1901, mention should be made of the Perret brothers' apartment house on the Rue Franklin and Sauvage's on the Rue Trétaigne (1903). Here, formal and technical innovation came together in a truly radical way not unrelated to an interest in Japanese architecture. Reinforced concrete—or more precisely, at the time, cement—was widely used, starting in the early twentieth century, to build terrace roofs on very prestigious constructions such as Boileau's Lutétia Hotel, his apartment building on the Quai d'Orsay, and Du Bois d'Auberville's two apartment houses on the Chaussée de la Muette. In the years that followed, the use of exposed skeletons spread, as seen in the Magasins Réunis on the Avenue Niel and early public housing projects. Henri

In 1913 the city organized a competition for a low-cost housing complex to be built on the Rue Brillat-Savarin and the Rue Henry-Becque. **1.** Project designed by Gonnot and Albeneque, façade and plan of the upper floors. **2.** Project designed by Dubost and Gautruche, view in perspective and plan of the upper floors. Paris, Bibliothèque des Arts Décoratifs, Maciet Collection.

Low-cost housing complexes were the beginning of public housing in France. The three projects shown here reflect the early-twentieth-century concern with "healthy" buildings. The designs show detached buildings with landscaped courtyards. The first project (which won the competition) is of a traditional type, with vaguely regionalist details, big roofs, and balconies. The second project, with its concrete roof terraces, was directly influenced by the theories of Anatole de Baudot and Henri Sauvage. The third project, more monumental, is heavy and massive; it includes roof terraces and an indented façade.

1

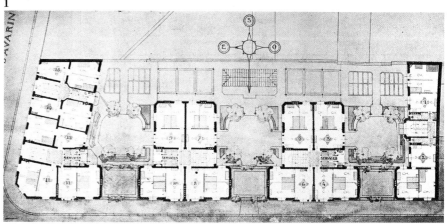

2

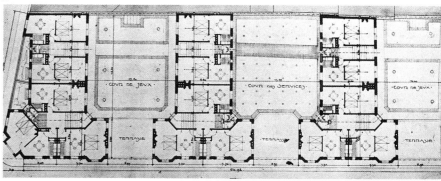

Elévation sur la rue Henri-Becque.

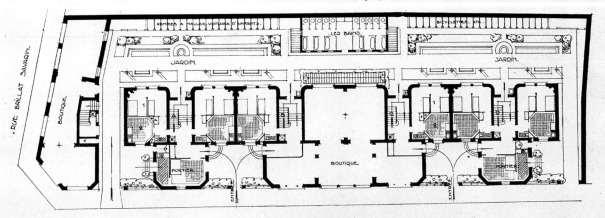

. RUE HENRI BECQUE.

Plan du rez-de-chaussée.

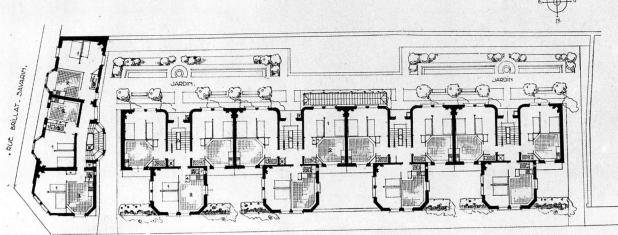

. RUE HENRI BECQUE.

Plan des étages.

4403. GILBERT (Henri) et POUTARAUD (Marcel). — *Projet d'habitation à bon marché.*

Villa Alexandre-Ribot.
Just as the first public-housing projects were being built, workers' cooperatives began to set up little neighborhoods of shallow brick houses with tiny gardens on the slopes of Belleville. In the background is the handsome Butte Rouge housing project, built between the wars.

Following pages:
1 and **2.** Rue Dieulafoy. **3.** Villa Alexandre-Ribot. The construction of houses peaked in the housing developments of the early 1920s.

445

Sauvage made particularly interesting use of the new principle of construction for the terraced design of his 1912 building on the Rue Vavin (the initial plans dated back to 1907-9).

Henri Sauvage's case is interesting. If he designed the Rue Vavin building, he was also responsible for a quantity of utterly conventional buildings with stone-faced façades—some of the most depressing examples of the deterioration of the nineteenth-century typology. Sauvage himself was deeply aware of this. The theoretical articles he wrote just after World War I on the changes that should be made in the Bonnier building code[20] are proof of how quickly and totally that code had been made obsolete by the dawn of modern architecture. Yet the bourgeois apartment house survived until World War II. Such architects as Lemaresquier and Dubouillon "modernized" the Bonnier type of building by skillfully using an art deco style with neoclassical tendencies. Art deco being just a geometrized version of art nouveau, that transposition was as logical as it was easy. A subtler revision using a modernist vocabulary was attempted during the same period by Michel Roux-Spitz in his best buildings, as for example on the Quai d'Orsay and the Rue Guynemer.[21]

Continuity

There were other reasons for the survival of the bourgeois apartment house. As brutal a shock as World War I was, it affected only the state of mind of the combatants; the home front remained isolated, its way of life unchanged. Parisian architecture was not so much affected by the war itself as by the slowdown in building activity imposed by it. Numerous projects came to a standstill, leaving unfinished façades throughout the city (e.g., Rue Chernoviz, Rue des Artistes, and Avenue du Maine). It took a long time to finish many buildings that had been started in 1914; indeed, some were just boarded up for the duration. After the armistice most building activity involved finishing up earlier projects. In some cases that meant bringing in a new contractor or architect, and the initial plans were significantly altered. In other cases, there was an effort to complete buildings in keeping with the original design. Thus for the Villa Patrice-Boudard, which begins on the Rue La Fontaine, the new architects faithfully executed the plans drawn up by their predecessor, who had been killed in the war, and named the street in his memory. Until about 1925, the year of the big decorative arts fair, there was a total continuity with the prewar period in the architecture of apartment houses, regardless of style. Not only did art nouveau continue, but the Louis XVI style of the 1910s flourished and became the bourgeois art par excellence of the roaring twenties. Indeed, stylistic continuity was so strong between 1910 and 1925 that it is extremely hard to say whether a building was built before or after World War I.

The modernist trend did not affect Parisian architecture any more

1. Quai des Orfèvres. **2.** 1-5 Rue Danton.

deeply than World War I did. Into the 1950s, the city's apartment houses continued to reflect the 1902 building code, which architects simply updated a bit in accordance with the tastes of the day. All kinds of styles were used: persisting neoclassical, toned-down 1900, art deco, bargain Louis XVI, mock antique. The twenty years between World Wars I and II can be divided into two quite distinct aesthetic periods—roughly, the 1920s and the 1930s. In the first period stylistic references were more in evidence and more varied; ornamental sculpture was still used abundantly; and buildings, even when of antique or geometrical inspiration, were still quite marked by the strong verticals that characterized art nouveau. During the 1930s, on the other hand, ornament was impoverished or commonplace. New construction techniques—such as nonload-bearing façades attached to reinforced-concrete skeletons—account for what happened. When load-bearing freestone façades disappeared, they took sculptors and stonecutters with them. By this time, the bulk of the cast-iron ornament produced was limited to simple volutes and bars. In 1930s architecture, huge window openings defined long horizontals on every floor. The terraced stories often used had nothing to do with the majestic curved roofs of art nouveau. Finally, basements were opened up with huge windows on both levels, protected by an enormous concrete awning.

Buildings of the 1930s did, however, fit in with 1920s buildings because building height and the use of a vertical façade rhythm did not change. In the 1930s, bay windows—updated as large semihexagonal projections in the style of Roux-Spitz—maintained a modulated façade plane, while the division of window openings by concrete mullions (based on the "Chicago window") broke the dominant horizontality of the voids. Finally, many ways of treating a building's top turned the

449

slopes into an element of dynamism even in the most modern buildings (Laprade, Roux-Spitz, Mallet-Stevens, Perret, Sauvage). Overall, the 1930s developments—such as the Avenue Paul-Doumer, Auteuil, and the public housing built at the city's edge—fit in perfectly with the aesthetics of the post-Haussmann approach, which they continued.

Corner of the Avenue René-Coty and the Rue des Artistes. The outbreak of war brought the construction of this building to a halt. It was finished ten years later on a very reduced budget, whence the small number of stories, the plaster façade, and the industrial-tile roof.

The Heyday of Public Housing

The use of block urbanism and great compositional coherence gave the public housing projects erected on the old Thiers fortifications a power that is all the more remarkable considering that their morphology evolved markedly by adapting original new features such as brick-and-stucco construction. Even before 1914, regionalism had led to new plastic approaches (most notably, the experimental projects of the Rothschild and Lebaudy foundations). Those approaches were used between the two world wars to build a number of big housing projects. The break with the city's architectural environment was much less radical than in the case of the modern school, for block urbanism basically fit in well with the 1902 building code by combining global unity with picturesque variety. One can even argue that the last great incarnation of the post-Haussmann approach is found in the housing projects built between the wars. Their design is diametrically opposed to the rationalist rigor underlying the functionalist approach to planning advocated by admirers of Le Corbusier's Charter of Athens. One need only look at the housing projects grouped together in heavy horizontal masses—rising above the deep trench formed by the loop highway around Paris—to realize how profoundly a spirit of unity and formal coherence inherited from the nineteenth century determined their forms.

Post-Haussmann Paris thus survived almost into the middle of our century. The collapse of the Third Republic in 1940 symbolically marked the end of a system that was itself the continuation of the late-nineteenth-century approach to the city and its buildings. A more objective assessment of this period than the one that has long prevailed would reveal its originality in decoration (a very appealing blend of regionalism and art deco) as well as in architecture and urban planning. In particular, a remarkable variety was introduced into the urban landscape by combining groups of individual houses with apartment buildings, often in a very convincing way. One reason for this is that a generation of regionalist architects had greatly benefited from the teachings of Camillo Sitte and his dynamic vision of medieval space.

The Disintegration of Paris

The 1967 building code sounded the knell of post-Haussmann architecture in Paris. From the Liberation to the early 1960s, buildings of a traditional type were still built. Increasingly impoverished in vocabulary, the mediocre landscapes formed by the apartment houses of that period can be considered the last metamorphosis of the aesthetics of the early twentieth century. But systematic disrespect of a row's alignment and ordonnance, a love of oversized forms, and the stylistic influence of prefabrication architecture gradually turned façades into flat, repetitive travesties of design. The traditional coordination of adjacent buildings was totally neglected, leading to kaleidoscopic alignments without the slightest coherence from one building to the next. In short, the urban landscape was shattered. In an attempt to restore unity, some architects did tackle the complicated problem of coordinating totally heterogeneous building sizes and typologies with the traditional forms of Paris. But one is rarely successful in mating cats and dogs, as many a modern cityscape demonstrates.

The 1967 Building Code

The urban model defined in Le Corbusier's Charter of Athens inspired the urban renewal projects of the 1960s and the 1967 building code, which was shaped by three concerns: automobile traffic, public health, and industrial mass production. The principle of separating functions led to the separation of different kinds of traffic: the city's old polyvalent streets were replaced by highly specialized routes designed for pedestrian use, neighborhood traffic, or crosstown transit. Parking ate up all the reserves of space at ground level and destroyed many of the green spaces planted in the name of hygiene. As in most European cities, Parisian city planners created residual green spaces, landscaped islands squeezed in between lanes of traffic. Use of the ground for automobile traffic and parking made the old notion of the lot totally obsolete, as the boundaries between public and private areas were blurred. Moreover, building alignment disappeared, leaving a number of very ambiguous spaces. The traditional division of space was challenged to such a point that all barriers—walls, fences, and landscaped borders—were eliminated in favor of an uninterrupted and undifferentiated space. As the public space disintegrated, the old structure of private space vanished with it; the hierarchy of depth (from the front to the back of the lot) disappeared, and the alignment of buildings was intentionally ignored. Application of the 1967 building code had a very negative effect on the structure of a block's interior: full utilization of the maximum building size eliminated courtyards.

Given the fact that the 1967 code encouraged setting buildings back from the building line, and allowed builders to make up for the loss in depth with an increase in height, one can see that this building code was the most anti-Haussmann text imaginable.[22]

The submission of urban space to the imperatives of traffic alone went unchallenged for a quarter of a century. Not until the failure of the Left Bank expressway, in 1974, did a real current of opposition emerge.[23] In point of fact, to privilege automobile traffic over everything else was to betray the Charter of Athens, of which the 1967 building code was only a crude caricature. The antiurban model that Le Corbusier and Russian city planners began to define in the 1920s did not focus on the problem of automobile traffic to the exclusion of everything else.[24] Indeed, they gave much greater priority to two other goals. The first, inherited from the nineteenth century, was to improve hygiene through access to sunlight. Application of the $H = W$ equation (building height equals street width) was a perfectly legitimate way of doing so (but not, as we now know, an effective way of structuring space). The second goal, the supreme motivating force of modernity, was to use standardized materials and plans—that is, to turn architecture into a mass-produced object. Based on the endless repetition of identical units stripped of ornament, the aesthetics of mass production is violently opposed to Europe's hierarchical tradition, since using identical elements makes it nearly impossible to subordinate some elements to others. This aesthetic ideal, whose sources were purely philosophical (and often tinged with the leftist politics of a certain European avant-garde), had nothing to do with the socioeconomic reality of French life in the 1960s. Le Corbusier's turnabout in the latter half of his career may be seen as tacit proof that he disapproved of the dominant trends in postwar architecture. (Regardless of what some have said, his early work is a far cry from the big apartment complexes of the 1960s.)

Rue du Ranelagh.

Order and Liberty

The aesthetics of mass production turned architecture into a purely formal exercise. Steeped in the nineteenth-century ideal of liberty, the architects of the 1960s had to *un*learn the golden rule of urban harmony. Every building was now designed to be a spectacular show of architectural prowess by architects whose main aim was to outdo the building next door. As the public space per se was abandoned, a new style of ornament devoted to the cult of industrial materials developed. The flashy luxury of polished marble and smoked mirrors—the "colonel style"[25]—was somehow supposed to be a statement of modernity. Though such meretriciousness might make sense for monuments (in their traditional interplay with vernacular architecture), it is absolutely unacceptable in residential architecture. Over the last thirty years, the proliferation of garish, contradictory architectural feats has not created fine cities.

Rue du Ranelagh.

Oddly enough, the modernist avant-garde alone defended the classical notion of order. Nothing could be more regular and coordinated than Le Corbusier's "city for a population of three million," which is based on a hierarchy of public spaces, a gradation in building heights, and the neutralization of private architecture. Unfortunately, Le Corbusier's plans, like Renaissance architectural drawings, were of a purely plastic order. The transposition of such ideal propositions into reality has never really been successful. Whereas the entire classical tradition was based on a compromise with urban reality to create a balance of order and disorder, the modernists ignored that reality and wore themselves out trying to impose a purely theoretical order. The ideal plans that looked so perfect on paper resulted in chaotic landscapes. In the few cases where they were realized as designed, the total uniformity of the resulting landscapes created a disastrous clash with the rest of the city.

The modernists doubtless failed because they overemphasized individual artistic expression. Their mistake was to lump all rules together and condemn them as unbearable constraints on creative liberty. Thus in 1961 Ionel Schein lavishly praised the Croulebarde skyscraper for destroying "one of the most antiarchitectural constraints imaginable: the alignment of buildings." And, describing Jean Balladur's glass-and-aluminum office building on the Rue de la Victoire in 1959, he saw "a fair and accurate protest against the city's nonsensical regulations on building size" (the 1902 height was still in effect at that time).[26]

1. Rue Linois. **2.** Avenue Alphonse-Humbert. **3.** Rue Gustave-Nadaud. **4.** Intersection of the Rue de Lourmel and the Rue de Javel. **5.** Avenue Félix-Faure. **6.** Rue de Lourmel.

Utterly indifferent to their environment, these edifices reveal the importance of attached, aligned buildings. Landscapes like these, numerous in the outer sections, forced the city to revise the 1967 building code.

458

The lesson to be drawn from the resounding failure of modern urban architecture can be summed up in one point: the fundamental distinction between *types* and *models*.[27] In contemporary architecture "perfect" works are designed and then used as models for many other buildings, whence the birth of "digest" architecture: every time an appealing design is shown in a review, it later crops up, more or less unchanged, in numerous other projects. The particularities of those projects, far from contributing to their design, mar the realization of the chosen model. Architects then rationalize the fact that their beautiful projects have produced mediocre buildings by complaining about the site or the demands of insensitive contractors and nagging clients. This litany, which architectural critics are all too familiar with,[28] does explain certain failures. But it is based on the very mistaken notion that what really counts in architecture is not the end product (doomed by various and sundry external constraints), but rather a project's ideal formulation on the drawing board (whence the superiority of Michel Ragon's "visionaries").[29] If, on the other hand, one assumes that constraints can generate interesting projects with a physiognomy of their own, one discovers what an architectural *type* is: a way of arranging forms and spaces that can be repeated from one construction to the next with multiple adaptations. By definition, a type calls for and welcomes variants, whereas models prohibit them. The nineteenth century was the golden age of typological architecture, its types ranging from the garden kiosk to the metal market. But on closer inspection, the unity of nineteenth-century architectural types dissolves into a multitude of variants so original in plan, material, and ornament that they cannot be considered mere reproductions of a standard form.[30] One can establish families of nineteenth-century edifices that are comparable in design, but one must also recognize how each construction was adapted to a particular site, environment, function, and budget. Architectural inventiveness lay not in the perpetual elaboration of new models (to be copied by lesser architects), but in fitting a project to a given set of circumstances.

Modern architects have turned the nineteenth-century approach around: starting with identical mass-produced parts, they have attempted to create original wholes. Such an attitude might be justifiable in questions of construction technique, but not in questions of project design, for it is hard to see why a single model need be applied in totally different circumstances. The purely conceptual systematization of project design resulted in a number of obvious absurdities in the early years of the Fifth Republic, and in some cases led to a total perversion of architecture itself. When Bossard and Faugeron came up with the idea of covering systematically arranged towers and strips of housing units with random decoration (on prefabricated sheets), they turned the relationship between ornament and architecture upside down: ornament was used not to accentuate architectural design, but rather to conceal its deficiencies. Based on a negative philosophy that sacrificed real design to an idealized, systematic norm, this kind of architecture reduced urban ordonnance to the simplistic repetition of oversized, identical objects.

Each of the forms created by modernity—the highway, the housing unit, the apartment complex, the green space—corresponds to some real need but satisfies it in a univocal way: highways are for driving, housing units and apartment complexes for shelter, and green spaces for fresh air. Moreover, each need is satisfied in a purely individual way: in his car or apartment, in front of his television set, or on a park bench, each individual is alone with a single need that is given a single response. In modern cities everyone is an island unto himself. On highways and buses, in the subway and parks, we encounter scores of individuals but never, strictly speaking, a group (the latter coming together only from time to time, in cases of mob violence).

Analysis of Old Paris shows that most public spaces used to be functionally mixed and sometimes fulfilled very contradictory needs, as for instance trade and traffic, which presuppose stopping and speed respectively. Streets, gardens, fountains, cafés, theaters, and churches were meeting places where one could speak to a stranger, say more to him than to somebody one knew better, and even make that stranger a friend. The destruction of places of interaction in big cities has created a plethora of social problems. Modern urban planners could unquestionably learn something from nineteenth-century Paris.

The preceding should not be seen as nostalgia. What is needed is not to turn back the clock, but to correct the mistakes in urban planning that have been made in our century. If it is true that Paris was once a very unhealthy place because of its high density and tiny courtyards, it is just as true that modern Paris suffers from inadequate public spaces and systematic, rigid architecture. Hygiene, sunlight, and nature are important, but a city also requires density, mixed functions, and places of social interaction. Experience has made it painfully clear that the mechanistic ideology of modernity has practically nothing to do with the real problems of urban planning. To design a city is to reconcile the irreconcilable, to deal with contradictory and changing needs, aspirations, and realities. A city cannot be set up once and for all; it must be constantly renegotiated. The various Parisian building codes from the French Revolution to the post-Haussmann period reveal an ongoing process of adjustment to complex demands. The Haussmann and post-Haussmann approaches were practical, not theoretical; problems were solved as they arose, in the light of past experience. The successive generations of the nineteenth and early twentieth centuries treated the city as a work in progress; each new generation assessed the contributions of preceding generations and tried to transcend them. When we began to doubt the value of the urban culture shaped by our forefathers, the city fell apart.

NOTES

1. From Delacroix to Bartholdi, the theme of liberty—a hodgepodge of individual liberty, artistic liberty, and the liberty of nations—characterized the entire nineteenth century. The peak came in the 1880s.

2. The fundamental primary source on city planning in the late nineteenth century is Camillo Sitte, *Der Städtbau nach seinen künstlerischen Gründsätzen* (Vienna, 1889), translated into French as *L'Art de bâtir des villes* (1918). Known through articles and partial translations, Sitte's ideas strongly influenced the fin de siècle generation. I have borrowed the concept of picturesque eclecticism from Carrol Meeks, who uses it—rather oddly—in *The Railroad Station: An Architectural History* (New Haven: Yale University Press, 1956). A critique of Meeks's positions can be found in Karen Bowie's unpublished doctoral dissertation, "'L'Eclectisme pittoresque' et l'architecture des gares parisiennes au XIXᵉ siècle," University of Paris 1, Panthéon-Sorbonne, 1986. My own use of the expression simply designates the merging of the picturesque tradition with the tradition of eclecticism. Curiously enough, my division of eclecticism into three phases (simultaneous, synthetic, and formal) in *Histoire de l'art* (Paris: Larousse, 1985), vol. 2, pp. 474-80, corresponds exactly to the division Meeks established, using slightly different adjectives (symbolic, synthetic, and creative) to designate the phases.

3. The construction of apartment houses developed all the more quickly because it was wise to diversify one's investments. Such diversification became the rule when the big insurance companies were required by law to invest part of their profits in real estate as surety for their stockholders' investments. This explains the insurance companies' huge real-estate holdings in Paris.

4. Conversely, architects working in the academic tradition, such as Guadet (240 bis Boulevard Saint-Germain) and Victor Laloux (64 Rue des Petits-Champs, 1889; 81 Avenue Bosquet, 1892), ended up totally assimilating the rationalism of the generation of 1830.

5. M. G. Jourdan and J. Bouvard, *Documents relatifs à la révision des décrets: 1ᵉʳ du 22 juillet 1882 sur les saillies permises dans la ville de Paris; 2ᵉ du 23 juillet 1884, sur la hauteur des maisons, les combles et les lucarnes dans la ville de Paris* (Paris: Préfecture de la Seine, Imprimerie et Librairie Centrale des Chemins de Fer, n.d. [1884]). The earlier regulation authorized metal bay windows (it was revised in 1893, when stone bay windows were authorized); the second concerned roofs. The importance of these two regulations, particularly the second, justifies our referring to them, a bit improperly, as the "1884 building code." Joseph Bouvard (1840-1920), the city's chief inspector of public works projects and an architect for the P.L.M. company, designed many primary schools and the magnificent Republican Guard barracks on the Rue de Schomberg. He also designed the Palace of Industry at the 1889 world's fair. A militant rationalist as well as a city official, Bouvard certainly had something to do with relaxing the Haussmann regulations. He found a worthy successor in Louis Bonnier.

6. It would seem that the regulation on 45-degree slopes had not been respected for some time. In the early years of the Third Republic, the lower slopes of many mansard roofs were raised to 60 or 70 degrees in order to improve use of the roof as living space. The first applications of the 1884 regulation involved giving a roof *two* lower slopes that traced the circular arc. The lower level, generally adorned with stone dormers, then became a bourgeois floor. More skillful architects used iron to construct stately curved roofs.

7. Viollet-le-Duc had a passion for bay windows and was already using them during the Second Empire in many projects for houses—in particular, those found in the eighteenth of his *Entretiens* (p. 319, published in 1872 but dating from 1869).

8. The maximum projection on bay windows authorized by the 1882 and 1893 regulations was forty centimeters, on a quarter of a façade's surface.

9. This is seen in the interest in the Louis XV style in both furniture and architecture at the end of Louis-Philippe's reign. The remarkable Lehon-Sabatier mansion at 9 Avenue des Champs-Elysées (today the *Jours de France* building) is beautiful proof of that interest.

10. Jacques de Caso, "Le Décor en 'motif détaché' dans l'ornement d'architecture et les arts décoratifs en France, 1840-1870," *Actes du XXIIᵉ Congrès International d'Histoire de l'Art*, Budapest, 1969 (Budapest: Akadémiai Kiado, 1972), vol. 2, pp. 293-301.

11. Iron and stone ornament are blended in the oddest ways in the work of the Lille architect Emile Vandenbergh, a student of Labrouste's. For the Cailletaux mansion in Lille, he got rid of garlands and flowers, and planted a wrought-iron composition on the magnificent gray stonework, using cast-iron pieces above the windows. This was an extreme and highly original approach that the nineteenth century did not dare to use as often as it might have.

12. In strictly chronological terms, my explanation might seem rather confused, for I have mentioned architects only from the generation of Louis-Philippe. It goes without saying that I am speaking here of eclecticism principally as a form of academicism. The architecture of Parisian apartment buildings was not meant to be original or new; throughout the second half of the nineteenth century, it followed trends defined by academic aesthetics as promulgated at the Ecole des Beaux-Arts. Even Garnier's revolution in ornament remained within the bounds of academicism. No movement could be said to have radically transformed architecture the way Impressionism did painting, unless one were to see Viollet-le-Duc's rationalism, the forerunner of art nouveau, as a theoretical redefinition of the art.

13. A similarity in decorative technique can be found in Gothic window frames, Louis XV motifs, and art nouveau, which are all based on the notion of framing and replace the classical hierarchy of proportion with a hierarchy of location. This explains why art nouveau—even when Louis XV in inspiration—is still art nouveau. The rules of this decorative repertoire were established, independently of the question of style, by Viollet-le-Duc.

14. The technique of embedding was used remarkably by Palladio in his churches—notably San Giorgio Maggiore in Venice. Embedding is one of the most characteristic elements of late-sixteenth-century manner-

ism. François Mansart was still using it, with phenomenal virtuosity, when he designed the Chapelle de la Visitation on the Rue Saint-Antoine around 1630.

15. For additional information, see François Loyer, "Art Nouveau Architecture in France," in the exhibition catalogue *Art Nouveau: Belgium/France* (Houston and Chicago, 1976), and the abridged version of that text in *Art Nouveau Architecture* (London: Academy Ed., 1979). Certain great sculptors like Pierre Séguin devoted themselves almost exclusively to making sculptures for buildings and became famous when their work was illustrated in the architecture and decoration reviews of the day. In the architectural production of the early twentieth century, the apartment building became a privileged form of expression, equivalent to what châteaus, churches, and public monuments had been in earlier times. The situation was such that E. Jalbert published in the directory of architect sentries mentioning the apartment buildings designed by the architects right alongside their prestigious edifices. From 1890 to 1930 the luxury apartment house was one of the major forms of European architecture. Art nouveau excelled particularly in this area, as it also did in the design of houses, at a time when housing was a high priority in the eyes of architects and the public alike (one proof being the size of investments in housing).

16. A. Cary, *Détails d'architecture contemporaine. Cent vingt consoles photographiées à grande échelle d'après nature et publiées par A. Cary* (Paris: Editions Photographiques d'Architecture, 1903).

17. François Gruson, Camille Hagege, and Rémi Koltirine, former students of Roger H. Guerrand's at the Ecole d'Architecture de Paris-Belleville, have embarked on an inventory of Third Republic architecture in Paris. François Gruson, "Inventaire de l'architecture parisienne sous la IIIᵉ République", thesis, 1986), though not exhaustive, is a helpful tool for researchers. When the inventory of Third Republic buildings is finished, we will have a better idea of the rich production of apartment buildings that marked the end of the nineteenth century and the first half of the twentieth century in Paris.

18. The first analysis was Jean Taricat and Martine Vilars, *Le Logement à bon marché. Chronique. Paris, 1850/1930* (Paris: Editions Apogée, 1982), which includes an excellent chronology of Paris from 1825 to 1930 (pp. 48-55). Since then the subject has attracted the attention of Jean-Louis Cohen, who is preparing a major study. All research on this topic has benefited from the excellent bibliographical research done by Roger H. Guerrand.

19. See Marc Emery, *Un siècle d'architecture moderne, 1850-1950* (Paris: Horizons de France, 1971).

20. Henri Sauvage, "Notes sur une simplification possible de certains articles du décret du 13 août 1902," in *L'Architecture*, January 10, 1923, pp. 79-81. For additional information, see Hélène Guéné and François Loyer, *Les Immeubles à gradins d'Henri Sauvage* (Paris and Liège: I.F.A.-Mardaga, 1987).

21. Michel Raynaud, "Michel Roux-Spitz," in *Architecture, Mouvement, Continuité*, no. 39 (1976), pp. 6-17.

22. The effects of the 1967 building code were perfectly analyzed by Jean-Louis Subileau in *Paris-Projet*, no. 13-14. If the city's 1974 urban plan drew very timidly on these observations, the 1986 revision followed them much more closely—thanks in particular to François Grether and Nathan Starckman who, under the direction of Nicolas Politis, maintained at the APUR the orientation provided by Pierre-Yves Ligen and Jean-Louis Subileau at the time of the 1974 regulations.

23. The authorities' determination to build freeways through the city reigned supreme until the death of President Georges Pompidou. They had, however, been contested for some years, giving rise in 1968 to the strange concept of "underground" urbanism, which M. Utudjian had already advocated in the 1930s in the columns of *Architecture d'aujourd'hui*. The Capitant Report recommended such an approach for the renovation of the Halles district, and Pierre-Yves Ligen was given the difficult task of putting it into effect.

24. Anatole Kopp, *Ville et révolution. Architecture et urbanisme soviétique des années vingt* (Paris: Editions Anthropos, 1967).

25. This is how Maurice Culot cruelly dubbed the style, in reference to television images of the former dictators of Greece and Argentina. I subscribe to it wholeheartedly.

26. Ionel Schein, *Paris construit* (Paris: Vincent & Fréal, 1961). The author's sincerity and love of architecture cannot be doubted, which may be part of the problem. Indeed, because he saw vernacular architecture as an occasion for individual artistic production, Schein overlooked the fact that the art of city planning does require certain conventions.

27. Bernard Huet first advised me to use the distinction between *type* and *model* during a discussion on the architecture of the detached house. It does seem to clarify.

28. During my years as a journalist in the late 1960's, I never met an architect who did not justify his failures with this kind of rhetoric, which I had already heard concerning contemporary architecture in Greece. After a while I began to suspect that the real problem lay elsewhere. On this point, my ideas are close to those of Henri Bresler who, along with Yann Keronnès, David Mangin, and Vincent Sabatier, has done an extremely impressive study of the problem: *Le Mur diplomatique* (Versailles: Ecole d'Architecture et d'Urbanisme de Versailles, 1986). That study is all the more relevant here since it is based on the example of the Parisian apartment building.

29. Michel Ragon, *Les Visionnaires de l'architecture* (Paris: Robert Laffont, 1965). Published twenty years ago, today this work seems almost unbelievable. At the time however, the cybernetic city, the cone city, floating urbanism, etc.—like Doxiadis's "megalopolis"—enjoyed considerable success in the media. Of course those were the years when Yona Friedman was blithely labeling the houses of Old Paris "slums" and calling for their systematic destruction.

30. This is, in any case, what I attempted to show in *Le Siècle de l'Industrie* (Geneva: Skira, 1983). Obviously, I had my reasons for doing so. To show that architectural unity can include a wide diversity of solutions was to oppose the very academic idea that the basic architectural option chosen is everything. Once one accepts that it is not, one can see architecture in a very different way, which will almost necessarily lead to a new interest in the "decorative" arts, belittled and scorned for far too long.

Place de l'Europe
Although its buildings range from the Second Empire to the 1930s, the Rue de Londres is a highly homogeneous patchwork. Differences in materials and detail are minimized by the strong alignment of similarly proportioned buildings, ensuring the kind of unity so sorely lacking in Paris today.

465

Conclusion

The Haussmann approach, which nobody ever took it on himself to conceptualize, was the victim of its own pragmatism. It was, moreover, severely attacked from the start. During the reign of Napoleon III, the accelerating pace of the city's transformation jostled age-old customs. When Jules Ferry, a young journalist opposed to the regime, attacked Haussmann's enormous expenditures,[1] he was expressing a widespread opinion and at the same time aiming at the Achilles' heel of capitalism. According to Ferry, the relentless pursuit of growth had thrust the economy into a dizzying spiral that would eventually reach the bursting point. However correct such a critique of free-market economics may be, it cannot be considered a critique of the actual principles of Haussmann city planning, which continued to be used throughout the Third Republic.

In point of fact, the Haussmann approach was eventually abandoned less for political and economic reasons (the autocratic regime and its free-market conception of the economy) than for strictly cultural ones. The strong dichotomy of past and present that still guides the way we think about the city began when the Department of Historic Monuments was set up during the July Monarchy and grew stronger as the Second Empire progressed. When the Commission on Old Paris was set up in 1897, the divorce between past and present was finalized. One either condemned the great prefect for destroying urban picturesqueness (more or less confused with the city's historical heritage) or enthusiastically applauded what he had done. "That genius of a man," Frantz Jourdain wrote of Haussmann, "made Paris the most beautiful city in the world by flying in the face of routine, casting the old prejudices aside, and freeing himself from our idiotic fixation on an uninteresting past shorn of beauty."[2] Along with a certain number of his art nouveau friends, the same Frantz Jourdain audaciously founded the Society of New Paris in 1903, an irreverent response to the creation of the Commission on Old Paris.

Posterity has made Haussmann bear the brunt of the blame for the "destroyed monuments of French art," to use Louis Réau's famous expression, and has conveniently overlooked the fact that he shared that honor with the Communards of 1871 and the Montagnards of 1792. He has also been saddled with responsibility for the economic and social changes brought about by the Industrial Revolution and has even been taxed with inventing the bad taste that, to hear certain critics tell it, is inherent in the bourgeoisie. The final irony—administered in the name of modernity—came when Louis Réau reproached Haussmann for having "thought too small."[3] *Tu quoque, fili* (You too, my son), our nineteenth-century Caesar could have answered, for the attack was perfidious indeed. Haussmann can hardly be said to have fared much better in the recent rehabilitation of nineteenth-century art, which has mainly benefited the Ecole des Beaux-Arts. Is it easier to appreciate art for art's sake than the realities of city planning?

There is a certain ambiguity about the Haussmann approach that may well explain why its true worth has seldom been recognized. If Haussmann, whom Jules Ferry blamed so virulently for his inordinate love of everything grandiose, was the last great figure in the classical tradition, he was also staunchly modern. When modernity and classical tradition parted company, and defending the city's historical heritage came to be seen as synonymous with fighting modernity (which was undeniably the case throughout the first half of the twentieth century), imperial art was rejected and even scorned because of its basic duality. One had to choose between tradition and modernity.

It might be wise, at this point, to call Le Corbusier to the stand. The great champion of modernity was in fact extremely close to Haussmann when he defined the hierarchy that so totally impregnates his 1922 plan for a city with a population of three million. And he was just as close when, for the 1937 world's fair, he thought of building a contemporary pavilion in the Kellermann bastion of the Thiers fortifications. Strongly opposed to razing the bastion, he wanted to turn it into a twentieth-century tribute (admittedly, a rather humorous one) to Napoleon III.[4] However, it would be a mistake to reduce the Haussmann approach to a brazen forerunner of modernity. Not only did the great prefect have nothing of an Attila about him, but his conception of city planning belonged to a long classical tradition. After the impossible confrontation between modernity and tradition that our century has lived through, the middle road that Haussmann represents is more appealing than ever. Only a neo-Haussmann approach that preserves the past without denying the present, and that unites beauty with efficiency, can get us out of the impasse we are in. Given the structureless spaces created by widespread use of the modernist ideology of liberty, Haussmann city planning cannot but be appreciated as a global, coherent, and unifying approach. Indeed, the order that the Haussmann approach requires is an absolute necessity, if we want to keep the industrial landscape of the suburbs from completely devouring the city. Whereas the previous generation invented the outrageous concept of "protected areas" (from which the rest of the city was by implication excluded!), today we want to restore urban unity by eliminating the city/suburbs dichotomy and reintroducing contemporary construction into the historical cycle of which it is by definition a part. For Paris to survive, the city's historical heritage must be allowed to live in the here and now!

As far as I can see, a neo-Haussmann approach is the only one capable of reunifying Paris. I hasten to add that such an approach strikes me as much less perverse than the postmodernists' anguished derision of cultural tradition. There is nothing wrong with going back to something that worked, and the Haussmann approach is an extraordinary lesson in city planning. It made the most contradictory formulations acceptable, because it never lost sight of the unity of the city as a whole. Indeed, the major quality of Haussmann's very flexible approach was that stylistic fluctuations did not detract from the unity of a city whose first priority was the public space. As noted earlier, the Haussmann approach lacked theorists, which has certainly damaged its reputation—especially in France, where art works are so often judged in terms of the theoretical writings they give rise to. But in these times of disillusion, pragmatism just may have a chance of winning out over the abstract beauties of theory. If European cities are to flourish again and not to sink into anarchic anonymity, a neo-Haussmann approach will have to be adopted. The admirable classical designs proposed by several contemporary architects (and not so admirably copied by others) have no chance of working in the real world, because they presuppose the disappearance of what already exists, as if some magic wand could conjure the city and its many liabilities away.[5] Faced with the same problem, the midnineteenth century came up with an extremely practical and efficient answer. One can but hope for the day when a similar approach will be applied to modern Paris and its many unattractive areas, which cry out for a little order.

Haussmann was utterly classical in realizing that beautification gives a city its dignity. Today, enjoyment of attractive urban spaces is the prerogative of the upper classes (the price of apartments in Paris makes this so obvious that I need not belabor the point). The most democratic approach to urban planning is one that will unify the city, get rid of the "sub-urban" spaces outside it, and set up public spaces of quality throughout the metropolitan area. In spite of everything, Paris is too beautiful a city for us to throw up our arms in despair. I do not advocate destroying what exists, but rather integrating it into a global form whose coherence will smooth over the city's many internal contradictions. For nearly a century urban planners have been guided by such profoundly antiurban notions as independence, isolation, and noncorrelation. The time has come to establish and respect a norm; without one, there can be no urban unity. Midtwentieth-century architects thought they had found such a norm in standardization. We now know that standardization alone is not enough. Values like beautification and hierarchization play a far greater role in maintaining a real urban community.

NOTES

1. Jules Ferry, "Les Comptes fantastiques d'Haussmann," in *Discours et opinions,* (Paris: Armand Colin, 1892-97), vol. 1 (reprinted by Guy Durier, 1979).

2. Frantz Jourdain, "Vers un Paris nouveau," in *Cahiers de la république des lettres et des arts*, Paris, n.d., quoted in Louis Réau, *Monuments détruits de l'art français* (Paris: Hachette, 1959), vol. 2, p. 158.

3. Louis Réau, *Monuments détruits*, vol. 2, p. 159: "his biggest mistake was that he thought too small." Whether they know it or not, even the most traditionalist of art historians have been influenced by the mentality of Haussmann's time, which ate up space as if it had no value and inordinately expanded the city's surface area. Réau's opinion is the exact opposite of what Haussmann's contemporaries thought; indeed, they severely criticized the prefect for building *oversized* streets, especially after the 1860 annexation.

4. Letter from Le Corbusier to Jacques Greber, head architect for the 1937 world's fair, October 4, 1935: "I do hope our antique bastion will be spared, so that we can bequeath it to posterity in memory of Napoleon III. If the barracks above it is torn down, the debris must not be used to fill up the moat, which we have other plans for. I don't know if there is any truth to the rumor, but I thought it a good idea to remind you of our desire to save the Kellermann bastion" (copy enclosed in Le Corbusier's letter to René Herbst, dated October 24, 1935, Musée des Arts Décoratifs de Paris, René Herbst Archives). Le Corbusier may be a bit off the mark when he credits Napoleon III with building the Thiers fortifications, as the decision was made during Louis-Philippe's reign; but his tribute is not without a certain respect for the city's great reformer.

5. Léon Krier will have to pardon this dig: I am obviously thinking of his propositions for Luxembourg and Washington. An admirer of Haussmann can sometimes feel rather ill at ease, knowing that his conceptions have no chance of pleasing either the neoclassicists or the postmodernists. These two schools, which are closer to each other than one might suspect, suffer from a slight overdose of formal idealism. Though more mundane, the neo-Haussmann approach is surely more operational, since it is not based on any particular aesthetic system; it is above all a mode of intervention.

Bibliography

Barroux, M. *Le Département de la Seine et la ville de Paris. Notions générales et bibliographiques pour en étudier l'histoire.* Paris; Conseil Général de la Seine, 1910.

Bastié, J. "Capital immobilier et marché immobilier parisiens." *Annales de géographie,* May-June 1960.

Belgrand. *La Seine.* 2 vols., 1 atlas. Paris: Institut Historique, 1869-1883.

Berty, A., and Legrand, H. "Topographie historique du Vieux Paris." *Histoire générale de Paris,* 70 vols. Paris: Bibliothèque Nationale, 1866-.

Boudon, F., Chastel, A., Couzy, H., and Hamon, F. *Système de l'architecture urbaine. Le quartier des Halles à Paris.* 2 vols. Paris: C.N.R.S., 1977.

Bresler, H. *Le Mur diplomatique.* Versailles; Ecole d'Architecture et d'Urbanisme, 1985.

Chevalier, L. *Les Parisiens.* Paris, 1967.

Couperie, P. *Paris au fil du temps.* Paris: Joël Cuénot, 1968.

Daumard, A. *La Bourgeoisie parisienne de 1815 à 1848.* Paris, 1963.

— *Maisons de Paris et propriétaires parisiens au XIXᵉ siècle (1809-1880).* Paris, 1965.

— "L'Avenue de l'Opéra de ses origines à la guerre de 1914." *Bull. Soc. Hist. de Paris et de l'Ile-de-France,* 1967-68.

Documents relatifs à l'extension des limites de Paris. Paris: Préfecture du Département de la Seine, 1859.

Dubech, L., and d'Espezel, P. *Histoire de Paris.* 2 vols. Paris, 1951.

Du Camp, M. *Paris, ses organes, ses fonctions et sa vie.* Paris: Hachette, 1875. Vol. 6, ch. 31: "La Fortune de Paris."

Feral, S. "L'Urbanisation du Paris contemporain: la plaine Monceau." Thesis, University of Nanterre, 1982.

Girard, L. *La Politique des travaux publics du second Empire.* Paris: Armand Colin, 1951.

Grison, C. "Evolution du marché du logement dans l'agglomération parisienne de 1880 à nos jours." Thesis, University of Paris, 1957.

Halbwachs, M. *Les Expropriations et le prix des terrains à Paris (1860-1900).* Paris, 1909.

— *La Population et le tracé des voies à Paris depuis un siècle.* Paris: P.U.F., 1928.

Haussmann, A. *Paris immobilier. Notions sur les placements en immeubles dans les zones parisiennes.* Paris, 1863.

Haussmann, E.-G. *Mémoires.* Vol. 1, *Avant l'Hôtel de Ville;* vol. 2, *La Préfecture de la Seine;* vol. 3, *Les Grands Travaux de Paris.* Paris: Victor Havard, 1890-93.

Hillairet, J. *Dictionnaire historique des rues de Paris.* 2 vols. Paris, 1963.

Hourticq, J. "Le Grand Paris d'Haussmann." *La Revue administrative,* no. 140 (April 1971).

La Tynna, J. de, *Dictionnaire topographique historique et étymologique des rues de Paris.* Paris, 1816.

Lavedan, P. *Histoire de l'urbanisme à Paris.* Nouvelle Histoire de Paris. Paris: Hachette, 1975.

Lazare, L. and F. *Dictionnaire administratif et historique des rues de Paris et de ses monuments.* Paris, 1844.

"La Maison. Espaces et intimités." Proceedings of the colloquium at the Ecole d'Architecture de Paris-Villemin, 1985. Special issue of *In extenso,* Paris, no. 9 (1986).

Marrey, B. and Chemetov, P. *Architectures Paris 1848-1914.* Exhibition catalogue. Paris: C.N.M.H.S., 1976.

Morizet, A. *Du vieux Paris au Paris moderne. Haussmann et ses prédécesseurs.* Paris, 1932.

Nomenclature des voies publiques et privées, especially the 7th (and last) edition, published in 1951 by the Services d'Architecture et d'Urbanisme, with the assistance of the surveying department of the Préfecture de la Seine.

Nouvelle Histoire de Paris. 5 vols. Paris: Hachette Diffusion, 1970-.

"Paris, croissance d'une capitale"; "Paris, fonctions d'une capitale"; "Paris, présent et avenir d'une capitale." Colloquium reports, *Cahiers de civilisation,* Paris, 1961, 1962, 1964.

Pinkney, D. H. *Napoleon III and the Rebuilding of Paris.* Princeton, 1958.

Poëte, M. *Une Vie de cité: Paris de sa naissance à nos jours. Vol. 1, La jeunesse;* vol. 2, *La Renaissance;* vol. 3, *Paris classique.* Album with 600 illustrations. Paris: Picard, 1924, 1925, 1927, 1932.

Pronteau, J. "Construction et aménagement des nouveaux quartiers de Paris (1820-26)." *Histoire des entreprises,* Nov. 1958.

— *Le Numérotage des maisons de Paris du XVᵉ siècle à nos jours.* Paris, 1966.

Rambuteau, Comte de. *Mémoires.*

Recueil des lois, ordonnances, décrets et règlements relatifs aux alignements, à l'expropriation pour cause d'utilité publique spécialement dans les voies de Paris. Established under the direction of M. Alphand, 1886.

Rochegude, Marquis de, *Promenades dans toutes les rues de Paris par arrondissements.* 20 vols. Paris, 1910.

Rouleau, B. *Villages et faubourgs de l'ancien Paris. Histoire d'un espace urbain.* Paris: Le Seuil, 1985.

Index

473

476

Maps And Diagrams

Construction Techniques And Materials

Photography Credits

Atelier Parisien d'Urbanisme, 211.
Nathalie Beaud, 30, 32, 38, 76, 84, 93, 95, 101, 117, 128, 139, 148, 155, 165, 181, 248, 274, 288, 295, 297, 298, 299, 302, 303, 315, 317, 324, 325, 329, 341, 359, 372, 396, 399, 401.
Bibliothèque des Arts Décoratifs (photos: Hubert Josse for the Maciet Collection), 73, 74, 75, 76, 88, 134, 142, 143, 145, 146, 147, 153, 154, 184, 186, 188, 189, 190, 194, 211, 212, 214-15, 216, 250, 251, 253, 254, 255, 256, 257, 259, 332, 333, 336, 340, 385, 386, 391, 393, 397, 409, 410, 411, 412, 413, 434, 439, 442, 443.
Bibliothèque Forney, 182, 183, 184, 185, 186, 189, 193, 194, 195, 247.
Bibliothèque Historique de la Ville de Paris (photos: Pierre-Noël Doyon), 2-3, 4-5, 16-17, 18, 20, 21, 28, 44, 45, 69, 70, 71, 72, 76, 80, 83, 87, 110, 111, 115, 116, 234, 269, 300, 305, 314, 322, 344-45, 348, 349, 352; (photos: Hubert Josse), 28, 29, 35, 36, 46, 47, 65, 82, 109, 122, 230, 304, 307, 308, 309, 310, 311, 316.
Bibliothèque Nationale, 25, 33, 34, 37, 38, 51, 55, 56, 57, 64, 67, 68, 71, 72, 75, 80, 112, 114, 119, 120, 123, 132, 147, 160, 233, 236, 241, 244, 245, 265, 284, 309, 323, 349, 365, 372, 396, 422.
Centre National des Monuments Historiques, 369.
Léonard de Selva, 127, 128.
Giraudon, 32, 42, 50.

François Hers, DATAR, 236, 290-91, 405, 441.
François Loyer, 26, 27, 31, 40, 52, 54, 56, 57, 77, 81, 86, 89, 90, 93, 94, 95, 98, 101, 103, 105, 117, 118, 132, 133, 135, 139, 140, 144, 163, 164, 165, 166, 169, 170, 172, 178, 179, 180, 181, 191, 193, 197, 198, 199, 200, 202, 203, 204, 205, 206, 207, 208, 235, 237, 238, 239, 240, 242, 243, 246, 248, 249, 252, 253, 256, 257, 258, 270, 271, 272, 273, 275, 277, 278, 280, 281, 282, 283, 286, 287, 288, 289, 293, 296, 297, 301, 305, 314, 315, 320, 328, 330, 331, 334, 335, 336, 338, 339, 340, 341, 342, 353, 354, 355, 356, 357, 358, 359, 377, 378, 379, 383, 384, 388, 392, 394, 395, 398, 399, 400, 401, 403, 404, 406, 408, 414, 415, 416, 417, 418, 419, 423, 425, 426, 427, 428, 430, 431, 433, 434, 436, 437, 438, 449, 450, 456, 457, 458, 459.
Sophie Ristelhueber, 78-79, 85, 96, 97, 266-67, 318-19, 328, 343, 351, 370-71, 380-81, 420, 444-45, 446, 447, 452-53, 454-55, 464-65.
Léonard de Selva, 127, 128.
Arthur Thévenart, 303.
Eric Uhlfelder, 36, 52, 53, 58-59, 100, 103, 125, 131, 175.
Roger Viollet, 107.

We would like to thank Marc Bruhat (Sillages) for developing many of the photographs in this book.

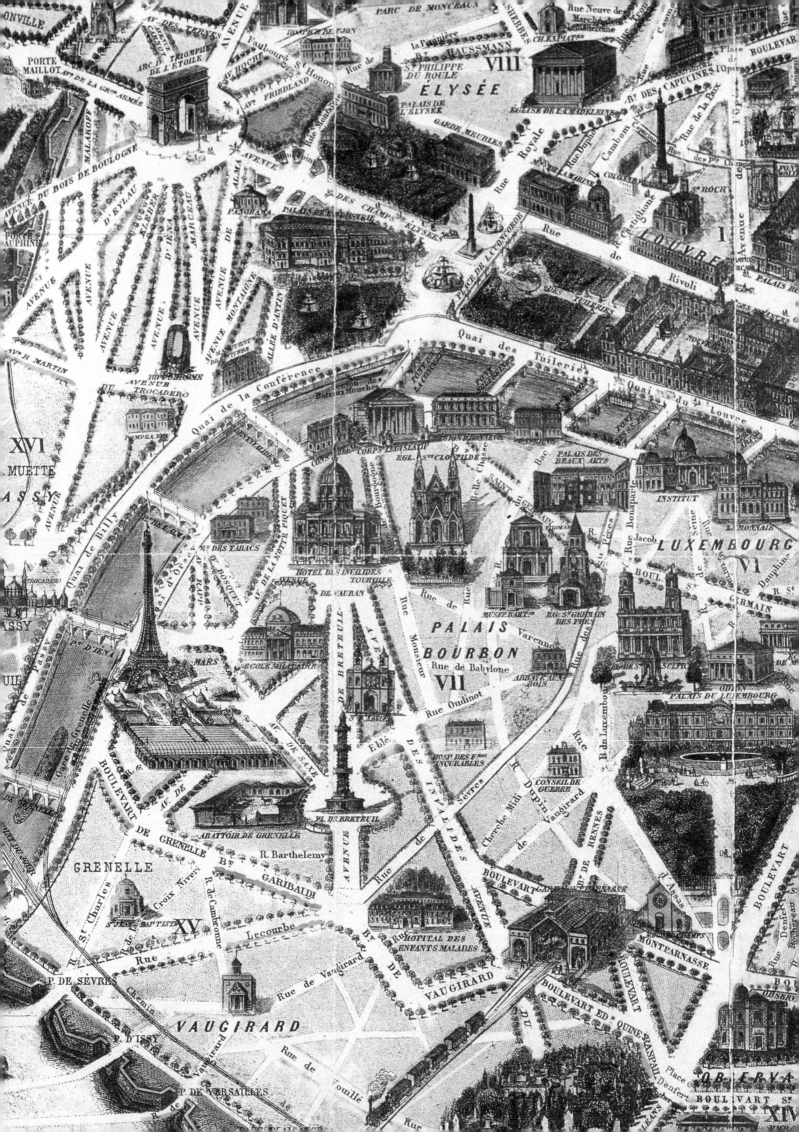